# Ryusuke Ishig[u]
# Tadeusz Janusze[wski]

# Japanese Special Attack Aircraft and Flying Bombs

STRATUS

# Table of contents

Published in Poland in 2009
by STRATUS s.c.
Po. Box 123,
27-600 Sandomierz 1, Poland
e-mail:office@mmpbooks.biz
for
Mushroom Model Publications,
36 Ver Road, Redbourn,
AL3 7PE, UK.
e-mail: rogerw@mmpbooks.biz
© 2009 Mushroom Model
Publications.
http://www.mmpbooks.biz

ISBN
978-83-89450-12-8

*Editor in chief*
Roger Wallsgrove

*Editorial Team*
Bartłomiej Belcarz
James Kightly
Robert Pęczkowski
Artur Juszczak

*Colour Drawings*

Artur Juszczak
Zygmunt Szeremeta
Krzysztof Wołowski

*DTP*
Artur Bukowski

*Translation*
Wojtek Matusiak

*Printed by:*
*Drukarnia Diecezjalna,*
*ul. Żeromskiego 4,*
*27-600 Sandomierz*
*tel. +48 (15) 832 31 92;*
*fax +48 (15) 832 77 87*
*www.wds.pl marketing@wds.pl*

PRINTED IN POLAND

*To Makiko and Takuya, my beloved wife and son*
*Ryusuke Ishiguro*

*All photos via the author*
*except where stated.*

# Japanese Special Attack

As long as air combat has taken place, there have been pilots who chose to use their aircraft as a weapon, sacrificing their lives to inflict damage on the enemy. For the most part this was an individual choice born of desperation or necessity. However, in the latter part of the Pacific war, Japan became the only nation to have ever developed this suicidal sacrifice as a policy. The Japanese Special Attack units - the *Kamikaze* in popular parlance - have since passed into legend as a weapon of unique terror. To Allied nations the dedicated units of suicide pilots represented an enemy that could not be deterred and a line that they themselves were unwilling to cross. For those fighting for the Allies, and succeeding generations of Western audiences, the attitude of those who ordered such strikes and the crews who went willingly to their deaths is difficult to understand. The basis for the relatively short-lived but now-legendary policy of suicide attacks lies not just in Japan's desperate situation late in the Pacific war, but in centuries of Japanese history and culture.

Perhaps ironically, development of a series of unmanned weapons followed the introduction of the Kamikaze. This measure was not, however, to save lives but a further measure of desperation - the Kamikaze was becoming increasingly ineffective due to ever better detection and defence. It is in these weapons that the full ingenuity and determination of Japanese designers can be found, which also has deep roots in Japanese culture.

## The culture of Kamikaze

The Japanese feudal system survived until the industrial revolution in the 1860s. Under fuedalism The Divine Emperor (*Tenno*) was the highest lord. The Emperor of Japan was, according to myth, a descendant of the first Emperor Jinmu (660-585 BC). He in turn was believed to be a direct descendant of Ninigi-no-Mikoto, grandson of the Goddess of the Sun (*Amaterasu-o-Mikami*), who was sent to Japan, or *Yamato* as it was called in legends, to establish a dynasty and to rule the chosen nation.

Considerable in-fighting, referred to in written accounts from the 5th century AD, resulted in the creation of the warrior class, the bushi otherwise known as samurai, who were the armed troops of a nobleman, or shogun - a contraction of *Sei-i-Taishogun*, or the 'great commander conquering barbarians'. The first Sei-i-Taishogun, Sakanoue-no Tamuramaro (758-811), was nominated in 797. From then until the mid-19th century shoguns ruled on behalf of the Emperors, supported by the samurai. At this time the Emperor Meiji (1852-1912) won power in a rebellion. He forced the last of the shoguns to resign in 1867 and established a modern army. This army, while following the

*Japanese woodcut depicting Amaterasu, the Goddess of the Sun.*

*Emperor Mutsuhito (1852-1912), posthumously named Meiji, also the name of the period of his rule (1868-1912)*

pattern of many western forces, inherited much of the samurai culture, including the moral code of *Bush*ido ('the Way of the Warrior'), which included concepts of obedience to one's master and a willingness to die in battle. The preamble of the *Bush*ido code announced 'we shall not die in silence and peace. We shall die by the side of the lord and creator. We shall sail out to sea, where water shall engulf our bodies. We shall walk up the mountains, where grass shall cover our bodies. We shall soar up to the Sun that will accept our souls. Our foremother Amaterasu shall accept us. Our life will never end, anywhere'.

After a failed rebellion by disenfranchised samurai in 1882, Meiji issued the military with the 'Imperial Rescript to Soldiers and Sailors' which demanded absolute obedience of all individuals in the military to the emperor. All personnel were required to learn the Rescript by heart. Shortly before Japan's entry into the Second World War, all personnel in the Imperial Japanese forces were issued with the *Senjinkun*, or 'Instructions for the Battlefield'. This was intended to complement the Imperial Rescript. It set out how the military should behave and refused to allow retreat or surrender.

A further significant element of Japanese culture was that of the gunshin - a form of deification under the Shinto state religion for soldiers who had given their lives for the emperor. The immense respect accorded to the honoured fallen was dramatically illustrated by the shrine built in Tokyo in 1869 to all the warriors killed in the rebellion that won power for the Emperor Meiji. The gunshin was a form of *kami*, a divinity or spirit, which is also a root of the word *Kamikaze*.

Another factor that adds to the context of the later Kamikaze units is that of ritual suicide in preference to dishonour - seppuku - which was part of the warrior code. The first to die the ritual death was the warrior Masashige Kusunoki who, in 1336 is said to have chosen to die rather than betray the Emperor Godaigo. His emblem was the chrysanthemum, which later became the symbol painted on the aircraft of suicide pilots.

The military held enormous power in Japan. Since Emperor Meiji came to power the head of the military was required to answer only to the Emperor and was not accountable to any of the elected civilian governments - much of the time, the civilian government relied on the military to support it. The military shaped the life of the nation and, significantly, controlled the education of the younger generation. A 1926 book by the nationalist Shūmei Okawa 'Japan and the Way of the Japanese', espoused theory of the superiority of the Yamato race that was created by gods' will and gave Japan the power to rule other states of the world. According to Okawa, a military state was the most ideal means of achieving such unanimity.

The compulsory education of young Japanese ended at the age of 20. Graduates of secondary schools had three options: to start work, to become university students, or to enter a military academy. These were open to anyone, irrespective of wealth, who passed a physical fitness test and entrance exam. The latter tested the candidate's knowledge of Japanese history in terms of samurai families and the protocol of customs and rules of behaviour. Entering the military was the duty of the eldest son in families with samurai traditions. Poor economic conditions encouraged many more Japanese families to send their sons for military service. The armed forces' numbers were supplemented by conscription of more than 15,000 recruits every year.

After an assessment of their abilities, recruits were assigned to one of three groups. The first of these, '*Ko-shu*' (group A) included the best recruits from whom future officers were selected. The core of the armed forces was formed by the group '*Otsu-shu*' (group B). This included the recruits with slightly poorer results. The final group, '*Hei-shu*' (group C), included all those unable to pass any of the tests, who were assigned to auxiliary services to be, for example, cooks or medics.

Apart from the training itself, ideological preparation was an important matter for the military. Young children were given four hours of Japanese history and an hour of patriotic songs every week. Soldiers, too, had history lessons every day, plus an hour of lectures on military history. Patriotic songs were also practised. This was accompanied by ideological training, mainly focused on the uniting of the 'eight corners of the world under one roof', under one ruler who would make the world one family. The next demand was the 'imperial way' under which the Emperor would define the most proper 'way' for everyone.

# Kamikaze - the last chance for the Japanese Empire

As well as elements of Japanese culture and history, and the tactical situation in the Pacific, a political struggle within the Japanese armed forces helped contribute to the conditions that created the Kamikaze.

Prior to the Second World War, the officer corps of the Japanese armed forces was polarised into two groups. Before 1916 only the sons of wealthy families could become officers, while later the officer ranks were opened more widely. Consequently, ideological divisions formed between the older officers from privileged backgrounds and younger officers from a more mixed background. There was never a truly open fight between these groups, but the opinions of the younger radicals, generally more uncompromising in their views and tactics, became more and more influential. Officers were bound by the principle 'Yamato Damashii', the spirit of Japan, and under nationalist ideology, the total superiority of the Japanese race. These principles demanded that servicemen show boldness and courage without regard for their own life.

It was potentially the result of this 'spirit', with the numerous other factors in Japanese culture and history, that the creation of *Tokubetsu Kogekitai or Tokko-tai*, special (suicide) attack units, could become reality. At a time of dire need, the creators of these units came to the fore.

# The creators of Japanese Special Attack

A number of individuals working together and separately contributed to the birth of the 'special attack' units, but three in particular are credited with being the chief founders.

Vice-Admiral Takijiro Ohnishi (1892-1945), is often credited as the father of the Kamikaze idea, and was the first to put the principle into practice. He was born in the village of Ashida into a family with long samurai traditions. He was a dedicated and successful student which, with his background, meant he had no trouble gaining acceptance to the Imperial Japanese Navy academy (*Kaigun Heigakko*) at Etajima. After graduating from the academy he was posted to the newly-formed naval aviation division, and immediately saw the potential that aviation presented. In 1916 he was one of the first Japanese pilots to serve on the seaplane carrier *Wakamiya Maru*. The carrier was sent against a German fortress on the Chinese coast, at the port of Tsingtao. With three other pilots, Ohnishi attacked German warships and during one of the low level raids he dropped a bomb on a German minelayer, which subsequently sank.

Ohnishi was by nature an innovator and keen advocate of new tactics, including the combat use of aeroplanes in combination with warships. He joined the naval intelligence service, which sent him to Hawaii where he obtained a great deal of information about the local naval base - Pearl Harbor - and about the warships and their Pacific cruises.

*Admiral Heihachiro Togo (1848-1934)*

Vice-Admiral Ohnishi studied in detail the psychology of behaviour in military circles. He was most interested in the NCOs and sailors under critical combat situations including their willingness to carry out their combat tasks even at the cost of their lives. His opinions were set down in the manual known as the 'Combat ethics of the Japanese Navy' 1938 which became an essential part of the education of young men in the Navy. In January 1941 he was commissioned by Admiral Isoroku Yamamoto, the Commander in Chief of the Japanese Fleet, to develop plans for an air assault on Pearl Harbor in order to knock out US Pacific sea power at the outset of any conflict.

Ohnishi was the chief of staff of the 11th *Koku Kantai*, based on Taiwan at Takao (Kaoshuing) at the beginning of the war in the Pacific. During his time in charge, an incident took place which foreshadows the beginning of the Kamikaze policy. A group of Mitsubishi G3M ('Nell') bombers of the 1st *Kokutai* attempted to bomb American bases in the Philippines. During the raid, one of the G3M crews was shot down and

taken prisoner by the Americans, though the squadron log book recorded that the members were killed in combat. With the rapid advance of the Japanese troops the crew were soon released and returned to their unit.

Under the codes of behaviour accepted by the Japanese military, the crew should not have allowed themselves to be taken prisoner. When the unit moved to Rabaul in the following month Ohnishi is said to have talked to the crew, restored their ranks and sent them on a reconnaissance mission over Port Moresby. Although it was officially a reconnaissance mission, the aeroplane was armed with bombs and departed without any fighter escort, despite the target's heavy defences. The crew did not return. Ohnishi heard the report then ordered that the crew should be regarded as heroes.

Another Kamikaze 'godfather' was Vice-Admiral Matome Ugaki (1890-1945). His background was similar to that of Ohnishi. The first son of the police chief at Mie, his family also had predecessors among the samurai. He, too, graduated with distinction from the academy at Etajima. A natural tactician and a strong advocate of close co-operation between the navy and the air force, he wrote several books which became official textbooks in military academies.

In early 1940 he was appointed chief of staff of the *Rengo Kantai* (Combined Fleet) commander, Admiral Isoroku Yamamoto. He took part in the battle of Leyte, as commander of a battleship division. Then he moved to Mabalacat, where together with Ohnishi he set up the suicide air units. When during late 1944 he took command of the 5th *Koku Kantai*, he immediately renamed it a special attack-suicide unit. His area of operations covered the island of Kyushu, where he commanded all the local air units. There he prepared the plan of suicide operations code named *Kikusui* (floating chrysanthemum).

Vice-Admiral Shigeru Fukudome (1891-1971) was the third father of the Kamikaze. He was an experienced staff officer who had graduated from the academy at Etajima before being appointed chief of staff of the 1st Battleship Division. It was at its head that he took part at the beginning of the war against China. For his outstanding achievements in the battlefield he was posted for studies at the Imperial Japanese Navy Academy. Once he graduated, he took the post of chief of staff under Admiral Yamamoto and his deputy, Admiral Mineichi Koga. In March 1944 he was promoted to Vice-Admiral and given command of the newly formed 6th Kichi *Koku Butai*, in the 2nd *Koku Kantai*, based in Taiwan. The unit took part in the *Sho*-Go plan at Leyte Gulf (see below).

# Establishment of the Kamikaze suicide units

On the morning of 19 October 1944, a group of senior officers gathered at Mabalacat, the base of the 201st *Kokutai*, the best Japanese naval aviation unit in the Philippines. They were Vice-Admiral Takijiro Ohnishi, Commander Rikihei Inoguchi (senior staff officer of the 1st *Koku Kantai*), Commander Asaichi Tamai (201st *Kokutai*), Lieutenant Commander Chuichi Yoshioka (senior staff officer of the 26th *Koku Sentai*), Lieutenants Ibusuki and Yokoyama (commanders of the squadrons) and Lieutenant Chikanoli Moji (adjutant to Vice-Admiral Ohnishi).

American soldiers had begun to land on several islands in Leyte Gulf two days previously - apparently the first step in a large scale invasion. Vice-Admiral Ohnishi opened the meeting and informed the group that a large fleet of battleships and cruisers was en route to attack the American invasion forces. He emphasised that everything must be done to prevent Allied air attacks stopping this fleet before its guns could destroy the American forces lying at anchor. Ohnishi proposed that fighter aircraft be fitted with bombs - however, to ensure the maximum destructive effect of each aircraft, the pilots would dive their mounts directly at a selected target and collide with it. The pilots would give their lives, but their sacrifice would guarantee destruction of the target.

As an example, he quoted the act of Vice-Admiral Masafumi Arima, commander of the 26th *Koku Sentai*. Arima was said to have been unsatisfied with the first wave of a strike against American ships off the Philippines. As a result, he directly led the second wave with the words:

"in a direct attack I will personally sink an enemy aircraft carrier. I will be led there by the samurai way and the rules of combat ethics, so I am calm. Long live His Highness the Emperor and Japan". Arima directed his aircraft towards the target, but during the dive his aircraft lost its rudder and crashed into the sea. The incident was later portrayed by Japanese propaganda as a progenitor of the Kamikaze attacks.

It was decided that volunteers should be sought, and those who came forward would be transferred from their units into new units called *Shimpū* Tokubetsu Kogekitai. This literally translates as 'divine wind special attack unit'. The *Shimpū* part of the name relates to the typhoons which had wrecked Mongol fleets attempting to attack Japan in 1274 and 1281. This was at the very least an apposite historical episode to call upon, given the Allied fleets massing to close on Japanese held territory. The 'divine wind' was also known as '*kamikaze*', after the Chinese derived pronunciation of the characters that make up the word *Shimpū* - although this term was never officially applied to suicide attacks. (An alternative explanation was provided by Commander Rikihei Inoguchi who suggested that the *Shimpū* in the units' name referred to the *Shimpū*-ryu school of kendo Japanese fencing in his home town).

*Vice Admiral Matome Ugaki, supporter of suicide attacks.*

It was decided that the honour of providing the first pilots in the special attack units would go to the 201st *Kokutai*. Two possibilities for the first of the new breed of combat pilots were identified by Commander Asaichi Tamai, Lieutenants Sadao Kanno and Yukio Seki. Kanno was, however, in Tokyo at that moment so with time running short, Seki was chosen.

Seki was the son of an antiquarian shopkeeper from the town of Iyo in Sikoku. The family had some samurai history, on Yukio Seki's father's brother's side, though Seki's father was a pacifist and refused to take part in any military action. Three of his four brothers were killed in China. Partly for this reason, Seki's father chose an academic path, the study of history, for his son. Yukio Seki graduated from his school as the best student. However, the intervention of Shigeo Iwamoto, known as 'the professor of war', saw that Seki would not take up his university place. Iwamoto demanded that schools lectured more about military matters and war. He discussed these subjects with students, and persuaded them to join the armed forces.

Despite protests from his family, Yukio Seki joined the Imperial Japanese Navy Academy at Etajima, starting in 1938. He graduated in late 1941, and was posted for service on the seaplane carrier Chitose, from which he took part in many combat operations in the Pacific including being in the second line at the Battle of Midway. In 1943 he was transferred to the air base at Kasumigaura, where he underwent further training. There he met the daughter of the commander, Mariko Watanabe, and they were married in May 1944. Soon afterwards Seki went to Korea, where he was trained on Mitsubishi A6M 'Zero' fighters at Nonsan. Later he was transferred to the base of Haneda, subsequently flying to Taipei. Later in the war he was posted to Mabalacat in the Philippines.

Commander Inoguchi personally introduced Seki into the room where all the officers waited. Inoguchi had been Seki's instructor at Etajima, and knew him very well. Commander Tamai spoke to Seki about their plan, and passed on the request of the unit commander that Seki lead the first Kamikaze unit into action. Seki is reported to have closed his eyes and paused for a moment before agreeing to to the appointment. In reality, Seki had little alternative - refusing would potentially have brought disgrace on his unit and family. In fact, he later told the war correspondent of the newspaper Domei that he was going to die for his wife, not for the emperor or for the country.

*Vice Admiral Jisaburo Ozawa.*

With the leader of the first kamikaze unit, and another 23 pilots, selected, Ohnishi quickly set about establishing additional volunteer units.

Seki first went into action with his special attack unit on 25 October, when when he and four others flew A6M5 Zeros, each loaded with a 250kg bomb, to attack four escort carriers. Seki is credited with sinking one of these, the USS St. Lo.

Kamikaze pilots had entered the war…

# Kamikaze pilot training

Detailed reports of impressive Kamikaze victories in the Philippines were sent to Tokyo by the war correspondent of the newspaper Domei, Masashi Onoda. He was called personally by Vice-Admiral Ohnishi who suggested that he tell the Japanese nation about the new combat units and their tactics. Tokyo Radio also broadcast information about the heroism of the naval aviation Kamikaze pilots, who became idols of the Japanese nation - at the same time causing many families to fear for their relatives in the Navy air service.

A communiqué was issued by the *Gunreibu* (General Staff) which suggested Kamikaze attacks could save Japan from enemy invasion. Imperial Orders No. 649 and 650 were issued to define the posthumous ceremonial for those who had carried out a Kamikaze attack. Emperor Hirohito was informed about the matter by Admiral Mitsumasa Yonai. The Emperor did not condemn the attacks, and Yonai immediately sent a report to Vice-Admiral Ohnishi in the Philippines. Ohnishi established the *Dai-ichi Rengo Kichi Kokubutai* (The first Combined Basic Air Group) composed of the 1st and 2nd *Kantais*. The formation was intended for suicide Kamikaze attacks. Vice-Admiral Ohnishi became the Chief of Staff of the new formation.

During the Pacific war the Japanese aircraft industry manufactured some 70,000 aircraft, but by mid-1944, the Navy had fewer than 10,000 while the Army had just over 11,000 combat aircraft. Seventy per cent of these were fighters and these would become the main equipment used for suicide Kamikaze attacks as, being faster and more manoeuvrable than bomber aircraft, they would have the best chance to evade attack by American fighters.

While the Imperial Japanese Navy's air arm embraced the Kamikaze attack, the Army's air wing was initially more cautious. While the Navy professed that suicide attacks should be carried out using aircraft only, the Army stressed the co-operation of air and ground forces in these attacks. For the Army a pilot was more valuable than an infantryman, so the army aviation did not see such mass suicide attacks in the same light as the Navy. The army did not use the term 'divine wind' in the title of their own suicide units, which were simply 'special attack units'. However, the Army did refer to individual suicide attacks as Tai-atari (falling thunder, also meaning 'direct attack').

*Mitsubishi A5M4-K two-seat fighter trainer, used for training of future Kamikaze pilots.*

Pilots were recruited for special attack units on a voluntary basis. In the Army this was not as forthcoming as in the Navy. Indeed, at the end of May 1945 a mutiny of Army pilots took place on Kyushu, sparked by orders that gave all units there suicide status. Compared to the Navy, Army units only sporadically undertook suicide attacks.

New pilots commenced training for the special attack units as soon as the orders establishing these units were issued. The Navy was the first to begin training. At the beginning of December 1944 Navy HQ announced that sending experienced pilots for suicide attacks was counter-productive, their numbers having shrunk significantly. It would be better to use the experienced pilots as escorts for the Kamikaze aircraft. Official propaganda helped the rapidly expansion of the Kamikaze force with enthusiastic youth, mostly students, volunteers.

The main training centre was located at Kagoshima on Kyushu. The training unit was named *Renshu Rengo Koku Sotai*. Training had little to do with standard Navy pilot training procedures. Although Kamikaze pilots had to have basic flying skills, they did not require much further knowledge or training. The training programme covered thirty take-offs with an instructor in a Mitsubishi A5M4-K trainer, a two-seat variant of the A5M4 ('Claude') carrier-borne fighter, and twenty take-offs and landings in a Mitsubishi A6M2-K two-seat trainer, a variant of the A6M2 'Zero' fighter. At the end of this brief course in flying, pupils listened to a few hours of lectures on navigation, behaviour in case of engine failure or during an engagement with the enemy, and how to carry out a correct suicide attack. Later the graduates received their Kamikaze pilot titles and were posted to their units. Here they would polish up their flying skills, take part in more training flying, and profit from the experience of other pilots.

Naturally, such rapid training had many shortcomings. Although the 'instant-pilots' were ready to destroy any enemy unit in a suicide attack, for most of them the major problem was how to locate it, due to their somewhat basic training in maritime navigation. Naval aviation HQ had assumed that the prospective targets would not be too distant, and navigation would not be important. Moreover, it was thought that the novices would be guided to their targets by experienced pilots, the latter also providing them with aerial protection. For this reason they were not taught air combat techniques. All this, coupled with the low number of solo flights, resulted in disappointing performance once these pilots found themselves in combat conditions. In the case of one unit, 150 aircraft flown by trainees left Kyushu to complete their training on Taiwan. The training was scheduled to last ten days, including the ferry flight to the Philippines, where they would be assigned to individual suicide units. The ferry route was via Okinawa, Amami O'Shima, to Taichu on Taiwan. During the flight, they unexpectedly encountered American fighters. This accidental engagement resulted in the loss of 20% of the force of which some were shot down and others lost over the sea. More losses were suffered during landing. The effects of these losses became clear to the naval aviation HQ on Taiwan, when, after ten days of their stay there it was not possible to establish a unit from the surviving pilots. Moreover, fuel shortages preventing continued training.

*Flag of Japan with signatures of the members of Mizugiwa Tokkotai (seaside suicide attack unit). This type of flag was initially carried by every pilot participating in a Kamikaze operation, and subsequently only by the formation leader.*

The result was clear from the outset: of the first 15 aircraft with these 'instant-pilots' only five reached Manila, and during landing all five of them damaged their undercarriages. It became clear that this was a waste of pilots and aircraft, and that Kamikaze pilot training procedures had to be significantly revised. For the time being, experienced pilots were reinstated for suicide attacks.

Training of future pilots for Kugisho Ohka rocket-powered suicide aircraft followed an even more simplistic procedure. Pilots graduated after only hours of sitting on a bench with a wooden stick to imitate the control stick. With their feet in sandals, they practiced pushing rudder pedals mounted on wooden trestles, accompanied by the sound of engines played from loudspeakers while receiving orders from their instructors. Following this stage of the training, prospective pilots would be given some experience in a two seat engineless Ohka trainer, towed aloft by another aircraft. It was considered that Ohka aircraft would be brought close to their targets by Mitsubishi G4M2 'Betty' bombers, and the final piloting of the suicide aeroplane would be

*A kamikaze pilot tying the hachimaki band, the symbol of courage, around his head.*

**12**

straightforward, with only adjustments of the dive required. Navy Kamikaze training therefore left much to be desired.

In the Army it was a different matter. Here, training followed all the rules of the elementary flying training syllabus, and speeding this up was not considered. Only skilled pilots were posted to special attack units.

Special attack unit pilots did not receive special additional equipment - their kit was mainly the same as regular pilots. Naval aviation pilots, however, did have one main distinguishing feature: a wide white cuff with the red hinomaru disc, Japan's symbol. A white strip was sewn onto the right strap of the parachute harness, and this carrying an inscription such as: 'member of a special attack unit, conquered the enemy for the glory of the Emperor and Japan'. Around their necks, pilots usually wore white scarves with signatures of the members of their unit. Volunteers from schools or young pilots had hachimaki around their heads - a white band – a symbol of courage - with the red disc that also symbolised the rising sun. Sometimes pilots wore a flag of Japan with signatures of all the members of their unit under their flying suit. Pilots of the army aviation wore around their necks the sennin-bari ('the scarf with a thousand stitches') for good luck. These touches were common only in the early days of the Kamikaze operations. Later only the hachimaki and sennin-bari were carried, while the Japanese flag was worn over the heart by leaders of attack groups.

## Last moments before a suicide mission

As already mentioned, pilots who joined special attack units lived with other pilots, and shared their schedule of activities. They did not have to take active part in everyday operational flying but waited, instead, for the order to fly their special mission. They were meant to spend their last days as pleasantly as possible with better food, no fatigue duties, and parties organised by HQ.

Kamikaze pilots awaiting their last missions spent their free time in discussions and recollections, devoted themselves to gardening, planting vegetables or decorative flowers. Some pursued their hobbies: painting pictures, writing poems, or calligraphy.

The day before the attack they ritually cut their hair and shaved. A ceremonial banquet was held, with all the officers of the unit invited. After the party, pilots usually wrote their farewell letters, which they handed to their commanders, often with a lock of their hair. These letters were rarely sad: pilots usually recalled joyful moments from their childhood at home, thanked their parents for their love and care, and advised their siblings how to care for their parents and respect them.

Before the sortie, they came to the table that stood in the middle of the roll-call square, where glasses with sake were prepared. Following a common toast, they marched in front of the unit to their aircraft and entered the cockpits - where the parachute was replaced on the seat by a plain cushion. At the leader's sign for take-off, pilots started their engines and taxied out. Other unit members waved farewell as the aircraft started their run for the last mission.

Army special attack pilots behaved in a similar way. Some Navy and Army pilots were not given sake, but a ceremony of 'water drinking', an old military tradition preceding major battles, was carried out. During this ceremony the unit commander poured pure water from a big jar, to purify the body and souls together with his comrades.

Soon after the special attack units were first established, each aircraft was fitted with a small radio transmitter. After take-off it started sending intermittent signals, assigned to each aeroplane. Each transmitter was set to a different frequency, so as not to confuse one pilot with another. When the signal disappeared, it indicated that the pilot had carried out his honourable duty.

As the Japanese became more desperate under American pressure, the Kamikaze ceremony became simplified, and eventually all that was left was the drinking of water or sake and the final march past unit personnel before take-off. The radio transmitters were abandoned - first, because they were in short supply and second, because suicide attacks became mass attacks and individual communication was no longer needed.

*Ritual shaving and haircutting.*

*...or writing his determination..*

*Kamikaze pilots writing farewell letters to their closest ones.*

...or donating their money to the country...

Army aviation pilots, Shimpū, before their last operation, during the ritual "water drinking", aimed at purifying their bodies and souls.

Navy pilots, Kamikaze, drank a cup of water during similar farewell ceremonies.

# Kamikaze over the Philippines

Suicide unit operations were generally confined to particular areas of activity, which were dictated by the situation at the front line: the Philippines, where suicide formations were first established, Formosa (Taiwan), Iwo Jima, Okinawa and the home islands of Japan could be considered as another area. American intelligence services first reported damage to ships inflicted by a Japanese suicide aeroplane on 27 May 1944, when a Japanese 'Zero' fighter damaged the transport ship SC.699. In fact, American records cite a number of examples of ships being attacked by suicide tactics before the 'official' beginning of Japanese special attack operations on the 25 October. Some of these are described below.

In October 1944, the US Task Force TF-38.4 under Rear-Admiral Ralf E. Davidson headed towards Taiwan. The task force included the aircraft carriers USS *Enterprise*, *Franklin*, *Belleau Wood* and *Belleau Wood*. Its objective was to attack the airfields and other military installations used by the Japanese 2nd *Koku Kantai* unit commanded by Admiral Fukudome. This unit had some 200 aircraft, at least half of which were Nakajima Ki-43 Hayabusa 'Oscar' and Nakajima Ki-84 Hayate 'Frank' fighters. The rest were bombers and training aircraft. The unit was subsequently reinforced with 100 Navy Mitsubishi A6M 'Zero' fighters and ten flying boats, which arrived from Kyushu on 11 October 1944. The first clash with the American force commenced the following morning, when Admiral Fukudome sent 230 aircraft against the Americans. Thanks to radar on the American ships, Japanese aircraft were detected and attacked long before they got close to the US vessels. American fighters quickly shot down at least one third of the Japanese aircraft and scattered the rest, and none got through to attack the American ships. On the morning of Friday 13 October 1944, at 0644, the American aircraft-carriers launched Grumman TBF/TBM Avenger and Curtiss SB2C Helldiver bombers to attack airfields and communication lines on Taiwan. Defending Japanese fighters were unable to put up much resistance because of the American escort of Grumman F6F Hellcat and Vought F4U Corsair carrier-borne fighters. Soon after the return of the attacking aircraft to the carriers, American radar detected Japanese aircraft.

These were mainly Mitsubishi G4M ('Betty') bombers armed with torpedoes. Four of these flew at wave top level and evaded detection by radar, arriving close to the aircraft carrier USS *Franklin* at the front of the American force. The tactics failed to confuse the gunners of the ship, as two of the Japanese bombers were destroyed by AA fire and Hellcat fighters. The third Japanese aircraft managed to launch its torpedo before being hit and blown apart by shells from American guns. The carrier made a sharp turn at maximum speed, causing some disarray below decks. This manoeuvre saved the ship, but the threat was not over. The fourth Japanese bomber approached from the other side and launched its torpedo, which disappeared into the water, but failed to hit the target. However, the attacking aeroplane itself collided with the carrier, and the burning Japanese bomber slid along the deck to fall into the sea near the port side. Damage to the aircraft carrier was minimal. Five US aircraft were dislodged into the sea, and 22 sailors who found themselves in the path of the Japanese aeroplane jumped overboard.

The light cruiser USS *Reno* was the next target of the Japanese attack. This ship was part of another US Task Force, TF-38.2, which included the aircraft carriers USS *Essex*, *Lexington*, *Langley* and *Princeton*. Commanded by Rear-Admiral F. Sherman, it sailed to assist TF-38.1. A relatively large group of Nakajima B6N Tenzan 'Jill' torpedo aircraft attacked, and one aimed at the flagship, the aircraft carrier USS *Lexington*, but thanks to skillful manoeuvring the ship avoided both the torpedo and the attacking aeroplane, which was hit by AA fire. The burning 'Jill' passed the aircraft carrier but hit the starboard side of the cruiser USS *Reno*, which was unable evade the attack in time. The aeroplane destroyed the *Reno's* forward AA gun positions. The resulting fire was quickly brought under control as soon as the damage control crews set to work. Six sailors suffered burns, while two AA gunners were killed.

The third attack before 25 October 1944 was carried out against TG-77.3, commanded by Rear-Admiral R. S. Berkley, which took up position off Leyte Gulf on the night of 21 October 1944. The

task group TG-77.3 was to support the landing operation that opened the actual American invasion of the Philippines. At about 06.00, American radar detected two aircraft. One of the attacking 'Zero' fighters was hit and exploded in mid-air, while another 'Zero' crashed on the bridge of the cruiser HMAS *Australia*. Burning petrol from the aeroplane spilled on the deck and poured underneath near the starboard side. The fire resulted in an explosion in a magazine and led to the death of 30 sailors. Captain Deschaineux, a staff officer of the Royal *Australia*n Navy, was also killed and another 64 members of the *Australia*n ship's crew were injured, most of them suffering burns. With help from other ships, the fire was extinguished, but *Australia* had to be taken at night to Manus Island for repair.

Further victims of Japanese suicide attacks before the official start of such operations were the ocean-Going tug Sonoma and the landing craft *LCI-1065*. Both of these ships were destroyed in Leyte Gulf on 24 October 1944. Sonoma was hit by a Mitsubishi G4M 'Betty' bomber that exploded, damaging the nearby fast transport ship *Augustus Thomas*. The LCI-1065 was hit by a Mitsubishi Ki-21 'Sally' that hit and exploded amidships. The ship started to burn and sank soon afterwards.

After Lieutenant Seki was chosen as the first Kamikaze pilot to carry out an attack, four air attack units were formed from volunteer Kamikaze pilots. According to Japanese tradition these were given names connected with Japanese literature. The organisers used a quote from a poem by Norinaga Motoori: '... *and when you insist that I tell what is the heart of Japan; I will tell that it is the smell of the mountain cherry blossom at sun rise*'.

The first attack unit was named *Yamazakura tai* (sakura mountain cherry). The second unit was called *Yamato tai*, the name of Japan at around the time of the Roman Empire. The third unit was named *Asahi tai*, referring to the morning sun and the fourth unit was named *Shikishima tai*, the name of Japan in native poetry. The entire strike group consisted of 26 Mitsubishi A6M 'Zero' fighters, half of which were allocated to carry out the attack itself, while the remaining aircraft would protect them from enemy fighters. *Shikishima tai* remained in the air base at Mabalacat, under command of Lieutenant Yukio Seki. *Yamato tai* under Sub-Lieutenant Yoshizane Kuno left for Cebu on the morning on 20 October 1944. These were four 'Zero' fighters with bombs attached under the fuselage. *Yamazakura tai* and *Asahi tai* left for Davao on 23 October 1944.

The situation at the front line was becoming more and more critical. On 24 October 1944 American troops commenced landing on the east coast of Leyte, and started to advance quickly inland. They broke through, getting within 10 miles of Tacloban. Tadashi Nakajima, staff officer of the 201st *Kokutai*, who had under his command the 'Zero' aircraft from Cebu, ordered the immediate establishment of a special attack unit, for which he started to recruit volunteers from among air crew based there. Those who volunteered immediately started writing farewell letters to their families and friends.

*Take-off of the first suicide unit Shikishima-tai, led by Lieutenant Yukio Seki. The attack ended in sinking of the aircraft carrier USS St Lo on 25 October 1944.*

*Reisen fighter about to strike the aircraft carrier USS* White Plains *on 25 October 1944.*

The 1st *Koku Kantai* had been decimated, for the main part by American carrier-borne aircraft. It had some 30 Mitsubishi A6M 'Zero' fighters and 30 bombers of various types remaining. For that reason Admiral Soemu Toyoda gave orders to transfer 350 aircraft of the 2nd *Koku Kantai*, commanded by Admiral Shigeru Fukudome, from Taiwan to the Philippines. On 23 October the aircraft landed in the Philippines, and the following day 250 aircraft attacked American ships. Bad weather and the strong AA defence of the American ships severely hampered the Japanese attack. Only five American ships were damaged, and those only slightly.

On 21 October 1944, the Japanese received information that an American fleet with six aircraft carriers was sailing 150 miles east of Suluan island. The *Yamato tai* unit started preparations for attack. Aircraft were rolled out from the edge of the jungle and five 'Zero' fighters were prepared for take-off - three intended for the suicide attack with the other two providing escort. While the aircraft taxied for take-off, American Hellcat and Corsair carrier-borne fighters appeared overhead, and within a few minutes all the Japanese aircraft had been destroyed. The American fighters were closely followed by Avenger and Helldiver carrier-borne bombers that completed the destruction at Cebu. After they departed, surviving ground crews tried to prepare a strike from some of the less damaged aircraft. With tremendous effort they managed to prepare three 'Zero' fighters - two to carry out suicide attacks and one escort. After a rapid take-off the three headed for Suluan. Due to bad weather conditions the pilots failed to locate any American ships and returned to base. Only two aircraft successfully found their way back. Sub-Lieutenant Kuno was missing having apparently lost his bearings.

Also at Mabalacat, suicide units of the *Shikishima tai* under Yukio Seki were preparing for an attack. Unit pilots included Iwao Nakano, Nobuo Tani, Hajime Nagamine and Shigeo Oguro. After the farewell ceremony, the pilots went to their aircraft and took off, but soon returned because bad weather made it impossible to locate American ships. The take-off was postponed for two days based on weather reports.

A big day for the new units arrived on 25 October 1944. Large numbers of American ships gathered around the Philippines, providing an ideal opportunity for use of Kamikaze units. The weather was still far from good, but as the sun rose, six aircraft took off from Cebu. At 0735 *Yamato tai* aircraft reported visual contact with the enemy. This was part of TG-77.4 sailing under command of Rear-Admiral Thomas L. Sprague. The group consisted of the 22nd Aircraft carrier Division that included USS *Sangamon*, *Suwannee*, *Santee* and *Chenango*, and the 28th Aircraft carrier division with USS *Petrof Bay* and *Saginaw Bay*. The carriers were escorted by five destroyers. Five minutes before the arrival of the Japanese aircraft American radar had identified the attack, and AA defences were ready for them.

Kamikaze pilots aimed at the aircraft carrier USS *Santee*. The first aeroplane dived straight onto her deck, so that sailors and gunners could do nothing as the explosion tore a huge hole five meters by nine in the main deck. Fires spread, endangering the 1,000lb bombs that were being prepared for the ship's aircraft, and only thanks to determined fire fighting was a further explosion prevented.

Flames and thick smoke rising from the burning aircraft carrier provided a beacon for other Japanese aircraft. Another attacking Kamikaze emerged from the clouds and aimed at the aircraft carrier USS *Sangamon*. This time American defences were faster, and as soon as the attacking 'Zero' got within the range of their guns it was destroyed. The fierce and determined barrage also accounted for the third 'Zero' which crashed near its intended target, the USS *Petrof Bay*. The fourth Japanese aeroplane that appeared above the American force was also destroyed, crashing into the sea at full speed. The last attacker was chased back into the clouds by the American AA defences.

The Japanese had lost five aircraft and failed to sink any American aircraft carriers. The fire on the carrier USS *Santee* was quickly brought under control, although 16 sailors were killed and 72 suffered burns. The damaged aircraft carrier was not able to launch any aircraft, but it remained with the fleet to help provide defence for other ships with its anti-aircraft guns.

The same day as the ill-fated *Yamato tai* took off, the *Shikishima tai* under Lieutenant Seki went into action. The unit took off from Mabalacat at 0725 and after three hours of flight, Seki spotted American aircraft carriers. This was the third American group, TG-72.4, formed from the 25th Aircraft carrier division under Rear-Admiral F. Sprague, including the escort carriers USS *St Lo*, Franshaw Bay, *White Plains* and Kalinin Bay, and the 26th Aircraft carrier division under Rear-Admiral R. A. Ofstie, including the escort carriers USS *Kitkum Bay* and Gambier Bay. The force was escorted by destroyers.

At 1005 the American force was attacked by the first 'Zero'. The aeroplane came in low over the water to avoid being spotted by American radar. Several hundred metres from the USS *Kitkum Bay*, the aeroplane rapidly gained height up to about 1,500m, and then, after a wingover, it dived directly onto the ship. The carrier desperately manoeuvred and initiated an AA barrage, but the 'Zero' hit the ship with its wing. The main part of the 'Zero' crashed and exploded in the sea, but some damage was done to the carrier. Two subsequent 'Zeroes' aimed at the USS *White Plains*. One of these broke apart under fire from 5 in. guns. The final 'Zero', flown by Seki, which was by this time trailing black smoke, broke away from the *White Plains* and aimed at the USS *St Lo*. It broke through the AA defence and hit the stern of the carrier, punching through the deck and igniting the aviation fuel tanks. The fire caught and spread until it reached seven torpedoes being readied, whereupon a huge explosion destroyed deck lifts and waiting aircraft. Further explosions below decks completed the destruction. At 1110 the ship's skipper, Lieutenant-Commander MacKenne, ordered the crew to abandon ship, and 15 minutes later the USS *St Lo* disappeared beneath the surface, taking 114 sailors with her - 784 crew members were saved, but many were wounded.

Based on the first reports from these Kamikaze attacks, Vice-Admiral Ohnishi introduced a substantial reorganization of special attack units. On the evening of 26 October 1944, a group of 12th *Koku Kantai* 'Zero' aircraft landed on the Philippine airfield of Clark Field. They were there to provide reinforcements for suicide units. The pilots were subsumed into the ranks of the Kamikaze, even though initially they were intended to provide escort cover during suicide attacks. The basic establishment of the special unit was set: three aircraft were allocated for the attack itself, while two others would provide cover. One of these aircraft would protect the group from above, the other from below. Escort pilots were instructed that they would have to remain in place until the end of the Kamikaze attack. They were to defend Kamikaze aircraft from enemy aircraft on their way to the target at all cost. For that reason the best pilots were selected for escort missions.

The *Dai-ni Shimpū Tokubetsu kogekitai* (2nd *Shimpū* Special Attack Unit) was formed with eight Kamikaze units with the newly-arrived aircraft. The basis was provided by pilots of the 701st *Kokutai*, part of the 2nd *Koku Kantai*, and the new units, named *Chuyu tai* (fidelity and courage),

*Seichu tai* (loyalty and patriotism), *Junchu tai* (true faith), *Giretsu tai* (bravery and chivalry), *Shisei tai* (heart and soul), *Jimmu tai* (the first '*Tenno*', or divine emperor), *Shimpei tai* (divine soldier), and *Tempei tai* (sky soldier) would be commanded by Colonel Satohiko Kida.

Meanwhile, Japanese reconnaissance aircraft detected a force of American ships in the bay of Surigao. *Yamazakura tai* prepared to attack, and at 0815 three 'Zero' fighters took off. They never reached their target, either because they lost their bearings or because they were shot down by American fighters patrolling the area. For the next attack, three attack aircraft took off with an escort of two 'Zero' fighters. At 1030 they established visual contact with the enemy, but before they reached the target they were attacked by 60 patrolling American Hellcat and Corsair fighters, which quickly shot down two Japanese aircraft. The third attacker managed to sneak through the AA fire and dived on the carrier USS *Suwannee*. Fire from American guns failed to destroy the Kamikaze, which hit a lift that was taking down an Avenger. The explosion of the Japanese aeroplane not only destroyed the American aeroplane on the lift, but also triggered more explosions and started a fire. This spread and started to threaten ten more Avengers, all of which were armed with depth charges. Fortunately for the crew of the *Suwannee*, the depth charges did not explode. However, some signal charges exploded and the resulting fire took over three hours to put out. The carrier was saved, but the damage was so serious that the ship had to withdraw from the combat area. Losses were high, with 150 sailors killed and 195 wounded.

The Americans reacted immediately to the Japanese attack. AA defence on all ships was reinforced, and fighter patrol sorties were strengthened. Bomber attacks against Japanese air bases intensified , with the focus of the Americans' attention being the 1st Tokubetsu Kogekitai, whose aircraft attacked carrier task force TF-38 sailing 60 km off Suluan island. When Kamikazes arrived over the American ships on the morning of 30 October 1944, American AA defences set a barrage which destroyed most of the attacking Japanese aircraft: of fourteen aircraft, only three managed to break through. Two Kugisho D4Y Suisei 'Judy' dive bombers damaged the carrier USS *Franklin* and one Mitsubishi A6M 'Zero' fighter crashed into the escort carrier USS *Belleau Wood*. None of the carriers under attack were damaged sufficiently to be put out of action.

*Nakajima B5N2 bomber from the Jobanchuka-tai takes off from Hyakuri-hara air base.*

# The last air combats over the Philippines

The next stage of the Japanese attacks by suicide aircraft commenced in late November 1944 when the units in the Philippines were reinforced with 450 aircraft from Taiwan. These were used immediately to form new Kamikaze units. One of these, the 3rd *Shimpū Tokubetsu Kogekitai*, assembled at Nichols Field and Mabalacat. The unit was equipped with Mitsubishi A6M 'Zero' fighters, Kugisho D4Y Suisei 'Judy' dive-bombers and twin-engined Kugisho P1Y Ginga 'Frances' land-based bombers. It began operations on 25 November 1944. The first to go into action was the Yoshino tai unit, under Sub-Lieutenant Masami Takatake. Six 'Zero' fighters and two 'Frances' bombers arrived over the American fleet commanded by Admiral Gerald F. Bogan at 1130, and two more attack groups followed.

The first group was met with heavy AA fire from the carrier USS *Cabot*, but two Kamikazes hit the ship. Only slight damage resulted, but 15 American sailors were killed and 16 were wounded. Two more Japanese aircraft hit the carrier USS *Intrepid*: the first struck a gun position and destroyed it, before falling onto the deck and causing a fire to start. The other Kamikaze exploded on the deck, from which 75 aircraft had just taken off. Damage to the deck was substantial meaning aircraft from the USS *Intrepid* had to find alternative places to land. The carrier lost 79 sailors killed and 43 wounded. The third target of the attack was the carrier USS *Hancock*, which came under attack by four 'Zero' fighters. Two of these were shot down by AA fire and the third burst into flames after American fighters intervened. When the fourth flew into the dense AA fire, its wings were shot off and most of the remaining wreckage missed the carrier but hit the destroyer next to her. The destroyer sustained slight damage. A few fragments of wing and fuselage fell onto the carrier, causing no damage.

The last to be attacked was the flag carrier, USS *Essex*. One of the attacking aircraft was shot down, but another crashed into the flight deck and 15 sailors were killed. A total of eighteen Kamikaze aircraft were shot down. The attacks continued into the next day and respite only came

*A damaged P1Y1 Ginga bomber from the 763rd Kokutai seen from the deck of the aircraft carrier USS* Ommaney *Bay.*

*During the suicide missions in October 1944 against the US fleet assembled near the Philippines, 250 kg bombs were attached under A6M Reisen fighters.*

for the Allied ships after the 25th Kamikaze attack, which was repelled with eight aircraft shot down and the others forced to withdraw.

These US ships faced the fiercest suicide attack on 27 November 1944. The attacking unit was the 3rd *Shimpū Tokubetsu Kogekitai* from Mabalacat. First to strike was Kasuga tai led by Kyoichi Inuzuka. The attack consisted of seven 'Zero' aircraft and two D4Y 'Judy' dive bombers. The *Hakko Dai-1 tai* army unit took off from Negros Island under Lieutenant Hideshi Tanaka at the same time as its Navy counterpart left Mabalacat. This group was made up of ten Ki-43 'Oscar' fighters, each carrying two bombs under their wings. They were escorted by six Ki-84 'Frank' fighters and twelve more Ki-43 'Oscar' fighters.

At 1125 Japanese pilots arrived above the twenty ships of the 7th Fleet of Admiral Hayler. Heavy AA fire greeted the Kamikazes as they commenced their attack, which was carried out simultaneously from different sides. The light cruiser USS *St Louis* was the first to be targeted. Two Kamikaze aircraft hit the ship, striking a gun turret and the floatplane catapult; 33 sailors were killed. The next to be attacked was another light cruiser, USS *Montpelier* which had been undergoing refuelling at the time. Three Kamikaze aircraft attacked, but all of their bombs failed to explode. The fourth Kamikaze aeroplane was destroyed by the ships' guns and only fragments fell onto the *Montpelier*.

The fifth suicide attacker fell on one of the cruiser's turrets. The gun crew was wounded, but the ship did not need to withdraw from combat. The sixth attacking aircraft exploded by the starboard side of the cruiser and inflicted no damage.

In addition to the damage to the light cruiser, the battleship USS *Colorado* also sustained damage in the attack, losing nineteen sailors. The transport ship SC-744 was sunk, and the crew of the cruiser USS *Montpelier* spent many hours fighting a fire on a deck covered with the remains of Japanese aircraft and bodies. The American damage control crew was able to ensure that the ship remained in combat condition. Optimistically, Tokyo radio announced that the American ships were completely destroyed. The American offensive continued.

Japanese suicide attacks off Leyte Gulf continued. The bases at Cebu, located some 100 km from Leyte, played a vital role for the Japanese. The local *Yamato tai* unit was reinforced with additional aircraft, the first of which came from the base at Mabalacat.

On the morning of 27 November 1944, seventeen Kamikaze aircraft took off, mostly 'Zero' fighters led by Lieutenant Kano. En route to Cebu they encountered sixteen Hellcats, and during

the air battle twelve American aircraft were shot down, while the Japanese only lost one 'Zero'. This was an unusual reversal in fortunes at this stage in the war, and the Japanese pilots showed the Americans that they should not be underestimated.

On the afternoon of 29 November 1944, more Japanese aircraft appeared over the 7th Fleet. Once again they were met by the massed anti-aircraft guns of the ships making a curtain of fire which the attackers would have to fly through. Kamikaze aircraft tried to break through to attack their targets, first striking at the battleship USS *Maryland*. Concentrated AA fire prevented any Japanese aircraft from posing any threat to her. The next target was the heavy cruiser USS *Portland*. Its attacker was also forced away, before switching to the destroyer USS *Aulick*. The Kamikaze hit the ship, causing

*Kugisho P1Y1 Ginga bombers of the 762nd Kokutai.*

fires to break out. Another 'Zero' crashed into a 6 in. gun turret on the battleship USS *Maryland*, but the explosion did not inflict serious damage. The destroyer USS *Saufley* was struck by a further Kamikaze which exploded and started fires. The crew fought the conflagration for over four hours before it was put out, but the destroyer had to be withdrawn from the battle zone.

The Japanese hoped that ultimately their attacks would break the American defences and destroy the US Navy invasion fleet's cohesion. However, the Navy responded quickly to the new style of attacks by equipping their ships with additional AA weapons, introducing a 'picket' of radar equipped ships in a perimeter around the fleet, and extending fighter patrols. The Sho-Go plan failed to take the Americans' improved defences into account.

According to official Japanese sources of the time, 50% of the American fleet had been destroyed in the Philippines. The Japanese commanders therefore considered that job of the Kamikazes was to finish the enemy off. In fact the fleet's capabilities had not been substantially harmed.

On 7 December 1944, US soldiers of the 77th Infantry Division landed in the bay some 4 miles from Ormoc, on Leyte. Kamikaze units were charged with preventing the Americans from landing at all cost, but the American ships managed to unload their cargo and subsequently could manoeuvre more freely. Kamikaze aircraft hit the destroyer USS *Mahan*, and a large explosion sank the ship.

*C6N1 Saiun reconnaissance aircraft of the 762nd Kokutai at Truk air base.*

The fast transport ship Ward was hit by three Kamikaze aircraft and the resulting blaze could not be extinguished so she was sunk by gunfire from US destroyers. The landing ship LSM-318 also sank and light damage was inflicted on three other landing ships. One 'Zero' fighter and one D4Y 'Judy' dive bomber were shot down.

Four days later, on 11 December 1944, a convoy sailing to Ormoc was attacked by Japanese aircraft. The *Shimpū Tokubetsu Kogekitai Kongo tai 1* commanded by Sub-Lieutenant Kiyoshi Suzuki with eleven Kamikaze aircraft took off first to attack the destroyer USS *Reid*. Two of them were shot down by American AA defences, but a third hit the ship and exploded in an ammunition magazine. The whole magazine detonated, and a few minutes later the ship took on a list and sank.

The following day, a Kamikaze aircraft struck the bridge of the destroyer USS *Caldwell*. The resulting fire was eventually extinguished, but damage to the ship was so serious that it had to make temporary repairs before returning to the US for more substantial work. The Japanese lost five aircraft to American AA defences during the day's attacks.

On the following morning, Japanese Kamikaze took off for further attacks. Their target was a large group of American ships, spotted off Surigao strait. Vice-Admiral Ohnishi prepared the strongest Kamikaze attack group so far: it consisted of 53 fighters, including thirty 'Zero' and 23 Kawanishi N1K-J Shiden ('George') aircraft, plus six Nakajima C6N1 Saiun ('Myrt') reconnaissance aircraft and 'Frances' twin-engined bombers. Upon receiving the news of American ships off Negros Island, Japanese aircraft took off in response. The assessment of the situation proved inaccurate, however. Some 120 km away the Japanese aircraft were intercepted by patrolling American fighters, and only the deteriorating weather allowed the Japanese to avoid an engagement.

Suicide attacks did however manage to locate American shipping on the Sulu Sea. This was the Visayan Attack Force. Their main target was the flagship, the light cruiser USS *Nashville*. The attack began at 1100 when the first aircraft dived on her. It crashed into the cabin of the commander, Admiral A. D. Struble, and leaking petrol caught fire. The ship was also attacked by other Kamikaze aircraft, suffering numerous explosions. Fires were put out, but the ship had to be withdrawn from operations and was out of action until April 1945. Out of the three 'Zero' fighters of the Kongo *Butai* 2, led by Acting Sub-Lieutenant Hiroshi Komatsu, at least two were shot down but one of these crashed just forward of the bridge where it exploded. Spilled petrol burst into flames and it was only thanks to enormous efforts by the crew that the cruiser stayed afloat and made it to Leyte Gulf for repair. Fourteen sailors were killed, and 28 were wounded.

On the morning of 15 December 1944, 28,000 Americans landed on Mindoro Island. Japanese Kamikaze aircraft arrived over the group the next day. This time they attacked from low altitude,

*Two D4Y4 Suisei dive bombers of the 252nd Kokutai. The housing for their fixed rockets is visible.*

and aimed for the landing ships LST-427 and LST-738, which they sank. However, these ships were empty, having already discharged their troops so casualties were minimal. Four more landing ships were damaged to varying degrees.

Losses by the Japanese in the last twenty attacks were so high that they were left virtually without aircraft. Deliveries of a wide variety of aircraft, mostly older and worn-out examples, were speeded up. Ironically, some of the most significant damage to the American 3rd Fleet occurred when it was struck by a typhoon on 18 December 1944, leading to the loss of three destroyers with most of their crews, and ten other ships were seriously damaged. Around 800 sailors were missing or dead, and 146 aircraft were destroyed, washed off the decks of carriers or smashed inside the hangars. This caused a number of planned air strikes to be cancelled. However, the Japanese were unable to capitalise on the damage caused to the Americans as the typhoon also prevented them from launching air strikes themselves until the storm had passed over Luzon.

On the last day of 1944 several small groups of Kamikaze aircraft attacked an American auxiliary convoy off Mindoro Island. The tanker *Porcupine* sank following a massive explosion and the ammunition ship Orestes was set on fire by the attacks. Several other ships in the convoy were damaged.

The beginning of 1945 was greeted with an attack by Kamikaze aircraft. On 2 January, a small group of Kamikazes attacked an American Auxiliary Fleet in the Surigao strait. The fleet consisted of 164 ships under the command of Vice-Admiral Oldendorf. During the attack, two 'Zeroes' were shot down, one of which fell on to the tanker Cowanesquep causing slight damage.

The American force encountered another Japanese attack two days later, on 4 January 1945, this time off Panay Island. The islands' proximity reduced the effectiveness of the US ships' radar,

*Scene following a Kamikaze suicide attack against USS* Bunker Hill.

which allowed the Kamikazes to approach undetected. Several Kamikaze aircraft were shot down before they were able to carry out a successful attack. However, a 'Judy', despite being ablaze from AA fire, crashed into the escort carrier USS Ommaney Bay. The 'Judy' was carrying two bombs, one of which detonated in the carrier's hangar, while the other penetrated the engine room and blew up there. After 18 minutes the entire ship was burning. Eventually the wreck was sunk by several torpedoes fired by an accompanying US destroyer. The casualties were 23 sailors killed and 65 seriously wounded. Another victim was the transport ship Lewis L. Dyche, sunk by three Kamikaze aircraft with 63 sailors killed. The commander of the Kyoku Jitsu tai, Sub-Lieutenant Mannen Kazama, celebrated a great victory for the suicide missions.

The next day the Kongo tai 19 under Lieutenant Yutaka Aono took off from Mabalacat, and attacked American ships off Cebu. The unit comprised fifteen bomb-carrying 'Zeroes' escorted by two 'Zero' fighters. Over the target it encountered numerous Hellcat fighters, which quickly decimated the Japanese formation. Only a few Kamikaze aircraft broke through to the American ships, but even these failed to cause significant problems. Their first target was the Australian destroyer HMAS Arunta which was struck, triggering internal explosions, but after four hours the crew managed to extinguish the fires and saved the ship. The next blow was delivered to another Australian ship, the cruiser HMAS Australia, but only slight damage was caused. American ships were also attacked by the Japanese aircraft: two Kamikaze aircraft fell onto the escort carrier USS Manila Bay, slightly damaging her but not preventing operations. The heavy cruiser USS Louisville and the destroyer USS Helm were both hit by Kamikazes, and other ships were targeted without success. The Japanese lost virtually all their available aircraft.

Vice-Admiral Ohnishi gave orders that the ground crews of the unserviceable aircraft still at the airfield should make as many of them as possible ready for flight, banking on the Americans being close to breaking point. Ground crews worked all night and managed to prepare 26 aircraft for take-off. On 6 January 1945, three suicide units took off to attack the American ships. The first was the Kongo tai 20 under Sub-Lieutenant Kunitame Nakao, which consisted of five 'Zero' and one 'Judy' aircraft. The second, the Kongo tai 22, flew under Sub-Lieutenant Teruhiko Miyake, and had five 'Zero' aircraft. The third unit, Kongo tai 23 under Sub-Lieutenant Shigeru Omori, had fourteen 'Zero' and one 'Judy' aircraft. The units took off from Mabalacat and Clark Field between 1100 and 1655. Their targets were the American ships anchored in the bay of Lingayen.

The first ship to be attacked was the minelayer USS Long, which was hit by two Kamikaze aircraft that started an enormous fire. Several minutes later the ship was hit by another 'Zero' suicide attacker, which exploded above the fuel tanks and the ammunition magazine. The force of the explosion substantially wrecked the ship. Finally, a fourth Kamikaze crashed into her, breaking the ship in half. The ship sank, taking 30 sailors with her. The rest of the crew escaped, many with burns. The next American ships to be hit were the minelayer USS Hovey and the fast transport ship Brooks. The heavy cruiser HMAS Australia, which had been hit by Kamikazes previously, received another blow. Two 'Zero' aircraft exploded almost simultaneously on her deck, killing 14 and injuring 16 sailors and putting three 4 in. guns out of action.

The battleships USS California and New Mexico were also subjected to successful Kamikaze attacks. A suicide attacker crashed into the New Mexico's bridge killing a number of officers including the ship's commanding officer Captain Robert W. Fleming and Lieutenant General Herbert Lumsden, Winston Churchill's military representative to General MacArthur. Another aircraft crashed into the light cruiser USS Columbia and three destroyers and one tanker were also hit, but were only slightly damaged and able to continue combat operations.

Another raid came together with more attacks by Kamikaze aircraft. The minelayers Long and Hovey were sunk, and a fire started on the fast transport ship Brooks. This assault, the heaviest Japanese suicide attack over the Philippines, lasted five hours. Late in the day the cruisers HMAS Australia and USS Louisville were attacked again, and although the crews managed to put out the resulting fires, the ships had to be withdrawn and the damage repaired. The Allies lost three ships and a further eleven were damaged, five seriously. The Japanese lost almost all their aircraft, some

200, based on various Philippine airfields. Therefore subsequent suicide attacks were carried out by pairs of Kamikaze aircraft rather than the massed attacks seen previously. One such pair took off on 7 January 1945 heading towards the bay of Lingayen on Mindoro, where troops of Rear-Admiral Daniel E. Barbey's 7th Fleet were landing. They managed to evade American radar and a patrol of Wildcat fighters from escort carriers. The Kamikazes ran into heavy AA defence the moment they spotted the landing troops, and the American fire accounted for both aircraft. One fell into the sea near the light cruiser USS Boise, which was carrying the Allied commander General Douglas MacArthur.

American landing troops were attacked once again in the afternoon of the same day by three more pairs of Kamikaze aircraft. The first of these exploded on the minelayer USS *Palmer*, which sank with the entire crew. Subsequent Kamikaze aircraft approached at low level and broke open the starboard side of the landing ship LST-912, detonating the ammunition the craft was loaded with. The still-floating wreckage was towed away as quickly as possible to make way for other landing ships. The transport ship Calloway was also struck, but damage was not significant.

On the next day, a Ki-46 'Dinah' reconnaissance aeroplane detected an American force sailing forty miles off Bataan. This was a part of Rear-Admiral Barbey's fleet. Further Kamikazes were dispatched to deal with the threat.

The first to successfully locate the ships was an Army fighter which, despite taking numerous hits from anti-aircraft fire, rammed the escort carrier USS *Kadashan Bay* on the waterline. The collision ruptured the carrier's aviation fuel tanks and started a large fire. The crew fought the fire for over three hours and saved the carrier, but it was so heavily damaged that it withdrew from combat. The only casualty was the Kamikaze pilot.

Kamikaze aircraft harried the American ships as far as the bay of Lingayen, where American Hellcat and Wildcat fighters operated. Several Japanese aircraft managed to sneak through these defences: two crashed onto the cruiser HMAS *Australia* that had just been repaired from damage sustained from the previous Kamikaze attacks. The Australian transport ship *Westfalia* came to help HMAS *Australia*, but this ship, too, was attacked by a Kamikaze aircraft that slid across her stern and fell into the sea. The transport had to withdraw to attend to the damage.

Also on the 8 January, Kamikaze aircraft attacked another force of American ships, a transport fleet sailing from the bay of Lingayen under Rear-Admiral Theodor S. Wilkinson. The ships were protected by two escort carriers, and FM-2 Wildcats from these ships succeeded in destroying four of the approaching Kamikazes. However, two more broke through the defences and collided with the carrier USS *Kitkum Bay*. One struck the open lift and exploded in the (fortunately empty) hangar below the deck. The other Japanese attacker skidded along the deck and exploded next to the island. The attack killed sixty crewmen, and eighty were wounded. The ship was seriously damaged and had to be taken in tow, although the next day it was able to move under its own steam.

Tokyo radio announced in the morning news that on 9 January 1945 the Americans had landed in the bay of Lingayen. The communiqué also included information about heavy fighting on the sea and in the air. A great Kamikaze victory was announced. Although the suicide missions were not a complete success, it seemed that the Kamikaze attacks had significantly increased in effectiveness.

Soon after sunrise on 9 January, three aircraft arrived over the bay of Lingayen. The ships were tightly packed in the bay and did not have a great deal of room to manoeuvre. Even so, the first of the attackers missed the leading destroyer and exploded immediately aft of her stern. Another aeroplane attacked the light cruiser USS *Columbia*, which had already been attacked by Kamikaze aircraft several days before. The previous damage had been significant but had not prevented *Columbia* from taking a part in the shore bombardment. This time the damage was more serious, and the Japanese aeroplane blew up deep in the hull, killing 30 sailors and damaging the command centre of the ship. The third attacker was hit by gunfire and broke up in mid air.

The large concentration of American naval forces in the bay of Lingayen was an irresistible target for Japanese suicide aircraft. More came every day of the landings, and American AA defences were stretched to the limit.

In the morning of 9 January, Kamikaze aircraft attacked the battleship USS *Mississippi*, which was taking part in operations for the first time. Two Kamikaze aircraft fell onto her starboard side, destroying a battery of AA guns and killing over 100 sailors. The cruiser HMAS *Australia*, just returned after patching up damage from a previous attack, received her fifth blow from Japanese suicide aircraft. Both ships spent the rest of the day fighting fires.

The last attacks by Kamikaze aircraft during the battle for the Philippines were carried out over five consecutive days. They were accompanied by Kaiten suicide boats, and the combined attacks damaged some 15 ships. All but one were able to remain in the area of the landings and continue operations, but the fast transport ship Belknap was so severely damaged by a Kamikaze on the 11 January 1945 that she had to be sunk by an American torpedo.

On the same evening that the Belknap was scuttled, American intelligence received information that the bay of Lingayen area would be subjected to a concerted attack by Kamikaze aircraft. Allied

*A6M Reisen fighter about to strike the battleship USS* Missouri.

commanders ordered smoke screens to obscure the transport ships in the bay, while larger ships were ordered to sail out to sea to avoid collisions whilst manoeuvring. Both ground troops and the Navy were put at the highest level of combat readiness. Wildcat, Hellcat and Corsair fighters carried out continuous patrols in the air. Eventually the predicted attack came, but it was made up of flying boats which, being slow and cumbersome compared to the American fighters, proved easy prey and were all destroyed.

On 13 January 1945 another Kamikaze attack led to severe damage to USS *Salamaua*, robbing the escort carrier of power and steering. Temporary repairs enabled the ship to get underway again, and she began the long journey back to San Francisco for the extensive work needed to bring her back to fighting trim. The last attack by Kamikaze aircraft over the Philippines took place on the morning of 16 January 1945. Japanese aircraft appeared near the fleet at low level. Two crashed into the landing craft LSM-318 whereupon the vessel listed and sank. Another 'Zero' hit the stern of the landing ship LST-700, and the succeeding explosion immobilised her. Eight Japanese aircraft were shot down.

During the battle of the Philippines, Kamikaze aircraft sank a total of 28 ships, and inflicted various degrees of damage to more than eighty others. They had not stopped the invasion and Japanese losses had been severe, in terms of ships, men and aircraft.

The inevitable defeat of the Japanese in the battle of the Philippines forced a meeting of their top commanders to review possible future action. At Clark Field Admiral Ohnishi, Rear-Admiral Sugimoto, the commander of the 26th *Koku Kantai*, and Admiral Fukudome, the commander of the 2nd *Koku Kantai* met. They decided that future air combat operations would be undertaken by units based in Taiwan, where the next American landing was anticipated. They then approved a programme of ground personnel hiding in the mountains to continue guerrilla war against the American troops.

Aircrews, on the other hand, were to fly to Taiwan using whatever aircraft were available, or would be ferried there by fast destroyers. On the night of 9 March 1945 at 0345 Admiral Ohnishi departed to Taiwan with his staff, in a Mitsubishi G4M4-L transport aircraft. Soon after sunrise they landed at Tainan air base.

Several days later Admiral Ohnishi started forming new *Tokubetsu Kogekitai* units. The first of these Kamikaze unit consisted of two 'Zero' fighters and two 'Judy' dive bombers with an escort of two more 'Zeroes'. The second units had only one 'Zero' for escort. The third unit had just two 'Judy' dive bombers with an escort of two 'Zero' aircraft. The entire formation was named Niitaka tai, after the highest mountain in Taiwan.

The ritual farewell ceremony was completed quickly. The American fleet had been detected approaching on 21 January 1945, a fine day with very good visibility. Ground crews prepared the aircraft for the first take-off by seventeen Kamikaze pilots. Their target was Admiral William Halsey's 3rd Fleet, 350 km off Tainan. However, American aircraft were already en route. Avenger and Helldiver bombers, together with Wildcat, Hellcat and Corsair fighters, attacked the south-east coast of Taiwan, where they sank ten Japanese ships anchored off Tainan, and destroyed sixty aircraft on the airfield. At exactly the same time the first aircraft of Niitaka tai were taking off. Only ten Japanese aircraft took off, and six of them were shot down by patrolling Hellcats.

The remaining four Kamikazes pressed home their attack, and two successfully rammed the carrier USS *Ticonderoga* and the escort carrier USS *Langley*. Fires broke out on both ships and serious damage was caused. Several minutes after the first damage, the USS *Ticonderoga* was hit by the third Kamikaze in the group. Fierce fires caused ammunition to explode and when the blaze was brought under control the new carrier made for Ulithi to disembark her wounded before returning to the US. She was accompanied by the destroyer USS *Maddox*, which had been hit by a previous Kamikaze attack. The Americans replied to that attack with bomber raids against harbours and airfields on Taiwan, carried out by Boeing B-29 Superfortress bombers. However, Taiwan was not the main focus of American attention - that target was located to the north, on Iwo Jima.

# Kamikaze in defence of Iwo Jima

After the Taiwan attacks, the Japanese commanders realised that the American invasion would be carried out closer to Japan, either at Iwo Jima or Okinawa - islands at the Southern fringe of the Japanese archipelago. Japanese forces urgently needed to find a way to prevent the Americans from realising their plans. Air defence for the islands' air bases was required. Air bases on the south coast of Kyushu, one of the four main islands of Japan, were found to be the most useful. From here, it was possible for Japanese aircraft to attack American bases located in the central Pacific, and could also provide support to Okinawa and Iwo Jima. To oppose the American invasion, the Japanese HQ elected to emulate the attack on Pearl Harbor to paralyse the invasion - an attack the main American base in the Pacific at Ulithi in the West Carolinas - although this was at very long range from the Japanese bases. To accomplish this plan, a new 5th *Koku Kantai* was formed to be based in the south of Kyushu, under Admiral Kimpei Teraoka.

The raid was planned for 19 February 1945, and the 601st *Kokutai* under Captain Riichi Sugiyama was selected to carry it out. The day before the raid was to take place, Admiral Teraoka named the unit *Dai-ni Mitate Butai* and Lieutenant Hiroshi Murakawa was appointed its commander. He had 32 aircraft at his disposal, divided into five groups. Aircraft allocated to the suicide attacks comprised twelve D4Y 'Judy' bombers and eight B6N 'Jill' torpedo bombers, escorted by twelve 'Zero' fighters.

Before the plan could be carried out it was abandoned because on the day it had been planned for the Americans commenced their landing on Iwo Jima. The target for the *Mitate tai* was changed, and on the morning of 21 February 1945 all five groups took off from Katori airfield and headed towards Iwo Jima, refuelling on Hachiyo island en route. After the long flight, the Japanese formation arrived over Iwo Jima in the afternoon. The island had been subjected to a vast naval bombardment, and over 30,000 Marines had landed by the time the *Mitate tai* arrived over the battle. By 1659, visibility was limited by smoke and the oncoming dusk. The approaching aircraft had in fact been detected at a range of around 75 miles, though they were initially identified as friendly. The mistake was only discovered when a Hellcat pilot reported shooting down two 'Zeroes'.

The carrier USS *Saratoga* was on approach to her planned operating area when she was attacked by six Kamikaze aircraft. Two were hit by gunfire, but one of these hit the water near the ship's starboard flank and skipped into the hull whereupon the bomb exploded. Another crashed into the forward flight deck and yet another was shot down without doing any damage, while the sixth and final Kamikaze hit the flight deck on the starboard side. Some of the aircraft lodged in a gun

*Kawanishi E7K2 seaplane of Kakumoto Squadron, at Takuma Air Base, just before taking off for a suicide mission on 3 May 1945.*

mounting while the rest fell over the side. The *Saratoga* could not recover her aircraft, which had to divert to nearby escort carriers - though a Wildcat from one of these same escort carriers accidentally landed on the *Saratoga*!

A further two Kamikazes aimed at the escort carrier USS *Lunga Point*, identified as B6N'Jill' torpedo bombers. One was shot down by the AA defences and the other exploded at the water line without doing serious damage. It was growing dark, which may have hampered defensive gunnery - *Lunga Point*'s sister ship USS *Bismarck Sea* was hit by a Kamikaze, followed by a second minutes later. The fires set off munitions, and the power of the explosions was such that they were felt on neighbouring ships. One of the aircraft broke through the deck and its bomb exploded inside the ship, immediately starting a fire. The other aeroplane hit the ship's island, damaging it seriously, and killing the captain, Captain J. L. Pratt.

Another Kamikaze aeroplane attacked the carrier USS *Lunga Point* that had already been damaged in the previous attack. The explosion destroyed the funnel, its pieces scattered all over the deck. Plunging Japanese aircraft also caused fires in the landing ships LST-477 and LST-809 and the fast transport ship *Keokuk* was also hit.

Of the three American ships damaged in the Japanese attack, only the USS *Lunga Point* returned to the line. Fires were still raging on the USS *Saratoga* a few hours after the Japanese attack, and they significantly damaged the interior of the ship. Heavily damaged, she had to go to Pearl Harbor for repairs, departing with 123 dead and 196 wounded sailors.

On the USS *Bismarck Sea*, fire-fighting squads continued their struggle, but fires rapidly spread under the deck, gradually approaching the ammunition magazine and fuel tanks. Eventually an explosion destroyed the ship's stern. After two hours the carrier sank, to the sound of a series of under-water explosions, taking with it 318 sailors. The first attack of the newly-formed *Mitate tai* ended with considerable success. However, the Japanese command failed to press further attacks as they had overestimated the extent of the damage caused.

As a result of reports by reconnaissance aircraft over the battlefield, the Japanese believed that the American fleet would have to withdraw from Iwo Jima and return to Ulithi because of losses sustained. Therefore the abandoned plan for a strike on Ulithi was reactivated. Within 24 hours

*Patrol unit of the 801st Kokutai led by Sub-Lieutenant Masaharu Sugita march past a Kawanishi H8K2 flying boat at Kanoya air base.*

a new formation was established at Kyushu to realise plan 'Tan'. The formation, called *Azusa Tokubetsu Kogekitai*, was prepared for the action which was to take place on 10 March 1945. It had 24 Kugisho P1Y 'Frances' twin-engine bombers split into two attack groups.

The first of these was led by Lieutenant Naoto Kuromaru, and the other by Lieutenant Koetsu Fukuda. Each aircraft carried an 800 kg bomb, with which the bombers could just reach the target. The formation was escorted by five Nakajima C6N-1 Saiun 'Myrt' reconnaissance aircraft. They were to take off from naval aviation bases at Kanoya and Konoike. Meanwhile, Kawanishi H8K2 'Emily' flying boats would be taking off from the bay of Kagoshima.

The order to take off came on the morning of 11 March 1945. An hour before that Admiral Ugaki himself flew to Kanoya, where he spoke briefly to the participants, and drank the farewell sake with them then the crews went to their aircraft. The weather was good, with just a few clouds in the sky.

The plan dictated that the flying boat crews would act as pathfinders for the main formation, and upon reaching the island of Jap they would return home. The 'Myrt' reconnaissance aircraft were detailed to keep the formation informed about the number and location of American ships in Ulithi. However, due to engine problems, only one 'Emily' flying boat could be prepared for take-off. The 'Myrt' reconnaissance aircraft reported that seventeen American aircraft carriers, the core of the US Navy in the Pacific, were anchored at Ulithi. The Japanese formation took off by 08.50, and at 09.10 it passed Cape Sada on the south coast of the Osumi peninsula. After thirty minutes of flying, six of the 'Frances' bombers turned back due to engine problems. Nineteen aircraft continued to their target. They cruised at optimum settings to ensure that they would have enough fuel to reach the target.

The flight continued in relatively good weather, and the light clouds allowed observation of landmarks, such as the Douglas coral reef. After eight hours of flight only fifteen aircraft remained – a further four had turned back because of various mechanical failures. By this time the aircraft were some 200 miles north of Jap Island, still in Japanese territory. It was there that they encountered an American convoy which requested identification codes. The Japanese did not react, but increased speed to pass it as quickly as possible.

Then, as the formation flew over Okinotori Shima island, the weather suddenly broke. Dark storm clouds and heavy rain rendered orientation impossible. At 19:10 the 'Myrt' reconnaissance aircraft and the 'Emily' flying boat turned back. Pilots of the 'Frances' bombers were left alone, and in the storm they did not really know where they were, as they could not see any landmarks.

Finally they saw an island, and identified it as Jap meaning they would still have an hour of flight to reach Ulithi. Meanwhile, four 'Frances' bombers left the group intending to land on the island, as their fuel tanks were almost empty. It is not clear what happened to these aircraft subsequently.

The other aircraft headed east, towards Ulithi. Finally, after twelve hours of flight, the crews saw ahead a well-lit American naval base. The Americans did not expect an attack, because by that stage of the war the Japanese had no aircraft carriers, or aircraft of the range that would be able to threaten the American base. There was, therefore, little in place to warn of an air attack, leaving the way open for the Kamikaze attack.

Most of the aircraft's fuel tanks were nearly empty, but it appeared success was within the formation's reach. The first to attack was Lieutenant Fukuda, who was forced to glide in as his aircraft ran out of fuel on the approach. The aeroplane crashed into the aircraft carrier USS *Randolph*, where a bomb exploded on deck. A hole 30 m by 18 m was torn in the deck, while 34 were killed and 125 wounded.

Many of the crew were watching a film in the hangar deck at the time of the attack and their first warning was when the 'Frances' plunged through the flight deck. The explosion woke the base up: searchlights and flares were aimed at the horizon, because an attack from the air had not been considered feasible, and because radar had missed the approaching raid. The initial reaction was that a miniature submarine had broken through into the harbour, an impression reinforced as the gliding 'Frances' could not be heard approaching. By the time the AA gunners were informed of the nature of the attack, it was over. All the remaining aircraft had crashed into the sea. Operation Tan, in which the Japanese had placed so much hope, ended in a fiasco. The USS *Randolph* was damaged, but not severely. The attack emphasised how burning fuel from a Kamikaze attack often compounded the damage by setting fires and detonating a ship's own munitions. Fukuda's 'Frances', with its utterly dry tanks, consequently did much less damage than might have been expected.

On the day after the attack a Japanese 'Myrt' reconnaissance aeroplane appeared over Ulithi. Its report revealed that the operation had been a failure, as all the American ships were still anchored safely in the harbour. This forced the Japanese HQ to reorganise attack units. As the Imperial Japanese Navy no longer had a fleet, it focused all of its attention on aviation. For that reason the 10th *Koku Kantai*, which included the 11th, 12th and 13th *Kokutai*, took over the bases and area of operation of the 5th *Koku Kantai*. The new operational deployment was therefore as follows:

1st *Koku Kantai* based on Taiwan, with 300 aircraft,
3rd *Koku Kantai* to defend the east coast of Japan, with 800 aircraft,
5th *Koku Kantai* to defend the west coast of Japan, with 600 aircraft,
10th *Koku Kantai* to defend the south coast of Japan, with 400 aircraft.

Altogether the Japanese Navy had 2,100 aircraft which it intended to employ against the US Navy and USAAF, with their overwhelming superiority in quantity and quality of materiel and crews. After its bitter experience in the battle of the Philippines the Navy demanded that its aviation units should destroy American ships at all cost – and so Kamikaze units became the principal means of combat. The 5th and 10th *Koku Kantai* therefore consisted entirely of suicide units.

On the 18 March around 100 American aircraft took off from their aircraft carriers to attack Japanese airfields and ports on the south coast of Kyushu, the southernmost of the main Japanese islands. Japanese reconnaissance observed this and considered that most of the American carriers were far out in the ocean: the Japanese HQ decided that this situation gave them the perfect opportunity to destroy the American fleet.

A group of fifty aircraft from the 5th *Koku Kantai* flew towards the target, the American task force TF-38 and its aircraft carriers. Vice-Admiral Marc Mitscher had sent his aircraft to bomb Kyushu and while the American aircraft were bombing targets on Kyushu, the first Kamikaze aircraft arrived over American aircraft carriers. They broke through the AA defences and attacked the USS *Intrepid* from several sides. The USS *Wasp* became the next target, and 102 sailors lost their lives and 269 were wounded on the two carriers. Worsening weather saved the American ships from more Kamikaze attacks.

Another Kamikaze attack took place the next day, on 19 March 1945. The first strike wave was made up of 45 Kamikaze aircraft, and the attack was carried out in the morning. This time the carrier USS *Franklin* was the target for the attack. During the first attack the lift and the island were damaged. The second blow was more serious. The bomb-laden aeroplane destroyed a catapult, and as the explosion reached nearby aircraft, almost the entire deck burst into flames, with 0.5in and 20mm ammunition and rocket projectiles set off by the fire.

Burning petrol soaked through the deck and caught fire underneath. At 09:52 the ship was shaken by a large explosion, as a D4Y 'Judy' aeroplane hit. Smoke and flames covered the ship, only thinning out only after subsequent explosions which marked the destruction of the ammunition magazine. The struggle to save the ship lasted the whole day. Eventually, in the evening, the crews put out the fires, but the carrier was no longer able to take part in operations, and was sent back to the USA for repair. 772 sailors were buried at sea, and 300 injured were sent to hospitals.

A further Kamikaze attack was carried out on 21 March 1945, when aerial reconnaissance reported American ships some 500km south of Kyushu. Admiral Matome Ugaki ordered that the attack should be carried out using Kugisho Ohka Model 11 rocket aircraft. The attack group was organised by Captain Motoharu Okamura, commander of the Ohka unit that had eighteen Mitsubishi G4M2e Model 24J 'Betty' bombers. Sixteen Betty aircraft carried Ohka aircraft underneath, while the remaining two were armed with bombs. These provided navigation backup. Escort was to be provided by fifty fighters, and the whole group was commanded by Lieutenant Commander Goro Nonaka.

The heavily laden Betty bombers took off first. The clock at Kanoya showed 1135. Due to a number of engine failures, only thirty 'Zero' fighters took off to escort the group.

After some two hours of flight, the Japanese aircraft found themselves 80km from the target. Before they could attack, American Hellcat and Wildcat fighters appeared, guided by radar. The American aircraft quickly dispersed the Japanese formation and started shooting the bombers down one after another. Fifteen Japanese bombers were shot down within twenty minutes while a further three sought cover in the clouds where they were able to hide for 15 minutes , until being located and shot down. Fifteen of the Japanese escort fighters were also shot down, and the surviving aircraft were so damaged that most crashed on landing. This was not an auspicious debut by the Ohka rocket-propelled aircraft.

*Mitsubishi G4M2 Model 24 Tei bombers of the Ohka-tai unit belonging to the 721st Kokutai with Ohka Model 11 flying bombs attached, ready for take-off on 21 March 1945.*

# Fighting at Okinawa

With the capture of Iwo Jima, it became evident that the Americans would next threaten Okinawa, one of the Ryūkyū chain of islands which stretches from Taiwan right to the edge of the Japanese main islands. Due to the closeness of the main American force to the Japanese homeland Admiral Ugaki, the Navy commander on Kyushu, demanded that all actions of the naval and army aviation be co-ordinated. This led to the formation of *Shimpū Tokko Kikusui Butai* which included aircraft of the 3rd, 5th and 10th *Koku Kantai* supplemented by *Sentai* units of the army. The main base was located at Kanoya, with support from all the airfields in the southern part of Kyushu. To confuse American reconnaissance, many dummy airfields were built throughout the island, with wooden aircraft mock-ups dispersed around them.

Technical equipment of the *Kikusui* formations varied widely, and consisted of a range of available aircraft, including civil aircraft as well as transport and liaison types. The shortage of fuel was becoming evident, and this meant that new candidates for suicide units would spend very little time in training. Army *Sentai* units were commanded by General Miyoshi, whose few volunteers had fortunately already been trained.

On 26 March 1945 the American invasion forces landed at Kerama Island, close to Okinawa. The Japanese put their forces onto the highest combat readiness. Thirty Japanese aircraft were used in the attack. The first Kamikaze aircraft took off to attack on the last day of March. They managed to penetrate the dense AA fire, and despite attacks by American fighters, they arrived over the enemy ships. The first fell onto Admiral Spruance's flagship, the heavy cruiser USS *Indianapolis*. This was struck by two D4Y 'Judy' aircraft that exploded, opening two large flaming holes in the deck. Explosions inside the ship followed soon afterwards. Admiral Spruance was forced to move his flag to the battleship USS *New Mexico* and the *Indianapolis* returned to the US. During the same attack the Japanese damaged two other American ships.

On 1 April 1945 at 0830 the first US Marines landed on Hagushi Beach, between the airfields of Yomitan and Kadena. The Japanese defence plan, *Ten*-Go, included a total of 4,500 aircraft, although the special Kamikaze units had only 355 aircraft at their disposal, with a further 344 aircraft for escort and reconnaissance duties. The first *Kikusui* action commenced the same day, at about 10:00.

The first Kamikaze crashed onto the battleship USS *West Virginia*, but because the 'Zero' hit the heavily armoured forward turret, damage to the ship was not major.

The next suicide aeroplane attacked the ammunition ship LST-884, killing ten and wounding 27 more. The burning ship was towed away so that an explosion would not damage other ships. The

*Shichisho-7-Tai formation at Wonsan base during preparation for action on 5 April 1945.*

*Last preparations for a suicide mission by a Mitsubishi G4M2 Model 24 Tei carrier aircraft from the 721st Kokutai (Jinrai Butai) at Kanoya air base in April 1945. An Ohka Model 11 rocket-powered flying bomb can be seen in the bomb bay. The crew was commanded by Captain Nonaka of the 721st Kokutai. The photo was probably taken on 21 March 1945.*

third ship to be hit was the transport Hinsdale, which was saved after a short struggle with fires, but was too badly damaged to remain on station. Thanks to effective AA defences, most Kamikaze aircraft were shot down or missed their targets.

The same day as the US troops landed on Okinawa, the British Royal Navy took part in operations for the first time in this campaign. Within TF-57, RN forces scouted south of Okinawa, where they could oppose any Japanese counter-attack from Taiwan. Indeed, on 1 April 1945, Kamikaze aircraft from Taiwan attacked the invasion forces. Two Japanese aircraft hit the battleship HMS *King George V*, the flagship of Vice-Admiral B. Rawlings, but they did little damage as the British ship was very heavily armoured. Two Kamikaze aeroplanes each crashed onto the carriers HMS *Indomitable* and HMS *Indefatigable*, and one on to the carrier HMS *Illustrious*. However, the three carriers were built with armoured decks so suffered little of the serious damage that had afflicted some of the US carriers struck by Kamikazes.

The next day, the 2 April, at 0830 Kamikaze aircraft arrived again, first attacking the fast transport ship *Dickerson*. A successful Kamikaze strike destroyed the bridge while the bomb broke free from the aeroplane and exploded below deck, triggering an ammunition explosion. To prevent damage to neighbouring ships, the transport ship was towed away near to the island of Kerama, where she was eventually sunk by destroyers.

Fifteen radar-equipped destroyers had been brought to the vicinity of Okinawa to escort the American fleet and the protect troops landing on the island. Their first line was located on a semi-circle of 75 miles and the second line 36 miles from the north-east cape of the Bolo peninsula, several

*Crew of a Mitsubishi G4M2 Model 24 Tei carrier aircraft from the 721st Kokutai (Jinrai Butai) awaiting take-off. An Ohka Model 11 flying bomb is already attached under the aircraft.*

miles north of Hagushi beach. Their early warning service significantly increased the protection of the American forces from attacks by the Japanese aircraft.

Over the course of a week, Admiral Ugaki prepared a mass attack of Kamikaze aircraft against this type of American defence. It was intended to be part of a great counter-offensive, which would involve 547 aircraft from the Navy and 188 from the Army. American aerial reconnaissance on 4 April spotted a significant concentration of Japanese aircraft on the bases in the southern part of Kyushu. Two days later the American HQ ordered its aircraft carriers to launch as many carrier-borne aircraft as possible against the Japanese bases. Early in the morning, several hundred American carrier-borne aircraft took off and attacked the bases on Kyushu. Upon their return, they reported that most of the Japanese aircraft were in flames and large numbers destroyed. However mostly only wooden mock-ups had been hit.

The core of the Japanese units remained untouched, and the Americans were not aware of the number of aircraft still available to the Japanese. On the morning of 5 April 1945, all the Japanese pilots were briefed for the attack, which was launched on 6 April 1945 after a Nakajima C6N 'Myrt' reconnaissance aeroplane reported that American ships had appeared south of Amami Oshima island. This was ideal for the Japanese, as the Americans had no carrier cover - the American carriers had moved away to attack the giant Japanese battleship *Yamato* which was approaching the island on a 'death or glory' mission.

The first wave of Japanese attack aircraft consisted of 195 naval aviation machines, including eighty Kamikaze aircraft. Included in the force were eight Mitsubishi G4M2 Model 24e 'Betty' bombers that carried Ohka Model 11 rocket-propelled aircraft. Escort of the formation was entrusted to Mitsubishi A6M 'Zero' fighters. The rest of the force consisted of standard bombers.

The radar destroyer USS *Colhoun* was in radar position no. 2, when at about 0230 Japanese aircraft first showed on her radar screens. Several minutes later the aircraft were noticed and the ship's AA fire opened up. No damage was caused in this initial attack. Later, a group of eleven Japanese aircraft arrived. It was 0700 and the sun was about to rise. A 'Betty' bomber dropped a torpedo in the direction of the destroyer, but the ship evaded it. Another group of Japanese aircraft arrived at Kerama Retto Island, where ammunition ships were anchored and being unloaded. Japanese aircraft arrived above the assault transport Logan Victory at the moment when the crew were offloading ammunition.

At this point an approaching aircraft was spotted by lookouts on the ships Hobbs Victory and Halaula Victory as it appeared from behind a small island. Both ships opened fire and the Japanese pilot returned fire with 20mm cannon, killing fourteen sailors aboard Logan Victory and wounding ten more. Under the strafing, ammunition boxes started to explode. Fire broke out on the ship and

*Briefing the crews of Nakajima B6N2 Tenzan torpedo bombers of the 254th Kogeki Hikotai of the 601st Kokutai, before a suicide mission. The briefing was conducted on the morning of 20 February 1945 by Lieutenant Hiroshi Murakawa.*

started to spread very quickly. At around midday, the ship exploded and sank. A Japanese 'Betty' bomber aimed at the transport ship *Halaula Victory*. The ship changed course, and the low flying aeroplane hit the sea before it reached its target. Some of the ships managed to find refuge in the harbour on the island of Kerama Retto where AA defences were ready. Two Japanese aircraft approached the island, but one of these was shot down immediately. The other, flying at extremely low level, suddenly changed direction and hit the side of the transport ship Hobbs Victory. This triggered an ammunition explosion. Fire-fighting squads continued to fight the fire for four hours after which the ship was destroyed by a second explosion.

At about midday, the radar destroyer USS *Colhoun* received a report that the Japanese had attacked task force TF-58. However, the radar operators could not see any Japanese aircraft. The formation of Japanese aircraft, approaching from Kyushu, was finally detected at 1219. It consisted of small groups, averaging six machines, which were constantly changing altitude. A similar picture was seen on the radar screens of the destroyer USS *Bush*, in radar position no. 1. Single aeroplanes could be seen around the main groups of Japanese aircraft, probably providing escort.

The first such aeroplane was spotted by the destroyer's captain, R. E. Westholm. This was a Nakajima B6N 'Jill' torpedo-bomber flying at wave top height directly at the destroyer. All the ship's guns opened fire. When it was some 1,500 m from the target, the ship made a rapid turn, but the Japanese aeroplane could not be shaken off. At 1515 the 'Jill' crashed into the destroyer and blew a large hole in the starboard side. The 'Jill's torpedo was torn loose and exploded in the engine room. In a further explosion shrapnel damaged the starboard side of the bridge, killing all of the officers and destroying medical rooms and other auxiliary facilities. The destroyer USS *Colhoun* went to the aid of the burning ship.

The *Colhoun* worked up to its full speed of 35 knots, and requested help from a group of American fighters on patrol. American aircraft arrived and engaged the Japanese, but they had to leave, as they were running short of fuel and ammunition. At about 1600 USS *Colhoun* found the burning USS *Bush*. They could also see fifteen Japanese fighters, circling the blazing ship. The landing ship LCS/L-64 also approached the burning destroyer, having heard the distress signal. USS *Bush* was motionless, shrouded in thick smoke. The landing ship started a rescue, as the destroyer was listing increasingly to starboard. USS *Colhoun* took over AA defence duties.

At 1700 one of the circling Japanese aircraft attacked USS *Colhoun*. The ship turned, and the bomb dropped by the Japanese dive bomber failed to hit the target. Other attacks followed the first – they included an Aichi D3A 'Val' bomber which dived on the ship, and a 'Zero' which flew in at low level. The first of these was hit by anti-aircraft fire and broke up, while the 'Zero' fighter crashed

*Aichi D3A2 Model 22 dive bombers of the Jimmu-tai take off for a suicide mission.*

some 50m aft of the destroyer's stern. Another 'Zero' approached the starboard side, unnoticed until it was too late, and hit the deck. Burning petrol flooded the deck, and the bomb penetrated the engine room where it exploded and opened a metre square hole below the water line.

At about 1730 the USS *Bush* was attacked again by more Kamikaze aircraft. Meanwhile, the USS *Colhoun* was set on by another 'Zero' accompanied by two 'Val' bombers. The attackers took separate paths, which divided the defensive fire - one attacked the ship from starboard, the second from port, and the third attacker aimed at the middle of the deck. One 'Val' fell some 200m behind the ship, and the second 'Val' fell into the sea out of control. The 'Zero' hit and damaged the ship at the water line, creating a hole that was 2m long and over 1m wide.

Japanese aircraft continued to circle the American ships, observing the results of their colleagues' attacks. Three further Kamikazes aimed at the destroyer USS *Colhoun*. Her AA fire had to revert to manual control, presumably due to problems with radar ranging, but they still shot down one of the attacking 'Zero' aircraft that aimed at the starboard side. A 'Val' came in from the port side, aiming at no. 3 gun turret, which it crashed into. The burning aeroplane fell beside the ship into the sea, where its bomb exploded and tore a large hole at the water line. Meanwhile USS *Bush* was struck by another Kamikaze and this time the damage could not be contained. Three hours after the *Bush* sank, the USS *Colhoun* turned over and followed her sister to the seabed.

As the destroyers suffered their ordeal, other Kamikaze aircraft broke through over Hagushi beach where they were met by heavy AA fire. Some of the aircraft attacked the ships that were coming to help the stricken destroyers. The minelayers USS *Emmons* and USS *Rodman*, were both attacked by Kamikazes and conventional attackers. One 'Val' crashed into the deck of USS *Rodman*, another crashed into the sea, while a 'Zero' dropped a bomb that exploded near the spot where the first 'Val' had crashed. Then the 'Zero' flew into the hole torn by the bomb, triggering a large explosion. Other Kamikaze aircraft were dispersed or shot down by patrolling Hellcat and Corsair fighters.

At about 1330 a group of 75 Army Kamikaze aircraft approached. One of them was shot down by an American Corsair fighter before the attack began. A twin-engined Kawasaki Ki-45 'Nick' bomber crashed into the minelayer USS *Emmons*, the resulting explosion tearing off the entire stern of the ship. One of the Nakajima Ki-43 'Oscar' fighters fell onto the bridge, where it exploded and destroyed the ship's command centre. Another 'Nick' crashed into a 5 in gun turret and destroyed it. The fifth Kamikaze aeroplane hit the bow of the ship and exploded at the water line. USS *Emmons* was now completely ablaze. The sixth Kamikaze aeroplane completed the destruction as it approached at very low altitude and rammed into the ship's bow. After an explosion the ship broke up and sank rapidly, taking 61 sailors with her.

Meanwhile the USS *Rodman* managed to reach Kerama Retto, where makeshift repairs were made. After another Japanese attack of over eight hours it was clear that the Japanese pilots were mostly inexperienced, for which they paid a high price. During the attack the Japanese used a total of 248 aircraft - of these, only a dozen escort aircraft and one 'Betty' bomber returned to their bases on Kyushu. This was one of the largest Japanese mass attacks, carried out almost entirely by suicide units. The Americans did not suffer enough damage to materially alter the battle, though the psychological effects on the men under attack may have been more significant.

Another Japanese attack was carried out the next day, 7 April 1945. It was much weaker than the previous day's efforts, due to high losses already suffered. This time, 114 aircraft approached Okinawa. It was late afternoon, and several dozen American fighters patrolled the air to intercept and destroy any Japanese formation. Despite this defence, several Kamikaze aircraft broke through. A 'Judy' crashed into the carrier USS *Hancock*, killing 50 sailors instantly, while the ensuing fire caused the death of a further 40. The fire was eventually extinguished, but the ship had to sail back to Ulithi and then Pearl Harbour to have the damage repaired.

Two aircraft, a 'Judy' and an 'Oscar', also hit the battleship USS *Maryland*. The ship burned for a few hours and could not continue combat operations, so withdrew. Serious damage was also inflicted on other ships, such as the carrier USS *San Jacinto* and two modern destroyers, USS *Haynsworth* and USS *Taussig*. A total of some twenty American ships were damaged that day, and the Japanese lost one hundred aircraft.

Two days of Kamikaze aircraft attacks gave the Japanese a 'priceless victory', as Japanese propaganda claimed. Kamikaze formations managed to sink five ships and damaged 34 more to various degrees. The price they had to pay did not seem to match the 'success' - the Japanese forces had lost 350 aircraft. Admiral Ugaki had increasing problems with the organisation of subsequent attack units, and he needed to collect aircraft and pilots wherever he could. Eventually, on 12 April

*On 21 March 1945 commanders and comrades bid farewell to crews flying off on a suicide mission. Pilots of the 723rd Kokutai sat in the cockpits of the Ohka Model 11 aircraft, and the carrier aircraft (Mitsubishi G4M2 Model 24 Tei) were from the 708th Hikotai.*

1945, he was able to dispatch 350 aircraft against the American fleet off Okinawa. These included 100 suicide aircraft from the Navy, and 60 from the Army. The formation also included ten 'Betty' bombers with Ohka suicide rocket aircraft attached, and 150 escort fighters. The *Kikusui* 2 formation commenced an attack. Landing ships grouped off Hagushi beach were their principal target.

The approaching Japanese formation was detected by radar on the destroyer USS *Cassin Young*, and later by the destroyer USS Purdy. Soon afterwards, Japanese aircraft went in to attack. Thirty Kamikaze aircraft of the first strike wave aimed for the USS *Cassin Young*, but only a 'Val' managed to press home the attack. It crashed into an ammunition magazine, setting off an explosion and the resulting fire caused severe damage to the ship, necessitating repairs at Kerama Retto behind the front line.

Just after midday, the main group of Japanese aircraft - 200 machines of various types - approached Okinawa. American AA defences were strong, but as the Japanese attacked from all sides the American defence was stretched. One of the attacking 'Judy' aircraft struck the carrier USS *Enterprise* a glancing blow, followed later by a second such aircraft which struck the flight deck and immolated an aircraft waiting to be catapulted off. Kamikaze aircraft attacked everything possible. The landing ship LCS/L-33 was also struck and sank with a big explosion as. The flagship, USS Tennessee, was hit, her crew having run out of luck after shooting down three previous attacking Japanese aircraft. One Kamikaze aeroplane fell onto the bridge and the next one crashed into the 4 in gun positions. Twelve gunners were killed, and 176 sailors were wounded. American pilots engaged the Japanese suicide aircraft - Major Hapsen from the USMC 'Wolf Pack' squadron shot down three aircraft, a 'Zero', a 'Jill' and a Nakajima Ki-44 'Tojo', within a few minutes. Lieutenant *Callaghan* also shot down three Japanese attack aircraft within five minutes. As the American defences responded to the initial overwhelming assault, the Japanese attack gradually lost momentum.

Nevertheless, the remaining Japanese pilots continued their attacks. The battleships USS *Missouri*, USS *New Mexico* and USS *Idaho* were damaged, and fires broke out on the light cruiser USS *Oakland* which had been hit by two Kamikaze aircraft. A total of thirteen destroyers, three minelayers and five other ships were damaged, most having to be sent away for repair.

It was not over. A formation of 'Betty' bombers and 'Val' dive bombers appeared on the destroyer USS *Mannert L. Able's* radar screens. The picket ship put up an AA barrage, which succeeded in dispersing the Japanese aircraft. Then, as three more groups of Japanese aircraft appeared on her radar screens, the destroyer requested help from American fighters. After fifteen minutes, the first Japanese aircraft were spotted from the destroyer, and a moment later the ship was hit by a 'Judy' aeroplane. Three 'Zero' aircraft were also spotted approaching, just above the water. Two were shot

*Souvenir photos of 1CPO Heiji Ueda in the cockpit of an Ohka Model 11 from the 721st Kokutai at Kanoya airfield in April 1945. The pilot carried out a suicide attack on 16 April 1945, against allied ships grouped south-east of Kyushu.*

down, but the third hit the American ship and damaged the engine room, causing the ship to lose speed and manoeuvrability. The ship's defences were, however, untouched. Eventually the fire in the engine room was extinguished and some of the machinery was repaired, restoring the ship's ability to manoeuvre fully. However, 90 sailors were killed, and 35 were wounded, mostly badly burned.

Just as it seemed that the Japanese attack was nearing its end, an Ohka ('Baka') aeroplane flown by 22-year-old Lieutenant Saburo Doi crashed into the side of the destroyer. His strike was the last blow for the American destroyer, which broke in half and sank within a few minutes leaving no survivors. This was the first American ship sunk by the Ohka rocket-propelled aeroplane. With night coming on, the remaining Japanese aircraft attempted to steal away in the darkness, but three more of them were shot down. The Americans requested reinforcements and expanded their patrols both at sea and in the air.

When Japanese aircraft re-appeared on 8 April 1945, many of them were shot down. Even given their relative success at warding off the Japanese, the Americans desperately wanted to end to this kind of threat. Therefore, two days later task force TF-58 launched an air attack on Japanese air bases on Kyushu. However, only 55 Japanese aircraft were destroyed, and Kamikaze units were left untouched, allowing the pilots of Admiral Ugaki to prepare for another attack by the Kokusui 3 formation.

This attack formation consisted of 44 Ginga bombers and six Betty bombers carrying Ohka rocket-propelled aircraft. Their escort consisted of eighty 'Zero' and Shiden fighters. The formation took off on 16 April 1945, and it was detected by the radar post no. 1 on the destroyer USS *Laffey*. Within a few minutes American fighters were in the air ready to repel the first attacks by the approaching Kamikaze aircraft. Six Japanese aircraft were shot down, but the next two Kamikaze aircraft, flying immediately above the water, got through. They hit the gun turret and the middle of the deck. A bomb fell through a hole in the deck and exploded inside the ship, igniting the fuel tanks and the auxiliary magazine. Thick smoke and flames caused serious problems as she was attacked by more Kamikaze aircraft. The USS *Laffey* defended herself bravely and effectively - she was hit by six Kamikazes and four bombs, but remained afloat and survived, shooting down nine aircraft in the 80 minute action.

Radar post no. 14, where the destroyer USS *Pringle* was on patrol, also came in for sustained attack. The *Pringle* was attacked simultaneously by three 'Val' dive bombers. The ship's defences destroyed one of these but the other two hit home. Their bombs exploded inside the ship, tearing the structure apart, and the destroyer sank within five minutes, taking around 100 crew members with her. The carrier USS *Intrepid* also took two hits by Kamikaze aircraft. By the time they were forced to turn back, the Japanese had damaged six other American ships.

Further Japanese suicide attacks were carried out during the next ten days, but only by single aeroplanes. During that time twelve ships were damaged, while the minelayer USS *Swallow* and the landing ship LCS-15 were sunk. The Americans, however, were expecting another massive attack by Kamikaze aircraft, and indeed such an attack began on 27 April 1945. Just before dawn, 115 Japanese aircraft arrived, fifty of them from the Army. In the frenzied attack, the destroyer USS *Hutchins* and transport ship *Canada Victory* were sunk.

However, the main attack was yet to come. This was made the following day, with the *Kikusui* 4 formation's 120 Navy aircraft and 45 Army aircraft, including 59 Kamikazes. Four 'Betty' bombers with Ohka aircraft also took part. The Japanese arrived over the target just after dawn, but their desperate attacks netted the Japanese very poor results with only a few ships struck, with mainly only slight damage suffered. The exception was the hospital ship USS *Comfort*, attacked by one of the Kamikaze aircraft despite the clearly lit Red Cross marking. The attack killed 28 people, including nurses and wounded patients. This attack infuriated American opinion, particularly the servicemen who might have to rely on the hospital ships. Nurse 2nd Lieutenant Louise Campbell noted: "*The hardest thing for the men to take was the fact that nurses had been killed, injured and horribly burned. They kept talking about it and muttering threats against an enemy that would willfully do such a thing.*"

The last attack by Kamikaze aircraft during April 1945 was carried out on the 29th. Only a few Japanese aircraft managed to break through the American AA defences to attack the destroyers USS *Haggard* and USS *Hazelwood* as well as two minelayers. Altogether, the April attacks cost Japan dearly, with 200 aircraft lost.

In May, when US Marine troops broke through the heavily fortified Japanese positions on Okinawa, in the Shuri area, Generals Mitsuru Ushijima and Isamu Cho decided to carry out an all-out attack. It was to commence on 4 May 1945. Air attacks to support the offensive commenced the day before, to prepare the ground for Japanese troops. The air attack was primarily aimed against Yomitan airfield and was carried out by Mitsubishi Ki-21 'Sally' bombers of the 6th *Sentai*, twelve of which had taken off from Kadena on Kyushu. The results of the attack were poor: the Americans were prepared, and their fighters, guided by radar on patrolling destroyers, dispersed the Japanese aircraft, and subsequently shot most of them down.

These destroyers on radar posts were problematic for the Japanese, so they became the primary targets for the *Kikusui* 5 formation that commenced its attack on the following day. 86 aircraft of the Navy and 37 of the Army took off from bases at Kanoya and on Formosa. The action also involved seven 'Betty' bombers with Ohka aircraft. The Navy aircraft group was led by Sub-Lieutenants Tadahide Tsuchiyama, Akira Horiie and Lieutenant Katsumi Murakami. Their target was Radar post no. 10, the destroyer USS *Little*, first attacked by Lieutenant Murakami with his 'Val' bombers. Three of these were shot down by the Americans, but the fourth aeroplane sneaked through the defences and flew into the superstructure, which was damaged. The bomb from the aircraft exploded under the ship's deck, triggering an explosion in the third and fourth boilers, which, in turn, tore off part of the deck, and the ship sank within twelve minutes, killing 30. That same day, the rocket-launching landing ship LSM/R-195 was attacked off Okinawa by a 'Judy' aeroplane. After the attack her rocket system exploded, destroying the landing ship completely.

Meanwhile, the crew of the minelayer USS *Aaron Ward* displayed commendable courage when, despite six Kamikaze aircraft hitting the ship, they managed to save the vessel and to sail away from the combat zone for repairs. Ten other ships suffered various degrees of damage.

Soon after midnight on 4 May 1945, sixty Japanese bombers attacked the US 10th Fleet. The attack was not very effective, and American losses were small. In the morning, a co-ordinated attack by ground and air forces of the Japanese was made. Once again, the radar destroyers were the first targets of the Japanese pilots. Destroyer USS *Luce* suffered a rapid attack at observation post no. 12, as within three minutes, two Kamikaze aircraft crashed into her: an 'Oscar' on the deck and a 'Zero' on the stern. Explosions resulted in a fire that started to spread very quickly and the boiler and fuel tank exploded after ten minutes, killing 148 sailors, and wounding 94. The destroyer turned on her side and slowly submerged.

*Aichi D3A2 dive bomber with a bomb attached under the fuselage and additional bombs under the wings readied for a suicide mission by ground crew. Note the white band on the wheel cover, showing flight leader.*

The destroyer USS *Morrison* on post no. 11 was the second to be attacked. Although the ship and a patrolling Corsair each shot down one 'Zero', two others fell on the ship simultaneously in almost-vertical dives. Their strikes triggered an explosion in one boiler. Despite the surviving crew's best efforts to defend the ship, it was hit by an Aichi E13A 'Jake' floatplane carrying a bomb. This new attacker's explosion completed the destruction as the ship sank with only 71 survivors out of 331 sailors on board.

Meanwhile, Kamikaze aircraft reached Hagashi beaches where they attacked anchored landing ships. The first explosion took place after one 'Zero' hit the rocket landing ship LSM/R-195, exploding the rockets with which the ship was shelling Japanese positions on the island. Only 25 sailors survived this attack, as the Japanese next turned to the landing ship LSM-190, which exploded when a 'Judy' hit her. The explosion was so powerful that the ship lost its stern and sank immediately. Kamikaze aircraft began by attacking everything they could see, and then the Ohka rocket aircraft started their attack. The first of these, flown by Lieutenant Susumu Ohashi, aimed at the destroyer USS *Willey*. The crew spotted it when it was some 200m from the ship, flying about 12m above the water. The ship opened fire with all guns. Their efforts succeeded, and the Ohka exploded 25m from the ship.

The remains of a 'Betty' bomber downed by one of the patrolling Hellcat fighters fell into the sea as another Ohka glided in from an altitude of 50m. The Ohka started to descend, plummeting to an altitude of 3m, then started its rocket engine. Again, the destroyer USS *Willey* was the target, but her 5in gun fire barrage destroyed the little rocket aircraft as it approached.

The third Ohka attacked the minelayer USS Grady that had already repelled an attack by two 'Zero' aircraft. The 'Betty' bomber that carried the Ohka had descended to 600m and launched its charge, after which it took evasive action. Meanwhile, the Ohka was some 250m from its target. The pilot successfully guided the aircraft to strike the ship, but it hit a gun post and fell into the sea with its undetonated explosive charge. Three men on the gun post were killed but otherwise the ship was unharmed.

The fourth Ohka hit the destroyer USS *Shea* that provided observation at radar post no. 14. The Ohka closed in at an altitude of 2m, so low that the crew could not see it. It exploded and destroyed the ship's rear superstructure, causing a fire that damaged the ship so much that it could not remain on station, and withdrew to undertake repair work. Twenty-seven sailors were killed and 91 wounded.

The other three Ohka aircraft were shot down with their carrier aircraft before they were able to enter action. Three 'Judy' aircraft damaged the light cruiser USS *Birmingham*. Turret no. 2 was destroyed, and internal explosions immobilised the ship, which had to be towed away for repairs along with the carrier USS *Sangamon*, whose deck was destroyed when two 'Zero' aircraft attacked.

The British aircraft carriers of TF-57 fared better when they were attacked off Miyako Retto. Thanks to their armoured decks and sturdier design than most contemporary aircraft carriers, they generally suffered minimal damage when they were attacked by Kamikazes. HMS *Formidable* was struck by a 'Zero' on the flight deck, suffering some damage to her boilers which reduced speed until repairs could be made, and also lost 11 aircraft to fire. She was operational again within hours, while HMS *Indomitable* only suffered a near miss and no damage.

On 9 May 1945, several dozen Japanese aircraft attacked Hagushi beach, targeting the escort destroyers USS Oberrender and England. Each ship was hit by two Kamikaze aircraft, and both had to withdraw. The next day, fourteen Japanese aircraft of the 762nd *Kokutai* attacked Hagushi beach again but their success was negligible, mostly due to bad weather.

Admiral Ugaki was stubborn. He prepared an attack by the *Kikusui* 7 formation for the 24th and 25th of May, 1945. This time, the attack would be carried out at night, and the targets would be lit by the landing lights fitted as standard to the aircraft. Flares were to be used, and on-board guns were to be used as much as possible. The attack was scheduled to focus on the landing ships. 182 Kamikaze aircraft took part in the attack, escorted by 311 fighters, with a second wave consisting of

*Trainer aircraft also participated in suicide missions, such as the one in this photo, which shows take-off of a Kyushu K11W1 Shiragiku from the Kochi Kokutai.*

twelve 'Betty' bombers carrying Ohka aircraft. The attacking group also included Kyushu K11W Shiragiku trainers.

The results of the attack were far from expected. Soon after take-off, a significant number of the aircraft had to turn back due to engine problems. The Japanese formation was detected by the destroyer patrolling at radar post no. 15, and the ship fired on a 'Betty' bomber before it was able to launch its Ohka aeroplane. The ships in the anchorage attempted to put up a wall of AA fire in front of the attacking aircraft. Two burning Kamikaze aircraft hit the fast transport ship Bates, which sank after a powerful explosion. A similar blow was delivered to the landing ship LST-135, and the ship broke up and sank after another attack by a Kamikaze. Altogether, eleven American ships were damaged during the night-time attack.

Japanese losses were relatively light, so the following day the *Kikusui* 8 formation was still able to operate. The radar-patrolling destroyers were the primary targets again, as the destroyer USS *Drexler* was attacked at observation post no. 2. The attack began as K11W Shiragiku aircraft, led by Sub-Lieutenant Shigeru Kawada, emerged from low rain clouds. In an intense attack, the destroyer received hits from five aircraft, and a series of explosions killed 158 sailors and wounded 51. Eventually, fuel tanks caught fire and, following a large explosion, the ship turned over and sank.

The USS *Braine* was the next destroyer to suffer, as one of the attacking aircraft fell on her deck and exploded in an ammunition store. The ensuing explosion killed 56 sailors, and the ship overturned and quickly sank. Other ships suffered light damage, and the Japanese lost over half of their aircraft. This ended the May attacks by the *Kikusui* formation.

By now, attacks were beginning to have a negative effect on Japanese morale. It was becoming apparent that the suicide attacks were futile. The Allies were quick at replacing their losses, and they brought in more and more weapons, including ships and aircraft. At the same time, the Japanese were experiencing more and more problems with their equipment. They could use only older types of aircraft and slow-speed training aircraft. The only thing that was not in short supply was the volunteer pilots for suicide units.

Combat operations on Okinawa were coming to an end, and it was becoming evident that the Japanese were breaking down. Admiral Ugaki planned another massive Kamikaze attack for 5 June 1945.

On that day, the *Kikusui* 9 formation took off. It was a black day for the US Navy. Three attack groups, led by Captain Momoda, amounted to fifty aircraft. Their attack commenced at 0520, and low visibility resulting from that morning's heavy rain clouds favoured them. The battleship USS *Mississippi* was the first target, and a turret and the radio and radar centre were put out of action. Similar damage was inflicted on the cruiser USS *Louisville*, and the radar destroyer USS *Anthony*, patrolling at post no. 1, was attacked. A burning 'Zero', that had been fired upon by AA defences, exploded and started a fire on the ship.

Soon after these attacks, a typhoon struck and caused more damage to the American fleet than did the Japanese. Three battleships, four aircraft carriers, three cruisers, thirteen destroyers and fifteen other ships were damaged to such a degree that 40% of the fleet had to withdraw to the USA for repair.

Admiral Ugaki learned about the result of the typhoon from a report by reconnaissance aircraft. He thought this could present an historic opportunity, and started organising another mass attack. He assumed they would meet disordered AA defences, and hoped that his attack could destroy whatever was left of the Americans after the devastating typhoon. However, his pilots found that the Americans were ready for them. The attack on 6 June 1945 caused only slight damage to the escort carrier USS *Natoma Bay* patrolling near post no. 2 even though a 'Judy' aeroplane hit her deck and exploded. The destroyer USS *William B. Porter* was attacked at patrol post no. 15 on 10 June 1945 by a lone 'Val' aeroplane. The aeroplane dived vertically into her deck, hitting the ammunition store. Following a large explosion, the ship sank. Meanwhile, the American carriers continued to carry out air strikes on the Japanese airfields.

The next Japanese attacks were carried out six days later. The destroyer USS *Twiggs* was attacked while on patrol at post no. 10. The ship had survived the April and May attacks by Kamikaze aircraft, but this time was less fortunate. She was attacked by a Nakajima B6N 'Jill' torpedo aeroplane and almost simultaneously by a 'Betty' bomber launching an Ohka aeroplane. After half an hour's struggle USS *Twiggs* sank, with 128 of her crew dead, including the captain George Philip.

The last attacks by the *Kikusui* formation in the battle of Okinawa commenced on 21 June 1945. Near Hagushi beach they attacked the transport ship LSM-59 and the destroyer USS Barry. Each was hit by three Kamikaze aircraft, and both ships were sunk. The attack continued the next day, when six Ohka-carrying 'Bettys' approached, escorted by 25 fighters. The results of the attack were disappointing: only three carriers were slightly damaged, while Japanese losses were high and only a few escort aircraft returned to Japan.

The Battle of Okinawa ended with American forces conquering the island and the Japanese suffering enormous losses. Of the total number of operational Japanese aircraft, 70% were intended for suicide attacks. During the Battle of Okinawa the Japanese lost 7,600 aircraft, while American losses were just 763 aircraft. A total of forty American ships were sunk or forced to withdraw to repair damage. 368 ships were damaged but continued to take part in combat.

# The last Kamikaze attacks in defence
# of the Japanese Islands

The fall of Okinawa meant that combat operations moved to the Japanese home islands. Admiral Ugaki established the last Kamikaze units on Kyushu. They had only one task: destroy whatever Allied craft around Japan that they could. This tactic was painfully brought home to the American destroyer USS *Callaghan*, which, three months and 27 days after taking up radar post no. 5, was attacked by a group of twelve Kamikaze aircraft. They attacked from ahead, diving almost vertically. The AA defences held until eventually an old Aichi D2A torpedo biplane hit the control room. After two hours of combat the destroyer sank with 37 crew members. This was the last ship lost by the USA in the war against Japan.

Kamikaze aircraft attacked once more on 13 August 1945, when two aircraft damaged the transport ship *Lagrance* in a suicide attack off Okino Erabu-jima.

It was not just ships that were subjected to Kamikaze attacks as the Allied assault moved to the Japanese home islands. Long range Boeing B-29 bombers had been striking at Japan since the Allies overran landing grounds on islands within striking distance. Japanese home defence forces therefore turned Kamikaze tactics against the airborne attack. The first such attack took place on 3 December 1944, when Lieutenant Toru Shinomiya, Corporals Masao Itagaki and Hatsumi Nakano, of the 244th *Sentai*, *Konoe Sentokitai* (Guards Fighter Unit) took off in Kawasaki Ki-61 Hien 'Tony' fighters against the incoming American B-29 Superfortress bombers. They quickly gained height, so that a few minutes later they found themselves right under two American aeroplanes and flew straight into them. Within fifteen seconds both aircraft were destroyed. The Japanese pilots were able return to base, albeit with damaged wings. A similar attack, but a true suicide attack this time, was carried out by 2nd Lieutenant Takashi Kono, also in a 'Tony', who destroyed a B-29 on 7

*Captain Shirai and his Kawasaki Ki-61 Hien fighter of the 244th Sentai awaiting interception of enemy aircraft.*

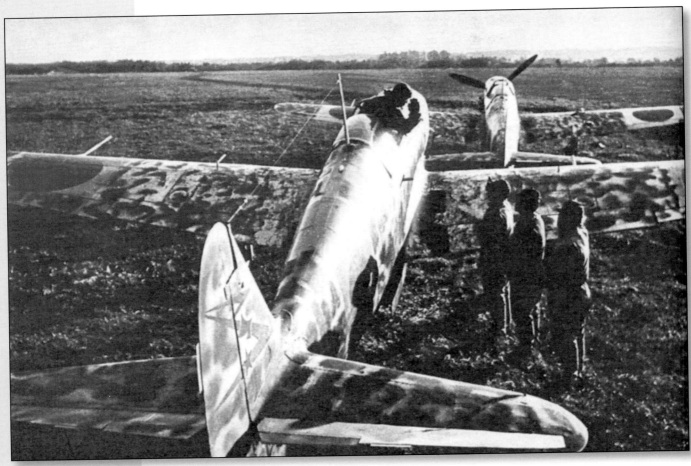

April 1945, crashing into it with his aeroplane. This suicide attack was carried out over the town of Kawaguchishi. A total of seven B-29s were destroyed by these ram attacks.

There was no Allied invasion of the Japanese home islands. After two atom bombs were dropped on Japanese cities, the Emperor surrendered unconditionally. The final assault against which the Kamikazes were expected to hurl themselves never came. Days after the armistice, Allied aircraft strafed the moored flotillas of suicide boats that had been prepared, to ensure they could not be used by fanatics ignoring the surrender. It was in this manner that the Kamikazes passed into history.

# The effects of Kamikaze

With a few exceptions, the effect of the majority of Kamikaze attacks can be described as not being materially significant. Suicide tactics undoubtedly shocked the Allies - generally the psychological effect of the Kamikaze operations was more significant than physical effects, as in Western attitudes voluntary suicide (even in the name of an ideology) was beyond comprehension. In terms of tactics, Kamikaze operations forced the Allies to put up more effective defences, complemented by close co-operation between the Navy and the other services of the US armed forces. In particular, the introduction of radar technology protected the Americans for the most part from the element of surprise in Kamikaze attacks, and was particularly useful during mass attacks by *Kikusui* formations.

# The fate of the Kamikaze godfathers

After introducing the Kamikaze concept into combat tactics, Takijiro Ohnishi was promoted to Admiral and appointed chief of staff for operations. He favoured fighting until the last soldier, so his orders gave no chance of survival.

After nuclear bombs were dropped on Hiroshima and Nagasaki, it was clear that the defeat of Japan was inevitable. Apathy was increasing among the inhabitants of the devastated and burnt

After the Kamikaze rules were introduced into combat tactics, Takijiro Ohnishi was promoted to the rank of Admiral and appointed the Chief of Staff for Operations. He supported fighting until the last soldier, so his orders gave no chance of survival.

out cities. On 15 August 1945, the Japanese nation heard its Emperor for the first time, when he announced to the world the unconditional surrender of Japan. During the night of 16 August 1945, Ohnishi planted a sword in his stomach. He had no assistance, and continued to suffer until his death on the following morning.

On the morning of 15 August 1945, Vice-Admiral Matome Ugaki gave orders to prepare his aeroplane, as he wanted to personally participate in an attack against enemy ships off Okinawa. When Captain Takashi Miyazaki, senior staff officer, learned about this request it became obvious to him what his commander intended to do. He informed Rear-Admiral Takatsugu Jyojima about these plans and they went to Vice-Admiral Ugaki. Although Ugaki welcomed them politely, he would not change his mind. Finally he said: "*I am a warrior and I have little time, I have to use the opportunity. I fly!*" In accordance with his orders, Lieutenant Tatsuo Nakatsuru prepared three 'Judy' dive bombers. Meanwhile, the radio broadcast the Emperor's announcement of the surrender of Japan. In the subsequent silence, the order to prepare all aircraft was given and ground personnel hurriedly attached bombs to other aircraft. A total of eleven aircraft were prepared for take-off, surprising even Vice-Admiral Ugaki himself, who had given orders to prepare only five aircraft. He found out that 22 Kamikaze pilots had volunteered to accompany him in his last mission. The Admiral climbed into the position normally taken by the gunner. Soon after take-off, four aircraft returned to the airfield due to engine problems, and the others flew on towards Okinawa. Ugaki's aircraft was last heard from when it issued a radio broadcast stating that the formation was diving on enemy warships. However, no Allied ships reported a Kamikaze attack on this day and it is unclear what the formation was preparing to attack. The following day, Allied servicemen found a wrecked aircraft on the beach of Ishikawajima, containing a body believed to have been Ugaki.

Vice-Admiral Shigeru Fukudome had been transferred to Singapore to command the 10th Area Fleet as the end of the war approached. After the war he was convicted of war crimes and sentenced to three years imprisonment. Fukudome came back to Japan in 1950 and he died in 1971.

Vice Admiral Matome Ugaki in front of his Kugisho D4Y4 Suisei Model 43 before the last suicide mission.

# *Kamikaze* effectiveness

The effect of suicide attacks is quantified by the numbers below. However, this can never be a complete reflection, as in addition to the officially recorded attacks by Kamikaze units, many suicide attacks were not recorded as they were performed by individual pilots or by small groups on their own initiative.

| Number of attack missions | 1944 | 31 |
|---|---|---|
| | 1945 | 75 |
| Number of ships destroyed | 1944 | 17 |
| | 1945 | 39 |
| Number of ships damaged | 1944 | 112 |
| | 1945 | 256 |
| Total pilot casualties , including: | 3,913 | |
| Imperial Japanese Navy | 2,525 | |
| Imperial Japanese Army | 1,388 | |

The Navy trained a total of 1,727 pilots, whose age varied between 18 and 20 (there were in fact several pilots aged 17). Of these, 110 pilots were students of the military academy. One Vice-Admiral and two Captains were killed, and the others were ranks between Warrant Officer and Lieutenant. Most of them had graduated from the military academy in 1943.

In the Army, most pilots had graduated from advanced flying schools. Most pilots were Sub-Lieutenants, and their average age was 25. Warrant Officers were generally aged 18 or 19.

The world learned more about the origin and operations of the Kamikaze units through the trials of Japanese commanders held after WWII. The principal trial was held in Tokyo by the International Far East Court between 3 May 1946 and November 1948, during which 28 Japanese commanders were tried for war crimes. The bill of indictment included 55 charges, mostly crimes against world peace, the conventions of war, and against humanity.

The 48th charge included the use of suicide units. It was agreed that this was not only a case of a crime against humanity, but also a crime against their own nation. However, on 25 October 1974, on the 30th anniversary of the establishment of the first Kamikaze unit at the Philippine base at Mabalacat, a monument with a memorial plaque was unveiled. Later, subsequent monuments were built, wherever Kamikaze units were based. A monument to Yukio Seki, the first of many subsequent pilots who gave their lives for Japan and the Emperor, was also erected.

There are more and more documents published about the actions of the special units, mostly memoirs of those who did not see their turn come. The Japanese have not forgotten their sons, sent to certain death in defence of their home.

*On 2 September 1945 on the USS Missouri in Tokyo Bay Lieutenant General Richard K. Sutherland received the unconditional surrender of the Japanese Empire, signed by Mamoru Shigemitsu.*

# List of the most important suicide units and formations

Suicide units of the Army and Navy participating in actions over the Philippines

| Naval suicide units | | |
|---|---|---|
| Name | Original unit | Notes |
| 1st *Shimpū* | 201st *Kokutai* | bases in the Philippines, A6M and Suisei |
| 2nd *Shimpū* | 701st *Kokutai* | A6M, Suisei and D3A |
| 3rd *Shimpū* | 201st, 221st, 341st, 634th, 653rd *Kokutai* | renamed from fighter *Kokutai*s, A6M and Suisei |
| 4th *Shimpū* | 701st *Kokutai* | A6M, Suisei and D3A |
| 5th *Shimpū* | 762nd and 763rd *Kokutai* | P1Y Ginga and A6M |
| *Jinmu-tokko-tai* | 601st *Kokutai* | D3A |
| *Shimpū*-tokko-tai Kongo-tai 1 to 30 | Formation originating from Genzan, Omura, Tainan, Takao, Tsukuba and Yatabe *Kokutai* | bases in Japan and on Formosa, A6M and Suisei |
| Niitaka-tai 1 to 3 | 317th *Hikotai* | operated from Formosa within 252nd *Kokutai*, A6M and Suisei |
| Army suicide units | | |
| Name of the formation | Original name of the unit | Notes |
| *Hakko-tai* 1 to 12 | Formed from several *Sentais* of the 4th *Kokugun* | Ki-43, Ki-51, Ki-45 Kai |

Suicide units of the Army and Navy participating in actions over Okinawa

| Army suicide units | | |
|---|---|---|
| Name | *Sentai* units | Notes |
| Makoto *Hikotai* | 15th, 16th, 17th, 31st to 39th, 41st, 71st, 114th, 116th, 119th, 120th, 123rd *Hikotai*s of the 8th Hikoshidan | Formosa, Ki-48, Ki-43, Ki-51, Ki-84, Ki-36, Ki-27, Ki-45 Kai, |
| *Sinbu-tai* | 18th to 24th, 26th to 30th, 40th, 42th to 46th, 48th to 70th, 72nd to 81st, 102nd to 113th, 141st, 144th, 159th, 160th, 165th, 179th, 180th, 213th to 215th, 431st to 433rd, 1st *tokubetsu*, Shitei of 6th *Kokugun* | Kyushu, except 102th and 104 th *Sentai* from Manse, Ki-43, Ki-51, Ki-45 Kai, Ki-84, Ki-27, Ki-61, Ki-36, Ki-55, Ki-79, Ki-46 |
| *Shinten-Seku-tai* | 10th *Hikoshidan* | Tokyo area, Ki-61 |
| *Katen-tai* | 12th *Hikodan* | |
| Naval suicide units | | |
| Name | Original unit | Notes |
| *Taigi-tai* 1 to 21 | 205th *Kokutai* | operated from Ishigaki, Formosa within 1st *Koku Kantai*, A6M |
| *Yubu-tai* | 401st *Hikotai* of the 765th *Kokutai* | P1Y Ginga and Suisei |
| *Chusei-tai* | 102nd and 252nd *Hikotai* of the 765th *Kokutai* | Suisei |

| Army suicide units | | |
|---|---|---|
| Name | *Sentai* units | Notes |
| *Sinten-tai* | 12th and 381st *Kokutai* | B5N and D3A |
| *Shimpū Ohka Tokko-tai* *Jinrai-butai* 1 to 10 | 708th and 711st *Hikotai* of 701st and 721st *Kokutai* | base at Kanoya airfield (Kyushu), G4M + Ohka |
| *Jinrai-butai Kenbu-tai* 1 to 11 | 721st *Kokutai* Ohka tai (Bakusen) | only A6M |
| *Jinrai-Bakusen-tai* 1 and 2 | 306th *Sentai* of the 721st *Kokutai* | A6M |
| *Kikusui-butai formation* | | |
| 2nd *Suisei-tai* | 103rd and 105th *Hikotai* of the 701st *Kokutai* | Suisei |
| *Kikusui-Raio-tai* | 251st *Hikotai* of the 931st *Kokutai* | Tenzan |
| *Oroku-Suisei-tai* | 103rd *Hikotai* of the 701st *Kokutai* | Suisei |
| 210th *Butai Suisei-tai* | 210th *Kokutai* | Suisei |
| 210th *Butai Zerosen-tai* | 210th *Kokutai* | A6M |
| *Tenzan-tai* | 251st, 254th and 256th *Hikotai* of the 131st and the 701st *Kokutai* | only B6N Tenzan |
| *Tenou-tai* | 251st *Hikotai* of the 701st, 901st and 931st *Kokutai* | only B6N Tenzan |
| Formations originating from fighter *Kokutai* units | | |
| *Tsukuba-tai* 1 to 6 | Tsukuba *Kokutai* and 721st *Kokutai* | Kanoya, A6M |
| *Shichisyo-tai* 1 to 7 | Genzan *Kokutai* and 721st *Kokutai* | Kanoya, A6M |
| *Shinken-tai* 1 to 6 | Omura *Kokutai* and 721st *Kokutai* | Kanoya, A6M and A6M2-K |
| *Syowa-tai* 1 to 7 | Yatabe *Kokutai* and 721st *Kokutai* | Kanoya, A6M and A6M2-K |
| Formations originating from bomber *Kokutai* units | | |
| *Hachiman-Goko-tai* 1 to 3 | Usa *Kokutai* | B5N and D3A |
| *Hachiman-Shincyu-tai* | Usa *Kokutai* | B5N |
| *Hachiman-Kanko-tai Shinbu-tai* | Usa *Kokutai* | B5N |
| *Seito-tai* 1 to 4 | Hyakurihara *Kokutai* | D3A |
| *Shōki-tai* 1 to 4 | Hyakurihara *Kokutai* | B5N |
| *Tokiwa-cyuka-tai* | Hyakurihara *Kokutai* | B5N |
| *Koka-tai Tenzan-tai* | Hyakurihara *Kokutai* | B5N |
| *Kusanagi-tai* 1 to 3 | Nagoya *Kokutai* | D3A |
| *Goko-Shirasagi-tai* 1 to 3 | Himeji *Kokutai* | B5N |
| *Shirasagi-Sekicyu-tai* | Himeji *Kokutai* | B5N |
| *Shirasagi-Youbu-tai* | Himeji *Kokutai* | B5N |
| Formations originating from floatplane *Kokutai* units | | |
| *Sakigake-tai* 1 and 2 | Kitaura and Kashima *Kokutai* | E13A and E7K |
| *Kotohira-Suishin-tai* | Takuma *Kokutai* | E13A and E7K |
| *Kotohira-Suitei-tai* | Fukuyama *Kokutai* | F1M |
| 12th *Koku Sentai* 2nd *Suitei-tai* | Amakusa *Kokutai* | A6M |
| Shiragiku formations | | |
| *Kikusui-butai Shiragiku-tai* 1 to 3 | Kochi *Kokutai* | Shiragiku |
| *Tokushima-Shiragiku-tai* 1 to 5 | Tokushima *Kokusai* and Kochi *Kokutai* | Shiragiku |
| Mixed formations (formed from units of the 3rd *Koku Kantai*) | | |
| *1st Mitate-tai* | 317th *Hikotai* of the 252nd *Kokutai* | Special strafing operations against the airfield in Saipan, only A6M |

| Army suicide units | | |
|---|---|---|
| Name | *Sentai* units | Notes |
| 2nd *Mitate-tai* | 310th *Sentai* and 1st and 254th *Hikotai* of the 601st *Kokutai* | Okinawa, only: Zero, Suisei and Tenzan |
| 3rd *Mitate-tai*, 706 *Butai* 601st *Butai* *Tenzan-tai* 252nd *Butai* | 405th *Hikotai* of the 706 *Kokutai* 308th and 310th *Sentai*, 1st *Hikotai* of the 601st *Kokutai* 210th *Kokutai* 304th and 313th *Sentai* and 3rd and 5th *Hikotai* of the 252nd *Kokutai* | Okinawa, only: Ginga, Zero, Suisei and Tenzan |
| 4th *Mitate-tai* | 1st *Hikotai* of the 601st *Kokutai* | Hyakurihara, only Suisei |
| 7th *Mitate-tai* Ryusei-tai 1 to 4 | 5th *Hikotai* of the 752nd *Kokutai* | Kisarazu and Miyazaki July-August 1945, only Ryusei |
| *Ginga-tai* formations | | |
| 1st and 2nd *Ginga-tai* | 501st *Hikotai* of the 762nd *Kokutai* | Miyazaki only: Ginga |
| 3rd *Ginga-tai* | 262nd *Hikotai* of the 762nd *Kokutai* | Miyazaki only: Ginga |
| 4th *Ginga-tai* | 262nd and 501st *Hikotai* of the 762nd *Kokutai* | Miyazaki only: Ginga |
| 5th *Ginga-tai* | 262nd and 501st *Hikotai* of the 762nd *Kokutai* | Miyazaki only: Ginga |
| 6th *Ginga-tai* | 262nd *Hikotai* of the 762nd *Kokutai* | Miyazaki only: Ginga |
| 7th *Ginga-tai* | 406th *Hikotai* of the 762nd *Kokutai* | Izumi only: Ginga |
| 8th *Ginga-tai* | 406th *Hikotai* of the 762nd *Kokutai* | Izumi only: Ginga |
| 9th *Ginga-tai* | 406th and 501st *Hikotai* of the 762nd *Kokutai* | Miyazaki only: Ginga |
| 10th *Ginga-tai* | 405th *Hikotai* of 752nd *Kokutai*, 406th *Hikotai* of 762nd *Kokutai* | Miyazaki and 2nd Miho only: Ginga |

## Organisation of some aircraft suicide units

| Name of the formation | Date, location of establishment and combat operations | Commander |
|---|---|---|
| *Asahi* | Formed on 19 October 1944 at Mabalacat (moved to Davao). Made up of volunteers from the 201st *Kokutai*. | Warrant Officer Keiichi Ueno |
| *Azusa* | Formed on 23 February 1945 at Kanoya. Intended to be used in operation Tan. | Lieutenant Naoto Kuromaru |
| *Banda* (cherry blossom) | Formed on 21 October 1944 at Kamata. Made up of graduates from the Kamata flying school. | Lieutenant Masuomi Iwamoto |
| *Chuyu* (fidelity and courage) | Formed on 26 October 1944 at Mabalacat, from volunteers of the 701st *Kokutai*. | Lieutenant Kyoji Yamada |
| *Fugaku* | Formed on 25 October 1944 at Hamamatsu. The 1st flight school unit equipped with specially converted Mitsubishi Ki-67 bombers. | Lieutenant Commander Tsunesaburo Nishio |
| *Giretsu* (bravery and chivalry) | Formed on 26 October 1944 at Nichols Field from volunteers of the 701st *Kokutai*. | Sub-Lieutenant Toshio Kondo |
| *Junchu* (true faith) | Formed on 26 October 1944 at Nichols Field from volunteers of the 701st *Kokutai*. | Lieutenant Kenji Fukabori |

| Name of the formation | Date, location of establishment and combat operations | Commander |
|---|---|---|
| *Kikusui* (floating chrysanthemum) | Formed in April 1945. General name of aviation formations that carried out suicide attacks from Kyushu against American troops landing on Okinawa. Made up mostly of volunteers from the 3rd, 5th and 10th *Koku Kantai*. Army aviation was only represented by pilots from the 6th *Kokugun*. | Formed by Vice-Admiral Matome Ugaki |
| *Kikusui* 1 | Attacks on 6-11 April 1945. A total of 547 naval aviation and 188 Army aviation aircraft took part, including 303 aircraft flown by suicide pilots. 34 ships were damaged and 6 sunk in the attacks. | |
| *Kikusui* 2 | Attacks on 12-15 April 1945. 500 aircraft altogether. | |
| *Kikusui* 3 | Attacks on 16-17 April 1945. A total of 155 aircraft. Sank one and damaged ten ships. | |
| *Kikusui* 4 | Attacks 22-30 April 1945. A total of 120 aircraft took part, including 50 of the Army, and 59 for suicide attacks alone. Ohka *Butai* 2 of four Ohka Model 11 aircraft was part of it. Sank one and damaged eleven ships. | |
| *Kikusui* 5 | Attacks on 3-9 May 1945. A total of 305 aircraft participated, including 75 for suicide attack. 50 aircraft came from the Army. Actions accompanied by 120 escort aircraft and 60 bombers armed with bombs. Six ships were sunk and 28 damaged. The Japanese lost 280 aircraft. This was the largest attack by Kamikaze units. | |
| *Kikusui* 6 | Attacks on 11-14 May 1945. 255 aircraft participated, including 40 of the Army. All aircraft used for suicide attacks. Damaged three ships. | |
| *Kikusui* 7 | Attacks on 24-25 May 1945. Equipped with 311 aircraft, including 182 for suicide attacks. Ohka *Butai* 3 with 12 Ohka Model 11 aircraft was part of it. Sank two and damaged eight ships. | |
| *Kikusui* 8 | Attacks on 27-29 May 1945. Mainly training units. Sank two and damaged 13 ships. | Sub-Lieutenant Shigeru Kawada |
| *Kikusui* 9 | Attacks on 3-7 June 1945. 50 aircraft participated. Damaged one ship. | |
| *Kikusui* 10 | Attacks on 21-22 June 1945. This was the last attack in defence of Okinawa. 55 aircraft participated. It included the Ohka *Butai* 3 with six Ohka Model 11 aircraft. Sank two and damaged six ships. | |
| *Mitate* | Formed on 18 February 1945 at Katori from volunteers of the 601st *Kokutai*. The first action was an attack by 32 aircraft against the Americans landing on Iwo-jima. | Lieutenant Hiroshi Murakawa |
| Ohka (cherry blossom) | Naval aviation unit formed exclusively of pilots flying Kugisho Ohka Model 11 rocket-powered aircraft. They attacked mostly within *Kikusui* formations. Formed on Kyushu. | Lieutenant Commander Motoharu Okamura |
| Ohka *Butai* | Eight Ohka Model 11 aircraft. Damaged 28 and sank two ships. | |
| *Sakon* | Formed on 5 November 1944 at Mabalacat from volunteers of 304th *Sentai* of 203rd *Kokutai*. | C.P.O Torao Otani. |
| *Seichu* (loyalty and patriotism) | Formed on 24 October 1944 at Mabalacat from volunteers of the 701st *Kokutai*. | Sub-Lieutenant Tomoyuki Goshima |
| *Yoshino* (unconditional fidelity) | Formed on 29 October 1944 at Mabalacat from volunteers of the 201st *Kokutai*. | Sub-Lieutenant Kimiyoshi Takatake |

Apart from the formations listed above, there were many other informal groups formed spontaneously at various air bases, depending on the situation, such as Kongo units of the naval aviation.

| | | |
|---|---|---|
| Kongo 19 | Formed in January 1945 at Mabalacat. Its commander led sixteen Reisen aircraft for an attack in Mindoro strait area. The unit was annihilated in that attack. | Lieutenant Yutaka Aono |
| Kongo 20 | Formed at Mabalacat. Five Reisen and one Suisei aircraft attacked the cruiser HMAS Australia. The unit ceased to exist after the attack. | Sub-Lieutenant Yuzo Nakano |
| Kongo 21 | Ceased to exist virtually the same day it was established, wiped out in a raid by American carrier-borne aircraft against Nichols Field. | |
| Kongo 22 | Formed in January 1945. Consisted of five Reisen aircraft. Destroyed by American aircraft while taking off from Clark Field. | Sub-Lieutenant Teruhiko Miyake |
| Kongo 23 | Consisted of two Reisen and one Suisei aircraft. Attacked as a first wave unit, and ceased to exist. | Sub-Lieutenant Shigeru Omori |

All of these and other similar formations were formed without any record in the naval aviation HQ reports. They were simply established within their parent units.

Ships damaged and sunk during attacks by **Kamikaze** or *Shimpū* suicide units

| Date | Ships sunk | Ships damaged |
|---|---|---|
| **1944** | | |
| 27.05 | | SC-699 |
| 13.10 | | CV-13 *Franklin* |
| 14.10 | | CL-96 *Reno* |
| 21.10 | | *Australia* (CA) |
| 24.10 | AT – *Sonoma* LCI-1065 | APD-11 *Augustus Thomas* |
| 25.10 | CVE-63 *St Lo* | CVE-26 *Sangamon*, CVE-27 *Suwannee*, CVE-29 *Santee*, CVE-66 *White Plains*, CVE-68 *Kalinin Bay*, CVE-71 *Kitkun Bay* |
| 26.10 | | CVE-27 *Suwannee* |
| 27.10 | | MC *Alexander Major*, MC *Ben. Ide Wheeler* |
| 28.10 | | CL-58 *Denver* |
| 29.10 | | CV-11 *Intrepid* |
| 30.10 | | CV-13 *Franklin*, CVL-24 *Belleau Wood* |
| 1.11 | DD-526 *Abner Read* | DD-411 *Anderson*, DD-527 *Ammen*, DD-571 *Claxton*, DD-593 *Killen* |
| 2.11 | | AG *Matthew P. Deady* |
| 12.11 | | AG *Egeria*, AG *Achilles*, MC *Jeremiah M.Daily*, MC *Leonidas Merrit*, MC *Morrison R.Waite*, MC *Thomas Nelson* |
| 17.11 | | APA-17 *Alpine*, MC *Gilbert Stuart* |
| 18.11 | | MC *Alcoa Pioneer*, MC *Cape Romano*, MC *Silvers Almirante* |
| 25.11 | | CV-9 *Essex*, CV-11 *Intrepid*, CV-19 *Hancock*, CVL-28 *Cabot* |
| 27.11 | SC-744 | BB-45 *Colorado*, CL-49 *St Louis*, CL-57 *Montpelier* |
| 29.11 | | BB-46 *Maryland*, DD-465 *Saufley*, DD-569 *Aulick* |
| 3.12 | DD-695 *Cooper* | |
| 5.12 | LSM-20 | DD-366 *Drayton*, DD-389 *Mugford*, LSM-23 |

| Date | Ships sunk | Ships damaged |
|---|---|---|
| 7.12 | DD-364 *Mahan*<br>APD-16 *Ward*<br>LSM-318 | DD-367 *Lamson*, DE-206 *Liddle*, LST-737 |
| 10.12 | MC *William S. Ladd*<br>PT-323<br>LCT-1075 | DD-410 *Hughes* |
| 11.12 | DD-369 *Reid* | CL-43 *Nashville*, DD-605 *Caldwell* |
| 13.12 | | DD-585 *Haraden*, DD-605 *Caldwell* |
| 15.12 | LST-472<br>LST-738 | CVE-77 *Marcus Island*, DD-390 *Ralph Talbot*,<br>DD-590 *Paul Hamilton*, DD-592 *Howorth*, PT-223 |
| 17.12 | | PT-84 |
| 18.12 | PT-300 | |
| 21.12 | LST-460<br>LST-749 | DD-511 *Foote* |
| 28.12 | MC *John Burke* | DD-665 *Bryant*, MC *William Sharon* |
| 30.12 | IX-126 *Porcupine* | DD-477 *Pringle*, DD-608 *Gansevoort*, X-73 *Orestes* |
| **1945** | | |
| 2.01 | | AO-41 *Cowanesquer* |
| 4.01 | CVE-79 *Ommaney Bay*<br>MC *Lewis L. Dyche* | |
| 5.01 | | CVE-61 *Manila Bay*, CVE-78 *Savo Island*, CA-28 *Louisville*, DD-388 *Helm*, DE-411 *Stafford*, *Australia* (CA), *Arunta* (DD), AVP-21 *Orca*, AT-26 *Apache*, LCI(G)-70 |
| 6.01 | DMS-12 *Long* | BB-40 *New Mexico*, BB-44 *California*, CA-28 *Louisville*, CA-36 *Minneapolis*, CL-56 *Columbia*, *Australia* (CA), DD-586 *Newcomb*, DD-692 *Allen M. Summer*, DD-664 *Richard P. Leary*, DD-723 *Walke*, DD-725 *O'Brien*, APD-10 *Brooks*, DMS-10 *Southard* |
| 7.01. | DMS-5 *Palmer*<br>DMS-11 *Hovey* | CL-47 *Boise*, APD-111 *Callowey*, LST-912 |
| 8.01 | | CVE-71 *Kitkun Bay*, CVE-76 *Kadashan Bay*, *Australia* (CA), *Westralia* (APD) |
| 9.01 | | BB-41 *Mississippi*, CL-56 *Columbia*, *Australia* (CA), DE-231 *Hodges* |
| 10.01 | | DE-414 *Le Ray Wilson*, APA-47 *Dupage* |
| 12.01 | | DE-342 *Richard W. Suesens*, DE-508 *Gilligan*, APD-34 *Belknap*, MC *Otis Skinner*, MC *Kyle V. Johnson*, MC *David Dudley Field*, MC *Edward N. Westcott*, MC *War Hawk*, LST-700, LST-778 |
| 13.01 | | CVE-96 *Salamaua*, APA-97 *Zeilin* |
| 16.01 | LSM-318 | CV-14 *Ticonderoga*, CVL-27 *Langley*, DD-731 *Maddox*, LST-700 |
| 5.02. | | MC *John Evans* |
| 21.02 | CVE-95 *Bismarck Sea* | CV-3 *Saratoga*, CVE-94 *Lunga Point*, MC *Keokuk*, LST-477, LST-809 |
| 11.03 | | CV-15 *Randolph* |
| 18.03 | | CV-11 *Intrepid* |
| 19.03 | | CV-18 *Wasp*, DD-686 *Halsey Powell* |
| 20.03 | | SS-292 *Devilfish* |

| Date | Ships sunk | Ships damaged |
|---|---|---|
| 27.03 | | BB-36 *Nevada*, BB-43 *Tennessee*, CL-80 *Biloxi*, DD-521 *Kimberley*, DD-725 *O'Brirn*, DD-792 *Callaghan*, DE-633 *Foreman*, DMS-1 *Dorsley*, DMS-10 *Southard*, ACM-74 *Skirmish*, APA-55 *Knudson*, APD-11 *Gilmer*, DM-23 *Robert H. Smith* |
| 31.03 | | CA-35 *Indianapolis*, ACM-79 *Adams*, LSM-188, LST-724 |
| 1.04 | | BB-48 *West Virginia*, DD-792 *Callaghan*, *King George V* (BB), *Indomitable* (CV), *Indefatigable* (CV), *Illustrious* (CV), APA-46 *Archenar*, APA-47 *Alpine*, APA-71 *Tyrrell*, APA-120 *Hinsdale*, LST-884 |
| 2.04 | APD-21 *Dickerson* | APA *Henrico*, APA *Chilton*, APA *Goodghue*, APA *Telfair*, LCI(G)-568, LST-599 |
| 3.04 | | CVE-65 *Wake Island*, DD-733 *Mannert L. Abele*, DMS-49 *Hambleton* |
| 6.04 | DD-329 *Bush* DD-801 *Colhoun* DMS-22 *Emmons* APA-111 *Hobbs Victory* APA-196 *Logan Victory* LST-477 | CVL-30 *San Jacinto*, DD-328 Mullany, DD-386 Newcomb, DD-417 Morris, DD-476 *Hutchins*, DD-481 *Leutze*, DD-573 *Harrison*, DD-591 *Twiggs*, DD-593 *Howorth*, DD-700 *Haynsworth*, DD-732 Hyman, DD-746 *Taussig*, DE-636 Witter, DE-640 Fieberling, DMS-44 *Rodman*n, ACM-16 Ransom, ACM-20 *Defense*, ACM-22 Recruit, ACM-47 Facility, LCS-64, YMS-311, YMS-321 |
| 7.04 | | CV-19 *Hancock*, BB-46 *Maryland*, DD-473 Bennett, DD-559 *Longshaw*, DE-84 *Wesson*, YMS-81 |
| 8.04 | | DD-802 *Gregory* |
| 9.04 | LCT-876 LST-447 | DD-407 *Sterett* |
| 10.04 | | DE-183 *Samuel S. Miles* |
| 11.04 | | **CV-6** *Enterprise*, BB-63 *Missouri*, DD-133 *Hale*, DD-660 *Bullard*, DD-661 *Kidd*, DD-702 *Hank*, DE-183 *Samuel S. Miles*, LCS(L)-36 |
| 12.04 | DD-733 *Mannert L. Abele* | BB-40 *New Mexico*, BB-42 *Idaho*, BB-43 *Tennessee*, DD-478 *Stanly*, DD-734 *Purdy*, DD-777 *Zellars*, DD-793 *Cassin Young*, DE-185 *Riddle*, DE-304 *Rall*, DE-412 *Walter C. Wann*, DE-634 *Whitehurst*, DM-32 *Lindsey*, DMS-27 *Jeffers*, AM-319 *Gladiator*, LSM(R)-189, LCS(L)-57 |
| 13.04 | | DE-306 *Connolly* |
| 14.04 | | BB-34 *New York*, DD-502 *Sigsbee*, DD-659 *Dashiell*, DD-674 *Hunt* |
| 15.04 | | DD-408 *Wilson*, LCS-51, LCS-116 |
| 16.04 | DD-477 *Pringle* | CV-11 *Intrepid*, BB-63 *Missouri*, DD-665 *Bryant*, DD-724 *Laffey*, DMS-61 *Harding*, DMS-65 *Hobson*, AO-101 *Taluga*, APD-40 *Bowers*, LCI-407, LCS-116 |
| 17.04 | | DD-796 *Benham* |
| 22.04 | AM-65 *Swallow* LCS-15 | DD-475 *Hudson*, DD-516 *Wadsworth*, DM-520 *Isherwood*, DM-30 *Shea*, ACM-16 *Ransom*, AM-319 *Gladiator* |
| 25.04 | | DE-635 *England*, MCS. Hall *Young* |
| 27.04 | APA-441 *Canada Victory* | DD-113 *Rathburne*, DD-390 *Ralph Talbot* |
| 28.04 | | DD-516 *Wadsworth*, DD-519 *Daly*, DD-591 *Twiggs*, DD-662 *Bennion*, DD-546 *Brown*, DMS-29 *Butler*, AH-6 *Comfort*, AH-10 *Pinkey*, LCI-580 |
| 29.04 | | DD-531 *Hazelwood*, DD-555 *Haggard*, DM-25 *Shannon*, DM-26 *Harry F. Bauer* |

| Date | Ships sunk | Ships damaged |
|---|---|---|
| 30.04 | | DD-662 Bennion, CM-5 Terror |
| 3.05 | DD-803 Little | DD-470 Bache, DM-34 Aaron Ward, MC Macomb, LCS(L)-25 |
| 4.05 | DD-552 Luce<br>DD-560 Morrison<br>LSM(R)-194<br>LSM-190 | CVE-26 Sangamon, CL-62 Birmingham, Formidable (CV), Indomitable (CV), Victorious (CV), AM-239 Gaety, DD-470 Bache, DD-546 Brown, DD-547 Cowell, DD-597 Wiley, DD-694 Ingraham, DD-770 Lowry, DD-778 Massey, DE-344 Oberrender, DE-635 England, DM-30 Shea, DM-33 Gwin, DMS-13 Hopkins, AV-9 St George, AG-81 Pathfinder, YMS-331, YMS-327 |
| 10.5 | | MC Harry F. Bauer |
| 11.05 | | CV-17 Bunker Hill, DD-552 Evans, DD-774 Hugh W. Hadley |
| 12.05 | | BB-40 New Mexico |
| 13.05 | | DD-470 Bache, DE-747 Bright |
| 14.05 | | CV-6 Enterprise |
| 17.05 | | DD-779 Douglas H. Fox |
| 18.05 | | APA-56 Sims |
| 20.05 | | APA-71 Chase, APA-33 Register, DD-514 Tatcher, LST-808 |
| 24.05 | APA-47 Bates<br>LSM-135 | DD-472 Guest, DD-780 Stormes, DE-188 O'Neill, DE-641 William C. Cole, DMS-29 Butler, AM-305 Spectable, APA-19 Barry, APA-44 Roper |
| 26.05 | | DMS-24 Forrest, PC-1063, AG-11 Dutton |
| 27-29.05 | DD-741 Drexler<br>DD-630 Braine | DD-268 Shubrick, DD-515 Anthony, DE-508 Gilligan, DMS-10 Southard, APA-89 Loy, APA-92 Rednour, APA-93 Sandoval, APA-98 Tatum, MC Brown Victory, MC Sosiah Snelling, MC Mary A. Livermore, AM-239 Gayety, LCS(L)-52 |
| 3.06 | | AT-6 Allegan, LCS(L)-52 |
| 5.06 | | BB-41 Mississippi, CA-28 Louisville |
| 6.06 | | CVE-62 Natoma Bay, DM-26 Harry F. Bauer, DM-31 J. William Ditter |
| 7.06 | | DD-515 Anthony |
| 10.06 | DD-579 William D. Porter | |
| 11.06 | | LCS(L)-122 |
| 16.06 | DD-591 Twiggs | |
| 21.06 | LSM-59<br>DM-93 Barry | DE-305 Halloran, AV-4 Curtiss, AV-5 Kenneth Whitting |
| 22.06 | | DMS-19 Ellyson, LSM-213, LSM-534 |
| 19.07 | | DD-514 Thatcher |
| 29.07 | DD-792 Callaghan | DD-561 Pritchett, DD-793 Cassin Young, APD-191 Horace A. Bass |
| 9.08 | | DD-704 Borie |
| 13.08 | | APD-144 Lagrange |

# Kamikaze (or Shimpu) aircraft

Suicide attacks continued uninterrupted until 15 August 1945 when Emperor Hirohito declared an armistice. In the last phase of the war the Japanese used all kinds of airworthy aircraft for suicide attacks, from training aircraft to flying boats, as well as the manned flying bombs such as the Ohka Model 11 rocket-powered aircraft.

The IJN used mostly Mitsubishi A6M 'Zero' fighters for suicide attacks. Prior to a suicide mission, a 250kg (25-*Ban*, or Number 25) bomb was attached under the wing centre section. Attaching a bomb under the fuselage reduced the aircraft's much-discussed manoeuvrability, as well as its air speed. This therefore increased the risk to the mission's chances of success when the Kamikazes met more and more advanced American carrier-borne fighters.

Another aeroplane used for suicide attacks was the Kugisho D4Y 'Judy' dive bomber. For a suicide mission, a 500kg (50-*Ban*) or 250kg bomb was attached in the bomb-bay. The 'Judy' had good performance but when used as a two-seater, crew losses were twice as high. By the end of 1944 a special version was developed, the D4Y4 Model 43 Suisei Kai, specifically for suicide attacks. This aeroplane was able to take a single 800kg bomb half-buried in the bomb bay, and it was fitted with three auxiliary take-off rocket boosters located under the rear fuselage. These could also be used to evade enemy fighters. The D4Y was used by, among others, Rear-Admiral Arima during his unsuccessful attack, and by Admiral Ugaki, when he took off with eleven other aircraft for his last mission.

The Nakajima B6N 'Jill' single-engined, three-seater carrier-borne torpedo-bomber was another type frequently used by suicide units. The aeroplane could take an 800kg bomb or a torpedo. For suicide attacks, it was fitted with a very sensitive contact fuse. In some cases aircraft of the type were manned solely by the pilot, although most suicide attacks were performed by crews of two.

Another commonly-used type was the Aichi D3A 'Val' carrier-borne dive bomber. A 250kg bomb was carried between the main wheel legs, while two 60kg bombs could be attached under the wings. At the end of the war a special suicide attack version of the aeroplane was developed. This version underwent flight trials led by Lieutenant Commander Shimizu in January 1945 at Yokosuka *Kokutai*. The modified aeroplane had its wing-mounted fuel tanks removed, and this reduced its range by almost half. After take-off and climb to the required altitude, the wing tips could be jettisoned to increase the diving speed. During one of the flight trials flown by test pilot Shigeo Tanaka, dropping the wing tips increased the speed of the aeroplane from 450km/h to 620km/h, and landing speed rose to 222km/h. In February 1945 another similarly modified D3A aeroplane was delivered for testing, but the further fate of the aeroplane is not known. This may in fact have been a test plane for the Ohka Model 43's wing tip jettisoning system.

In May or June of 1945 a programme was started to develop aircraft of all-wooden construction. A version of the fast reconnaissance aircraft the Nakajima C6N Saiun ('Myrt') reconnaissance aeroplane designated C6N6 Saiun Kai 4 was intended to be used for suicide attacks against American landing ships operating off the Japanese home islands.

In the final stage of the war a shortage of aircraft forced the Navy to use virtually all airworthy aircraft

*2nd Lieutenant Eizo Nakamura of the Showa-3-tai in the cockpit of a Mitsubishi A6M2 Reisen fighter with a 250 kg bomb attached. He took off for his last sortie on 16 April 1945.*

types in suicide units, such as the Mitsubishi K3M3 high-wing monoplanes that had seen their best days in the early 1930s. Training aircraft and flying boats were also used for suicide missions, partly because they were available and airworthy, but also because the Japanese were starting to save fighters for the anticipated air battle over mainland Japan.

The Army declared the Nakajima Ki-43 Hayabusa 'Oscar' fighter as the standard suicide aeroplane in *Shimpū* units. It was the standard Army fighter in China and south-east Asia, and it had a very good reputation thanks to its excellent manoeuvrability and the ease with which it could be maintained. It could carry two 250kg bombs under the wings.

The IJAAF specialised in suicide attacks against American Boeing B-29 Superfortress four-engined bombers. These aircraft, able to carry up to 6 tonnes of bombs, were systematically bombing Japan by the end of the war. The Japanese encountered many problems trying to combat the B-29s, as the Japanese AA defence was relatively weak and disorganised mainly due to the short-sighted policy of the Japanese High Command, which did not even consider the possibility of air attacks against Japan. Even the raid by Colonel Doolittle's B-25 Mitchell bombers in the spring of 1942 failed to push the High Command into improving defences. The B-25s had taken off from the aircraft carrier USS *Hornet* and dropped bombs on Tokyo, Yokohama, Kobe and Nagoya.

The Japanese arms industry started updating AA guns, but production capacity was limited, and there were not enough cannon produced. They could therefore rely only on fighters. The first specially developed interceptor fighter was the Nakajima Ki-44 Shōki ('Tojo'), which was able to reach a service ceiling of 11,000m. However, its 20mm cannon were ineffective against American bombers. The Kawasaki Ki-61 Hien ('Tony') fighter and the twin-engined Kawasaki Ki-45 Toryu ('Nick') fighter were both pitched against the American bombers, and both of these aircraft successfully engaged the American giants by ramming them, as well as using more conventional attacks.

To destroy large and important objects in the last months of the war, the Army used two types of aircraft. These were the Kawasaki Ki-48 ('Lily') light bomber and the Mitsubishi Ki-67 Hiryū ('Peggy') heavy bomber. Both of these aircraft will be discussed later.

The Army and Navy used the same bombs types. These were standard aircraft bombs manufactured by Mitsubishi at their No. 23 plant in Nagano. Different types of bomb were available, with TNT (high explosive) warheads being used for suicide attacks.

The designation '25-*Ban*' denoted a 250 kg bomb. By early 1945, all bombs featured a new, more sensitive fuse system, making them more likely to explode with a near miss or glancing blow. Tests proved that an explosion with this sort of bomb could inflict very serious damage or even eliminate a ship from combat operations if it exploded up to 10m away from the target.

*Manshu Ki-79 Otsu with 250 kg bomb of 113 Shimbu-tai, 10 Koku Sokogeki, 6 June 1945, flown by col. Nakajima. See also colour profile.*

In August 1944 the *Kaigun Koku Hombu* (Imperial Japanese Navy Air Service) prepared a strategic plan which called for three categories of special aircraft, under the code name of *Kokoku Heiki* – The Emperor's Weapon. This referred to the tactic consisting of mass suicide attacks against enemy units. To discuss the plan, the *Kaigun Koku Hombu* invited representatives of companies such as Kawanishi, Mitsubishi and Nakajima for discussions. The representatives were informed of details of the plan, which stipulated that the first category (*Kokoku Heiki* 1-Go) included those aircraft that could be adapted to carry one 800kg bomb, such as the Mitsubishi J2M Raiden 'Jack', Kawanishi N1K2-J Shiden 'George' and Kugisho D4Y 'Judy'. The second category (*Kokoku Heiki* 2-Go) included rocket and jet-powered aircraft, and the third category (*Kokoku Heiki* 3-Go) would include special attack aircraft, called the Tokubetsu Kogeki-ki (shortened to Tokko-ki), which were developed by Kawanishi. These would have conventional propulsion, namely 1,280hp Mitsubishi Kinsei 14-cylinder radial engines. Their role would be to perform suicide attacks against Allied ships. The Navy never received any aircraft from the latter category, and though the Army took delivery of Nakajima Ki-115 Tsurugi aircraft built along these lines, these were never used in anger.

Production combat aircraft were converted under *Kokoku Heiki* 1-Go, while the other two projects covered new, purpose-built suicide aircraft. The specifications were issued in early 1945 and called for the new designs to be simple and easy to build, using the materials that were still available, able to take off from roads, highways, and hardened surfaces and be catapulted, and able to be built in small workshops by unskilled workers.

Several designs were developed to these specifications, but none of them were used in combat. Individual projects are described in more detail below.

*Tachikawa Ki-9 trainer in the suicide version.*

*Kawasaki Ki-45 Toryu.*

Until the moment of Japan's surrender, its leaders continued to develop and plan for various methods of attacking the American continent, such as wind-borne balloons which would carry bombs across the Pacific and a giant six-engined bomber which would bomb the US then carry on to land in German-occupied France. Naturally, the Kamikaze concept was also considered for these attacks on US soil. One project involved the use of submarines to launch attack aircraft.

Aircraft that were able to take off from submarines were built in Japan and used in practice during the 1930s. During the Sino-Japanese war of 1938-1942 they patrolled the East China Sea, successfully attacking Chinese transports. In 1942, the Japanese submarine I-25 made a raid off the US coast of Oregon, launching a Kugisho E14Y1 ('Glen') floatplane that dropped incendiary bombs on a forest not far from the coastline. This kind of activity had little effect on the course of the war, but it meant that the possibility of deploying aircraft on submarines was developed further. Consequently, the Aichi company was given the task of developing a special floatplane bomber for submarines. This was built as the Aichi M6A1 Seiran . Easy to strike down and set up, it could be carried in a special watertight hangar on Japanese I-400 class submarines and each submarine could take three aircraft. The M6A1 was able to carry one 800kg bomb. Eighteen aircraft were built, but by December 1944 only two submarines were ready to launch an attack.

In May of 1945, Japanese strategists revived the idea of an attack against the American continent. This time, the Panama Canal was selected as the target because the largest American shipyards were located on the Atlantic coast, and they continued to launch more effective and more modern ships that reinforced the US Pacific fleet. The Japanese thought that an attack on the Panama Canal would delay the US fleet sending reinforcements into the Pacific. A single attack on the canal was planned, to destroy its facilities and render it useless.

It was planned that the M6A1s be launched from submarines without their floats, so that the operation would effectively be a suicide mission. A special submarine division was established for this plan, led by Ryunosuke Ariizumi, and it was intended that Submarines I-400 and I-401 would each carry three M6A Seiran aircraft. On 17 August 1945, the ships were redirected to attack US aircraft carriers in Ulithi instead of carrying out the planned attack on the Panama Canal. The planned attack on Ulithi was prevented by the Emperor's declaration of the surrender of Japan.

In parallel with the development of unmanned flying bombs, some aircraft companies developed unmanned missiles, some of which were radio-controlled. In Japan work was carried out on a series of guided flying bombs, known in the Army as the I-Go-1. The Navy focused on the development of a series of Funryu rocket missiles, to be used for attacks against enemy ships and later against B-29s.

# Special attack aircraft of the Imperial Japanese Army

## Kawasaki Ki-48 ('Lily')

The Kawasaki Ki-48 was a twin-engined medium bomber which was approaching obsolescence at the end of the war and consequently was available for suicide attacks. It was among the first aircraft to be considered for a dedicated suicide variant.

During the Second Sino-Japanese War, which began in 1937, the Japanese Army Air Service became very impressed with the Tupolev SB fast medium bomber, which the Chinese had obtained from the Soviet Union.

In December 1937 Kawasaki and Mitsubishi were given the task of creating a Japanese answer to the SB, which should have a maximum speed at an altitude of 3,000m of 480km/h and a cruising speed at 3,000m of 350km/h. It should be able to climb to an altitude of 5,000m within 10 minutes, carry a defensive armament of 3-4 machine guns and a bomb load of 400kg. It should be powered by two Nakajima Ha-25 radial engines, and be able to operate in extremely difficult winter conditions, such as on the Manchukuo-Siberia border. To speed the process the manufacturers were encouraged to modify aircraft that they already had on the drawing board.

The Mitsubishi Ki-47 was eliminated at the preliminary project stage of the competition. Mitsubishi, busy at the time with numerous research and development projects, did not have the time to work on another aeroplane. Kawasaki commenced work in January 1938 on the new aeroplane, known as the 'Experimental Army Light Twin-engined Bomber Ki-48'. The new aeroplane was a cantilever mid-wing monoplane. The fuselage, with a characteristic bulged forward section, housed the crew compartment and the bomb bay. Aft of the trailing edge the fuselage merged into a narrow boom, ending with the tail. The crew of four included the pilot, the bomb aimer/gunner manning a flexible 0.303in. (7.7mm) Type 89 machine gun mounted in the forward glazed position, the radio-operator/gunner manning a 0.303in. (7.7mm) Type 89 machine gun mounted in the rear compartment, and the navigator/gunner also manning a 0.303in. (7.7mm) Type 89 machine gun, mounted in the retractable under-fuselage position. The normal bomb load included 24 bombs, each 15kg, or six 50kg bombs. The aeroplane was powered by two 940 hp Nakajima Ha-25 radial engines, driving three-bladed metal variable pitch propellers. The undercarriage was retractable, the main wheels retracting completely into the spacious engine nacelles while the tail wheel was only partly retracted into the rear fuselage

The assembly of the first prototype was delayed due to numerous problems during testing of the Ki-45 heavy fighter, which distracted the efforts of Takeo Doi's team. The first prototype Ki-48.01 was not ready until July 1939, and by September of that year the results of the first test flights of the prototype Ki-48.01 were showing satisfactory results in terms of speed, manoeuvrability and flying characteristics. However, tail flutter proved a problem. The forward fuselage design affected the centre of gravity and forced an extension of the fuselage aft of the trailing edge. Between September and November four more prototypes were built, each differing in the reinforced rear fuselage and carrying varying tail configurations. Eventually, the tailplane flutter was cured by raising the fin 0.4m higher than in the first prototype, and strengthening the fuselage structure.

Prototype and pre-production Ki-48 aircraft were successively handed over to the *Rikugun Kokugijyutsu Kenkyujo at Tachikawa* (Army Air Technical Research Institute) for further testing.

Flight trials were conducted there by Army test pilots, and testing was completed successfully in November 1939. After the final configuration of the aeroplane was defined, five more pre-production machines were built for final operational testing. The aeroplane was approved for series production by the end of 1939 and given the official designation 'Type 99 Army Twin-engined Light Bomber Model 1 Ko" (Ki-48-I Ko). However, the decision to start series production was not taken until 11 May 1940, after the operational trials had ended.

The first production Ki-48-I Ko was completed in July 1940 at the Kawasaki plant in Gifu. The first Ki-48s entered service in China in early 1941 and experiences in combat led to various developments improving the basic machine. With the declaration of war against the Allies in December 1941, Ki-48s saw action in the Phillippines, Burma, Malaya and Indochina. Development of the Ki-48 continued and variants appeared with better defensive armament, larger bomb load and even a dive-bomber version. However, as the war progressed, the Ki-48 became increasingly obsolete. Production of the Ki-48-II continued until November 1944, by which time 1,408 machines of the type had been built.

Despite its numerous shortcomings, the Ki-48 remained in Army Aviation service virtually until the end of 1944. It bore the brunt of tactical tasks, and even though it fulfilled its role with more and more difficulty, the Ki-48 had no successor. From the Allied point of view, the Ki-48 initially had two different Allied code names: it was called 'Julia' on the Chinese front and 'Lily' in Burma, Sumatra and Java. In December 1942, when codenames of Japanese aircraft from various operational areas were unified, the more widespread name of 'Lily' was accepted.

As the campaign in the Philippines came to a close, the Kawasaki Ki-48 light bomber became rare outside Burma and Indochina. The 3rd and 75th *Sentais* commenced re-equipment with the Kawasaki Ki-102 heavy fighter following the losses suffered in the Philippines, while the 16th *Sentai* was reformed as a heavy bomber unit and equipped with Mitsubishi Ki-67 Hiryūs. In the home islands, Ki-48s were left only in the 6th and 208th *Sentais*.

In April and May 1945 a number of machines of the type were first used for suicide attacks. The Ki-48s were employed to strike against the Allied fleet around Okinawa, and they were also used for night raids against airfields on Okinawa after these airfields were captured by Allied forces. They flew sporadic daylight missions in the area, but surviving Ki-48s were retained for suicide attacks during the planned final battle of the home islands, where they were captured by American occupation forces.

*Kawasaki Ki-48-I twin-engined light bomber.*

In July 1944, some three months before Kamikaze suicide attacks commenced, Colonel Masaki (the head of the *Dai-San Koku Kenkyujyo*, or 3rd Air Research Institute, reporting to the *Rikugun Koku Hombu*, (the body responsible for testing of bomber armament and explosives) put forward a proposal to convert the obsolete Ki-48 bomber into a suicide aeroplane. According to the specification, the machine would be modified to carry 800kg of bombs in the forward fuselage rather than in the bomb bay, and would be used for attacks against enemy vessels. Colonel Masaki's idea was received favourably by the *Rikugun Koku Hombu*, who at the time approved many similar initiatives, and it was earmarked for production by the *Dai-Ichi Rikugun Kokusho* (1st Army Air Arsenal) at Tachikawa. According to the specification, twelve machines were going to be converted to the suicide version, termed 'special'. They were designated the Ki-48-II Otsu Kai. (Some sources state that this version was called Ki-174. However, if this was the case it was unofficial as the actual Ki-174 designation was given to a planned Tachikawa light bomber.) The engineering project called for pole-mounted contact detonators in the forward fuselage to trigger the bombs when the aeroplane hit its target. The work was supervised by an experienced officer, Major Hideo Sakamoto. In September the first prototype of the new version was ready, and it was sent for testing at the *Rikugun Koku Shinsa-Bu* (Army Flight Testing Division) at Fussa. There, the prototype was assigned high priority and testing commenced immediately. Major Takeshita was responsible for flight testing the Ki-48-II Otsu Kai.

The first test flights were made on 12 September 1944, but the test results were not promising. In their report, the test pilots said that fitting 800kg bombs resulted in a reduction of the top speed to 460km/h, and reduced the manoeuvrability of the aeroplane. In addition, the take-off run increased from 1,000 to 1,400m. In fact, the weight of the 800kg bombs stretched the lifting capability of the airframe to the limit, and consequently all defensive armament had to be removed which made the aeroplane highly vulnerable to enemy fighters.

Despite this unfavourable feedback, the *Rikugun Koku Hombu* ordered that work on the suicide version should speed up, and that

conversion of the remaining eleven machines should proceed. Clearly, the rate at which the Ki-48-II Otsu Kai was introduced into operations was influenced by the September strike by American carrier-borne aircraft, which forecast an imminent invasion. With this in mind, the *Rikugun Koku Hombu* expanded its order to cover conversion of another 100 machines of the type. These would form the equipment of three 'special' strike units, known as the *Rikugun Koku Tokubetsu Kogekitai*. At the same time, work continued on a similar conversion of the Nakajima Ki-49 Donryu heavy bomber.

At the end of September 1944, the first three modified Ki-48-II Otsu Kai aircraft were delivered to the special unit called Banda-Tai, commanded by Captain Iwamoto. The unit was undergoing training when the Americans landed in the Philippines. Although the training was not complete, the unit was transferred in emergency to the Philippines at the end of October and on 5 November, the first two aircraft of the Banda-Tai took off for a suicide mission. However, on the way to the target both machines were intercepted by a formation of F6F Hellcat fighters. The absence of defensive guns made them easy prey for the American fighters, who shot them down without realising that they had just encountered a new, suicide version of the 'Lily'. As a result of the unsuccessful first mission, the conversion of subsequent aircraft was cancelled.

**Specifications:**

Description: twin-engine mid-wing monoplane light bomber, dive bomber (Ki-48-II Otsu) or special attack aeroplane. All metal construction with fabric covered control surfaces and ailerons.

Crew: four (pilot, co-pilot, bomb aimer/gunner, radio-operator/gunner), three in the Ki-48-II Otsu dive bomber and Ki-148 bomb carrier, or two in the Ki-48-II Kai special attack aeroplane.

Power plant: two Nakajima Ha-25 (Army Type 99) 14-cylinder air cooled radial engines rated at 940hp (690kW) for take-off and 970hp (715kW) at an altitude of 3,000m; three-blade variable pitch metal propellers, diameter 2.86m; fuel tank capacity 1360l. (Ki-48 prototypes, Ki-48 pilot batch and Ki-48-I).

*Ki-48-I of 16 Sentai at Chosen airfield, Korea.*

*Ki-48-II Otsu Kai bomber during trials provided by test pilots at Fusa Air Base, under the command of Major Hideo Sakamoto.*

One of the variants of the
Ki-48-II Otsu Kai with
three probe fuses.

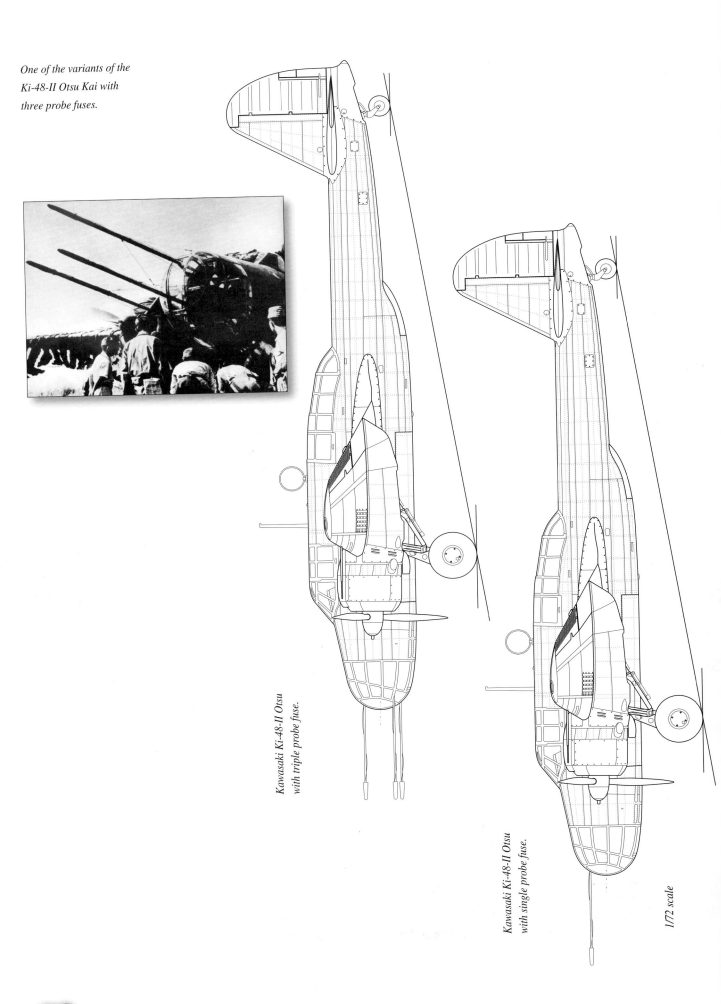

Kawasaki Ki-48-II Otsu
with triple probe fuse.

Kawasaki Ki-48-II Otsu
with single probe fuse.

1/72 scale

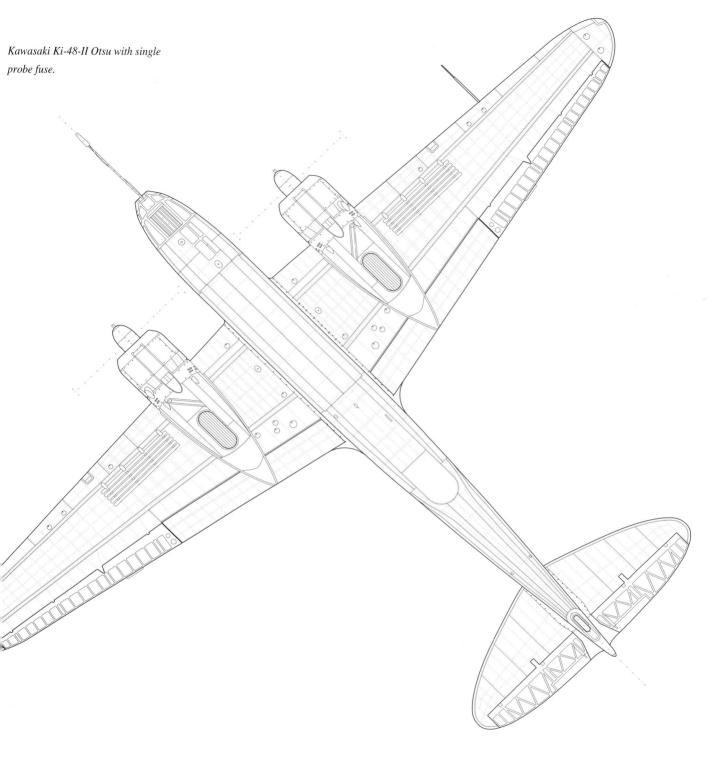

*Kawasaki Ki-48-II Otsu with single probe fuse.*

Two Nakajima Ha-115-I (Army Type 100) 14-cylinder air cooled radial engines rated at 1,130hp (830kW) for take-off, 1,070hp (785kW) at an altitude of 2,800m and 980hp (720 kW) at an altitude of 6,000m; three-blade variable pitch metal propellers, diameter 2.900m; fuel tank capacity 2,680l. (Ki-48 -I and Ki-48-II Kai),

Armament: three 0.303in. (7.7mm) Type 89 machine guns (Ki-48-I Ko, Ki-48-I Otsu, Ki-48-II Ko, Ki-48-II Otsu). One 0.5in. (12.7mm) machine gun, three Type 1 machine guns, and 0.303in. (7.7mm) Type 89 machine guns.

Bomb load: 300-310kg (Ki-48-I Ko), 400kg (Ki-48-I Otsu), 500kg (Ki-48-II Ko, Ki-48-II Hei, Ki-48-II Tei), 800 kg (Ki-48-II Otsu, Ki-48-II Otsu Kai) or Ki-148 guided bomb.

*1/72 scale*

| Type | Ki-48-I Ko | Ki-48-II Ko | Ki-48-II Otsu Kai | Ki-48-II Hei |
|---|---|---|---|---|
| Wing span (m) | 17.47 | 17.47 | 17.47 | 17.47 |
| Length (m) | 12.875 | 12.875 | 14.050 | 12.875 |
| Height (m) | 3.8 | 3.67 | 3.67 | 3.67 |
| Wing area (m$^2$) | 40 | 40 | 40 | 40 |
| Empty weight (kg) | 4,050 | 4,550 | 4,470 | 4,650 |
| Maximum take-off weight (kg) | 5,900 | 6,750 | 6,620 | 6,500 |
| Useful load(kg) | 1,850 | 2,200 | 2,150 | 1,850 |
| Wing loading (kg/m$^2$) | 147.5 | 168.75 | 165.5 | 162.5 |
| Power loading (kg/hp) | 3.21 | 2.99 | 3.06 | 2.88 |
| Maximum speed (km/h) | 480 | 505 | 504 | 485 |
| at an altitude of (m) | 3,500 | 5,600 | 5,000 | 5,550 |
| Cruising speed (km/h) | 350 | 395 | 368 | 350 |
| at an altitude of (m) | 3,000 | 3,500 | 3,000 | 5,000 |
| Landing speed (km/h) | 120 | 125 | 130 | 129 |
| Time of climb | 9 min. 00 sec. | 8 min. 05 sec. | 9 min. 56 sec. | 9 min. 30 sec. |
| to an altitude of (m) | 5,000 | 5,000 | 5,000 | 5,000 |
| Ceiling (m) | 9,500 | 10,100 | 10,000 | 10,000 |
| Normal range (km) | 2,400 | 2,400 | 2,400 | 2,400 |

Production: during 1939-1944 Kawasaki Kokuki Kogyo Kabushiki Gaisha at Gifu built 1,997 Ki-48s, including:
- 4 – Ki-48 prototypes (1939)
- 5 – Ki-48 pilot batch (1940)
- 557- Ki-48-I production aircraft (July 1940-June 1942)
- 3 – Ki-48-II prototypes (February 1942)
- 1408 – Ki-48-I production aircraft (April 1942-October 1944)
- Plus:
- 3 – Ki-48-II Otsu Kai converted from production aircraft
- 4 – Ki-48-II Otsu modified to carry the Ki-148 guided bomb

# Kawasaki Ki-119

The Kawasaki Ki-119 bomber was one of the first to include suicide attacks in its specification. It also presaged an increasing desire to commission aircraft that were simple to build, and maintain, using non-strategic materials.

In the first months of 1945, when Allied invasion forces approached the Japanese home islands, the Army Aviation HQ issued an urgent request for a special light bomber which could be used for both conventional and Kamikaze missions. To meet this new requirement, the *Rikugun Koku Hombu* prepared specifications that stipulated, among others, that the aeroplane should be easy to produce and maintain, and that it should be simple enough to be flown by less experienced pilots. One of the requirements was that it should use engines that were already in production. Since range was a secondary issue in this case, a single-engined low-wing monoplane design was chosen, designated the 'Experimental Light Army Bomber' and given the classification Ki-119.

In March of 1945, the *Rikugun Koku Hombu* changed its requirements dramatically. This time the specification called for a fast light bomber that would be able to perform dive-bombing attacks on enemy ships far away from the coast and also act as an escort fighter. The new Ki-119 aeroplane was required to have a radius of operation of at least 600km carrying a 800kg bomb, and was to be armed with two 20mm cannon; it needed to have good flying, take-off and landing characteristics, to be easy to maintain, and of simple construction. The aeroplane would thus complement existing fighters and bombers, and it would be possible to manufacture two such light attack fighters with the resources required to build one heavy bomber, making better use of available engines and the ever-shrinking number of aircrew.

To speed up design work, it was proposed that the new machine should make maximum use of parts made for other aircraft of all metal construction, such as castings, forgings, and machined parts made of light metals. These could be supplied quickly by the many small dispersed workshops, located in tunnels or mines, which already produced sub-assemblies for these aircraft.

The work was entrusted to the Kawasaki design team, which was headed by Takeo Doi and Jun Kitano. Within three months the Ki-119 project had been developed and a full-scale mock-up was built. It was a single-engined cantilever low-wing monoplane of all metal construction, with tapered wings of high aspect ratio and large area. It had widely spaced main undercarriage units with long stroke shock absorbers, which were adapted from the Kawasaki Ki-102 twin-engined heavy fighter. This layout made for safe take-off and landing (when required), even when the aircraft was flown by less experienced pilots. The fuselage design used similar technology to that used in production of the Kawasaki Ki-100 single-engined fighter, and equipment from that aeroplane was also used. The cockpit was enclosed by a tear-drop canopy (similar to that of the Ki-100-I Otsu), which was located over the wing centre section leading edge to provide good forward visibility. Power was provided by a 2,000hp Mitsubishi Ha-104 18-cylinder radial engine driving a three-bladed propeller.

It was not difficult to develop a simplified airframe design, but using subassemblies from the Ki-100-I Otsu was more problematic for the designers. Eventually, only a few existing components were used, chiefly the hydraulics for lowering the undercarriage and flaps, engine cooling shutter control and oil cooler.

The Ki-119 was intended to be fitted with an automatic pilot, but as this system was still at a prototype stage, the initial production aircraft were designed to be fitted with automatic rudder control only.

Design work commenced in mid-March 1945, and on 4 April, Kawasaki received an order to prepare a schedule to move the production tooling for the new aeroplane to plants located in tunnels at Mino, Wachi and Togari. The latter tunnel would be employed for final assembly of the Ki-119. As it was, the war in the Pacific came to an end before the assembly plant there was set up.

In early June 1945, a wooden mock-up of the Ki-119 was built at Kagamigahara and was subjected to evaluation by *Rikugun Koku Hombu* experts, who noted their approval of the design. Following

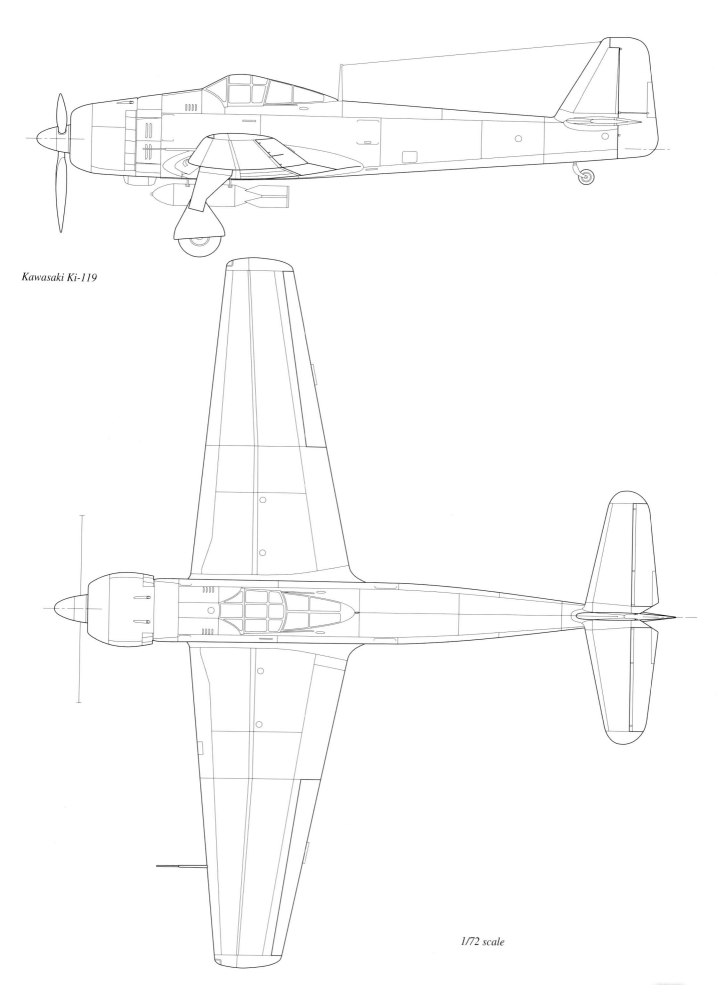

*Kawasaki Ki-119*

*1/72 scale*

**73**

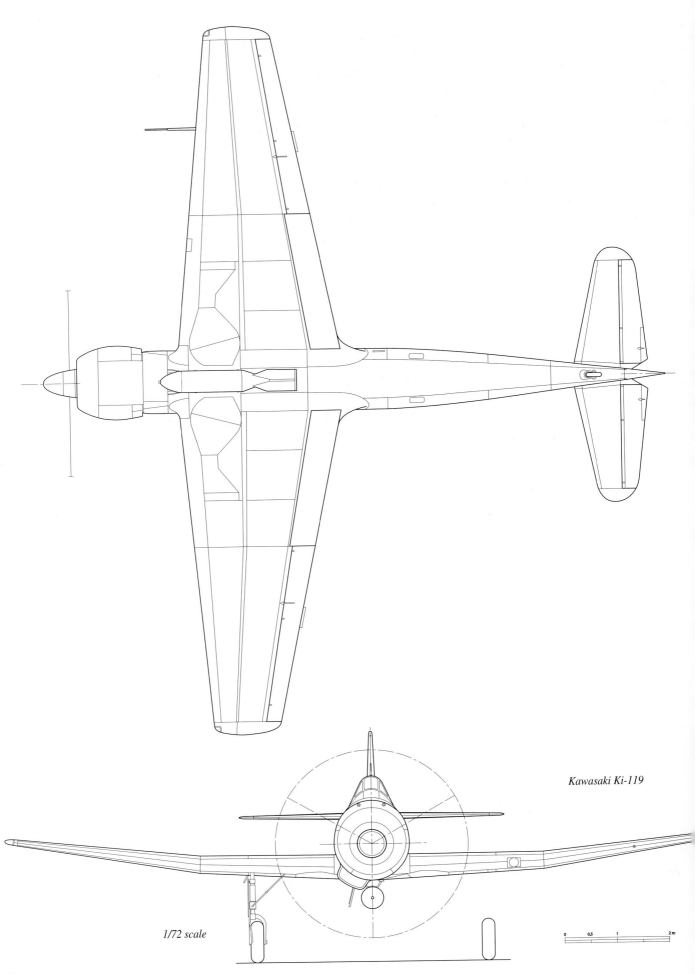

*Kawasaki Ki-119*

*1/72 scale*

0    0,5    1    2 m

this it was decided that the primary prototype would be prepared for flight in early September 1945, and that at the end of that month pre-production assembly would commence.

In the light bomber version, the armament would consist of two 20mm Ho-5 cannon fitted in the forward fuselage, and one 800kg bomb on an external carrier under the fuselage. For dive bombing missions, two 250kg bombs could be carried under the wings. The same under-wing carriers could be used to carry additional 600l fuel tanks instead of bombs, to increase the radius of operation to 1,200km. The planned escort fighter version would have two additional Ho-5 cannon in the wings.

The first flight of the prototype could not take place in September 1945 as the Kagamigahara plant was almost completely destroyed during four days of bombing from 22 June 1945, which totally destroyed the plant. Almost all of the documentation regarding the Ki-119 was lost. Nevertheless, immediately after the raids, the designers decided to recreate a new set of documentation, hoping that the prototype of their aeroplane would be completed by November 1945 and pre-series production could start. The war ended before further progress could be made.

**Specifications:**

Description: single-seat low-wing monoplane light bomber, dive bomber or escort fighter with an enclosed cockpit and retractable undercarriage with tail wheel. All metal construction with fabric covered control surfaces and ailerons. Conventional tail surfaces.

Crew: pilot in an enclosed cockpit.

Power plant: one Mitsubishi Ha-104 18-cylinder air cooled radial twin row radial engine rated at 2,000hp (1,470kW) for take-off, 1,900hp (1,395kW) nominal output and 1,720hp (1,265kW) at an altitude of 5,400m, driving a three-blade variable pitch metal propeller.

Armament: in the bomber version – two fixed 20mm Ho-5 cannon in the forward fuselage and one 800kg bomb on an external carrier under the fuselage or two 250kg bombs on external carriers under the wings,

In the fighter version – two fixed 20mm Ho-5 cannon in the forward fuselage and two fixed 20mm Ho-5 cannon in the wings.

| Type: | Ki-119 |
| --- | --- |
| Wing span m | 14.0 |
| Length m | 11.85 |
| Height m | 4.5 |
| Wing area m² | 31.9 |
| Empty weight kg | 3,670 |
| Take-off weight kg | 5,980 |
| Useful load kg | 2,310 |
| Wing loading kg/m² | 187.46 |
| Power loading kg/hp | 2.99 |
| Maximum speed km/h | 580 |
| at an altitude of m | 6,000 |
| Cruising speed km/h | 475 |
| Climb to 6,000m | 6 min. 9 sec. |
| Ceiling m | 10,500 |
| Normal range km | 600 |
| Maximum range km | 1,200 |

Production: Kawasaki Kokuki Kogyo Kabushiki Gaisha at Kagamigahara developed and built a mock-up Ki-119 - no prototypes were completed and production never began.

# *Kokusai* Ta-Go

In Japan many ideas were put forward on how to repel, or inflict heavy losses on, the forces of the imminent Allied invasion. These included new aircraft designs for Kamikaze pilots, the most effective weapon of the disintegrating Empire. The Ta-Go was actually two aircraft designs, intended from the start to be simple, cheap and to use meagre resources sparingly. Each was designed to use a lower-power engine.

Although the Nakajima Ki-115 Tsurugi suicide aeroplane had been officially accepted, young officers of the *Rikugun Kokugijyutsu Kenkyujo* (Army Air Technical Research Institute) at Tachikawa offered other solutions. In view of the shortage of light metal alloys, and the scale of the destruction of the Japanese aircraft industry by Allied strategic raids, an even simpler design was offered. The new suicide aeroplane would not be built in normal aircraft factories, but in small workshops from generally available materials, such as wood and steel, by unskilled personnel. For this reason the design of the aeroplane was required to be very simple, and even performance was of secondary importance. It was simply necessary for the aircraft to be able to take off and carry out its single suicide attack.

Supporters of the new suicide aeroplane, known as the Ta-Go (Ta was short for *Take-yari* – bamboo spear), were led by Captain Yoshiyuki Mizuyama. He suggested the construction of two types of simple Ta-Go aircraft, to be powered by any available aircraft engine. A review was undertaken of the power plants that were available at the time, and the specifications of the two aircraft were drawn up based on the review's findings.The first variant was designed to use an engine rated at some 500hp , while the second variant used a much less powerful one, rated at 150HP.

Initially, Captain Mizuyama's initiative failed to obtain the approval of the *Rikugun Koku Hombu*. However, ignoring this lack of official support, Captain Mizuyama met representatives of the Tachikawa and *Kokusai* companies, which specialised in construction of light aircraft, in February 1945. According to Captain Mizuyama's concept, Tachikawa would build an aeroplane powered by a 500hp engine, and *Kokusai* would build the lighter aeroplane with a 150hp engine. Also in February 1945, Captain Mizuyama visited *Nihon Kokusai Koku* at Kyoto to present his concept. Talks with *Kokusai* were significantly more successful than those with Tachikawa, whose management had agreed to build a prototype, but only on receipt of an official order from the

*Side view of the Kokusai Ta-Go suicide aircraft.*

*Rikugun Koku Hombu*. *Kokusai* imposed no such conditions, and started work on the Ta-Go right away. Almost simultaneous with the design work, workshop documentation was prepared.

The Ta-Go project was a small low-wing monoplane of compact design, built entirely of wood. The wooden framework was covered with plywood and fabric. Because the project requirements stipulated that the aeroplane must be mass produced by unskilled personnel, the use of sophisticated shapes in the design was prevented. To simplify production, the vertical and horizontal tail surfaces were identical. The fuselage was rectangular, not only in its side elevation, but also in cross-section. The pilot was seated in a very cramped open cockpit, fitted with a small windscreen. Wings were also of very simple wooden construction: they could be folded at hinges placed just outside the centre section for better concealment of the aeroplane from aerial reconnaissance and for storage in caves and small buildings. The main undercarriage and the tail skid were simple in design, and power was provided by the Hitachi Ha-47 Hatsukaze inverted in-line air cooled engine, rated at 110hp for take-off, as used by *Kokusai* in the Ki-86 trainer. The engine was fitted with a wooden propeller adapted from that of the Ki-86. A 100kg bomb could be fitted under the fuselage.

The first (and only, as it would turn out) prototype of the Ta-Go suicide aeroplane was built by students of the *Rikugun Kokugijyutsu Kenkyujo* (Army Air Technical Research Institute) at Okubo near Kyoto. It was first flown on 25 June 1945 by a *Kokusai* test pilot, but flight trials did not continue for long because the simplified design caused handling problems. Despite this, efforts were made to start series production, even though the aeroplane still had no official approval from the *Rikugun Koku Hombu* and therefore had no Ki designation. The plan was to assemble these aircraft in railway tunnels and caves, from which they would take off, but by the time of the cessation of hostilities, no production aeroplane of the type had been built. Had series production started, it was expected that Ta-Go aircraft would be used for defence of the Kansai area, and in the Osaka and Kobe regions.

By the end of the war, *Kokusai* were reputedly developing more projects, designated Tsu-Go and Gi-Go. However, no credible information on these has surfaced so far, and there are no photos or drawings.

**Specifications:**

Description: single-engined low-wing monoplane. Wooden construction, fabric covered.

Crew: pilot in an open cockpit.

Power plant: one Hitachi Ha-47 Hatsukaze (GK4A Model 11) 4-cylinder air cooled in-line engine rated at 110hp (80kW) for take-off; wooden two-blade fixed pitch propeller, diameter 2.180m.

Armament: one 100kg bomb.

| Maximum speed km/h | 580 |
|---|---|
| at an altitude of m | 6,000 |
| Cruising speed km/h | 475 |
| Climb to 6,000m | 6 min. 9 sec. |
| Ceiling m | 10,500 |
| Normal range km | 600 |
| Maximum range km | 1,200 |

Production: in 1945 Nippon *Kokusai Koku Kogyo Kabushiki Gaisha* built only one prototype Ta-Go.

Ta-Go Go with wings folded, to facilitate hiding it in tunnels or under viaducts.

Head-on view of the Ta-Go with manually folded wing. The aircraft was propelled by a Hitachi Ha-47 Hatsukaze (GK4A Model 11) 4-cylinder air-cooled in-line engine with take-off rating of 110 KM (81 kW), driving a 2.180 m fixed pitch wooden propeller. Note the cranked pitot tube.

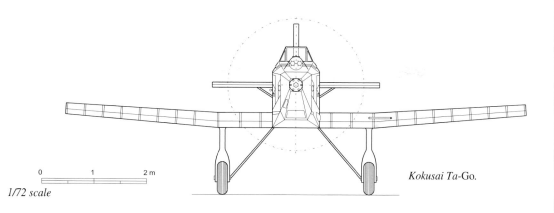

0       1       2 m

*1/72 scale*

*Kokusai Ta-Go.*

*The first and eventually the only prototype of the Kokusai Ta-Go suicide aircraft was built by students of the Rikugun Kokugijyutsu Kenkyujo at Okubo near Kyoto. It was first flown on 25 June 1945 by a Kokusai company test pilot.*

*The Ta-Go was of all-wooden construction. It could carry a single 100 kg bomb under the fuselage.*

*Ta-Go with 100 hp engine completed at Kokusai Koku in Kyoto. The person in the center with his hands crossed is the designer, Mr. Masuura.*

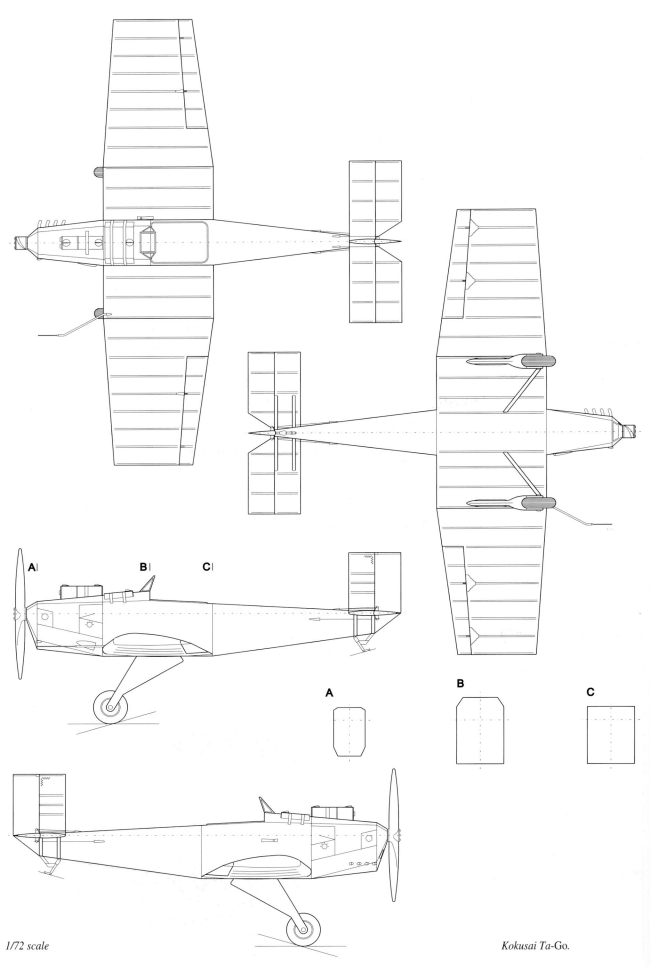

A    B    C

A    B    C

1/72 scale

*Kokusai Ta-Go.*

# Nakajima Ki-49 Donryu (Helen)

The Nakajima Ki-49 was considered largely unsuccessful as a bomber, and the war ended before it could achieve much as a suicide aircraft, despite a promising start.

The largest Japanese aircraft manufacturer, Nakajima, did not achieve much success during the first half of the 1930s. Its primary competitor, Mitsubishi, won most of the bids announced by the *Rikugun Koku Hombu* and *Kaigun Koku Hombu* for new Army and Navy aircraft. Particularly painful for Nakajima was that both the Army and the Navy decided to introduce into service Mitsubishi twin-engined bombers, which at the time were considered to be the most important part of Japanese air power, in preference to Nakajima designs. The LB-2 bomber developed by Nakajima, based on the American Douglas DC-2 airliner, lost out to the Mitsubishi G3M. In another competition for a similar aeroplane for the Army, the designs for the Nakajima Ki-19 narrowly lost to the Mitsubishi Ki-21. All that Nakajima was left with was the contract for licence production of the Ki-21. Following these disappointments, Nakajima prepared particularly carefully for the next bomber competition.

Specification for the Ki-21's successor were defined by the *Rikugun Koku Hombu* in early 1938. The primary requirement, based on experience gained during the war in China, was that this should be a heavy bomber, able to operate independently, deep within enemy territory and without fighter escort. To achieve these aims, the aeroplane would need not only to possess performance superior to that of the Ki-21, but would also have to have very heavy defensive armament, able to repel attacks by enemy fighters. The following requirements were therefore included in the specification:

maximum speed – 500km/h

range with 750kg bombs – 3,000km

bomb load – normal 750kg, maximum – 1,000kg

defensive armament – one 20mm cannon and five machine guns

armour protection of crew positions and self-sealing fuel tanks

crew – six, but room for eight.

At the end of 1938, less than a year after series production of the Ki-21 commenced, Nakajima had produced a mock-up of the new design, which was designated Ki-49. The project involved Dr Hideo Itokawa, the chief designer of Nakajima, Tei Koyama, known for his advanced ideas, and Dr Setsuro Nishimura, who had the most experience in the company with the design of twin-engined aircraft.

In early 1939, the engineering committee of the *Rikugun Koku Hombu* approved the mock-up and projected performance of the Ki-49, and approved the project for further development. The aeroplane received its name of Donryu ('Thundering Dragon'), a name derived from a Shinto

*Hamamatsu training unit was formed on 20 June 1944 to train bomber crews, mainly on Ki-49-1 Donryus.*

81

temple near Nakajima's base in Ota. The first prototype Ki-49.01 was ready in August 1939, and was flown that month.

The aeroplane was a mid-wing monoplane. The wing centre section had a larger span than the outer wings, to give room for six self-sealing fuel tanks (three on each side of the fuselage). Two more self-sealing fuel tanks and the oil tank were located in the fuselage. Fowler flaps were fitted between the engine nacelles and the fuselage, to improve take-off and landing characteristics. The spacious fuselage housed a crew of six to eight. The defensive armament consisted of one 20mm Ho-1 cannon in a dorsal turret and five 0.303in. (7.7mm) Type 89 machine guns fitted individually in the nose, two waist, and ventral positions, and in the tail turret. The maximum bomb load, depending on the bomb type used and the distance to the target, was between 750 and 1,000kg. The bomb load was carried entirely inside a spacious bomb bay that extended along the entire chord of the wing centre section. It had been intended to fit the Ki-49 with the latest Nakajima engine, the 1,200hp Ha-41. However, when the construction of the first prototype was completed, these engines were not available, and it was decided to test fly the first prototype with Ha-5 Kai engines, rated at 950hp for take-off, and driving Hamilton Standard three-bladed two-pitch propellers (built under licence by Sumitomo) to prevent delays to the programme. Two subsequent prototypes, Ki-49.02 and Ki-49.03, completed in November 1939, received the Ha-41 as planned.

Flight trials of the prototype Ki-49.01 were satisfactory in terms of flying characteristics and manoeuvrability. On 20 November 1940, after some changes were introduced, the aeroplane was approved for series production. It then received the designation 'Type 100 Army Heavy Bomber Donryu Model 1' (Ki-49-I).

The first production Ki-49-I left the Nakajima assembly hall in August 1941, three years after *Rikugun Koku Hombu* approval of the preliminary Ki-49 project and nine months after approval of the Ki-49 for series production. Even so, production of the older Ki-21 was gaining momentum after new Ki-21-I versions entered operations, and the Ki-49 was only ever built in small numbers.

It took until mid-1942 for the first combat unit to become operational with the Ki-49. The unit in question was the 61st *Sentai* (heavy bomber regiment), which began receiving Ki-49s from February 1942 and completed conversion training in June 1942. Soon afterwards, the 61st *Sentai* moved to Kendari on Celebes.

The role of the unit was to perform bomber attacks on *Australia*. Due to its recent type conversion and relocation, the unit was not ready for combat until June 1943. The first combat operation took place on 20 June 1943, when 18 Ki-49s of the 61st *Sentai* flew a raid against Darwin. The type's combat debut was not a success: two Ki-49s were lost over the target, another crashed on the return leg, force-landing on Timor, and two more were damaged during landing. At the end of 1942, Ki-

*Army aviation aircraft at Kalidjati airfield in Java, used mainly for transport duties. In the background Nakajima Ki-49-II Ko Donryus.*

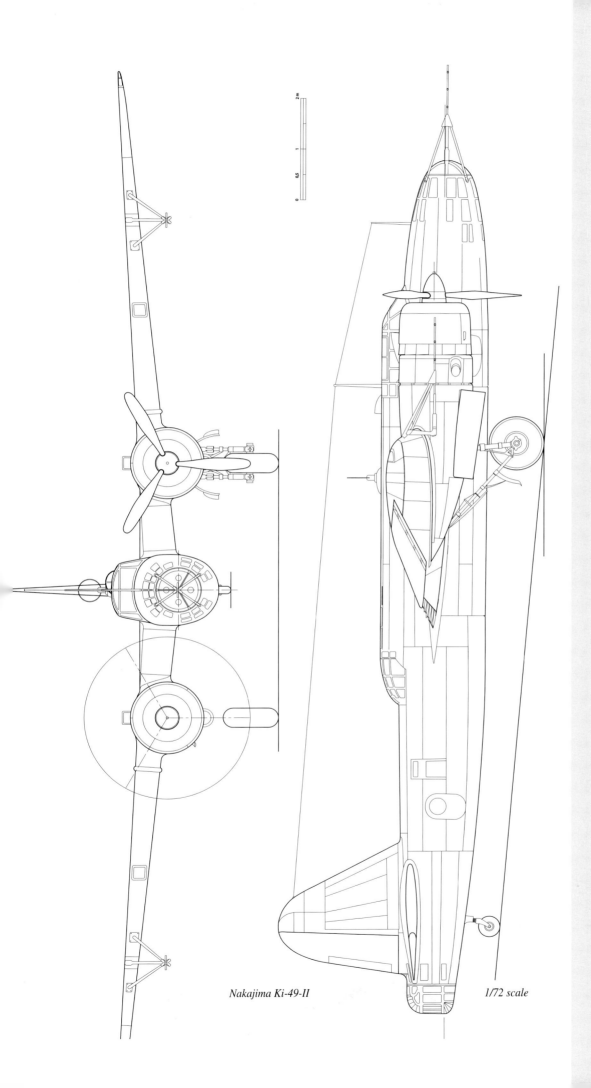

*Nakajima Ki-49-II*

*1/72 scale*

2 m

1

0,5

0

83

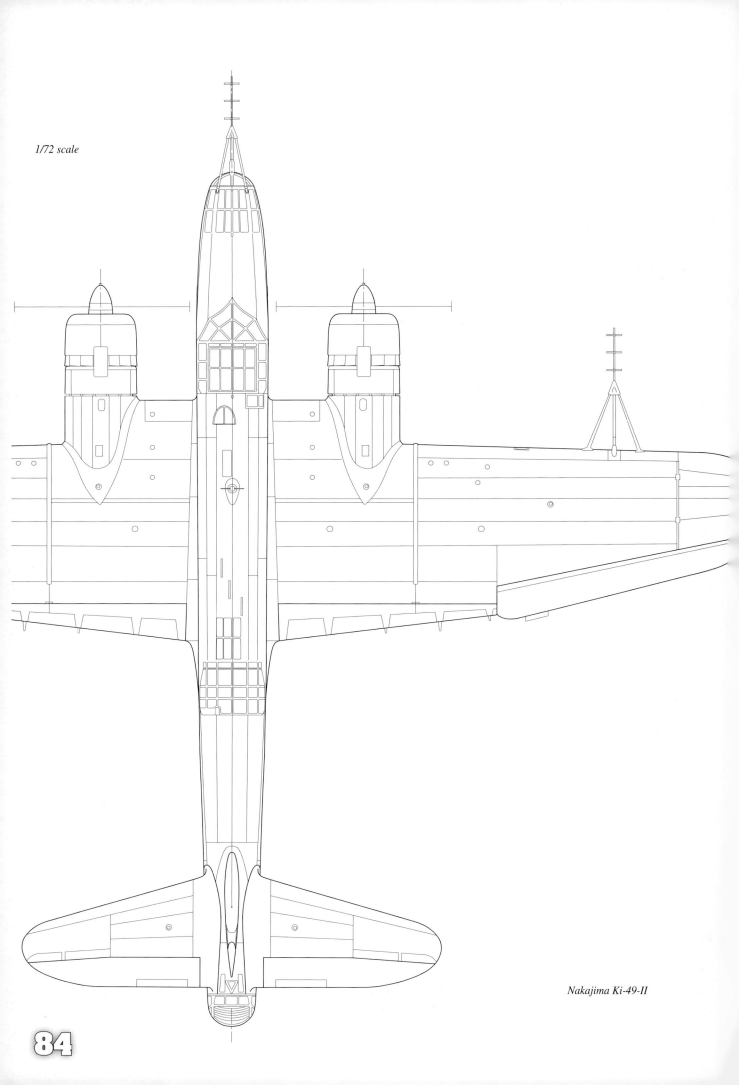

*1/72 scale*

*Nakajima Ki-49-II*

49-Is were also allocated to the 74th *Sentai* based in Manchukuo (Manchuria), far from any combat action area. This was the only other unit to be armed with the Ki-49-I.

In mid-1941, before the first Ki-49s started to reach active units, work on a new version of the aeroplane commenced. The Ki-49-II Ko had more powerful Ha-109 engines, improved self-sealing and armour protection of the fuel tanks, and a new bomb sight to allow night bombing. In June 1943, the 7th *Sentai* was re-equipped with the Ki-49-II Ko. However, after a few weeks of combat the unit had only six remaining aircraft. In December 1943 Ki-49-IIs replaced the earlier version for the 74th *Sentai* based in Manchuria and the 61st *Sentai* on Celebes.

In September 1943, a slightly improved bomber variant, the Ki-49-II Otsu, started to come off the production lines. This was similar to the Ki-49-II Ko, but had 0.5in. (12.7mm) machine guns in the nose, tail and ventral positions in place of the earlier .303in. machine guns, and an improved bomb sight. (A further improved version, the Ki-49-III, was planned with the major change from earlier versions being still more powerful engines. However, the anticipated Nakajima Ha-117 powerplants had not entered production by the war's end).

The first Ki-49-II Otsus were delivered to the 4th *Kokugun* in early April 1944. The new aircraft were used for night attacks against Allied troops participating in the invasion of Hollandia. The aircraft usually operated in formations of one to four machines, from airfields at Menado, Kendari and Makasser.

By early 1944, the Ki-49-II equipped the 62nd *Sentai* operated in Burma. Their first action took place on 27 March 1944, but out of nine machines despatched, none returned to base. Eight Ki-49-IIs were shot down by Allied fighters, and the ninth, heavily damaged, force-landed in Burma. By May 1944, the unit performed sporadic attacks against targets in India, including Imphal. However, faced with heavy losses, it had to be rapidly withdrawn to the Philippines. At the same time, most of the units of the 4th *Kokugun*, including Ki-49 units, were withdrawn from New Guinea to the Philippines. Ki-49s were delivered to the 7th and 74th *Sentais*, and the newly formed 95th *Sentai*, which was deployed to Manchuria to replace the 74th *Sentai*. In October 1944, during the Allied invasion of the Philippines, all Ki-49 units in the region were based at Clark Field and Lipa on Luzon. Most aircraft were destroyed on their airfields by Allied aircraft in the first days of the invasion, and those that survived operated only at night. Starting in December 1944, Ki-49s started to be used for suicide attacks .

After the successful employment of the special Banda corps that used converted Kawasaki Ki-48s, it was decided to modify other aircraft types for such attacks. Among the aircraft selected for the purpose were twelve Ki-49-IIs. Compared to a standard machine, the modified aeroplane had its crew reduced to two, the entire defensive armament removed, and the forward fuselage modified to include an 800kg bomb with a long probe fuse instead of the nose gunner/bomb aimer position. The first aeroplane of the type, designated 'Type 100 Army Heavy Bomber Donryu Model 2 Kai' (Ki-49-II Kai), was converted by Nakajima in August 1944. Training of a selected group of volunteers commenced in the summer of 1944, before Ki-49-II Kai aircraft were ready. At the news of the invasion of the Philippines, the first of two special units was formed from airmen of the 74th *Sentai*, and it was sent to the fighting area at the end of October. Soon it was joined by a second suicide unit, based on the 95th *Sentai*, and both units were regarded as the strategic reserve of the 4th *Kokugun*. They carried out their first action on 6 December 1944 and the success of the suicide action resulted in a plan to establish eighteen more suicide units equipped with a total of 216 Ki-49-II Kai aircraft. Although this idea was quickly accepted, it was never realised, due to the end of fighting in the Philippines.

By the time fighting had reached the Philippines at the end of 1944, the frontline career of the Ki-49 was virtually over, as the new Mitsubishi Ki-67 Hiryū 'Peggy' entered service. During the fighting on Okinawa in May 1945, the idea of using obsolete bombers as transport aircraft for special commando suicide groups was put forward, so some of the surviving Ki-49-IIs were converted to transport aircraft. The machines were to land on airfields in enemy hands and deploy groups of commandos, who would destroy aircraft and facilities on the airfields. However, after an unsuccessful mission of this type, using Ki-21 aircraft at Yomitan on Okinawa, the idea was abandoned.

Many Ki-49s survived combat operations, and after the war Ki-49s were used to ferry Japanese troops from China. The Ki-49 had been identified by Allied intelligence in September 1942, when it received its allied code name, 'Helen'. The first aeroplane of the type was captured by the Allies on 20 June 1943, which was a machine of the 61st *Sentai*, shot down over Darwin in Australia. Another aeroplane, in slightly better condition, fell into the hands of the Americans in December 1943 at Cape Gloucester on New Britain. One Ki-49, assembled from several machines, was used after the war in the

*Ki-49-II Kai with special probe fuse.*

*Ki-49-II Kai suicide bomber of the 74th Sentai, with the probe fuse at the front of the fuselage, to detonate the 800 kg bomb.*

Dutch East Indies by the Indonesian People's Revolutionary Forces. It remained in service until 1947.

The Ki-49 was not well liked by the pilots of the Army Aviation section. It was too heavy, and was always underpowered, which caused problems during flight. Its performance was not much better than that of its predecessor, the Ki-21. During night actions, which were common due to Allied supremacy in the air, crews complained about glare from the exhaust, as the engines were in line with the cockpit. It was more complicated to maintain and more time-consuming to produce than the Ki-21, and machines of the Ki-49 type equipped only one training and five combat regiments.

**Specifications:**

Description: twin-engined mid-wing monoplane heavy bomber (Ki-49) or transport airplane (Ki-49 Kai) or special attack aeroplane (Ki-49-II Kai). All metal construction with fabric covered control surfaces and ailerons.

Crew: eight (pilot, co-pilot, bomb aimer/gunner, radio-operator/gunner, navigator and three gunners).

Power plant: Two Nakajima Ha-5 Kai 14-cylinder air cooled radial engines rated at 950hp (699kW) for take-off and 1,080hp (794kW) at an altitude of 4,000m; three-blade variable pitch metal propellers, diameter 3.175m; fuel tank capacity 2,350l, oil tank capacity 150l (Ki-49.01). Two Nakajima Ha-41 14-cylinder air cooled radial engines rated at 1,200hp (883kW) for take-off and 1,260hp (927kW) at an altitude of 3,700m; three-blade variable pitch metal propellers, diameter 3.175m; fuel tank capacity 2,350l; oil tank capacity 150l (Ki-49.02 – Ki-49.10, Ki-49-I and Ki-49-I Kai). Two Nakajima Ha-109 (Army Type 2) 14-cylinder air cooled radial engines rated at 1,520hp (1118kW) for take-off and 1,440hp (1059kW) at an altitude of 2,150m and 1,310hp (963kW) at an 5,250m; three-blade variable pitch metal propellers, diameter 3.175m; fuel tank capacity 2,700l; oil tank capacity 150l (Ki-49-II). Two Nakajima Ha-117 14-cylinder air cooled radial engines rated at 2,420hp (1,779kW) for take-off and 2,370 hp (1,742 kW) at an altitude of 4,000m; three-blade variable pitch metal propellers, diameter 3.200m; fuel tank capacity 2,700l; oil tank capacity 150l (Ki-49-III).

Armament: One 20 mm Ho-1 gun and five 7.92 mm Type 89 machine gun (Ki-49 prototypes, Ki-49-I and Ki-49-II). One 20 mm Ho-1 gun and three 12.7 mm Type 1 (Ho-103) machine guns and two 7.92 mm Type 89 machine guns (Ki-49-II Otsu and Ki-49-III). Three 7.92 mm Type 89 machine gun (Ki-49-I Kai) and Ki-49-II Kai)

Bomb load: normal – 750 kg; maximum – 1000 kg

*Ki-49-II Otsu Donryu bomber wreckage at Nicholson Field in the Philippines. March 1945.*

| Type | Ki-49-I | Ki-49-II | Ki-49-III |
|---|---|---|---|
| Wing span m | 20.424 | 20.424 | 20.424 |
| Length m | 16.808 | 16.808 | 16.808 |
| Height m | 4.25 | 4.25 | 4.25 |
| Wing area m² | 69.33 | 69.05 | 69.05 |
| Empty weight kg | 6,250 | 6,070 | 6,750 |
| Normal take-off weight kg | 10,225 | 10,150 | 10,680 |
| Maximum take-off weight kg | 10,675 | 11,400 | 13,50 |
| Useful load kg | 3,975 | 4,080 | 3,930 |
| Wing loading kg/m² | 153.93 | 147.00 | 158.22 |
| Power loading kg/hp | 5.38 | 3.39 | 3.76 |
| Maximum speed km/h | 466 | 492 | 540 |
| at an altitude of m | 5,000 | 5,200 | 5,300 |
| Cruising speed km/h | 350 | 350 | 350 |
| at an altitude of m | 3,000 | 3,500 | 4,000 |
| Landing speed km/h | 131 | 133 | 133 |
| Climb to 5,000m | 14 min. 5 sec. | 13 min. 39 sec. | 10 min. 30 sec. |
| Ceiling | 8,650 | 9,300 | 8,500 |
| Normal range | 2,000 | 2,950 | 2,000 |
| Maximum range km | 3,070 | 3,500 | 3,120 |

Production: a total of 814 Ki-49s of all versions and variants were built, including:

- Nakajima Hikoki Kabushiki Gaisha at Ota:
- 3 - Ki-49 prototypes (August 1939),
- 7 - Ki-49 pilot batch (January-December 1940),
- 129 - Ki-49-I production aircraft (August 1941-August 1942),
- 2 - Ki-49-II prototypes (August 1942-September 1942),
- 587 - Ki-49-II production aircraft ( March 1943-December 1943),
- 6 - Ki-49-III prototypes (March 1943-December 1943),
- Tachikawa Hikoki Kabushiki Gaisha at Tachikawa:
- 50 - Ki-49-II production aircraft (January 1943-December 1943),
- Mansyu Hikoki Seizo Kabushiki Gaisha in Harbin:
- 30- Ki-49-II production aircraft.

# Mitsubishi To-Go and Ki-167

The Mitsubishi Ki-67 'Peggy' originated as a twin-engined bomber and torpedo bomber. It was used in strikes against the US fleet at Formosa and the Ryuku Islands, but subsequently became one of the many types of aircraft selected for conversion for suicide attacks. On 18 August 1944, the *Rikugun Koku Hombu* issued specifications for the development of a suicide version intended to be used with a high-tech 'shaped charge' explosive for maximum destructive effect.

On the basis of a preliminary analysis of the requirements, the task was split into two stages. The first stage was to produce a hasty modification of the Ki-67 airframe to carry two 800kg bombs, designated the Ki-67-I Kai or To-Go (short for Tokubetsu Kogeki – special attack). The second stage was to build a special version, the Ki-167, fitted with a thermal (hollow charge) bomb. This version of the aircraft was given the suffix '*Sakura-Dan*' (Cherry Blossom).

In August 1944, with great secrecy, the order came for the conversion of several Nakajima Ki-49 'Lily' and Mitsubishi Ki-67-Ia 'Peggy' bombers into suicide aircraft. The Ki-67-I Kai variant was a simple adaptation of the existing Ki-67 airframe. In accordance with the recommendations, its bomb load was increased to 1,600kg and a fuse was fitted to a long probe ahead of the forward fuselage. All unnecessary equipment was removed. The waist and tail gun positions and the ventral turret were removed, and the openings faired over. The glazed forward fuselage was replaced by a solid section housing one 800kg bomb, while the second bomb was carried in the existing bomb bay. The crew was limited to three: pilot, co-pilot and radio-operator. By September 1944, ten machines had been converted this way. The modification was carried out by the Tachikawa and Kawasaki plants, supervised by the *Dai-Ichi Rikugun Kokusho* at Tachikawa. The modified aircraft were allocated to the Fugaku *Sentai* special unit.

In October 1944 the *Fugaku Sentai* arrived in the Philippines. It was formed at the Hamamatsu flying school, comprising six instructors selected from volunteers of the 1st Training Flight, commanded by Captain Miura. In the Philippines the unit was reinforced with additional personnel from the 7th *Sentai*. The recognition marking for the unit took the form of a Mount Fuji motif on the vertical tail. The unit attained operational capability at the end of October, by which time it had 26 crew members, all volunteers, and was equipped with the ten converted Ki-67-I Kai (To-Go) suicide aircraft. The unit reported to the 4th *Koku Sentai*, also based in the Philippines, whose commander decided to retain the Fugaku *Sentai* as a strategic reserve.

The Fugaku *Sentai* entered action on 7 and 13 November 1944, at which time only five of the machines were serviceable. The last suicide attack of the Fugaku *Sentai* took place on 12 January 1945. The effects of the unit's attacks are not known, although the conversion of another five Ki-67s to the To-Go suicide version in December 1944 was authorised. These machines were quickly deployed to the Philippines, where they equipped the decimated 74th *Sentai*. At that time the unit was using Nakajima Ki-49 bombers, but at the end of 1944 the 74th *Sentai* was designated for suicide attack duties, and received some To-Go aircraft on 9 January 1945. The plan to launch suicide operations failed when the To-Go aircraft were destroyed at Lingayen airfield on Luzon before the unit had a chance to carry out any missions. The remaining wreckage of the To-Go aircraft subsequently captured in the Philippines was mistakenly identified by the American Technical Air Intelligence Unit (TAIU) experts as belonging to reconnaissance versions of the Ki-67 'Peggy'.

The second suicide adaptation based on the Ki-67 was designed to carry the Sakura-Dan thermal bomb. This aeroplane received the designation 'Experimental Army Attack Aeroplane' (Ki-167), though it was not the official Ki-designation. (The official Ki-167 designation was given to a proposed experimental trainer.) The Sakura-Dan thermal bomb was based on a similar weapon supplied by the Germans. In October 1942, a bomb of the type, along with associated documentation, was brought to Japan by the submarine I-30. This was probably the same warhead used in the German Mistel composites. Japanese research and development work on the bomb was carried out in utmost secrecy at Pai-Chengi-zi in Manchuria. A hollow charge flame extending 1,000m from the point of impact was obtained during trials. The bomb could completely destroy the average tank within

300m range. Later on, trials of the Sakura-Dan bomb's effectiveness against warships were carried out. During the tests, the hollow charge flame of the Sakura-Dan bomb penetrated four armour plates 6, 40, 172 and 35mm thick, spaced at 6m intervals and angled at 45°.

Analysis of the trial results revealed that there was virtually no warship at the time that could withstand a direct hit by the bomb. However, one problem remained: how to use the 2,900kg Sakura-Dan bomb effectively. Because it was too heavy to be carried by the Ki-67 'Peggy', a special version of the bomb, the Sakura-Dan 2 was produced, with a reduced weight of 1,300kg. This version was shaped like a truncated cone, with a base diameter of 1.12m, and a height of 1m, a thin covering for the explosive charge at the front and 4mm armour on the sides. The rear part of the bomb housing had a 500mm armour plate which was designed to properly direct the hollow charge stream.

The Sakura-Dan 2 bomb was fitted into the structure of the Ki-67. It was located aft of the cockpit in place of the gun turret, to maintain the centre of gravity. The bomb was angled downwards at 15°, the angle considered the most appropriate for attacks against naval targets. Fitting the Sakura-Dan 2 in the Ki-67, however, required substantial changes to the fuselage: the upper decking was cut away and, after the bomb was fitted, faired in with metal sheeting. This gave the Ki-167 a characteristic 'humpback' fuselage profile. The crew was reduced to two, pilot and a navigator/radio-operator. All of the gun positions were removed and faired over, and for reasons of economy, the forward fuselage and the fin were made of wood.

The first two Ki-167 prototypes armed with the Sakura-Dan 2 were built at the experimental plant at Nagoya in February 1945, and in March they were subjected to flight testing at Kagamigahara, supervised by representatives of the Army Scientific-Research Aircraft Arsenal at Tachikawa (*Rikugun Kokugijiutsu Kenkyujo*). Upon completion of the tests the Ki-167s were handed over to the 62nd *Sentai* based at Nishi Tsukuba. Later, when the unit moved to Tachiarai, it received additional Ki-167s.

In March 1945 several To-Go machines went to the 62nd and 98th *Sentais*, based on the Japanese home islands. On 17 April 1945, the 62nd *Sentai* used the Ki-167 with a Sakura-Dan 2 hollow charge bomb in combat for the first time, when one Ki-167 flown by Lt Kozaburo Kato, accompanied by two To-Go aircraft, took off from Kanoya, at the far south of the home islands, heading for US Navy ships off Okinawa. The Japanese aircraft were fortunate enough to avoid enemy fighters, but immediately before the attack the Ki-167 was suddenly destroyed by a spontaneous explosion. This alarming phenomenon was noted by the formation commander, Captain Maemura, who was accompanying the Kamikazes in a conventional aircraft.

The second action of the 62nd *Sentai* Ki-167s was flown on 27 May. A formation of two Ki-167 and two To-Go aircraft intended to attack enemy ships off Okinawa. The To-Gos failed to locate the enemy and returned, while the Ki-167s located the ships and reported commencing their attack. No further news was heard from the Ki-167s and there was no indication of the success of otherwise of the attack.

Not many of these To-Go aircraft were built; at least one was lost in an accident, and several others were destroyed in sabotage actions. One aeroplane of the type was on the inventory of a suicide unit, name unknown, formed in June 1945 at Hamamatsu under the command of Major Isamu Katano. Eventually, the intention was that the unit would operate 16 Ki-167s. The unit planned to mount suicide attacks against American airfields in the Marianas, and the take-off was scheduled for midnight on 16 August 1945. It was believed that at least six machines would reach the target, but the action never took place because the armistice was declared on the day before.

Ki-167 aircraft were shrouded in secrecy. Only one photo of the aeroplane survives to date, and all surviving Ki-167s were destroyed before American occupation troops entered Japan. Similarly, the engineering documentation and details of the Sakura-Dan bombs were lost and the existence of this version of the Ki-67 Hiryū only became apparent to the West after the war.

**Specifications:**

Description: twin-engined cantilever mid-wing monoplane suicide aeroplane. All metal construction with fabric covered control surfaces.

Crew: three (To-Go), two (Ki-167).

Power plant: two Mitsubishi Ha-104 (Army Type 4) 18-cylinder air cooled radial engines rated at 1,900hp (1,395kW) at 2,450rpm for take-off; 1,810hp (1,330kW) at 2,350rpm at an altitude of 2200m; 1,610hp (1,185kW) at 2,350rpm at an altitude of 6,100m; four-blade variable pitch metal propellers, diameter 3.6m; fuel tank capacity 5,116 l (To-Go, Ki-167),

Armament: defensive – none

Bomb load: 1,600kg (2 x 800kg) (To-Go), 1,300kg Sakura-Dan 2 (Ki-167) thermal bomb.

| Type | To-Go (Ki-67-I Kai) | Ki-167 |
|---|---|---|
| Wing span m | 22.5 | 22.5 |
| Length m | 18.7 | 18.7 |
| Height m | 7.7 | 7.7 |
| Wing area m² | 65.85 | 65.85 |
| Empty weight kg | 8,650 | |
| Take-off weight kg | 13,765 | |
| Useful load kg | 5,115 | |
| Wing loading kg/m² | 209.04 | |
| Power loading kg/hp | 2.81 | |
| Maximum speed km/h | 537 | 535 |
| at an altitude of m | 6,100 | 6,100 |
| Cruising speed km/h | 400 | |
| at an altitude of m | 8,000 | |
| Landing speed km/h | 120 | |
| Time of climb | 14 min. 30 sec. | |
| to an altitude of m | 6,100 | |
| Ceiling m | 9,470 | |
| Normal range km | 3,800 | |

Production: it is not known exactly how many Ki-67 Hiryū aircraft were converted to suicide versions, but at least fifteen To-Go (Ki-67-I Kai) and five Ki-167 aircraft were built. The aircraft were built by the experimental plant of the Mitsubishi Jukogyo Kabushiki Gaisha factory at Nagoya and by Kawasaki Kokuki Kogyo Kabushiki Gaisha and Tachikawa Hikoki Kabushiki Gaisha.

*Take-off of the Fugaku Sentai To-Go suicide aircraft.*

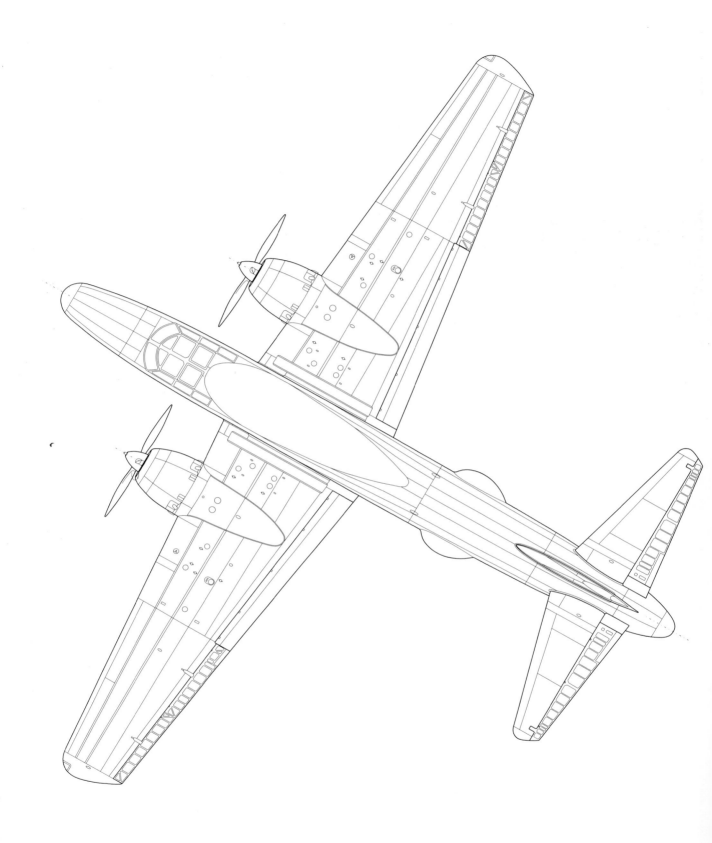

Ki-167

*1/100 scale*

*Wreckage of a To-Go aircraft with the probe fuse at the front of the fuselage.*

Ki-167

*1/100 scale*

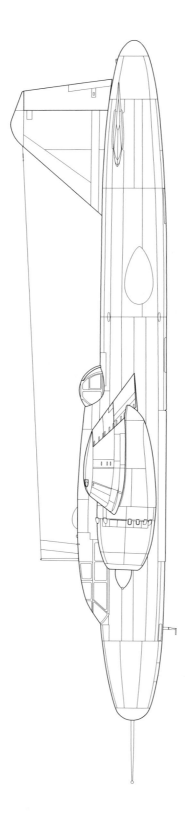

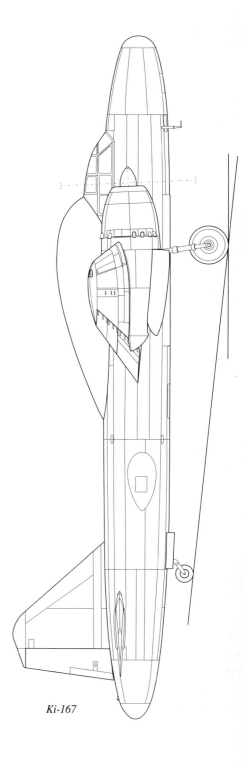

*Mitsubishi To-*Go

*Ki-167*

# Nakajima Ki-115 Tsurugi

The Ki-115 was one of a number of aircraft designed specifically for suicide missions towards the end of the war, but one of only a few to have actually reached production. Even so, the Ki-115 was never used in anger.

After Japan was occupied, Allied engineering committees undertook a review of aircraft factories, and found large numbers of aircraft that were unknown to their intelligence until that time. These turned out to be Nakajima Ki-115 Tsurugi suicide aircraft, which were intended to be used in group suicide raids against Allied targets, particularly against Allied invasion fleets.

At the end of August 1944, at a joint conference of the Naval and Army Aviation HQs, the decision was made to commence suicide attacks and to prepare three categories of aircraft for that purpose. The first category of aircraft included existing aircraft types that were modified for special attacks, their structure lightened by removing unnecessary equipment to allow for an increased bomb load. The second category of aircraft covered rocket-powered (Ohka, Baka) or jet-powered (Kikka) suicide aircraft developed using technologies from Germany and from local studies. The third category was intended to cover development of very simple aircraft to be powered by existing radial engines (already in production), and which could be manufactured using a minimum of strategic materials. The aircraft were intended for mass attacks. As noted earlier, work began straight away on the first two categories of suicide aircraft.

The American invasion of the Philippines surprised Japan with its speed and intensity. Suicide units were not fully prepared, but they were employed to as great an extent as their hasty organisation allowed. After the defeat in the Philippines, the schedule of work on special aircraft designs for the *Shimpū* units was significantly accelerated and priority was given to the third category of aircraft. Priority was given to these - the simple aircraft - because of the extreme shortage of strategic materials resulting from the American sea blockade, and the lack of surviving skilled aircraft industry labourers, after sustained Allied strategic bombing severely affected Japanese industry. It was it necessary to productively employ a labour force largely consisting of unskilled personnel. Production needed to be prioritised, furthermore, because an accelerated mass training of volunteers for *Shimpū* units was planned.

On 20 January 1945, the *Rikugun Koku Hombu* issued the following official specifications for the new special aeroplane for *Shimpū* units:

- technically simple, its individual elements suited for mass production in dispersed workshops by unskilled personnel
- easy to fly, even for a minimally-trained pilot
- made of generally available materials, with minimum use of aluminium and non-ferrous metal alloys
- able to take-off easily from makeshifts air strips
- armament: one medium size bomb
- power plant: adaptable to use any available radial engine from 800hp to 1,300hp
- maximum speed with the bomb load and with fixed undercarriage: 340km/h
- maximum diving speed: 515km/h.

Design work on the new aeroplane was carried out at Mitaka *Kenkyujo* (Research Institute at Mitaka) in co-operation with the Ota Seisakusho company at Ota (a nationalised subsidiary of Nakajima). The team was headed by Kunihiro Aoki from Nakajima. The design team developed an aeroplane which received the designation "Experimental Army Special Attack Aeroplane Tsurugi" (Ki-115 Tsurugi). Originally the project was designated Ken-ichi (experimental No. 1). As the sound of the ken character also means tsurugi (sword), the second meaning was adopted as the official name.

The Ki-115 was technically very simple, in accordance with the specifications. Wings were of all metal construction, and were made of aluminium alloys. The fuselage featured a framework welded

*Head-on view of the Ki-115 Ko. Note the under-fuselage bay that could partly enclose a 500 or 800 kg bomb.*

from steel tubes. The forward section was covered with duralumin skin, and the rear part with thin sheet steel, while the tail was of wooden construction, covered in plywood. Control surfaces and ailerons were covered with fabric. Only four attachments points were used for the engine, which allowed the use of various types of radial engines, although all Ki-115s that were built were fitted with Nakajima Ha-115-II radial engines rated at 1,130 hp for take-off, driving three-bladed constant speed propellers. The pilot was seated in an open cockpit, equipped with only the most essential flight instruments and engine controls, and shielded only by the windscreen. The aeroplane was fitted with a fixed undercarriage without shock-absorbers, with the main wheel leg assembly welded from steel tubes, designed to be jettisoned after take-off and re-used. This was understandably kept as simple as possible as the aircraft were not expected to need to land after taking off for their first and only mission, though many problems arose as a result of the undercarriage's basic nature. An 800kg bomb was carried under the fuselage, partly buried in the fuselage. It was assumed that 250 or 500kg bombs could also be used, depending on their availability. This was the Ki-115's only armament.

Assembly of the first prototype Ki-115.01 was complete on 5 March 1945, and it was immediately subjected to flight testing. The results of the trials were not satisfactory. A number of problems were discovered, caused by the stiff undercarriage, which had no shock-absorbers or brakes. This was even more troublesome as the aeroplane had poor visibility from the cockpit. Another problem was the wing, which was too small in area and was not fitted with flaps. This made take-off difficult, greatly extending the take-off run. The overall assessment of the aeroplane was negative, as it was unsuitable even for experienced pilots. Kunihiro Aoki's team was charged with improving the design.

The modified prototype was ready by June 1945. It was now fitted with shock-absorbers on the main undercarriage legs, and simple flaps were fitted aft of the wing trailing edge to improve the take-off characteristics - though these worsened the already-unsatisfactory visibility from the cockpit. However, the modified prototype underwent a series of preliminary tests in the air, and was approved by the qualification committee. At the same time, series production of the Ki-115 Ko commenced, even though it had not successfully passed all flight trials. Between March and August 1945 Nakajima plants at Iwate and Ota assembled 104 Ki-115 Ko aircraft from externally supplied components. Design changes were introduced during production. Although Series Ki-115 Ko aircraft did not differ much from the prototype, they were not fitted with shock-absorbers, and the undercarriage remained stiff. However, they did receive drum brakes, which significantly improved ground handling.

The Army training programme for new volunteers, using Ki-115 Tsurugi aircraft, commenced at the end of June 1945. Several prospective suicide pilots were killed during training as the aircraft was very difficult to fly, and soon afterwards all further training was halted.

No production Ki-115 Ko aircraft reached combat units. Even so, plans for a further-developed version designated Ki-115 Otsu were underway. The Otsu variant had a new wing which had increased span and area. The plan was to fit it with normal flaps, and the cockpit was relocated slightly forward to improve visibility. It was going to be built entirely of wood, to minimise the use of duralumin. However, although design work had been completed, no prototype of the Ki-115 Otsu was built as the project was overtaken by the end of the war.

The Ki-115 Hei variant also remained on paper. This featured significantly improved visibility as a result of locating the cockpit even further forward than on the Otsu. It was also going to be fitted with a manual bomb release so the pilot could jettison the bomb, or use the aircraft like a conventional bomber - previous versions of the Tsurugi had no option to release the bomb from the cockpit, which would have made landing in the event of an aborted mission impossible.

Two production Ki-115 Ko aircraft were completed and tested with two solid fuel rocket boosters under the wings. The rockets were intended to accelerate take-off of the aeroplane from hastily prepared air strips, or to increase diving speed in the final phase of the suicide attack.

The Navy was also interested in the Ki-115 Tsurugi. The *Kaigun Koku Hombu* issued Nakajima its own specification for a similar aeroplane type and placed an order, giving the machine the designation of "Experimental Navy special aeroplane Toka" (Wisteria Blossom). Changes included, among others, an increased wing area of 13.10m², and a number of minor modifications in the equipment (mainly the re-scaling of instruments to knots rather than km/h). According to Nakajima's calculations, the introduction of the changes requested by the *Kaigun Koku Hombu* would reduce

*One of eight Ki-115 prototypes with main undercarriage fitted with shock-absorbers.*

*Although 105 Nakajima Ki-115 Tsurugi suicide aircraft were built, none took part in combat operations. This is one of the production aircraft in the assembly hall.*

One of the production Ki-115 Ko Tsurugi aircraft. The photo was taken after occupying forces entered the Nakajima plant at Ota. The Hinomaru is applied over dark green primer on the side of the fuselage and the upper wing surfaces. Matt black antiglare panel is applied forward of the cockpit.

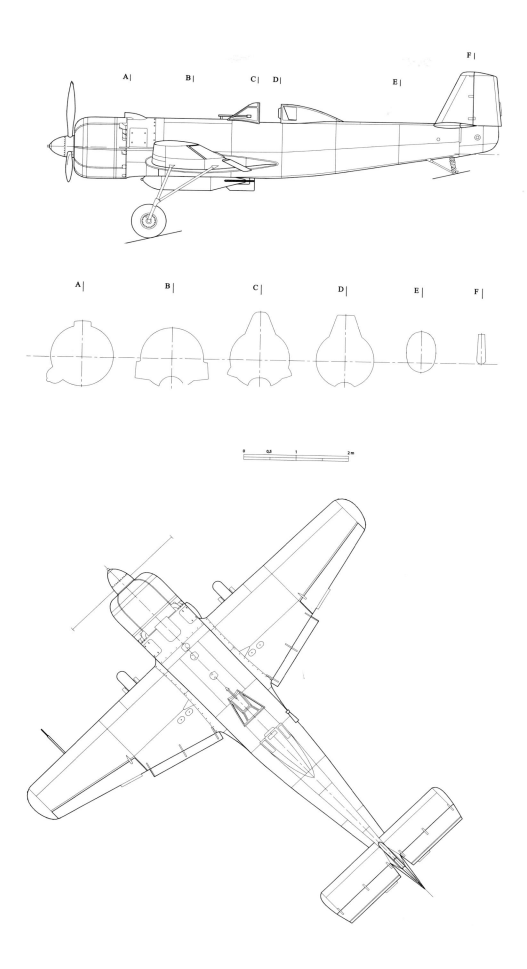

A|    B|         C| D|                E|          F|

A|        B|         C|         D|         E|      F|

0    0,5    1         2 m

*Nakajima Ki-115 Ko*
*Tsurugi*

*1/72 scale*

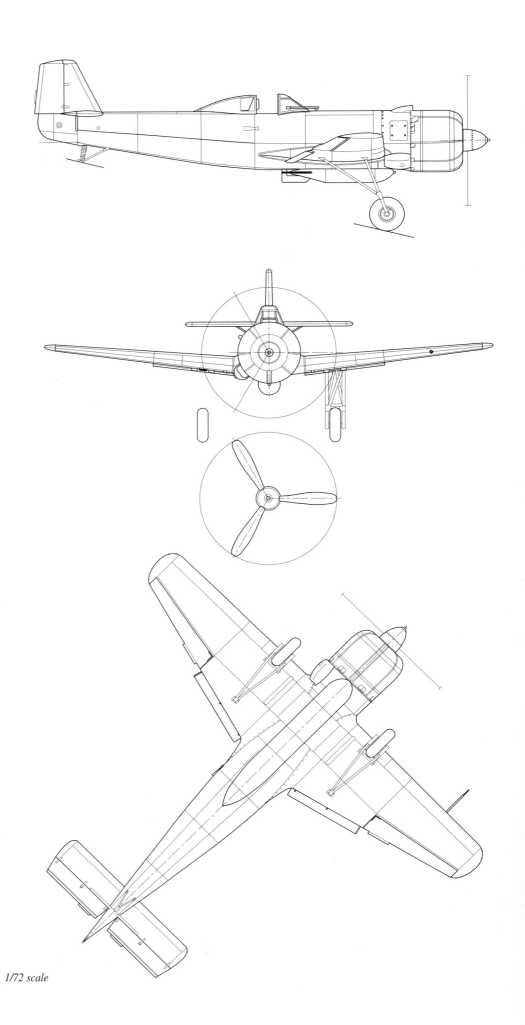

*Nakajima Ki-115 Ko
Tsurugi*

*1/72 scale*

the useful bomb load to 700kg. Production for the Navy was to be undertaken by the Showa Hikoki factory near Tokyo, and to this end Nakajima supplied full engineering documentation and two Ki-115 Ko aircraft in component form, to be modified there according to the Navy specifications. However, by the end of hostilities the documentation was not complete, and the two Ki-115 Kos were never modified to Navy standard. Aircraft built for the Navy were intended to be powered by various types of new or overhauled radial engines, and consideration was also given to manufacturing a Ki-115 of all-wooden construction, in consideration of which the *Rikugun Koku Hombu* put pressure on the Tanuma subsidiary of Nakajima to undertake a comprehensive redesign of the aeroplane.

The Army Aviation HQ planned to use the Ki-115 in defence of Okinawa and the home islands. These plans came to nothing, however, even though 104 aircraft had been built. The Aviation HQ now considered that tactical operations of the Ki-115 suicide aeroplane would be very limited. For example, if a formation of Ki-115s failed to locate their target, they could not return to their base as their endurance was limited, and they could not land. This would have meant the aircraft and their crews would simply have been wasted. Even if they Ki-115s could ditch successfully in the sea, the Japanese had no search and rescue operation to recover the pilots. Furthermore, the Ki-115 had no defensive armament and would have been extremely vulnerable to interception by Allied aircraft if they were not well protected by fighter escort. Therefore the Ki-115 remained nothing more than an unusual example of aircraft design for a very specific purpose.

After the war, one Ki-115 Otsu Tsurugi was shipped to the USA for technical testing. Later it became an exhibit at the Garber Facility of the National Air and Space Museum, where it is currently stored in a dismantled state.

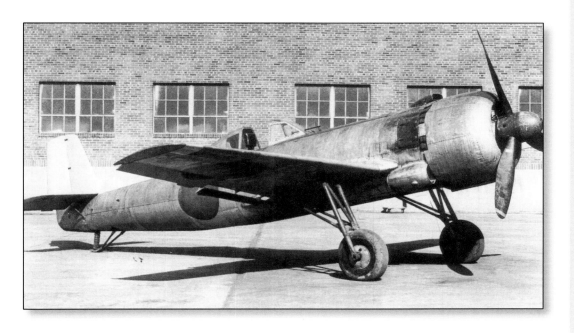

Colour schemes

When, in August 1945, occupation forces entered the Nakajima plant at Ota, they found a number of production Ki-115 Ko Tsurugi aircraft in three different paint schemes on the factory airfield.

Most Ki-115s had no disruptive camouflage, being painted light grey overall. The upper forward fuselage up to the cockpit was covered with a matt black anti-glare panel. Oil and fuel fillers located in this area were painted red and yellow. Hinomarus were applied on both wing surfaces, and on the sides of the fuselage immediately aft of the cockpit. Propellers of all aircraft were dark brown, including spinners. Yellow warning stripes were applied at the tips of the propellers.

Several of the captured Ki-115 aircraft wore partial camouflage, consisting of dark green areas on the upper wing surfaces and on the sides of the fuselage underneath the Hinomarus. In this case all Hinomarus featured a white outline. A matt black anti-glare panel was applied ahead of the cockpit.

Several Ki-115s featured the standard Army camouflage scheme. The upper wing surfaces and the top and sides of the fuselage were dark green, while the lower surfaces were light grey. The Hinomarus on the upper and side surfaces featured white outlines. A matt black anti-glare panel was applied ahead of the cockpit.

**Specifications:**

Description: single-seat low-wing monoplane suicide aeroplane. Mixed construction with fabric covered control surfaces and ailerons.

Crew: pilot in a partly enclosed cockpit.

Power plant: one Nakajima Ha-115-II (Army Type 99 Model 2) 14-cylinder air cooled radial engine rated at 1,130hp (1,105kW) for take-off, 1,100hp (810kW) at an altitude of 2,850m, and 980hp (720kW) at 6,000m; three-blade constant speed metal propeller, diameter 2.9m; fuel tank capacity 450l.

Armament: one 250, 500 or 800kg bomb.

| Type | Ki-115 Ko | Ki-115 Otsu | Ki-115 Hei |
|---|---|---|---|
| Wing span m | 8.572 | 9.72 | 9.72 |
| Length m | 8.55 | 8.55 | 8.55 |
| Height m | 3.3 | 3.3 | 3.3 |
| Wing area m² | 12.4 | 14.5 | 14.5 |
| Empty weight kg | 1,640 | 1,690 | |
| Maximum take-off weight kg | 2,880 | | |
| Useful load kg | 940 | 940 | |
| Wing loading kg/m² | 208.06 | 182.64 | |
| Power loading kg/hp | 2.24 | 2.29 | |
| Maximum speed km/h | 550 | 558 | |
| at an altitude of m | 2,800 | 2,800 | |
| Cruising speed km/h | 300 | | |
| at an altitude of m | 3,000 | | |
| Operational ceiling m | 6,500 | 6,500 | |
| Normal range km | 1,200 | 1,200 | |

Production: a total of 105 Ki-115 Tsurugi aircraft were built, including:

Mitaka *Kenkyujo*:
- - Ki-115 prototype

Nakajima Hikoki Kabushiki Gaisha at Iwate:
- - Ki-115 Ko production aircraft

Nakajima Hikoki Kabushiki Gaisha at Ota:
- 82 - Ki-115 Ko production aircraft

Showa Hikoki Kabushiki Gaisha: did not start production before the end of the war

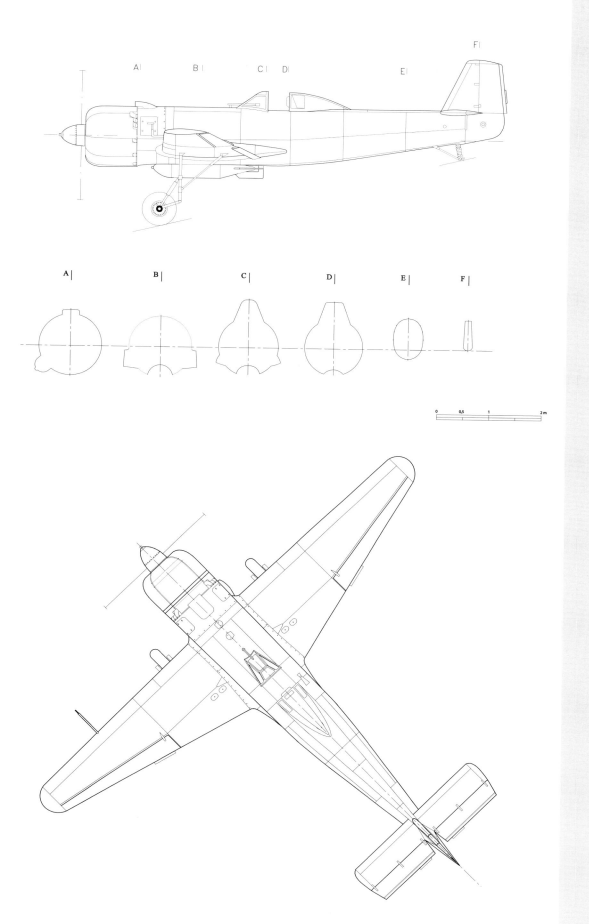

A  B  C  D  E  F

A| B| C| D| E| F|

Nakajima Ki-115 Ko Kai
Tsurugi  prototype with
shock absorber.

0   0,5   1   2 m

1/72 scale

Nakajima Ki-115 Otsu
Tsurugi

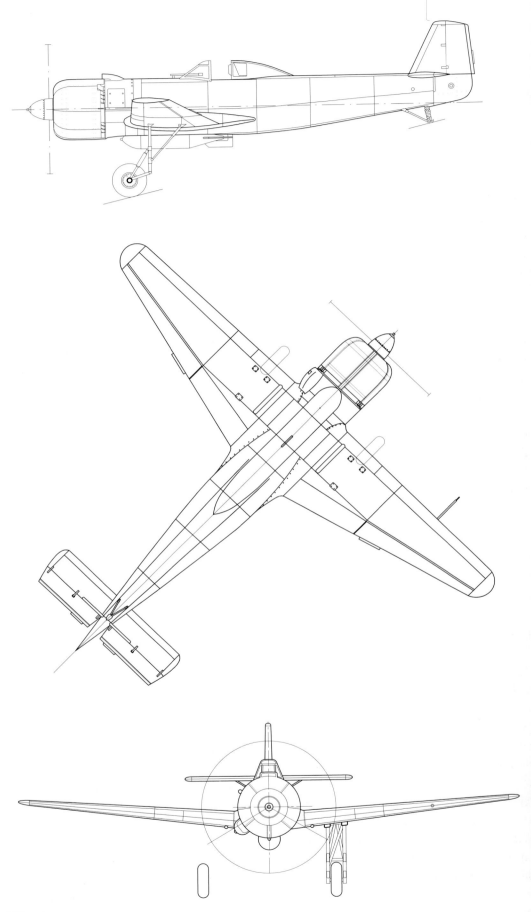

*Nakajima Ki-115 Otsu*
*Tsurugi*

*1/72 scale*

# Rikugun single jet-engine fighter

One of numerous 'paper projects' under consideration at the war's end, the Rikugun single jet-engine fighter was a turbojet powered single seater designed with suicide missions in mind. Before the armistice, when Japan was faced with substantial destruction of the principal aircraft factories by Allied bombardment, various small workshops planned on starting mass production of suicide aircraft. At the same time various design bureaux raced to develop more and more suicide machines.

While Nakajima was developing the Ki-201 Karyu, the *Rikugun Koku Kosho* (Army Air Arsenal) ordered the experimental manufacture of a jet-powered fighter which would apparently achieve similar performance to the German Messerschmitt Me 262 Schwalbe. It would be powered by a single jet engine, and its flight endurance would not be less than 30 minutes.

Two design teams worked on the preliminary project. The first team was headed by Captain Hayashi, and the second by Lieutenant Ieda. The aeroplane designed by Captain Hayashi featured a streamlined aerodynamic form with the jet engine under the rear fuselage. Lieutenant Ieda developed another project with a short fuselage with twin vertical tails. The jet engine was located in the rear part of the central fuselage nacelle, near the centre of gravity. Major Yoshio Segawa from the *Rikugun Koku Hombu* technical committee analysed both projects and approved the project of Captain Hayashi, which maybe received the official designation of Ki-203. However, by the end of hostilities the aeroplane had not proceeded beyond preliminary design work.

**Specifications:**

Description: single-seat low-wing monoplane suicide aeroplane. Mixed construction.
Crew: pilot in an enclosed cockpit.
Power plant: one jet engine.
Dimensions and performance data: not known.
Production: None.

# Tachikawa Ki-74 'Patsy'

The Tachikawa Ki-74 'Patsy' went through numerous changes of purpose from long range, high-altitude reconnaissance, reconnaissance bomber, fast transport and, eventually, one-way 'America bomber'.

In the mid-1930s, the Japanese armed forces were divided into the followers of either the "southern strike" or the "northern strike". The former was preferred by the Imperial Japanese Navy, and the latter by the Imperial Japanese Army. Their preference for one or the other direction for further territorial expansion was connected with the fact that whichever branch of service that would play the leading part would obtain more funding. To realise the expansion towards the south they needed a strong fleet and numerous landing units, while expansion in a northerly direction meant the capture of Siberia, rich in raw materials. With this in mind, the Imperial Japanese Army issued a requirement for a long-range strategic reconnaissance aeroplane that would be able to penetrate the territory of the future enemy, in anticipation of a conflict with the Soviet Union.

Preliminary specifications were prepared by the *Rikugun Koku Hombu* in the spring of 1939. According to these requirements the future strategic reconnaissance aeroplane should be a twin-engined monoplane that would be able to range as far as the western banks of Lake Baikal from advance airfields in Manchuria. At the end of the year the requirements were confirmed, and range was considered the primary factor, the specification requiring at least 5,000km at a cruising speed of 450km/h. The aeroplane would operate at high altitudes, and for this reason it was stipulated that it should be fitted with a pressurised cockpit. High altitude and high maximum speed should ensure the aeroplane immunity from enemy fighters, so defensive armament could be reduced to a minimum. The new aeroplane received the designation "Experimental Army Long-range High Altitude Reconnaissance Aeroplane" (Ki-74).

The development of an aeroplane to these requirements was entrusted to Tachikawa, where design work was undertaken by the design team of Dr H. Kimura. Designing and constructing an aeroplane with such performance capabilities was no mean feat in 1939, so it is even more remarkably that Tachikawa was entrusted with the task without any competition. This was not a matter of chance: in 1938, a team headed by Dr Kimura had developed a single-engined long-range aeroplane named Koken-ki, which made a flight over a distance of 11,651km, and their experience was considered to guarantee success. Almost at the same time Tachikawa, in cooperation with the Aircraft Faculty of the Imperial University in Tokyo, worked on a similar project, the A-26 (also known as the Ki-77), which was planned to make a record-breaking flight to celebrate 2,600 years of the Japanese Empire. While working on the Ki-74 they used their experience from work on the A-26.

The design team working under Dr Kimura realised that the key to success was to use an appropriate power plant, which would achieve its best performance at high altitudes. It was therefore decided that the aeroplane should be powered by the Mitsubishi Ha-214 Ru turbo-charged radial engine, then in an early stage of development. The Ha-214's expected maximum rating was 2,400hp at sea level. Thanks to the turbo-charger, at an altitude of 9,500m it would still produce 1,700hp. The engines were to drive six-blade propellers. However, when the preliminary design project was ready, the Ha-214 was not, so further work was halted.

Meanwhile, Tachikawa continued work on the A-26 (Ki-77) and SS-1 aircraft, which allowed for the testing of some design features planned for the Ki-74. For example, a pressurised cockpit was tested, although unsuccessfully, in the A-26. Work was slowed down even further in 1941 when the engineering department of the *Rikugun Koku Hombu* came to the conclusion that high altitude reconnaissance was not very effective, given the fairly underdeveloped reconnaissance systems of the time. They ordered Tachikawa to focus on the Ki-70 fast reconnaissance aeroplane project, planned to replace the Mitsubishi Ki-46. Politics also had a part to play in this decision. Faced with the tough attitude of the USA, proponents of the southern expansion concept (towards the oil fields of the Dutch East Indies) started to get the upper hand, while the prospect of a conflict with the Soviet Union seemed to fade away.

The outbreak of war in the Far East gave a new impetus to the push to develop the Ki-74. This time the aircraft's role was redefined: as a result of the overwhelming successes of the first phase of the war in the Pacific, Japan occupied territories scattered over vast areas, and any further expansion required aircraft with increased range. In this situation the *Rikugun Koku Hombu*, ordering Tachikawa to redesign the Ki-74 aeroplane as a reconnaissance-bomber. To adapt the aeroplane to its new role, the design team and Dr Kimura slightly altered the existing preliminary project: a bomb bay was added to the fuselage to hold up to 1,000kg of bombs (4 x 250kg, 9 x 100kg or 1 x 500kg and 3 x 100kg); the previous integral fuel tanks were replaced with self-sealing ones, and armour protection was provided for the crew of five. Due to the lack of availability of the Ha-214 Ru engines it was decided that they would be replaced with the Mitsubishi Ha-211-I, rated at 2,200hp for take-off and driving four-blade variable-pitch propellers.

In September 1942 the *Rikugun Koku Hombu* approved the preliminary project, and ordered construction of three prototypes. However, work on the prototypes was very slow. The first prototype Ki-

*Technical inspection of the Ki-74 (Patsy) in US markings performed by Japanese ground crew prior to shipment to America*

74.01 was not ready until March 1944, and then its flight trials were not satisfactory. Nevertheless, the Army put great faith in the Ki-74 and made sure that the work continued. Soon, two more prototypes were completed, and these were fitted with turbo-supercharged Ha-211 Ru engines for improved performance at high altitudes. However, both versions of the Ha-211 engine were still under-developed and they caused problems. This led to another change of power plant, this time to more reliable turbo-supercharged Mitsubishi Ha-104 Ru engines rated at 2,000hp for take-off. It was decided that the pre-production batch of aircraft would receive this new power plant.

Thirteen aircraft were built in the pre-production batch, and these aircraft were subjected to comprehensive trials until the end of the war. The Ki-74 was a large twin-engined mid-wing monoplane of all-metal construction. Wings, in common with the A-26, had a laminar-flow section and high aspect ratio. The conventional tail surfaces of large surface area were designed to ensure good manoeuvrability at high altitudes. The crew of five was housed in a large pressurised cockpit in the forward fuselage and, compared to the initial project, the cockpit was significantly longer to accommodate two additional crew members. The armament consisted of a single remote controlled 0.5in (12.7mm) Type 1 machine gun with 500 rounds, mounted in the tail, which was operated by the air gunner seated in the rear part of the cockpit. The aeroplane could take up to 1,000kg of bombs in the various combinations of 100kg, 250kg and 500kg bombs.

By the end of the war it was intended that Ki-74s would be the main equipment in the detached air units charged with bombing American strategic bomber bases in the Marianas. However, none of the prototypes and or pre-production aircraft achieved operational capability before the end of hostilities.

A plan to develop the Ki-74 into a long-range transport aeroplane designated Ki-74 Toku, to ensure air communication between Japan and the other Axis powers, came to nothing. However, the two aircraft undergoing conversion were later considered for suicide missions of an unusual sort.

In April 1944, while trials of the first three prototypes continued at Tachikawa, work commenced on a developed version designated the Ki-74-II. This was going to be a long-range bomber. The new version was to have a redesigned wing, with the span increased to 29.60m. The fuselage was also considerably redesigned: the cockpit was repositioned forward and blended in to the fuselage outline for improved aerodynamics, the remote controlled machine gun in the tail was replaced by a standard gun position, and the air gunner would operate two 0.5in (12.7mm) machine guns manually. The bomb load would rise to 2,000kg and the crew was increased to seven. Additional equipment would include the Mu-5 long-range radio, a radio direction finder, and a radio transmission jammer. Faced with the unavoidable weight increase, the design showed the single undercarriage units replaced with twin ones.

The aeroplane received the designation Ya-Go, and it was anticipated that it would allow revenge raids on the USA. Although the expected range of around 8,000km would only allow a

*Ki-74 aircraft during engine trial runs.*

*Ki-74 long range bomber.*

one-way trip, this was thought justifiable for propaganda reasons. The Ya-Go would be built in two versions: Project A, with increased range, was intended for bombardment of the US. Its crew was reduced to three, and the pressurised cockpit was made smaller. It would be able to take only two 500kg bombs because extra space in the bomb bay was used to fit additional fuel tanks. Total fuel capacity in the Ya-Go version A would reach 12,000 litres. Completion of the first prototype was

*Forward fuselage of the Ki-74 with a pressurised cockpit.*

planned for August 1944, four months after the design work commenced. The Ya-Go version B, the first prototype of which was going to be completed in October 1944, should have been able to carry twice the bomb load, that is up to 2,000kg depending on bomb fit (3 x 500kg, 4 x 250kg, or 2 x 1,000kg), in exchange for a reduced range. However, the Ki-74-II did not progress beyond a full-size wooden mock-up by the end of hostilities.

Late in the war the *Rikugun Koku Hombu* decided to suspend work on the Ki-74 once more, in order to divert resources into developing the more promising "Project Z", a four-engined heavy bomber with a range of over 17,000km, which would be able to bomb the USA. The Tachikawa company continued to push the Ki-74, and offered a modified Ki-74-II Kai project to the *Rikugun Koku Hombu*. This modification could carry 1,000kg bombs as far as the US West Coast. The Ki-74-II Kai was still unable to fly a return trip, but Tachikawa proposed that the machine could bomb a West Coast city, following which the crew would fly to a remote area, bale out and conduct guerrilla warfare against the US. To assist with these operations, the aeroplane would carry food rations for one week, plus relevant equipment and armaments.

However, there were delays in testing the pre-production Ki-74s, compounded by the difficult situation at the front line. With this in mind, it was considered that the Ki-74-II would not be ready soon enough. Therefore the role of a special duty bomber for bombardment of the USA would be performed by two converted Ki-74 long-range transport aircraft. These long-range transports were given the name Ya-Go, originally reserved for the Ki-74-II. On 9 August 1945, by top secret order, several Army Aviation officers were posted to the 114th *Hikotai* based in Saitama prefecture. There they were informed that they had been selected for a special mission, a strike on New York. The mission would be flown in a special long-range aeroplane, apparently designated the Ki-114. However, this designation had been reserved for the Tachikawa Ki-114 transport aeroplane project developed from the Ki-92. It is more probable that it was planned to fly the mission using the Ya-Go or Ki-77. However, the mission was never flown.

Allied intelligence obtained its first information about the Ki-74 while the prototype was still under construction. However, due to lack of information, it was assumed that this was a long-range high altitude heavy fighter. For that reason the Ki-74 was given a boy's name, in accordance with the designation system: 'Pat'. After subsequent intelligence reports revealed the true role of the aeroplane, the name was changed to a girl's name, 'Patsy', appropriate to bombers and reconnaissance aircraft.

**Specifications:**

Description: twin-engined cantilever mid-wing monoplane strategic reconnaissance aeroplane (Ki-74 preliminary project), high altitude heavy long-range reconnaissance bomber (Ki-74 and Ki-74-II), special attack aeroplane (Ya-Go and Ki-74-II Kai) or courier aeroplane (Ki-74 Toku). All-metal construction with fabric covered control surfaces.

Crew: three (Ki-74 preliminary project, Ya-Go, Ki-74-II Kai), five (Ki-74-I and Ki-74-II), seven (Ki-74-II).

Power plant: two Mitsubishi Ha-214 Ru 18-cylinder air cooled radial engines with a turbo-supercharger, rated at 2,500hp (1,840kW) for take-off, 2,310hp (1,700kW) at an altitude of 7,600m; 1,930hp (1,420kW) at an altitude of 8,300m; six-blade variable pitch metal propellers, diameter 3.80m; fuel tank capacity 3,886l (Ki-74 preliminary project),

The thirteenth prototype of the Ki-74 (Patsy) prepared for shipment to the USA for technical trials

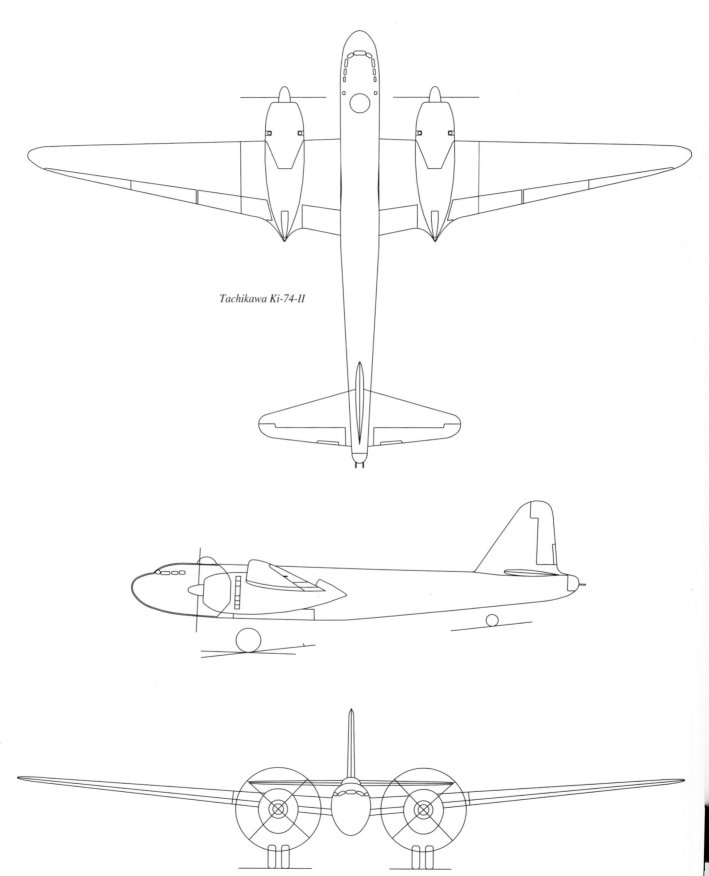

*Tachikawa Ki-74-II*

Not to scale.

Two Mitsubishi Ha-211-I 18-cylinder air cooled radial engines rated at 2,200hp (1,620kW) for take-off, 2,070hp (1,520kW) at an altitude of 1,000m; 1,930hp (1,420kW) at an altitude of 5,000m; four-blade variable pitch metal propellers, diameter 3.80m; fuel tank capacity 9,200l. (Ki-74.01),

Two Mitsubishi Ha-211-I Ru 18-cylinder air cooled radial engines with a turbo-supercharger rated at 2,200hp (1,620kW) for take-off; 2,130hp (1,565kW) at an altitude of 1,800m; 1,720hp (1,265kW) at an altitude of 9,500m; four-blade variable pitch metal propellers, diameter 3.80m; fuel tank capacity 10,900l. (Ki-74.02 and Ki-74.03, Ki-74-II, Ki-74-II Kai),

Two Mitsubishi Ha-104 Ru 18-cylinder air cooled radial engines with a turbo-supercharger rated at 2,000hp (1,470kW) for take-off; 1,900hp (1,395kW) at an altitude of 2,000m; 1,810hp (1,330kW) at an altitude of 7,360m; four-blade variable pitch metal propellers, diameter 3.80m; fuel tank capacity 10,900l (Ki-74.04-Ki-74.16 and Ki-74-II) or 12420l (Ki-74 Toku),

Armament: one remotely-controlled 0.5in. (12.7mm) Type 1 machine gun (Ki-74),

Two flexible 0.5in (12.7mm) Type 1 machine guns in a tail turret (Ki-74-II),

Bomb load: 1,000kg (Ki-74.04 – Ki-74.16, Ki-74-II Kai); 2,000kg (Ki-74-II).

| Type | Ki-74.01 | Ki-74-03 | Ki-74-07 | Ki-74-II |
|---|---|---|---|---|
| Wing span m | 27.0 | 27.0 | 27.0 | 29.6 |
| Length m | 17.65 | 17.65 | 17.65 | 20.0 |
| Height m | 5.1 | 5.1 | 5.1 | 5.5 |
| Wing area m² | 80.0 | 80.0 | 80.0 | |
| Empty weight kg | 9,232 | 8,078 | 10,200 | |
| Normal take-off weight kg | 18,524 | 19,025 | 19,400 | |
| Maximum take-off weight kg | 9,292 | 9,947 | 9,200 | |
| Useful load kg | 231.55 | 237.81 | 242.50 | |
| Wing loading kg/m² | 4.21 | 4.33 | 4.85 | |
| Power loading kg/hp | | | | |
| Maximum speed km/h | 600 | 540 | 570 | |
| at an altitude of m | 10,000 | 9,000 | 8,500 | |
| Cruising speed km/h | 400 | 400 | 400 | |
| at an altitude of m | 8,000 | 8,000 | 8,000 | |
| Landing speed km/h | | | 150 | |
| Time of climb | 10 min. 01 sec. | 17 min. 00 sec. | 17 min. 00 sec. | |
| to an altitude of m | 5,000 | 8,000 | 8,000 | |
| Ceiling m | 12,000 | 12,000 | 12,000 | |
| Normal range km | 8,000 | 8,000 | 8,000 | |
| Maximum range km | 9,000 | 12,000 | | |

Production: Tachikawa Hikoki Kabushiki Gaisha at Tachikawa built a total of sixteen Ki-74 aircraft, including three prototypes and two Ki-74 Toku (Ya-Go).

# Tachikawa Ta-Go

The Tachikawa Ta-Go was a dedicated suicide aircraft conceived with the same rationale as the Ki-115 Tsurugi - an easily and quickly produced aircraft for mass suicide attacks in defence of the home islands, built from non-strategic materials. However, the Ta-Go was even more basic in this regard than the Ki-115.

A group of young officers from the Army Scientific-Research Aircraft Arsenal at Tachikawa (*Rikugun Kokugijiutsu Kenkyujo*), represented by Captain Yoshiyuki Mizuyama, proposed a new special aeroplane for suicide units, termed the "weapon of last resort". The new aeroplane would have an even simpler design than the Ki-115, making maximum use of generally available materials, such as wood and zinc-coated sheet, and production could be achieved in small workshops by largely unskilled labour. The aeroplane could be powered by any available low-power engine. It was proposed to produce two aircraft types under the common name of Ta-Go. The heavier aeroplane, to be powered by an engine rated at approximately 500hp, would be built by Tachikawa, while the lighter one, with the engine rated at approximately 150hp was to be manufactured by *Kokusai*.

In February 1945, Captain Mizuyama met the manager of Tachikawa, Koguchi, and presented his concept. Koguchi said that for Tachikawa development of a suitable design and starting its production would not be a problem, but due to current production plans the company needed an official order from the *Rikugun Koku Hombu*. However, the *Rikugun Koku Hombu* had no interest in Captain Mizuyama's idea, as it backed the Nakajima Ki-115 project. Rejection of the Ta-Go by the *Rikugun Koku Hombu* prevented Tachikawa from undertaking engineering design work and starting production. This did not discourage Captain Mizuyama, however. He located an appropriate warehouse where he and his co-workers started construction of the prototype.

As the principal idea of the Ta-Go was to have a simple design, to be produced under any conditions, even hastily-arranged carpenter's workshops, the framework of the fuselage was wooden, braced with steel wires. Around the cockpit the fuselage was covered with plywood, while the rest of the fuselage was fabric-covered. To simplify production, the dimensions and shape of the fin were the same as those of the horizontal tail surfaces. Only essential flight instruments were fitted in the cockpit. The main undercarriage was to be jettisoned upon take-off and no radio

*The second prototype Tachikawa Ta-Go suicide aircraft during assembly at the Tachikawa woodwork shop. It was captured by the Allied occupation forces in this state in September 1945.*

*Internal structure of the Ta-Go fuselage, looking aft.*

*Botom: Forward fuselage structure of the Ta-Go with engine and main undercarriage attachments visible.*

would be fitted. Power would be provided by the Hitachi Ha-13a radial engine rated at 510 hp for take-off. A 500kg bomb under the fuselage was the only armament.

Design work proceeded smoothly, and after a month's work the first prototype was ready. The machine was shipped to Tachikawa to undergo strength tests, but during one of the many Allied air raids, the Tachikawa test station was destroyed and with it the first Ta-Go.

This was not the end of the development of Captain Mizuyama's concept. A meeting of representatives of the Army Scientific-Research Aircraft Arsenal at Tachikawa with delegations of the Tachikawa and *Kokusai* companies regarding production took place just before the end of the war. The meeting was arranged by the Koku Hombu Gunjusho (Ministry of War Supply) which had previously opposed Captain Mizuyama's concepts, but who were now positive enough to initiate plans for production. However, the war ended before production was underway, and the only progress made was the beginning of construction of a second prototype. After the end of hostilities, American occupation forces found the unfinished second Ta-Go in the warehouse rented by Captain Mizuyama. Apart from a few photos of the fuselage framework, no drawings or specifications of the aeroplane survive.

### Specifications:

Description: single-engined monoplane. Wooden construction, fabric covered.
Crew: pilot in an open cockpit.
Power plant: one Hitachi Ha-13a 9-cylinder air cooled engine rated at 510hp (790kW) for take-off
    and 470hp (345kW) at an altitude of 1,700m; wooden two-blade fixed pitch propeller.
Armament: one 500kg bomb.
Dimensions and performance: no data.
Production: in 1945 one prototype Ta-Go was built, the second prototype was not completed by the
    end of the war.

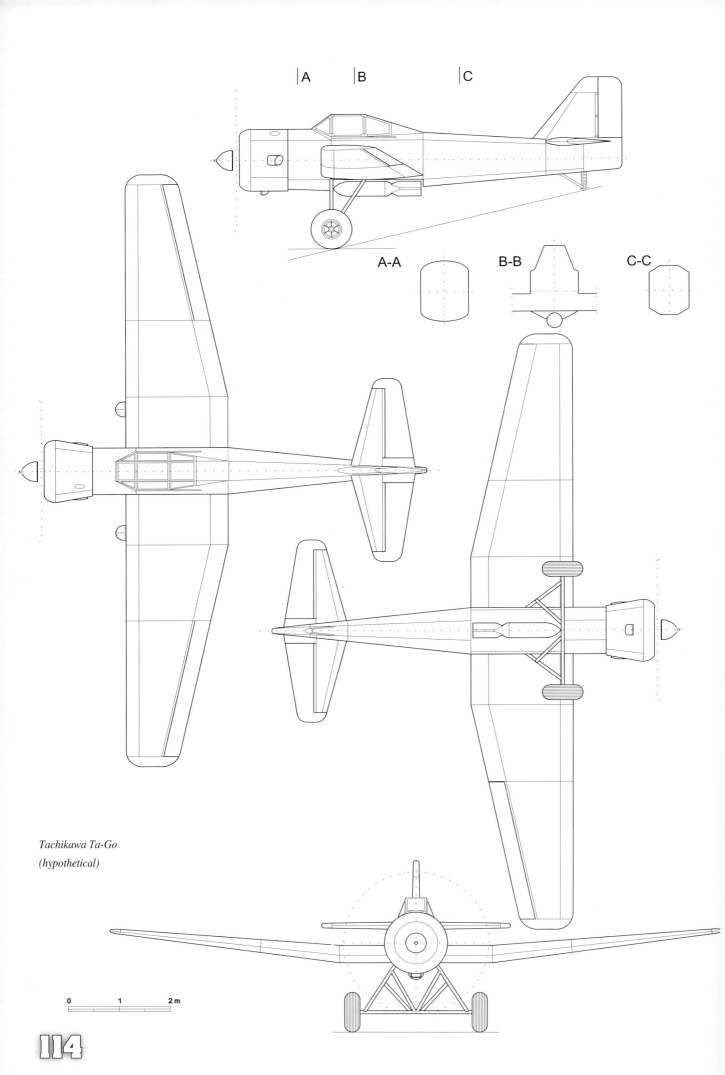

A    B    C

A-A          B-B          C-C

*Tachikawa Ta-Go*
*(hypothetical)*

0    1    2 m

114

# The Experimental Single-seat Attack Aeroplane

The un-named and undesignated aircraft known only as 'Experimental Single-seat Attack Aeroplane' was intended to be a joint Army and Navy strike aircraft with a not-dissimilar concept to the Nakajima Ki-115, but was more aerodynamically refined and potentially corrected some of the faults of the Nakajima aircraft. In the last days of April 1945, during the fighting in Okinawa, a meeting of representatives of the *Rikugun Koku Hombu* and *Kaigun Koku Hombu* took place in Singapore during which local production capacity was reviewed and general rules laid out for using the existing stock of 1,000hp radial engines and propellers for some 250 attack aircraft to be used in suicide attacks both by the Army and Naval Aviation.

Design work was entrusted to the design team headed by Shinroku Inoue, who began work in early May 1945. Shinroku Inoue, who had previously worked for a small aircraft company called Tokyo Koku, undertook close collaboration with the *Rikugun Kokugijyutsu Kenkyujo* (Army Air Technical Research Institute) with regard to production technology and assembly of aircraft in field conditions.

A single-seat attack low-wing monoplane of streamlined profile, of mixed construction, was developed. Like the Ki-115, power could be provided by any radial engines rated at around 1,000hp, turning propellers available from stock. Wings and tail were wood, covered in plywood, and the framework of the fuselage was welded from steel tubes, also plywood-covered. Tapered wings with small dihedral were fitted with flaperons of a similar design to those on the Ki-107. Control surfaces and ailerons were covered with fabric. The cockpit was protected by a tear-drop hood offering very good visibility, and the aeroplane had a fixed streamlined cantilever undercarriage with a tail wheel, fitted with shock absorbers, unlike the very simple welded steel undercarriage of the Ki-115. Unusually, the aircraft was designed to be able to incorporate appropriate subassemblies from existing damaged aircraft. The designers planned to add a 250kg bomb carrier under the fuselage, with the possibility of dropping the bomb from a 60 degree dive. This design was put in production as an attack aeroplane in field workshops near Singapore. However, ten weeks after assembly of wings and fuselages commenced, the war ended, terminating all work.

## Specifications:

Description: single-seat low-wing monoplane attack aeroplane with fixed undercarriage. Mixed construction, wings and tail of all-wooden construction, fuselage with plywood covered steel tube structure. Fabric-covered control surfaces and ailerons.

Crew: pilot in an enclosed cockpit.

Power plant: one air cooled radial engine rated at 1,000hp for take-off, four-blade variable pitch metal propeller.

Armament: one 250kg bomb under the fuselage.

| Type | Attack Aeroplane |
|---|---|
| Wing span m | 11.35 |
| Length m | 8.35 |
| Wing area m$^2$ | 20.0 |
| Empty weight kg | 2,500 |
| Take-off weight kg | 3,000 |
| Wing loading kg/m$^2$ | 150.0 |
| Power loading kg/hp | 3.0 |

Production: by July 1945 field workshops near Singapore had made only a few wings and fuselages, no complete airframes.

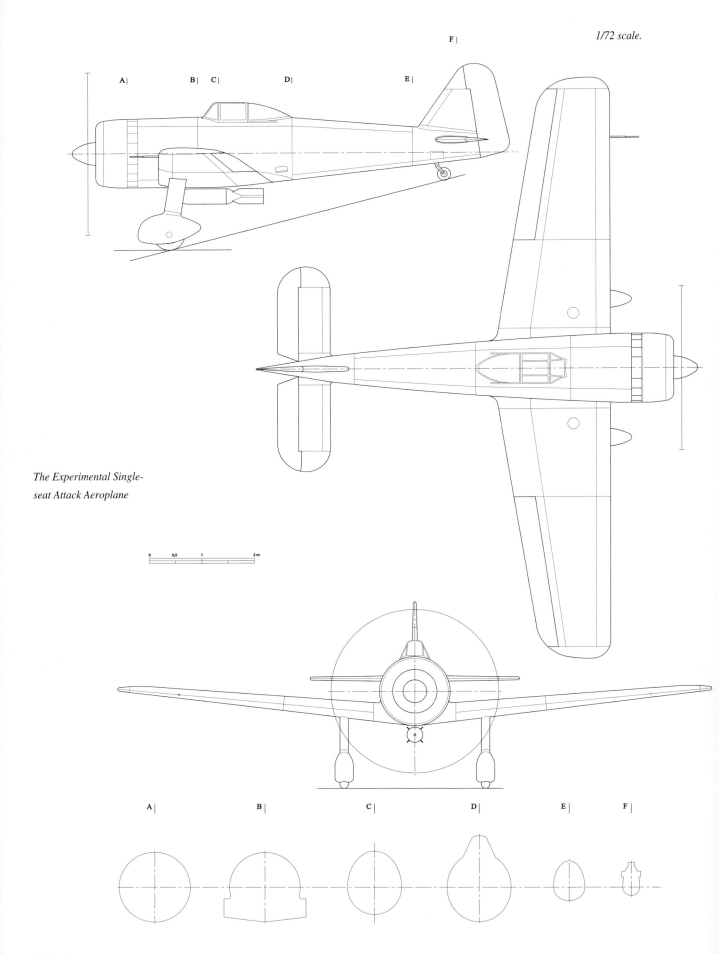

1/72 scale.

A|  B| C|  D|  E|  F |

The Experimental Single-
seat Attack Aeroplane

0   0,5   1   2 m

A |   B |   C |   D |   E |   F |

# Special attack aircraft of the Imperial Japanese Navy

## Aichi M6A Seiran/Nanzan

The Aichi M6A was designed around a very different kind of 'special attack' than the 'conventional' Kamikaze. Designed to launch from a submarine, the M6A could launch sneak attacks on the US. Like many Japanese aircraft of the time, the Aichi M6A was developed to carry out one-way missions.

The concept of an aeroplane that could be carried by a submarine is an idea almost as old as naval aviation itself. On 15 January 1915, the Friedrichshafen FF29a floatplane took off for the first time from the forward deck of the U-12 submarine, and following this there were numerous experiments in various countries. From the end of WW1 until the end of WW2 there was a great deal of interest in the capabilities offered by a submarine-based aeroplane. The interest in the aeroplane-submarine combination waxed and waned, and only the Imperial Japanese Navy stuck to it as a viable concept until the very end of the Pacific war. It was in Japan that this kind of aeroplane was developed into a strike aircraft, rather than a reconnaissance tool.

The novel tactic of direct attack by a submarine-based aeroplane led to the development of the Seiran (Mountain Haze). From the very beginning of its development the aeroplane was intended to form an integral part of the submarine, as a form of strategic weapons system. This would be used against American cities and other targets that lay outside the range of a conventional air force, and could also employ the element of surprise to the full.

The concept was created in the *Kaigun Gunreibu* (Operational Headquarters of the Navy) several months before the outbreak of the Pacific war, as one of the special weapon types for attacks across the Pacific or in other far away regions. Specification prepared by the *Kansei Hombu* (Ship Construction Bureau of the Navy), code-named *Maru-Yon*, called for very large ocean-Going submarines with the capacity to carry and launch attack aircraft. This new weapon required the establishment of a flotilla of submarine aircraft carriers with enough range to cross the Pacific. When the submarine came within range of effective aerial attack against the enemy, the aircraft would be launched, and the submarine would submerge to avoid detection. After the attack, the aircraft would go to a pre-arranged rendezvous with the submarine flotilla, and would alight to be recovered aboard. A few minutes later the ships could be out of sight beneath the waves. Such operational tactics were considered to cause surprise and confusion in the enemy, as there would be no trace of the attacker. Above all, the effects would be psychological as the American population in coastal cities would live under constant stress, uncertain when another attack would take place.

Further to this, the suggestion was put forward that an advanced base could be set up in enemy-held territory, where the flotilla could replenish with aircraft, ordnance and fuel after each attack. This would allow an increased frequency of raids without the need to return home. As an alternative, the submarines could be fitted with torpedo launchers and operate conventionally to disrupt coastal shipping for as long as their fuel permitted.

The project was developed in utmost secrecy so enemy intelligence would not even guess of its existence. The project was categorised as a priority by the Daihonei, and by early 1942 designers working for the Imperial Japanese Navy commenced work on the design of what would become the world's largest submarines prior to the advent of nuclear-powered vessels. The project was called *Toku-gata Sensuikan* (*Toku-gata* in short – special submarine), and the preliminary project was scheduled to be completed by April 1942. Eighteen of these powerful submarines were planned to be built, and the programme was known as the *Kai Maru-5* Plan of the Navy.

*Toku-gata* class submarines would have a surface displacement of 4,550 tonnes and would be able to carry two floatplanes on board. The first keel was laid at the Naval Shipyards at Kure on 18 January 1943, but in 1944 the specifications were changed to increase the number of aircraft. The surface displacement was increased to 5,223 tonnes and the number of floatplanes to three plus spares. Once the specifications for the *Toku-gata* submarine had been defined, it became possible to start work on the aeroplane which was the purpose of the construction of the submarines.

The *Kaigun Koku Hombu* (Naval Aviation Headquarters) held talks with the Aichi company which had, under manager Kamataro Aoki, developed aircraft exclusively for the Imperial Japanese Navy since the early 1920s. Talks were held in the early spring of 1942 with the aim of defining the main specifications of this entirely new kind of combat aircraft, based on the Navy's requirements as well as the limitations set by the size of the submarine hangar.

The Navy was sure that the success of the submarine aircraft carrier would depend on the capabilities of her aeroplane. The aeroplane needed to perform well enough to evade interception, and so performance requirements were ambitious. The required top speed was defined as 300 knots (556km/h) at 4,000m, without external stores. It would also need to take off at some distance from the US Pacific coast and fly inland until it reached the target so a range of 800 nautical miles (1,480km) was therefore considered necessary. The Naval Aviation HQ considered that this would now be a single-sortie aeroplane, so undercarriage would be unnecessary ballast. The diameter of the cylindrical, water-tight hangar to house the aircraft was defined as 3.5m, and the length as 34m. The Navy preferred that any part of the aeroplane larger than the diameter should be folded, rather

*Full size wooden mock-up of the AM-24 hydroplane, prepared for assessment by the qualifying committee of the Kaigun Koku Hombu on 15 January 1943.*

*In combat conditions fitting the floats took merely two and a half minutes. Assembling the entire Aichi M6A1 Seiran floatplane did not take more than seven minutes.*

than detached. This preference was as a result of experience with the operation of Kugisho E14Y1 (Glen) floatplanes.

The Aichi design team, under Takuichiro Gomei, the manager of Experimental Programmes, saw these specifications as a great challenge. On 15 May 1942, the Navy requirement became a formal specification known as the 17-Shi, and the task of running the project was entrusted to the chief designer, Norio Ozaki, and his assistants Yasushiro Ozawa and Morishige Mori.

The aeroplane received the factory designation of AM-24 and the official military name of '17-Shi Experimental Naval Attack Aeroplane' (M6A1), with the name Seiran added fourteen months after development commenced. Work advanced relatively smoothly, considering its innovative character. As agreed with the Navy, the Aichi Atsuta (name of a temple in Aichi prefecture) 12-cylinder, liquid-cooled, inverted V engine, developed from the German Daimler-Benz DB 601, was selected as the power plant. Already at this initial stage of development the design team decided to fit detachable floats as the only separable components of the aeroplane, to increase the operational capabilities of the aeroplane. It was agreed that the floats should be able to be jettisoned in flight should this be required by the combat situation. The design of the *Toku-gata* was changed by adding on each side of the catapult a small recess to facilitate attachment and detachment of the floats and fitting of the transport trolleys.

During the summer of 1942 a full-scale wooden mock-up was built, intended from the outset to provide a basis for work on improved wing and tail surface folding methods. A rotating connection was set on the central portion of the main pivot base, allowing the wing to swivel hydraulically by 90° backwards, while rotating its leading edge down so that the entire wing lay flat along the fuselage. This operation was preceded by manual folding of the outer portions of the horizontal tail and folding the tip of the vertical tail to starboard. Following this the overall width was 2.46m, and the overall height of the aeroplane on its catapult trolley was 2.10m. All connections were painted with phosphorous paint to facilitate night assembly. The aeroplane could be warmed up in its hangar by a lubricating oil pre-heating circulation system while the submarine was still submerged. It was calculated that after surfacing, the aeroplane without floats could be prepared for catapult launch by four men within 4.5 minutes, and it would take 2.5 more minutes to fit the floats.

The M6A1 was of conventional all-metal design, with the exception of the wing tips made of wood, covered with plywood and externally finished with varnished fabric. Ailerons, elevators and the rudder were of metal structure, covered with fabric. Flaps of special design were optimised for ditching. They allowed the aeroplane to alight at a speed of 113 km/h, while the rearmost flap sections could be rotated by 90° to operate as air brakes for alighting, or in a dive. Two crew members were located in a cockpit covered by a two-piece detachable sliding hood. Initially, the aeroplane was armed with a single fixed forward firing 7.7mm (0.303in.) machine gun plus a similar one in a flexible mount, but in January of 1943 the armament was limited to just one moving 13mm Type 2 machine gun in the rear cabin. It was planned that the attack warload of the aeroplane would

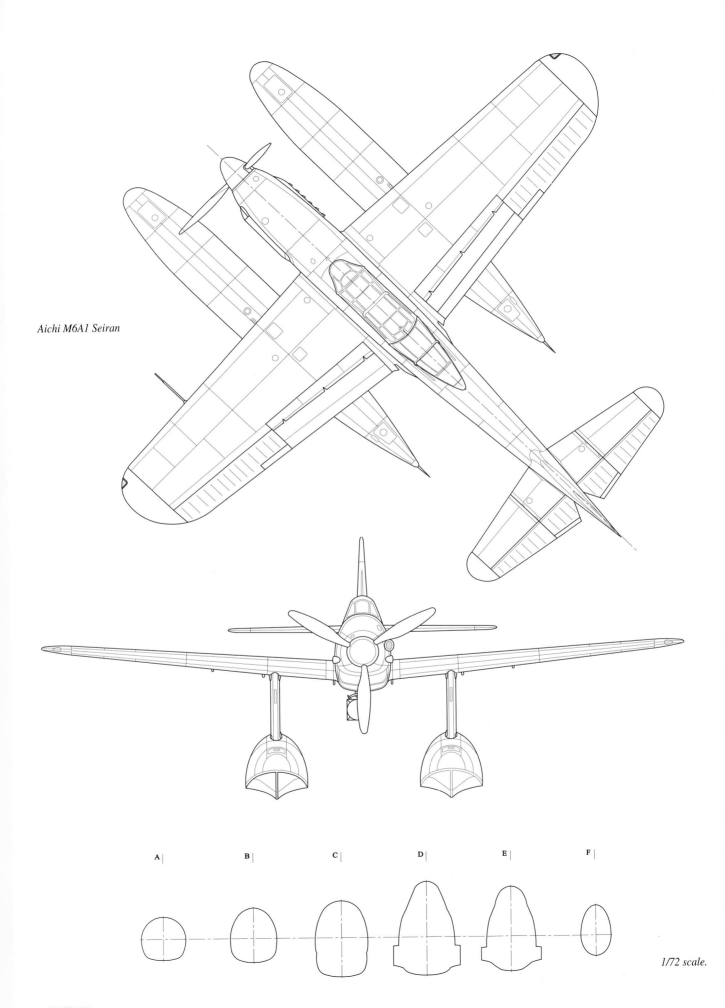

*Aichi M6A1 Seiran*

A|    B|    C|    D|    E|    F|

*1/72 scale.*

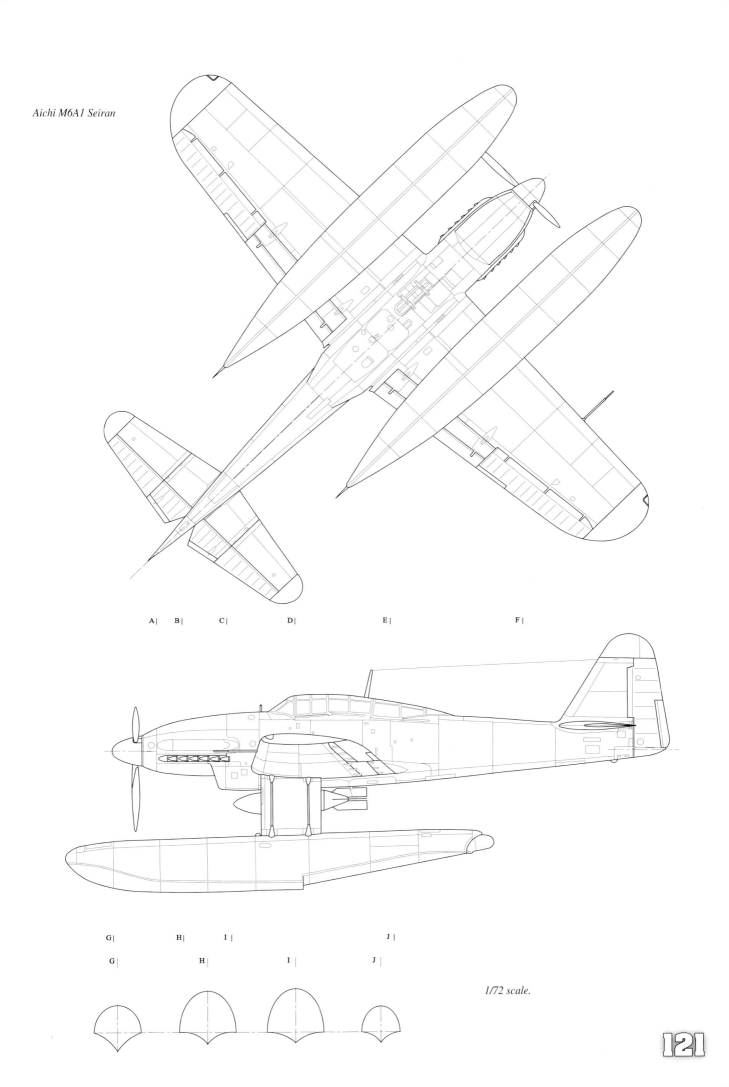

Aichi M6A1 Seiran

A| B| C| D| E| F|

G| H| I| J|

G| H| I| J|

1/72 scale.

121

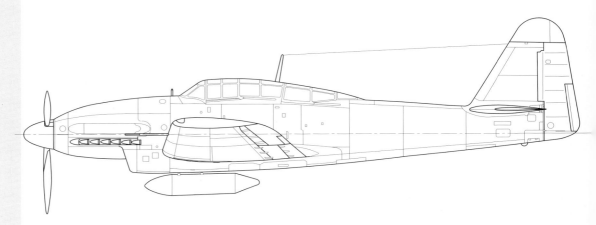

include a single 850kg Type 91 Model 2 aircraft torpedo, or a single 800kg bomb, or two 250kg bombs.

In early 1943, the Eitoku plant of the Aichi company at Nagoya built six prototype airframes, the last two being earmarked for conversion to trainers and designated M6A1-K, named Nanzan (southern mountain), although initially they were known as the Seiran-Kai. The M6A1-K had no folding components, and was fitted with a retractable undercarriage. Apart from the removal of the upper fin, necessary to restore aerodynamic stability without the floats, the M6A1-K was identical to the standard version even to the point of having the catapult trolley attachments. These latter allowed for it to be used for catapult training on land.

Meanwhile, the *Toku-gata* submarine programme gained momentum. The first ship, which commenced construction in 1943, was designated I-400, while two more submarines, I-401 and I-402, were laid down at the Sasebo Shipyard. Preparations to build two more, I-404 and I-405, were under way at the Kure shipyard and at Kawasaki Shipyard in Kobe. The construction of twelve subsequent *Toku-gata* submarines had been planned, and at the same time it was decided to build ten AM class submarines, also known as the *Ko-gata Kai* 2, each of them carrying two M6A Seiran attack aircraft. The AM submarines had a surface displacement of 3,217 tonnes. Construction of the first ship in this class commenced in February 1943. This version had a hangar for just one reconnaissance floatplane. During construction at the Kawasaki Shipyard in Kobe the ship was redesigned and work commenced on two more.

In November 1943 the Aichi plant at Eitoku completed construction of the first prototype M6A Seiran, and the following month flying trials commenced. In February 1944 the second prototype joined in. The M6A Seiran was carefully developed in terms of aerodynamics. It is sometimes thought that Norio Ozaki and his team developed their design based on the Kugisho D4Y 'Judy' carrier-borne dive bomber, developed by Kugisho at Yokosuka and produced in volume by Aichi. While true that initially studies into the conversion of the D4Y to a submarine-carried attack aeroplane were conducted, at an early stage this was found impractical. The design of M6A Seiran used to some degree the experience of Yokosuka in aircraft design, but otherwise there was no similarity between these two aircraft.

The lack of AE1P Atsuta 32 engines led to the two first prototypes being fitted with the less powerful Atsuta 21 rated at 1,400hp for take-off. Although no trial results survive, it seems they were satisfactory, as in early spring of 1944 the Eitoku plant started tooling for series production. The third and fourth prototypes were completed almost at the same time. These were similar to the two earlier prototypes and were fitted for airfield landing. Designated M6A1-K, they were powered by Atsuta 32 engines. Assembly of these aircraft was completed in May and June 1944.

The first batch of M6A1 Model 11 Seiran aircraft was completed in October 1944, and four more aircraft had been built by 7 December, when a strong earthquake in the Nagoya area stopped production at the Eitoku plant, destroying jigs and causing significant other damage. The damage had only just been repaired, and the production programme regaining momentum when, on 12 March, the Eitoku plant was destroyed by fire following a bombing raid on Nagoya. The situation was worsened by the fact that various local subcontractors had been destroyed. At the time of the attack, the Eitoku plant was already partly dispersed, and this process, started a month earlier, was accelerated for fear of renewed attacks. Further production was underway when on 17 May the Nagoya area suffered another bombing attack. However, despite these setbacks, the ultimate termination of M6A Seiran production was caused by a general change in Imperial Japanese Navy priorities.

The decision to stop production of the M6A Seiran resulted from a re-evaluation of the probable effects of the submarine aircraft carrier operations. By 30 December 1944 the I-400 was completed, and almost a week later, on 8 January, work was also completed on the I-401, and a decision was taken to convert the I-402, still under construction. The I-402 would be transformed into a submarine tanker, to carry oil from the Dutch East Indies to Japan through the American blockade. The I-403 was damaged in an air raid during construction, which was halted as a result. Construction of the I-404 would be completed by March 1945. Construction of the I-405 was not completed, and construction of the other submarines, I-406 to I-417, was abandoned.

The decision, in March, to stop the *Toku-gata* production programme also affected the AM class submarine construction programme of four boats. The I-1 was launched at Kobe on 10 June 1944 but, despite being 70% complete, never finished fitting out. The I-13, the first in the AM series, was completed on 16 December 1944, and the I-14 was completed on 14 March 1945. Construction of the I-15, even though 95% complete, was abandoned. With the Navy in possession of just a few submarines able to carry aircraft, there was no reason to built large numbers of attack aircraft for these boats. It was anticipated that a batch of 44 aircraft would be ready by the time the programme was terminated, but due to stoppages of the assembly line, only fourteen M6A Seiran aircraft had been delivered by the end of March 1945. The programme continued as components for this aeroplane continued to be produced, but the aircraft's role was changed to more conventional operation from the ambitious strikes at the continental US. As a result, just six more M6A Seirans were built at Eitoku, although a few more machines of the type reached varying stages of construction.

During late autumn 1944, the Imperial Japanese Navy started forming a special air corps to fly the M6A Seiran aircraft from submarines. Both the deck and flying crews were selected carefully, much attention being paid to their previous experience. On 15 December 1944, command of the 631st *Kokutai* was entrusted to Captain Ryunosuke Ariizumi. This *Kokutai* was an integral part of the 1st *Koku Sentai*, a unit that formed part of the 1st Submarine Division in 6th *Koku Kantai* (6th Fleet). The flotilla would include two *Toku-gata* class ships (I-400 and I-401), supported by the AM class vessels I-13 and I-14, the latter of which was still undergoing trials. They would carry a total of ten M6A Seirans among them.

*Rear view of the proto-type Aichi M6A1 Seiran floatplane. A standard 250 kg aircraft bomb is attached under the fuselage.*

Training was carried out for the most part at the 1st Aircraft Technology Arsenal at Yokosuka. The first training voyage with a practice catapult launch of a M6A Seiran was carried out in January 1945. Generally, exercises were performed in the area of Iyo-Nada in the Inner Sea, south of Kure, while Seiran flying training was done at the Fukuyama naval air base where six aircraft were stationed. There were a number of problems, many of them relating to the M6As' Atsuta engines. Combined training of the submarines and their aircraft commenced on 2 April only on paper, as there was virtually no fuel, all supplies being reserved for combat use. Therefore the I-401 was sent in haste to Dairen in Manchuria, where fuel was still available. For this trip the huge submarine was given a camouflage structure to imitate a frigate, but having passed Ube the ship hit a magnetic mine and was forced to return to Kure for repair. The masking superstructure was transferred onto the I-400, which sailed to Dairen and back bringing fuel to continue the programme, if only temporarily.

Though work on submarines and aircraft was halted in January 1945, the completed machines were assembled for missions of a more limited scope than originally intended. On 11 May 1945, two *Toku-gata* submarines accompanied by the I-13 and I-14 left Kure and, passing through the Kan-mon straits, entered the Sea of Japan. They were heading for the port of Maizuru in Kyoto prefecture, which was selected as the main base of the 1st Submarine Division. It was intended that they would be joined by their M6A aircraft in Nanao Bay for operational training. Six weeks were to be spent on training for catapult launches. The training revealed that it took 30 minutes from the moment the floats were attached until all three M6A Seirans from the *Toku-gata* were airborne, half of the time being spent on the third aeroplane, because moving it out of its hangar took the most time. It was calculated that under operational conditions, and if the Seirans took off without floats, the time from surfacing to diving could be brought down to 14.5 minutes.

The target identified for the first combat mission of the 1st Division was the Gaton lock in the Panama Canal, which was being used extensively by the Allies to transfer forces to the Pacific after the victory over Germany. Should such an attack succeed, it would stop the flow of men and materiel on their way to fight Japan. The attack was going to be made by ten M6A Seirans led by Lieutenant Atsushi Asamura, six of them armed with torpedoes, and the other four with high-explosive bombs. Two aircraft would attack each lock system. Seirans carried out dummy attacks on a large-scale Gaton lock model, the crews learning by heart every feature of the area. During these exercises two M6A Seirans crashed. The flotilla was to take the same heading Admiral Nagumo's force took three and a half years earlier on their way to attack Pearl Harbour, then from Oahu steer for the Colombian coast and finally head north along the American coast. Two smaller AM class submarines, their fuel tanks insufficient for the whole trip, would be re-fuelled by the large submarines en route.

This ambitious attack, more an act of despair than a mission that could really alter the results of war, would never be accomplished. The critical situation of Japan and the threat of invasion of the home islands forced a change of plans. It was considered that a main strike against the Allied forces near Japan would be more effective than a strategic attack that would probably produce effects

*Front view of the Seiran.*

too late to relieve the besieged Japanese forces. The orders no. 95 of 25 June 1945 directed the 1st Division to use all of its M6A Seirans for solo suicide attacks against US aircraft carriers anchored at Ulithi.

The new plans were twofold. At Ominato naval base at the northern tip of Honshu the *Toku-gata* submarines would rendezvous with two AM submarines carrying disassembled C6N1 'Myrt' reconnaissance aircraft in their hangars. The C6N1s would then be shipped to Truk, at this time still in Japanese hands, where they would be erected and used for reconnaissance of targets at Ulithi. This part of the mission was code-named Operation *Hikari* ('Light').

The information passed to the M6A Seirans based on I-400 and I-401 would be used to plan strike missions. Submarines I-13 and I-14 would be the first to sail, but the former was damaged on 16 July by aircraft from the aircraft carrier USS Anzio and only I-14 reached Truk, where on 4 August the C6N1 aircraft were unloaded and prepared for reconnaissance missions. This element of the mission was codenamed Operation *Arashi* ('Storm').

Meanwhile, the I-400 and I-401 submarines left Ominato. At Maizuru Navy Yard, six Seirans of I-400 and I-401 had been painted silver to disguise them as US aircraft for surprise attack. At Ominato Bay, the crew added the US national marking on Seirans, and they even removed the fins of bomb to make it look like a fuel drop tank. On 6 August the I-401, the flagship with Captain Ariizumi aboard, suffered a fire caused by a short circuit in the electrical system. Until the damage was repaired, the submarine could not submerge. Probably as a result of this situation, Captain Ariizumi sent a signal that moved the rendezvous spot further away from the target, 100 miles (185km) off Ponape island in the Eastern Carolinas. Operation *Arashi*, the attack against Ulithi, was scheduled to take place on 17 August, but Captain Ariizumi was unaware that the captain of I-400, Toshio Kusaka, never received the signal and followed his original orders, awaiting I-401 east of their target.

Two days before the planned start of Operation *Arashi* Japanese forces in Asia and in the islands of the Western Pacific ceased fire, but Navy HQ simply postponed the attack until 25 August. On the morning of 16 August the submarines were informed about the armistice and ordered to return to Japan. Four days later Commander Ariizumi was ordered to destroy the entire offensive armament and the three M6A Seirans. The latter were catapulted, unmanned and unpowered, off the I-401, while the Seirans of I-400 were simply rolled out of their hangar and pushed overboard. The submarines surrendered at sea on 27 and 29 August. This was the end of one of the more unlikely strategic plans invented during WW2.

**Specifications:**

Description: single-engined submarine-based attack bomber floatplane (M6A1) and attack bomber trainer (M6A1-K). All metal construction with fabric covered control surfaces and ailerons and wooden wing tips.

Crew: two, in an enclosed cockpit.

Power plant: one Aichi AE1A Atsuta 21 (Ha-60-21) 12-cylinder liquid-cooled inverted Vee engine rated at 1,400hp (1,030kW) for take-off, 1,250hp (920kW) at an altitude of 1,700m and 1,290hp (950kW) at an altitude of 5,000m (M6A1 – prototypes),

One Aichi AE1P Atsuta 32 (Ha-60-32) 12-cylinder liquid-cooled inverted Vee engine rated at 1,400hp (1,030kW) for take-off, 1,340hp (985kW) at an altitude of 1,700m and 1,290hp (950kW) at an altitude of 5,000m (M6A1 Model 11, M6A1-K).

Three-blade variable pitch metal propeller, diameter 3.20m; fuel tank capacity 934l, oil tank capacity 49l.

Armament: one 13mm Type 2 machine gun in the observer's cockpit,

Bomb load: two 250kg bomb or one 800kg bomb or one 850kg Type 91 aircraft torpedo.

| Type | M6A1 AM-24 | M6A1 Model 11 | A6M1-K |
|---|---|---|---|
| Wing span m | 12.262 | 12.262 | 12.262 |
| Overall length m | 11.640 | 11.640 | |
| Length of the fuselage m | 10.640 | 10.640 | 10.640 |
| Height m | 4.580 | 4.580 | 2.940 |
| Wing area m$^2$ | 27.00 | 27.00 | 27.00 |
| Empty weight kg | 3,362 | 3,301 | 3,002 |
| Normal take-off weight kg | 4,250 | 4,040 | 3,642 |
| Maximum take-off weight kg | 4,900 | 4,445 | 4,225 |
| Useful load kg | 888 | 739 | 640 |
| Wing loading kg/m$^2$ | 157.41 | 149.63 | 134.89 |
| Power loading kg/hp | 3.04 | 2.88 | 2.60 |
| Maximum speed km/h | 439 | 444 | 575 |
| at an altitude of m | 4,000 | 4,200 | 3,000 |
| Cruising speed km/h | 277 | 277 | 295 |
| at an altitude of m | 3,000 | 3,000 | 3,000 |
| Landing speed km/h | 115 | 113 | 124 |
| Climb to 3,000m | 5 min. 55 sec. | 5 min. 48 sec. | 8 min. 9 sec. |
| Ceiling m | 9,000 | 9,900 | 9,600 |
| Endurance | 3 hrs 58 min. | 4 hrs 15 min. | |
| Take-off run m | 215 | | |

Production: Eitoku plant of Aichi Kokuki Kabushiki Gaisha built a total of 28 M6A aircraft, including:

| | |
|---|---|
| 8 | M6A1 – prototypes (October 1943 – October 1944) |
| 18 | M6A1 Model 11 Seiran – production aircraft (October 1944 – July 1945) |
| 2 | M6A1-K Nanzan – prototypes (1944) |

*Port front view of the same prototype of the Aichi M6A1-K Nanzan.*

*The front cockpit of the preserved Seiran.*
*T. Hortmann*

*M6A1 Seiran floatplane at Eitoku plant of Aichi company near Nagasaki. Note the absence of vertical tail, which had been removed to introduce structural alterations.*

*Starboard front view of the prototype of the Aichi M6A1-K Nanzan trainer version.*

# Front Instrument Panel

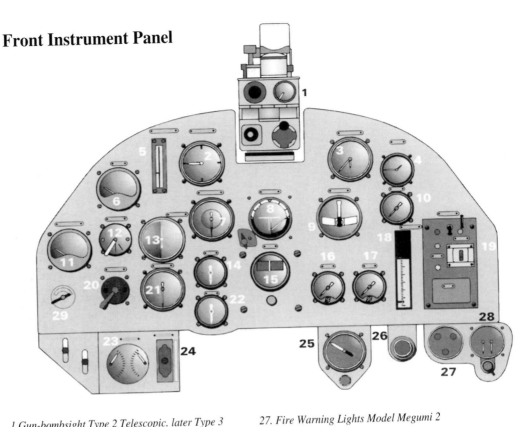

1. Gun-bombsight Type 2 Telescopic. later Type 3 Mk I Model 1.

2. Rate ofClimb Indicator Model 1.

3. Altimeter, Sensitive Model 1.

4. Chronometer.

5. Inclinometer Model 2.

6. Fuel Quantity Gauge.

7. Airspeed Indicator Model 3 Kai 1.

8. Artificial Horizon Model 2.

9. Turn and Bank Indicator Model 2.

10. Vacuum Pressure Gauge Model 1.

11. Exhaust Gas Temperature Gauge Model 1.

11. Fuel Tank Reading Selector Switch.

13. Manifold Pressure Gauge Model 1.

14. Fuel Pressure Gauge Mk 1 Model 4.

15. Directional Gyro Model 1.

16. Engine Coolant Temperature Gauge Model 2.

17. Oil Temperature Gauge Mk 1 Model 5.

18. Accelerometer Model 2.

19. Engine Starting Panel.

20. Engine Magneto Switch.

21. Tachometer Model 1 Kai I.

22. Oil Pressure Gauge Mk I Model I.

23. Dive Brake and Wing Flap Position Indicator.

24. Landing Flap Switch.

25. Compass Magnetic Type 0, later Remote Reading Model 1.

26. Engine Primer Fuel Pump.

27. Fire Warning Lights Model Megumi 2

28. Oxygen Flow Regulator Model 2.

29. Fire Extinguisher Director Switch.

*Instrument panel: gun/ bombsight Mk. 1 and control column. To the right are: elevator trim wheel, aileron trim (aft), rudder trim (forward) throttle quadrant (above trim controls). The darker (red) knob is for mixture control and lighter (silver) is for propeller pitch control.*

*T. Hortman.*

# Kawanishi Baika

The Kawanishi Baika, or 'Plum Blossom', was intended as a replacement for the rocket-powered Ohka ('cherry blossom') and jet-powered Kikka ('orange blossom') suicide aircraft. Unlike either of these aircraft it was to be powered by pulse-jet, similar to the German Fieseler Fi-103 V-1 'Doodlebug'.

Just before the end of hostilities, on 2 July 1945 the *Kaigun Koku Hombu* issued to Kawanishi their specifications for the development and production of a new aeroplane, which received the designation 'Experimental Navy Special Attack Aeroplane Baika'. The new design was to replace the existing Ohka Models 11 and 22 and Nakajima Kikka special attack aircraft. Similar specifications were also received by *Dai-Ichi Kaigun Koku Gijyutsusho* (generally shortened to Kugisho) at Yokosuka, in response to which a development of the Ohka Model 22, designated the Ohka Model 43 Otsu, was designed.

According to Japanese staff officers, both of the aircraft under development were soon to be used to repel the anticipated Allied invasion at the home islands. They would be catapulted from special launch pads or take off from coastal air strips. The main difference between the two aircraft designs was in the propulsion unit. The Ohka Model 43 Otsu was intended to be powered by the Ne-20 turbojet engine, while it was planned that the Baika would use the Ka-10 pulse-jet.

At the time, the Japanese aircraft industry was experiencing massive disruption from the Allied bombing onslaught and was a shadow of its former self. Daily raids by American B-29 Superfortress bombers had destroyed most Japanese aircraft factories. Consequently, aircraft production was dispersed and moved to underground factories. Also at that time, a number of new suicide aircraft concepts were developed. They would become a 'weapon of last resort' for the crumbling Japanese Empire. One example, the Ohka Model 11, had been in production since August 1944, but due to its low combat effectiveness, production was halted in March of 1945, after several hundred were built.

The Ohka Model 43 Otsu project was an improvement on the Model 22, to be powered by the Ne-20 turbojet in place of the Model 22's rocket engine. Its design was, however, rather complex, and could not be put into mass production using the dispersed locations, unskilled labour and lack of strategic materials that were facts of life for aircraft production at this time. Faced with the prospect of the enemy landing in Japanese home territory, time was a key factor, and the complexity of the design prevented rapid development and production.

At the same time, at the Aircraft Institute of the Imperial University in Tokyo, Professors Taichiro Ogawa and Ichiro Tani were following German designs such as the Fieseler Fi-103 flying bomb and the Heinkel He-162 jet fighter, and they developed their own project for a similar aeroplane, matching the specifications for the Baika. Both the Kugisho project and that of the Aircraft Institute were to be powered by the Ka-10 (Kantetsu Nensho Rocket) pulse-jet, similar to the German engine that powered the V-1 flying bomb. The main factor influencing the selection of this propulsion unit was its simplicity and ease of mass production. Additionally, this engine did not required high quality fuels, unlike the Ne-20 turbojet engine. It was even possible to use fuels obtained from other somewhat unconventional sources, such as pine resin. The loud noise of the engine, which made it vulnerable to detection by the enemy, the tendency to vibrate massively, and the short useful life of the fuel straight-run valve were considered its only shortcomings. The latter was solved by replacing the valve after each use of the engine, and the vibrations were cured by fitting adequate shock-absorbers. Eventually, Kugisho and the Aircraft Institute pooled their resources and worked on a single design.

On 5 August 1945, a meeting of all interested parties took place at the Aircraft Institute. The *Kaigun Koku Hombu* was represented by Admirals Wada and Katahira, the Aircraft Institute by its manager Mr. Nakanishi and Professors Taichiro Ogawa and Kihara, and the manufacturer, Kawanishi, was represented by the deputy manager Vice-Admiral Katahira and the chief designer Tamenobu Takeuchi. The meeting was to discuss the schedule of the design work and the progress

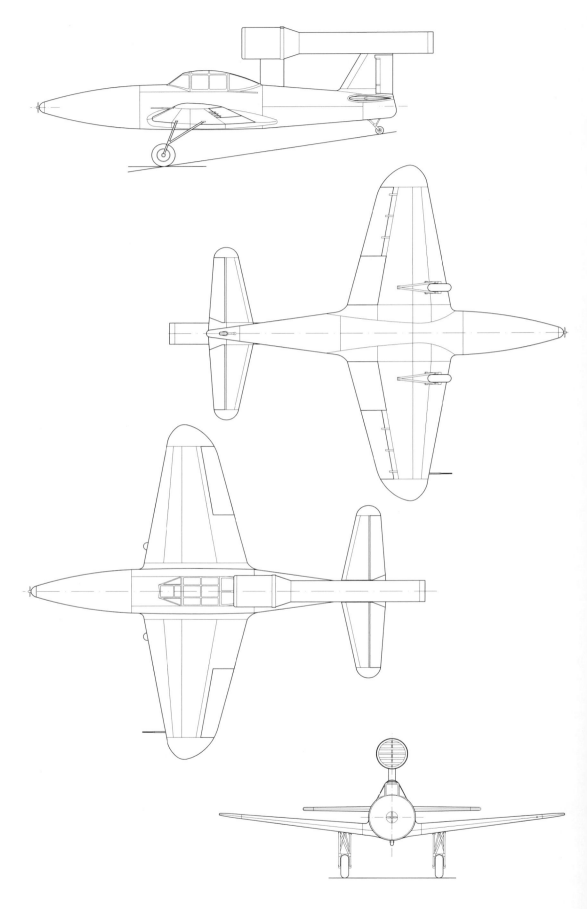

*Kawanishi Baika 2*

*1/72 scale.*

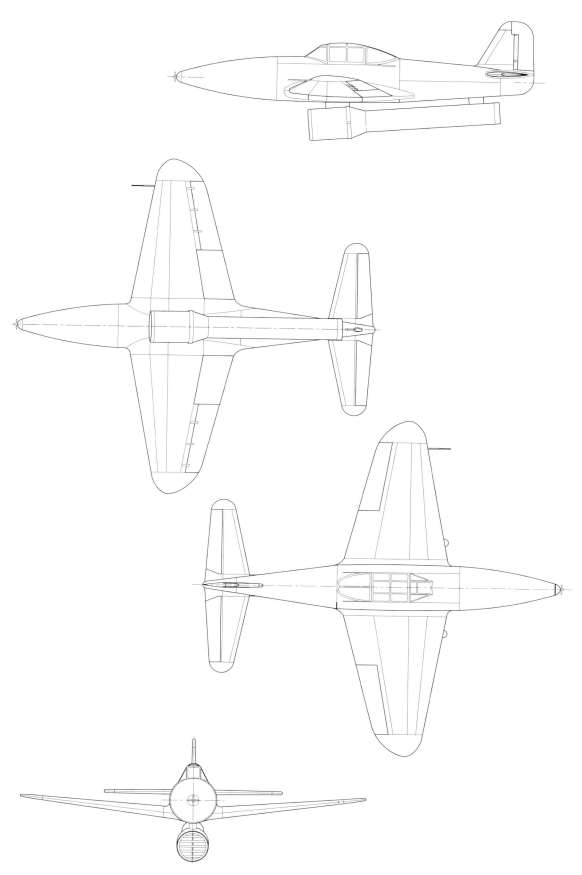

*Kawanishi Baika 3.*

*1/72 scale.*

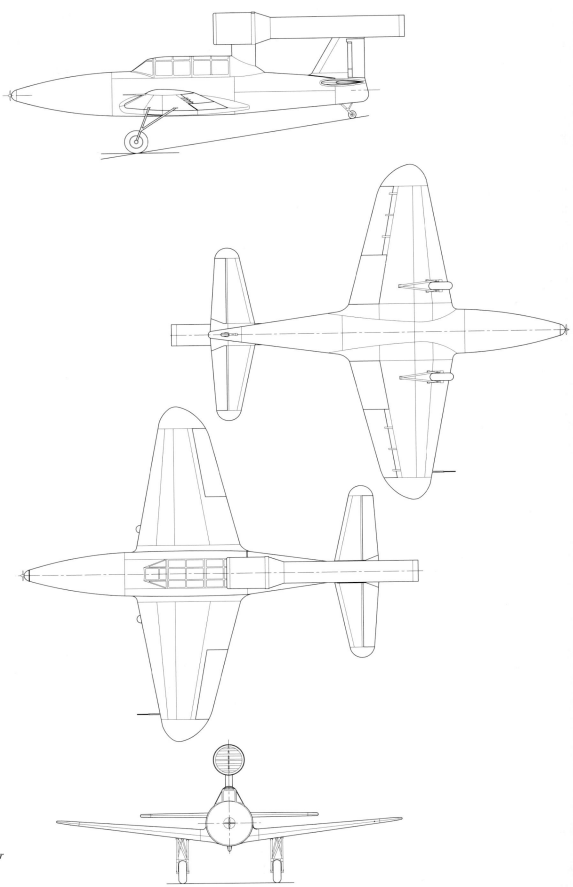

*Kawanishi Baika trainer
version (hypothetical).*

1/72 scale.

toward preparing for mass production. At the meeting, a final choice between the two preliminary projects was made. Two main factors were considered during the selection of the project: simplicity of design and ease of operation. The Kugisho project was thought to be better overall considering these criteria, but several engineering solutions developed for the Aircraft Institute project were promising and the meeting considered that these should be pursued.

The fuselage shape of the Baika was slim and circular in cross section; similar to that of the German Fi-103 (V-1) flying bomb. The cramped cockpit was covered with a canopy that offered good visibility. Various locations for the engine were proposed, and depending on which was chosen, the cockpit could be opened to one side or slid rearwards. The wings were tapered with round tips, and were fitted with standard slotted ailerons. The construction was entirely of wood, with the exception of steel joints. Two basic layouts were developed: the first layout (Baika 1) had the engine located immediately above the cockpit or positioned slightly rearwards of the cockpit. The fuselage was fitted with a non-retractable undercarriage which could be jettisoned after take-off, using explosive charges fitted in the main wheel leg attachment joints.

In the second basic layout (Baika 2) the engine was located under the fuselage. This version had no undercarriage, and was intended to be launched from a special catapult initially designed by Kugisho for the Ohka Model 43 Otsu. A modified take-off trolley for the Baika 2 was developed which be powered by a less powerful solid fuel rocket engine than the Ohka version, producing a thrust of 800kg for 9 seconds. Both versions of the Baika were designed to accept a 250kg explosive charge fitted in the forward fuselage.

Both versions had advantages and drawbacks. The catapulted variant could be used in virtually any spot on the coast, while the wheeled variant was easier for inexperienced pilots. It was therefore decided that the wheeled variant would be used for pilot training, and the catapulted variant would be used in combat. During the meeting, Kawanishi also received precise deadlines for individual stages of the work. The design documentation was supposed to be ready by the end of September 1945, and series production was going to commence in October. At the same time an order was placed for construction of one combat Baika and ten Baika 3 two-seater trainers.

During the same meeting the design specifications were updated as follows:
- Role: land-based attack aeroplane taking off from a simple and cheap catapult, for attacking enemy landing craft.
- Layout: pulse-jet powered monoplane.
- Principal dimensions: as small as possible – width with wings folded: 3.6m, overall length 8.5m, height no more than 4.0m (including the catapult, the height could be up to 5.0m).
- Propulsion unit: one Ka-10 pulse-jet.
- Crew: pilot.
- Performance: maximum speed at least 463km/h (250 knots) at sea level; range at full engine power in flight at sea level no less than 130km; service ceiling up to 2,000m; visibility and control during a dive better than the A6M 'Zero'.
- Catapult specifications: flight path 0 degree (or 12 o'clock) (with engine at head wind up to 44 m/s)
- Armament: over 100kg explosives.
- Armour: 8mm armour plate behind the pilot.
- Flight instruments: engine (fuel gauge, fuel level indicator, rev counter) and navigation (airspeed indicator, altimeter, compass, turn-and-bank indicator).

Soon afterwards, the range requirement was dropped and the armour for the pilot was deleted, while the explosive charge was increased to 250kg.

During another meeting on 6 August 1945, methods of construction using such materials as wood and steel were discussed. The subject was presented by Mr. Masayama, the representative of the *Kaigun Koku Hombu*. Additional priorities were also defined, such as good controllability, ease of mass production and range.

The next meeting took place two days later, on 8 August 1945, this time at the Kawanishi company facilities. A design team was named, working under Tamenobu Takeuchi and consisting of 60 engineers, mainly from Kugisho. On 11 August the first ten designers under Mr. Tokuda arrived. The second group of twenty designers arrived on 15 August, and the third and last group, on 20 August, including all of the remaining engineers. However, at midday on the day the second group arrived - and five days prior to the arrival of the last group - the armistice was announced and construction work on the Baika was therefore never undertaken.

**Specifications:**

Description: cantilever low-wing monoplane special attack (suicide) aeroplane. Mixed construction.

Crew: pilot in an enclosed cockpit or pilot and instructor (training version).

Power plant: one 360kg Ka-10 pulse-jet; fuel tank capacity 600 l.

Armament: 250kg explosive.

| Type | Baika 1 | Baika 2 | Baika 3 |
|---|---|---|---|
| Wing span m | 6.6 | 6.6 | 6.6 |
| Length m | 7.0 | 7.58 | 7.0 |
| Height m | | | |
| Wing area m² | 7.59 | 7.59 | 7.59 |
| Empty weight kg | 750 | | |
| Max take-off weight kg | 1,430 | | |
| Useful load kg | 680 | | |
| Wing loading kg/m² | 188.00 | | |
| Thrust loading kg/kG | 3.97 | | |
| Maximum speed km/h | 648 | | |
| at an altitude of m | 2,000 | | |
| Cruising speed km/h | 485 | | |
| at an altitude of m | 6,000 | | |
| Landing speed km/h | 111 | | |
| Climb to 2,000m | 3 min. 55 sec. | | |
| Service ceiling m | 6,000 | | |
| Normal range km | 278 | | |
| Take-off run m | 900 | | |

Note: the designations of Baika 1, Baika 2 and Baika 3 were not applied by the Japanese. They are for information only, to identify individual variants of the design.

Production: in August 1945 Kawanishi Kokuki Kabushiki Gaisha at Naruo commenced work on production documentation for the Baika. No prototypes had been built by the time of the armistice.

# Kugisho D3Y Myojo

The D3Y Myojo started life as a bomber-trainer built from non-strategic materials, but like many Japanese aircraft of the period, it was eventually developed as a dedicated suicide aircraft.

When Japan entered the war in the Far East it was counting on a quick end to the conflict. Lightning invasions were supposed to capture vast new territories, rich in raw materials needed for further expansion. At the beginning of the war a great deal of territory was captured, but the merchant fleet, busy with transporting troops, could not cope with the demand for supplying raw materials to an industry switched to a war footing. As time went by, the Allies slowed and then stopped the Japanese offensive, while US submarines and air strikes gradually reduced the inflow of raw materials from the occupied territories. The Japanese arms industry started to look for substitute materials as their stocks of strategic materials shrank.

From 1943 such limitations also affected the aircraft industry. Initially the deficit in light metal alloys affected production of training and transport aircraft but later, as stocks diminished further, principal combat aircraft were affected. Numbers of skilled personnel were also shrinking as more able-bodied men were drafted into the armed forces. All this led to a search for replacement materials and simplified designs.

At the *Dai-Ichi Kaigun Koku Gijyutsusho* (Kugisho), work commenced on an aeroplane with the factory designation Y-50. This was a bomber trainer of all-wooden construction, based on the design of the carrier-borne dive-bomber Aichi D3A1 Model 11 'Val', once perfectly satisfactory but now obsolete. The original was of all-metal construction, but in accordance with the necessity to conserve strategic materials and manufacture aircraft with less skilled personnel, the designers of the new aeroplane made it as simple as possible. For this reason, the characteristic elliptical wings and tail of the 'Val' were replaced by a straight-tapered planform with rounded tips. Dive brakes were also fitted under the wings. To ensure stability, the fuselage was lengthened over that of the 'Val', which could be achieved because the trainer was not required to fit into an aircraft carrier's lift.

The Y50 was powered by the 1,300hp Mitsubishi Kinsei 54 radial engine. To enable the aircraft to be used for gunnery training two fixed 0.303in (7.7mm) machine guns were mounted in the engine cowling. Four 30kg practice bombs could be fitted to racks under the wing centre section. The fixed main undercarriage was fitted with shock-absorbers, and covered by spats.

In July 1944, the first prototype was built, and the second appeared a month later. The aeroplane then received the designation 'Experimental Navy Dive Bomber Trainer Myojo' (D3Y1-K). During flight trials the aeroplane proved to be too heavy and had poor flight characteristics which disqualified it as an advanced trainer.

*D3Y1-K Myojo Model 22 dive bomber trainer found in an assembly hall by American occupation troops.*

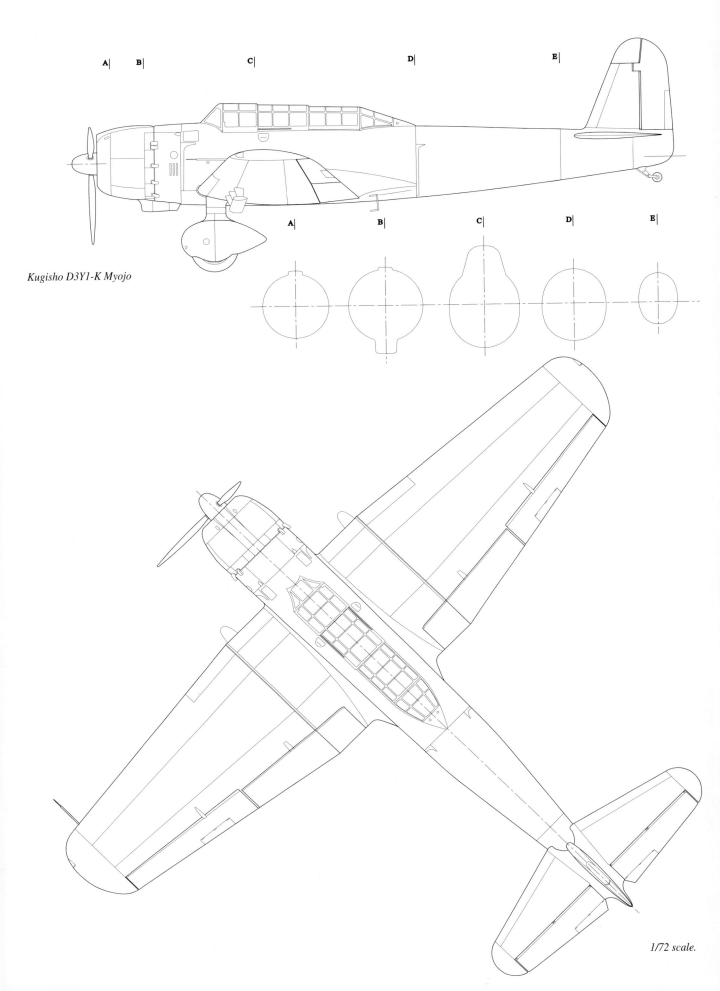

Kugisho D3Y1-K Myojo

1/72 scale.

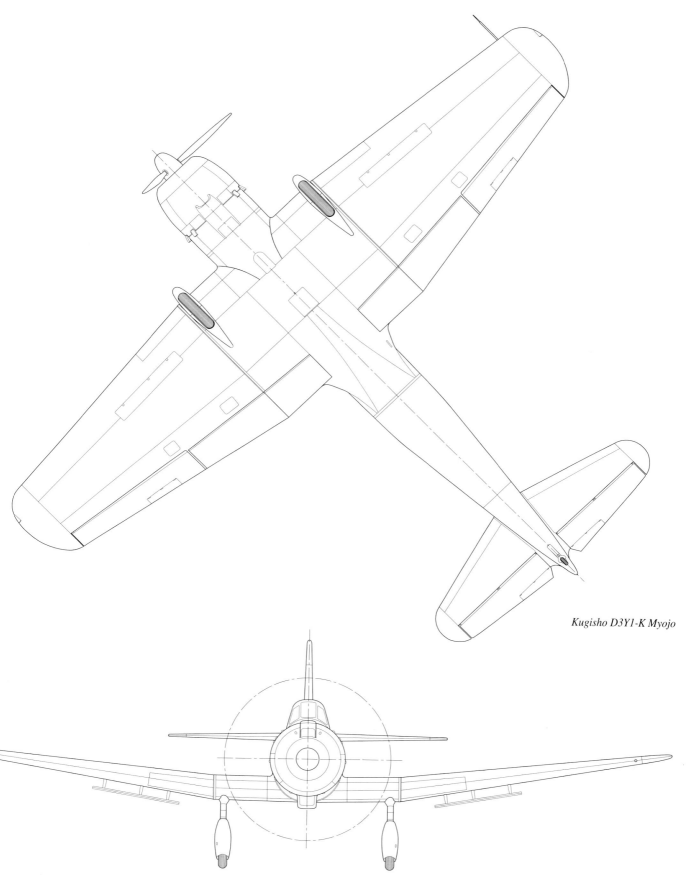

Kugisho D3Y1-K Myojo

1/72 scale.

0   0,5   1   2 m

137

A programme of weight reduction was undertaken. The *Kaigun Koku Hombu* anticipated that the redesign work would be successful and ordered the Matsushita company to start preparations for series production. Reducing the weight of the design proved to be troublesome, but eventually the Myojo's flight characteristics were improved. Unfortunately this necessitated the removal of all armament, which rendered it unable to be used for gunnery training. Changes concentrated on stretching the fuselage by some 0.30m and reducing the wing area from 32.8m² to 30.5m². This reduced the overall weight by 150kg. The aeroplane, now approved for series production, received the designation 'Type 99 Navy Dive Bomber Trainer Myojo Model 22' (D3Y1-K Model 22). By now, however, there was little official interest in the aeroplane, and the withdrawal of the D3A to second-line units meant that there was a plentiful supply of suitable training aircraft. Only seven production machines of the type were to be built by the end of the war.

However, the increased use of suicide tactics breathed new life into the Myojo. By early 1945, in accordance with the guidelines of the *Kaigun Koku Hombu*, Kugisho designers started to develop a single-seat special dive bomber, with the designation D3Y2-K Model 23 Myojo Kai, intended for suicide attacks. The project was based on the D3Y1-K trainer, but the more powerful Mitsubishi MK8F Kinsei 62 engine was selected. The Myojo Kai had an 800kg bomb fixed under the fuselage, and its armament included two 20mm Type 99 cannon under the engine cowling. Before the suicide pilot hit an enemy ship, he could fire at the target to help judge the distance. This innovation was introduced at the request of the *Kaigun Koku Hombu*, who received many reports from escort fighters that the Kamikaze attacks were unsuccessful due to inaccurate judgement of distance. The Myojo Kai was fitted with an undercarriage which could be jettisoned after take-off. Thanks to the reduced drag, the aeroplane could then attain a higher maximum speed. A retractable undercarriage was considered an unnecessary piece of luxury in a 'disposable' machine. However, operational practice showed that many suicide attacks came to nothing due to inefficient reconnaissance, and the prospective suicide pilots were forced to return. Despite these hurdles, it was planned to start series production, estimated at 30 aircraft a month. Production machines would receive the official designation 'Navy Special Dive Bomber Myojo Kai' (D5Y1). By the time of the armistice in August 1945 no prototype of the D3Y2-K had been completed.

### Specifications:

Description: single-engined cantilever low-wing monoplane two-seat dive-bomber trainer (D3Y1-K) or single-seat special attack aeroplane (D3Y2-K). Wooden construction with fabric covered control surfaces and ailerons.

Crew: pupil-pilot and instructor in an enclosed cockpit (D3Y1-K), pilot in an enclosed cockpit (D3Y2-K )

Power plant: one Mitsubishi MK8E Kinsei 54 (Ha-33-54) 14-cylinder air cooled radial engine rated at 1,300hp (955kW) for take-off, 1,200hp (885kW) at an altitude of 3,000m, and 1,100hp

*One of seven prototypes of the D3Y1-K Model 22 during ceremonial handover to the armed forces.*

*The D3Y1-K Model 22 during take-off run.*

(810kW) at an altitude of 6,200m; three-blade variable pitch metal propeller, diameter 3.20m; fuel tank capacity 1,190l, oil tank capacity 60l (D3Y1-K).

One Mitsubishi MK8F Kinsei 62 (Ha-33-62) 14-cylinder air cooled radial engine rated at take-off 1,560hp (1,145kW) and 1,350hp (995kW) at an altitude of 2,000m, and 1,190hp (875kW) at an altitude of 5,800m; three-blade variable pitch metal propeller, diameter 3.20m; fuel tank capacity 1,200l (D3Y2-K),

Armament: two fixed 0.303in. (7.7mm) machine guns (D3Y1-K),two fixed 20mm Type 99 cannon (D3Y2-K)

Bomb load: four 30kg bombs (D3Y1-K), one 500-800kg bomb (D3Y2-K).

| Type | D3Y1-K Model 22 | D3Y2-K Model 23 |
|---|---|---|
| Wing span m | 13.918 | 14.0 |
| Length m | 11.515 | 11.515 |
| Height m | 4.185 | 4.2 |
| Wing area m$^2$ | 32.84 | 30.5 |
| Empty weight kg | 3,200 | 3,150 |
| Normal take-off weight kg | 4,200 | 4,630 |
| Useful load kg | 1,000 | 1,580 |
| Wing loading kg/m$^2$ | 128.05 | 151.80 |
| Power loading kg/hp | 3.23 | 2.97 |
| Maximum speed km/h | 450 | 470 |
| at an altitude of m | 6,200 | 5,000 |
| Cruising speed km/h | 296 | 296 |
| at an altitude of m | 3,000 | 3,000 |
| Landing speed km/h | 130 | 124 |
| Climb to 6,000m | 13 min. 23 sec. | 11 min. 45 sec. |
| Ceiling m | 9,000 | 9,250 |
| Normal range km | 1,780 | 1,760 |
| Maximum range km | 2,360 | 2,315 |
| Landing run m | 228 | |

Production: *Dai-Ichi Kaigun Koku Gijyutsusho* built two D3Y1-K prototypes, and Matsushita Koku Kogyo Kabushiki Gaisha built seven production D3Y1-K Model 22 aircraft. Construction of the prototype D3Y2-K Myojo Kai attack aeroplane was not completed.

# Kugisho D4Y Suisei ('Judy')

Like most front-line aircraft of the Imperial Japanese Navy, the Kugisho D4Y Suisei was adapted for suicide attacks, initially in impromptu conversions and later with more dedicated adaptations. The suicide applications of the D4Y, as noted in the section 'The fate of the Kamikaze godfathers', are chiefly associated with Vice-Admiral Matome Ugaki, who took off on his last mission on August 15 1945, and was never heard from again.

The 'Judy' was an unusual aeroplane in the Imperial Japanese Navy in using an in-line liquid-cooled engine in its early versions, as opposed to the generally favoured air-cooled radial. Although designed as successor to the famous Aichi D3A 'Val', the D4Y actually made its combat debut as a carrier-borne reconnaissance aircraft.

Representatives of the Imperial Japanese Navy visiting Germany in 1937 purchased the licence to build the Heinkel He-118, which had lost the competition for the Luftwaffe standard dive bomber to the Junkers Ju87. In February 1937 the fourth He-118 V4 prototype (D-OMOL), powered by a Daimler-Benz DB-601A of 1175hp, was sent to Japan and later test-flown by the pilots of the Yokosuka *Kokutai*. It received the Japanese designation of 'Type He experimental Navy dive bomber' (DXHe1). The *Kaigun Koku Hombu* planned to begin production of the DXHe1, but it was too big and heavy for use on aircraft carriers and its performance was not good enough. The domestic production plan was cancelled after the V4 crashed in 1938.

In spite of this, the *Kaigun Koku Hombu* obtained much useful experience from operating the He-118, which was employed in the '13-Shi carrier-borne dive bomber' designed by *Dai-Ichi Kaigun Koku Gijyutsusho* (Kugisho) at the end of 1938. Among others, the following requirements were specified: a maximum speed of 518km/h; cruising speed of 426km/h; range of 1,480km with a 250kg bomb; range in reconnaissance missions 2,220km; ability to operate from small aircraft carriers; smaller dimensions than those of the He-118.

In order to meet the above requirements, the design team under engineer Masao Yamana, the chief designer of Kugisho, designed a relatively small cantilever mid-wing aircraft. It was an all-metal, two-seat, carrier-borne dive bomber which received the designation '13-Shi Navy experimental carrier-borne dive bomber Suisei' (D4Y1). Although the D4Y1 had a similar span and wing area to the Mitsubishi A6M2 'Zero', it could carry larger amounts of fuel, similar to its predecessor the D3A2. The small wingspan of 11.5m did not require the installation of a wing folding mechanism, which reduced weight significantly. Also, the D4Y1 Suisei was designed with high-lift devices in the wing. During the dive, the speed of the 'Judy' could be controlled with the use of three electrically powered air brakes. The main landing gear and wheel doors were also electrically controlled. The designers of the D4Y1 also took care to ensure an aerodynamically clean profile; to reduce drag, a bomb of up to 500kg size could be carried in an internal bomb bay rather than the external carriage of the 'Val'. It was also possible to carry 30kg light bombs or markers on underwing racks. The planned power unit for the D4Y1 was the licence-built version of the German Daimler Benz DB-601A engine, the Aichi Atsuta 12 rated at 1,175hp. Initially none of the Atsuta engines was ready, forcing the designers to use another German engine the Daimler Benz DB-600G rated at 960hp on the early prototypes.

The first prototype of the D4Y1 was assembled in November, 1940, just before the outbreak of war in the Far East. It was test-flown a month later at the airfield in Yokosuka, and performance exceeded the original requirements for the 13-Shi specifications. The impressive performance, along with the likelihood of war, influenced the decision to accelerate the programme of flight tests and assembly of the next prototypes. By the end of 1941, four more prototypes with Atsuta 12 engines were built. Armament consisted of two fixed 7.7mm (.0303 in) Type 97 machine guns installed in the fuselage above the engine, and a movable 7.7mm (.303 in) Type 92 machine gun in the gunner/radio-operator's cockpit.

Before it was officially accepted as 'Carrier-borne bomber Suisei Model 11' (D4Y1 Model 11), a critical fault emerged during dive-bombing trials. Vibration in the rear fuselage caused the mid-air disintegration of the fifth prototype during a shallow dive. As diving was essential to the aircraft's purpose, preparations for series production by Aichi were suspended pending strengthening of the structure. The D4Y1 was officially accepted in December 1943.

In 1942, the *Kaigun Koku Hombu* commissioned the conversion of the third and the fourth prototypes to carrier-borne reconnaissance aircraft on the strength of their high speed. The D4Y1-C was equipped with a K-8 fixed automatic camera and an additional fuel tank in the bomb bay. It could also carry two fuel tanks under the wings.

Two D4Y1-C were carried on the aircraft carrier Soryu and took part in the Battle of Midway. One of them was lost in an accident. After the Soryu was damaged, the second D4Y1-C landed on the sister carrier Hiryū and continued reconnaissance flights until the Hiryū itself was sunk. The performance of the D4Y1-C during the Battle of Midway was very promising, so the *Kaigun Koku Hombu* decided to adopt the plane as 'Type 2 carrier-borne reconnaissance aircraft Suisei Model 11' (D4Y1-C) and ordered series production at Aichi on July 6, 1942. Production developed quite slowly, since the number of carrier-borne reconnaissance aircraft needed was not great. By March 1943, Aichi had managed to produce only 25 D4Y1 and D4Y1-C Model 11 aircraft. By the end of 1943, only a few D4Y1-Cs were operational on aircraft carriers. However, first impressions of the D4Y1 in front-line units were positive about the aircraft's good flight performance. It lacked defensive armour for the fuel tanks and the cockpit, but this was an 'Achilles' heel' of many Japanese aircraft. The Atsuta 12 engine caused problems but this was mainly due to lack of experience with liquid-cooled in-line engines.

The development of the D4Y continued. The main spar of the wing was reinforced and the air brakes were improved. These changes were implemented into series production in March, 1943. The performance of the D4Y1-C Suisei considerably exceeded that of the outdated Aichi D3A2 dive bombers, and so it was decided to speed up series production of the D4Y1 now it could perform its intended role as a dive-bomber. From April 1943 to March 1944, Aichi produced 589 D4Y1s and D4Y1-Cs. In June 1944, during the battle to repel the American invasion of the Marianas, 81 D4Y1s and D4Y1-Cs participated in the action from aircraft carriers, while a further D4Y1s from the land-based Palau *Hikotai* and Tinian *Hikotai* took part in the battle. A small number of D4Y Model 21s (D4Y1 Kai) also participated. They could be catapult-launched, and the fuselage was strengthened but the dive brakes were omitted. Only a few were produced. The majority of Japanese aeroplanes participating in the battle were shot down, and the D4Ys did not sink any ships.

Further versions were developed, but these did not sufficiently incorporate the lessons of the Marianas battle which had highlighted the extreme vulnerability of aircraft with little armour and non self-sealing fuel tanks. The D4Y2 merely gained 15mm of armoured glass on the canopy, while its more powerful Atsuta 32 engine was even less reliable than the Atsuta 12. A slightly improved version with a 13mm (.5 in) Type 2 machine gun in place of the 7.7mm (.303 in) machine gun was produced in parallel with the D4Y2 and was designated D4Y2a. With the later addition of catapult equipment the D4Y2 became the D4Y2 Kai and the D4Y2a became the D4Y2a Kai. These two variants, in addition to the Model 21 (D4Y1 Kai), were manufactured especially for the aircraft carrier battleships (BB/CV) *Ise* and *Hyuga* - hybrid warships with heavy guns on the fore part of the ship, with a landing-on deck aft.

A reconnaissance version was also built, differing from its predecessor the D3Y1-C only in the installation of the Aichi Atsuta 32 engine. It received the designation 'Type 2 carrier-borne reconnaissance plane Suisei Model 12' (D4Y2-R), and a further variant with Type 2 movable machine gun was the 'Type 2 carrier-borne reconnaissance plane Suisei Model 12 Ko' (D4Y2a-R).

All the above versions were used during the battle for the Philippines, during which they were decimated by US Navy fighters. The majority of D4Ys were used for Kamikaze missions.

From the very beginning the D4Y experienced problems with maintenance and operation of the Aichi Atsuta engines. For this reason, commanders of the units equipped with D4Ys suggested replacing the liquid-cooled in-line engine with a more reliable unit. The designers at Aichi analysed the possibility of fitting a radial engine and chose the Mitsubishi Kinsei 61 (later 62), which best fitted the small cross-section of the fuselage. In order to keep the fine aerodynamic lines, the engine was closely cowled, with a smooth transition to the narrow mid section of the body, but the increased frontal area decreased the speed of the aircraft by 16.7km/h.

This experimentally-converted D4Y2, Shi-sei Suisei Kai, began flight tests in May 1944. This confirmed the validity of the idea, and the *Kaigun Koku Hombu* commissioned Aichi to start series production of this aeroplane under the designation Suisei Model 33 (D4Y3). The D4Y3 armed with a Type 2 13mm (0.5in) movable machine gun received the designation Suisei Model 33 Ko (D4Y3a). The new engine was much more reliable, and bomb load was increased to 750kg (one 250kg bomb in the bomb bay and two 250kg bombs under the wings). The arrestor gear was removed, since most Japanese aircraft were now operating from land bases.

The final production version of the D4Y Suisei was Suisei Model 43 (D4Y4). It used the Mitsubishi Kinsei 62 radial engine, but maximum speed was reduced to 552km/h because of an increase in weight. This version was crewed only by the pilot, and the bomb load was increased to 800kg, with the main bomb semi-recessed in the bomb bay rather than being completely enclosed as in earlier versions. Because of recent combat experience, crew protection was increased with 75mm bullet-proof glass in front of the canopy, plus 5mm and 9mm thick armour plates fore and aft of the cockpit. Fuel tanks also gained added protection. The movable machine gun was left out, and the canopy above the rear seat could be faired with metal plates. Two types of auxiliary rocket engines, for assisting take-off and for emergency acceleration to evade enemy fighters, were installed. Two 4FR Type 110 rockets with a maximum thrust of 1,200kg were placed under the nose section to assist take-off and three 4FH Type 121 rockets, with maximum thrust of 2,000kg, were under the rear fuselage for emergency acceleration. The two 7.7mm (0.303in) Type 97 machine guns in the nose were removed from April 1945. After February 1945, 296 of this type were produced. This version may have been intended as a dedicated suicide version.

From April 1944 until the end of the war, the *Dai-Juichi Kaigun Kokusho* (11th Navy Aircraft Factory) in Hiro also undertook the production of 'Judy' D4Y1, D4Y2 and D4Y3 versions, and a total of 215 D4Ys were produced here.

A few D4Y2s were converted to night fighters at the Iwakuni branch of the *Dai-Juichi Kaigun Kosho*, receiving the designation Suisei Model 12 Hei (D4Y2-S) or Model 12 Hei (D4Y2-S). In this variant, the crew was reduced to the pilot alone, with a single 20mm Type 99 Model 2 inclined obliquely upwards at an angle of 30o mounted in the rear cockpit. A few of these received underwing racks for light phosphorous air-to-air bombs, which were dropped on the big formations of B-29 Superfortress or B-24 Liberator heavy bombers. At the beginning of 1945, the 302nd *Kokutai* possessed nine planes of this type. However, without radar to locate hostile bombers at night, and because the aircraft had a poor climb rate, the D4Y2-S had no success in the new role. There was also a night fighter 'Judy' Model 33 Hei (D4Y3-S), converted from Model 33 with the same armament.

The last proposed version of the D4Y Suisei was the Suisei Model 54 (D4Y5) with a Homare 12 engine rated at 1,825hp. Because of problems with the Homare 12, no prototype was produced.

Many D4Ys ended their days in suicide attacks, particularly in defence of the Philippines and Iwo Jima. The aircraft's speed and ability to carry a heavy bomb load made it an obvious choice in this role where the ability to evade interception and maximum destructive power were paramount.

**Specification:**

Description: single-engine carrier-borne dive bomber (D4Y1, D4Y2, D4Y3, D4Y4, D4Y5), carrier-borne reconnaissance (D4Y1-C, D4Y2-R, D4Y2a-R), or night fighter (D4Y2-S, D4Y3-S); cantilever mid-wing aircraft of all-metal structure, control surfaces covered with fabric.

Crew: pilot and radio-operator/gunner within a closed cockpit (most versions) or pilot only (D4Y4).

Power unit:

One 12-cylinder liquid-cooled inverted-V Daimler Benz DB-600G engine of 960hp (706kW) take-off power, three-blade variable-pitch metal airscrew of 3.2m diameter; fuel tank capacity 1,070l (D4Y1 prototypes);

One 12-cylinder liquid-cooled inverted-V Aichi AE1A Atsuta 12 (Ha-60-12) engine of 1,200hp (883kW) take-off power, 1,010hp (723kW) at 1,500m and 965hp (690kW) at 4,450m, three-blade variable-pitch metal airscrew of 3.2m diameter; fuel tank capacity 1,070l (D4Y1, D4Y1 Kai, D4Y1-C);

One 12-cylinder liquid-cooled inverted-V Aichi AE1P Atsuta 32 (Ha-60-32) engine of 1,400hp (1,030kW) take-off power, 1,250hp (920kW) at 1,700m and 1,290hp (949kW) at 5,000m, three-blade variable-pitch metal airscrew of 3.2m diameter; fuel tank capacity 1,660l (D4Y2, D4Y2a, D4Y2-R, D4Y2a-R, D4Y2 Kai, D4Y2a Kai, D4Y2-S);

One 14-cylinder air-cooled Mitsubishi MK8F Kinsei 62 (Ha-33-52) radial engine of 1,500hp (1,103kW) take-off power, 1,350hp (993kW) at 2,000m and 1,190hp (875kW) at 5,800m, three-blade variable-pitch metal airscrew of 3.000m diameter; fuel tank capacity 1,660l (D4Y3, D4Y3a, D4Y3-S, D4Y4);

One 18-cylinder air-cooled Nakajima NK9B Homare 12 (Ha-45-12) radial engine of 1,825hp (1,342kW) take-off power, 1,670hp (1,228kW) at 2,400m and 1,500hp (1,103kW) at 6,600m, three-blade variable-pitch metal airscrew of 3.0m diameter; fuel tank capacity 1,660l (D4Y5);

Armament:

Two fixed 7.7mm Type 97 machine guns in the fuselage above the engine and one 7.7mm Type 92 flexible machine gun in gunner/radio operator's cockpit (D4Y1 prototypes, D4Y1, D4Y1 Kai, D4Y1-C, D4Y2, D4Y2 Kai, D4Y2-R);

Two fixed 7.7mm Type 97 machine guns in the fuselage above the engine and one 7.9mm Type 1 flexible machine gun in gunner/radio operator's cockpit (D4Y3);

Two fixed 7.7mm Type 97 machine guns in the fuselage above the engine and one 13mm Type 2 flexible machine gun in gunner/radio operator's cockpit (D4Y2a, D4Y2a Kai, D4Y2a-R, D4Y3a, D4Y5).

Two fixed 7.7mm Type 97 machine guns in the fuselage above the engine and one oblique 20mm Type 99 Model 2 cannon in the rear cockpit (D4Y2-S, D4Y3-S).

Two fixed 7.7mm Type 97 machine guns in the fuselage above the engine (D4Y4).

Bomb load:

Standard – 310kg. One 250kg bomb under the fuselage and two 30kg bombs under the wings. (D4Y1, D4Y1 Kai, D4Y2, D4Y2 Kai, D4Y2a).

Maximum – 560kg. One 500kg bomb under the fuselage and two 30kg bombs under the wings, or 750kg – one 250kg bomb under the fuselage and two 250kg bombs under the wings (D4Y3, D4Y3a).

One 800kg bomb (D4Y4). Instead of bombs, the planes could take two additional 380l fuel tanks under the wings for reconnaissance missions.

*Among the aircraft found by the Allies at this airfield was a suicide variant of the D4Y4 Suisei Model 43 dive bomber with rocket boosters to accelerate it in the last stage of the suicide attack (aircraft on the left).*

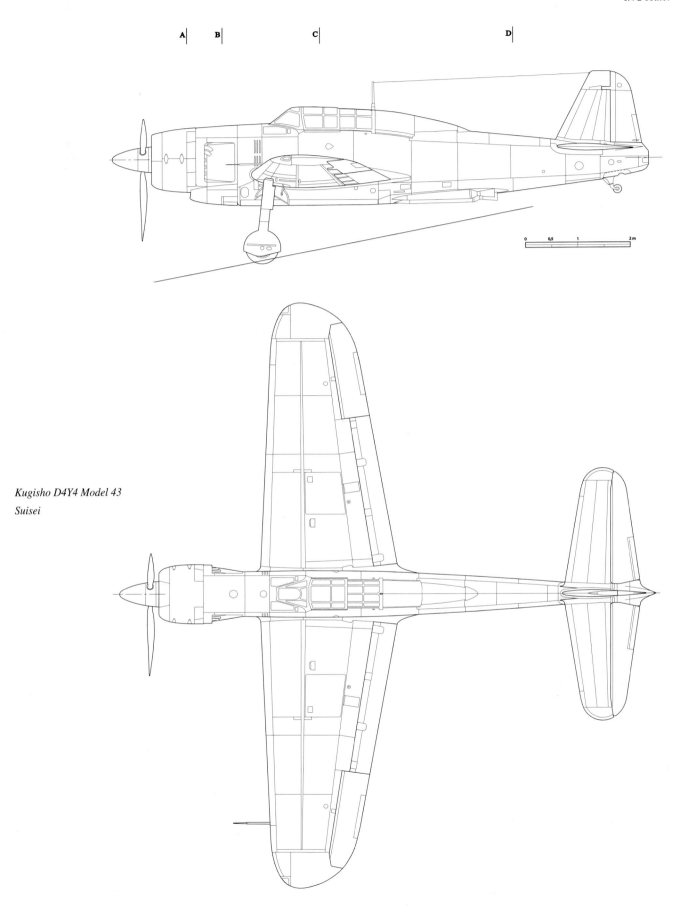

*1/72 scale.*

A  B  C  D

*Kugisho D4Y4 Model 43*
*Suisei*

0  0,5  1  2 m

*1/72 scale.*

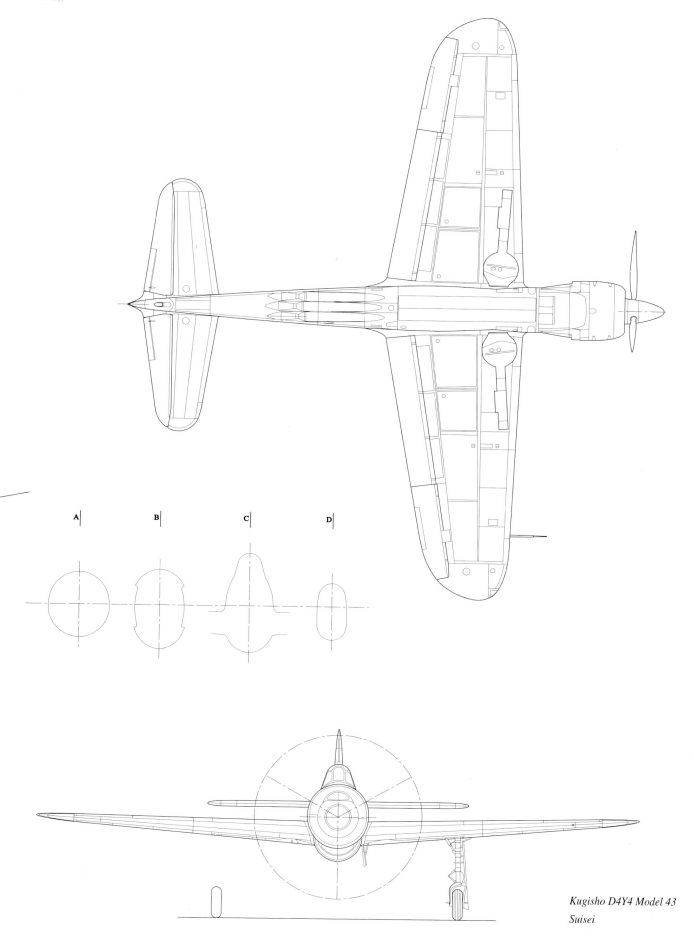

A    B    C    D

*Kugisho D4Y4 Model 43*

*Suisei*

*Rear view of the D4Y4 Suisei Model 43.*

*D4Y4 Suisei Model 43 photographed after the war.*

*Fuselage bays that housed the three rocket boosters.*

| Type | D4Y1 13-Shi | D4Y1-C Model 11 | D4Y2 Model 12 | D4Y2-S | D3Y3 Model 33 | D4Y4 Model 43 | D4Y5 Model 54 |
|---|---|---|---|---|---|---|---|
| Span m | 11.5 | 11.5 | 11.5 | 11.5 | 11.5 | 11.5 | 11.5 |
| Length m | 10.22 | 10.22 | 10.22 | 10.22 | 10.237 | 10.237 | 10.237 |
| Height m | 3.295 | 3.295 | 3.295 | 3.295 | 3.74 | 3.74 | 3.74 |
| Wing area m. | 23.60 | 23.60 | 23.60 | 23.60 | 23.60 | 23.60 | 23.60 |
| Empty weight kg | 2,390 | 2,440 | 2,635 | 2,456 | 2,470 | 2,630 | 2,750 |
| Standard take-off weight kg | 3,650 | 3,650 | 3,835 | 3,750 | 3,850 | 3,960 | 4,200 |
| Max. take-off weight kg | 4,250 | 3,960 | 4,353 | 4,750 | 4,250 | 4,646 | 4,630 |
| Payload kg | 1,260 | 1,210 | 1,200 | 1,294 | 1,380 | 1,325 | 1,450 |
| Wing loading kg/m. | 154.66 | 154.66 | 163.35 | 158.90 | 163.14 | 167.80 | 177.97 |
| Power loading kg/hp | 3.80 | 3.04 | 2.74 | 2.68 | 2.57 | 2.64 | 2.30 |
| Max. speed km/h | 552 | 552 | 579 | 580 | 571 | 551 | 563 |
| At m | 4,750 | 4,750 | 5,250 | 5,250 | 6,000 | 5,600 | 5,900 |
| Cruising speed km/h | 426 | 426 | 426 | 370 | 304 | 333 | 370 |
| At m | 3,000 | 3,000 | 3,000 | 3,000 | 3,000 | 3,000 | 3,000 |
| Landing speed km/h | 140 | 140 | 145 | 145 | 145 | 145 | 145 |
| Climb min | 5'14" | 5'13" | 7'40" | 4'36" | 9'18" | 9'22" | 7'30" |
| To m | 3,000 | 3,000 | 5,000 | 3,000 | 5,000 | 5,000 | 5,000 |
| Ceiling m | 9,900 | 9,900 | 10,720 | 10,700 | 10,500 | 8,500 | 9,000 |
| Normal range km | 2,590 | 2,590 | 2,390 | 1,510 | 1,520 | 1,650 | 1,400 |
| Max. range km | 3,890 | 3,890 | 3,600 | 2,400 | 2,900 | 2,600 | |

Production:

A total of 2,038 D4Y Suisei was built including:

- Dai-Ichi *Kaigun* Kuku Gijyutsusho in Yokosuka:
- 5 - D4Y1 prototypes (1940-1941).

Aichi Tokei Denki Kabushiki Gaisha in Eitoku, Nagoya:

- 660 - D4Y1 (1942 – 04.1944),
- 326 - D4Y2 (04.1944 – 08.1944),
- 536 - D4Y3 (05.1944 – 02.1945),
- 296 - D4Y4 (02.1945 – 08.1945).
- *Dai-Juichi Kaigun Kokusho* in Hiro:
- 215 - D4Y1, D4Y2, D4Y3 (04.1944 – 07.1945)

The D4Y4 Suisei Model 43 special single-seat attack aircraft is in the foreground. Rocket booster nozzles can be seen under the fuselage.

Close up photo of the rocket booster on D4Y4 Suisei.

# Kugisho MXY7 Ohka (Baka)

The Ohka, or 'Cherry Blossom', known to the Allies as 'Baka' ('fool'), was one of the few aircraft designed from the very beginning as a suicide attacker which was actually used in anger. The rocket-powered single seater was extremely innovative, but did not prove to be the decisive weapon hoped for.

Suicide unit operations were initially regarded as a makeshift solution, but soon they became established practice. As the Japanese aircraft industry could not produce sufficient numbers of modern aircraft matching their American counterparts, the Kamikaze came to be increasingly relied upon. Many ideas were put forward for aeroplane designs that were simple in production, cheap, and effective for Kamikaze missions. One of the ideas put forward was presented by Lieutenant Mitsuo Ohta, a transport pilot from the 405th *Kokutai*. His concept was for a rocket-powered suicide aeroplane, which could be carried into action by a specially converted Mitsubishi G4M twin-engined bomber.

In mid-1944 Japan was planning unmanned flying bombs similar to those being used with some success by Germany. Captain Tadanao Mitsugi of the *Dai-Ichi Kaigun Koku Gijyutsusho* (Kugisho) received an order to develop a remote guidance system for flying bombs, similar to the German V-1, for which incomplete design documentation was delivered to Japan by submarine. However, when Lieutenant Ohta presented his idea for a rocket-powered, piloted suicide airplane to his superiors, who approved it, the unmanned flying bomb project was circumvented by 'solving' the problems inherent in the remote guidance such weapons - by using pilots instead!

Lieutenant Ohta had worked on the project since 1943, and it was subjected to detailed verification by Captain Tadanao Mitsugi. Eventually the idea was approved, and Lieutenant Ohta received permission to develop the idea. The preliminary project was given the code name Maru-dai, or 'Project O', from the first letter of its designer's name. Lieutenant Ohta, together with workers of the Aircraft Institute at the Imperial University in Tokyo, developed a preliminary design that was presented for approval to the *Kaigun Koku Hombu* in August 1944. This was received positively and the project was immediately earmarked for production. This task was entrusted to Kugisho, and control over the entire programme was given to Captain Tadanao Mitsugi, with project engineers Masao Yamana and Rokuro Hattori. The aeroplane under development received the designation 'Experimental Navy Attack Aeroplane Ohka' (MXY7) – Cherry Blossom.

The Ohka was to be an anti-invasion suicide aeroplane, principally for the defence of the home islands. It was intended to be brought to the vicinity of the target by a carrier aeroplane and independently controlled after release by the pilot. Initially it was planned to use a liquid fuel rocket engine that would give it a long range, but the Japanese did not have an engine of that type of their own design and were reliant on German experience. However, the two-component German fuel posed a serious technical problem for the Japanese chemical industry, which was considered unable to maintain regular deliveries of liquid fuel. The design team therefore decided use a set of three solid fuel rocket engines fitted in the rear section of the aircraft. This decision proved very important for the further fate of the MXY7 as the short operational range of the Ohka was responsible for limiting its success on operations.

The Japanese, forced by the deteriorating situation at the front lines, worked at an incredible rate. Before production documentation was complete and the prototype was built, the *Kaigun Koku Hombu* had already

*The cramped cockpit of the Ohka Model 11 was equipped with only the basic instruments on the panel. Photo of the a preserved aircraft.*

A. Lochte.

approved the new aeroplane for series production under the designation 'Navy Special Attack Aeroplane Ohka Model 11'. During development it was intended that aeroplane would have a very simple design, suitable for mass production by unskilled workers.

The Ohka Model 11 was a cantilever low-wing monoplane with twin vertical tails. It was powered by a cluster of three Type 4-1 Model 20 (4FH120) solid fuel rocket engines with a total thrust of approximately 800kg, maintained for 8-10 seconds of operation. The Ohka Model 11 consisted of fuselage, wings, tail including the power-plant housing, and warhead with its housing. The three-piece fuselage was of all metal construction, with duralumin frames and longerons. The skin was formed of duralumin panels fastened with countersunk rivets. Similar skin panels formed the housing of the propulsion unit and of the explosive charge. The wings and tail surfaces were wooden: the two-spar wings were plywood covered and the ailerons were also of wooden construction, fitted with counterweights. The tail consisted of a tailplane and elevator fitted with mass balances, and two fins and rudders, also with mass balances. The warhead housed a 1,200kg explosive charge (TNT), attached by bolts to a special mount. It was fitted with four inertial fuses and one contact fuse at the nose. Fuses were made safe for the flight. The nose fuse was armed upon release from the mother aircraft, while four highly sensitive 'base' fuses (intended as a failsafe if the impact fuse did not function) were unlocked by the pilot after the Ohka's glide angle had been set.

The cockpit was armoured with 6mm or 8mm steel panels that protected the pilot from the rear. Only essential instruments were fitted, including airspeed indicator, altimeter and compass. (Prototypes also had a turn-and-bank indicator, which was deleted on production models). The control panel also included an electric five-position engine start-up switch, to control the three rocket engines in the rear fuselage and two optional auxiliary boosters under the wings. The aeroplane was guided towards its target using a simple optical sight fitted forward of the windscreen.

The Ohka Model 11 could be carried by a specially-converted Mitsubishi G4M2e Model 24J 'Betty' bomber. The Ohka was carried partially recessed in the 'Betty's' bomb bay by an attachment located on top of the fuselage in front of the Ohka's cockpit. The pilot of the Ohka usually travelled

*The Ohka Model 11 suicide aircraft (construction no. 1022) found in Okinawa after it was captured by allied forces, disarmed, with partly removed skin panels. The housing of the explosive charge displayed the code number and the stylised chrysanthemum motif, the symbol of suicide units.*

inside the carrier aeroplane, and only boarded the Ohka via the bomb bay when in the vicinity of the target. However, if the flight to the target was of relatively short distance, the pilot would board his machine before it was attached to the carrier. The two aircraft were connected by an intercom system and oxygen pipe. As the suicide aircraft could be released at an altitude of over 8,000m, a small oxygen cylinder was provided to provide oxygen for the independent section of the flight. The Ohka Model 11 was taken to the carrier aeroplane on a tricycle trolley, which could lift the Ohka 0.45m high to facilitate fitting it in the bomb bay.

In September 1944, the *Kaigun Koku Hombu* decided that the 721st *Kokutai* would be the first unit to transport Ohka Model 11 aircraft into attack. The unit was commanded by Captain Motoharu Okamura, a dedicated proponent of the suicide attack idea. Initially the unit was based at Konoike, and then, after re-organisation it moved to Kanoya. Meanwhile, work on the Ohka continued. Even before the production documentation was completed, the construction of ten prototypes commenced. They were completed in September 1944, after just a few weeks of construction. The first unpowered flight trials of the prototype MXY7 Ohka commenced on 23 October 1944 at Sagami, and the first powered flight took place a month later from Kashima aerodrome. The flight trials were successful, and during tests in January 1945, the MXY7 Ohka achieved a maximum speed of 648km/h in level flight at an altitude of 3,500m, and in an unpowered dive it reached 462km/h.

Production of the Ohka Model 11 was technically very simple. It was split between several subcontractors, with the fuselage built by Kanagawa K.K., where the propulsion unit and warhead were fitted, while the wings and tail were built by Fuji Hikoki K.K. and the cast parts were manufactured in Osaka and near Hiroshima. Other parts and assemblies were supplied from the

*The Kugisho Ohka Model 11 (code no. 10) found by American occupation troops in bush near the naval air arm base at Kadena (Yontan) in Okinawa.*

*Ohka K-1 trainer gliders in a hangar occupied by allied forces. Water ballast was carried in the forward fuselage and aft of the cockpit. Note the characteristic painting scheme of training aircraft of the naval aviation. Upper surfaces and sides were orange, lower surfaces were light grey. The wavy colour division line can be seen on the fuselage. Hinomaru was only applied on sides of the fuselage.*

*Ohka Model 11 (code no. I-13) undergoing measurements. In the background is Ohka Model 11 (code no. 18), later also subjected to detailed technical inspection.*

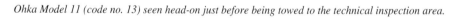

*Ohka Model 11 (code no. 13) seen head-on just before being towed to the technical inspection area.*

*Above*: Ohka Model 11 s/n 1020 on Okinawa.
*via A. Lochte.*
*Left*: Souvenir photo of 1CPO Heiji Ueda in the cockpit of an Ohka Model 11 from the 721st Kokutai at Kanoya airfield in April 1945. The pilot carried out his suicide attack on 16 April 1945 against allied ships assembled south-east of Kyushu.

Ohka Model 11 (code no. I-18) under camouflage netting, captured in Okinawa, photographed during technical inspection.

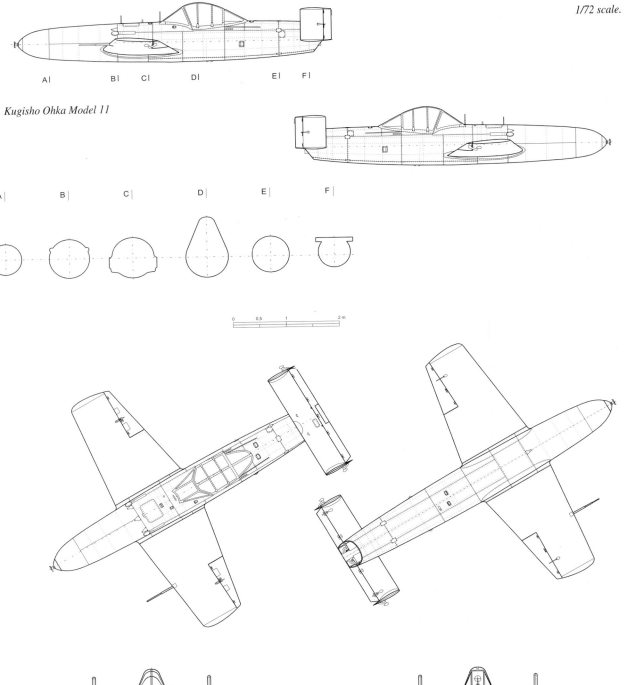

*1/72 scale.*

*Kugisho Ohka Model 11*

A|      B| C|    D|      E| F|

A|       B|       C|       D|       E|       F|

0    0,5    1  &nbs  2 m

*Ohka Model 11 on its transport trolley.*

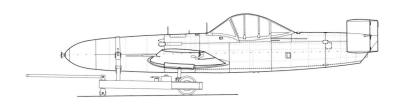

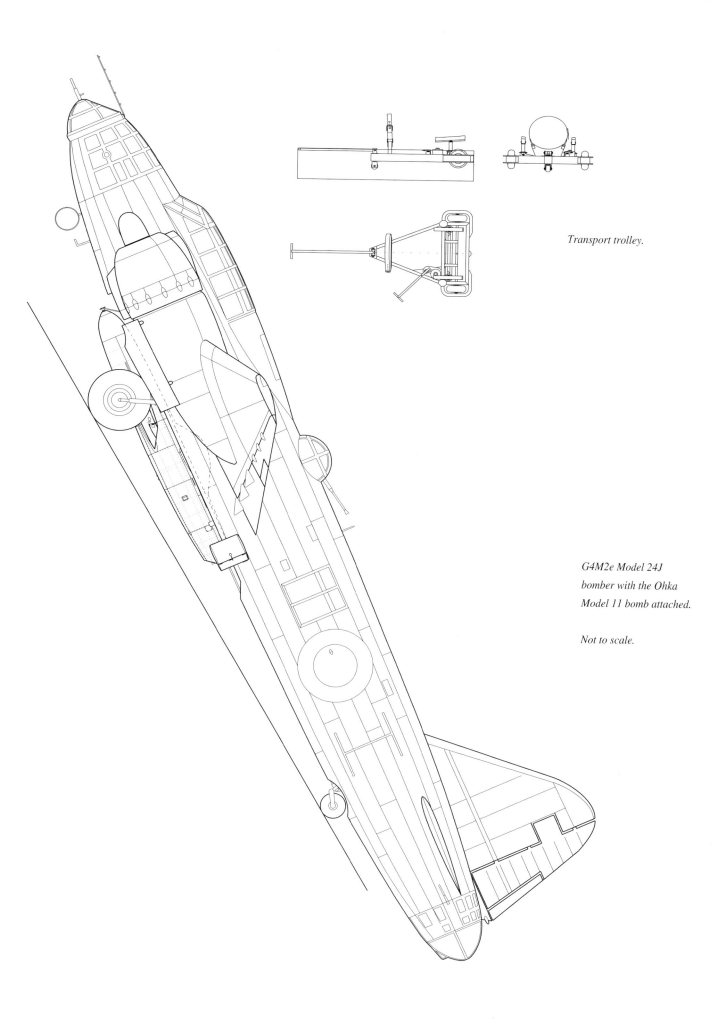

*Transport trolley.*

*G4M2e Model 24J
bomber with the Ohka
Model 11 bomb attached.*

*Not to scale.*

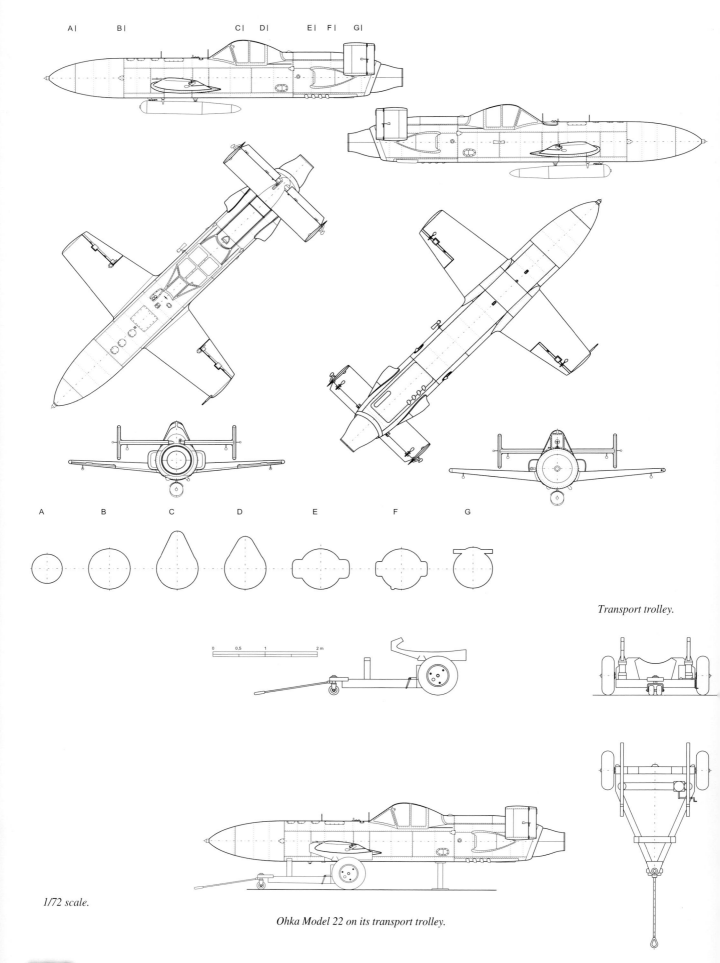

A  B  C  D  E  F  G

Transport trolley.

0   0,5   1   2 m

1/72 scale.

*Ohka Model 22 on its transport trolley.*

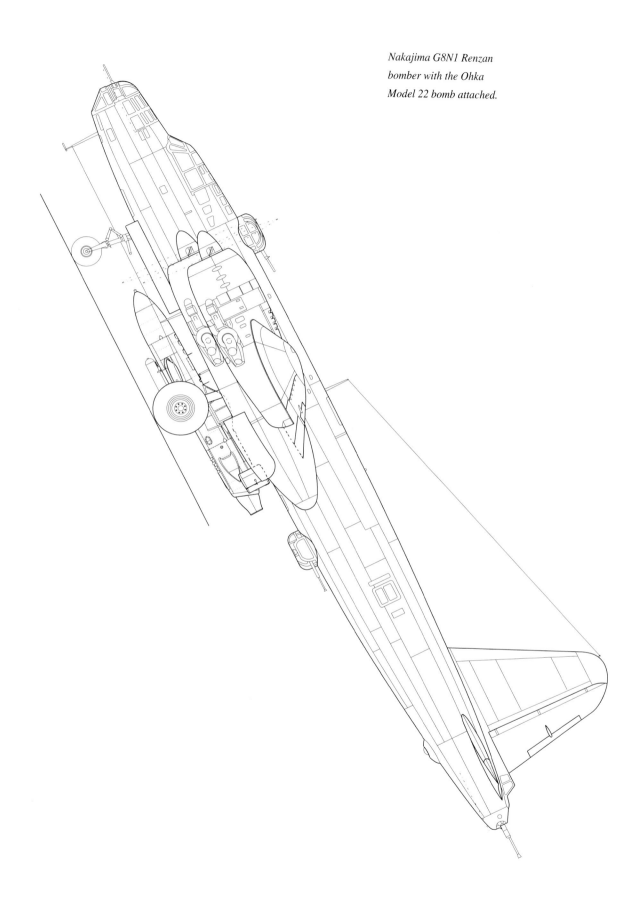

Nakajima G8N1 Renzan
bomber with the Ohka
Model 22 bomb attached.

1/100 scale.

Tokyo area. The final assembly and trials were carried out at Kugisho in Yokosuka, and from there the partly disassembled aircraft were shipped in crates to the front line, to individual suicide units. The first units to receive the Ohka Model 11 aircraft were named *Jinrai Butai* (Divine Thunder).

Unfortunately, fifty Ohka Model 11 aircraft were lost before the type ever went into action. On 29 November 1944, the submarine USS *Archerfish* sank the largest aircraft carrier of WW2, the Shinano, which was carrying the Ohka aircraft. They were to be delivered to the Philippines, to commence operations against the invasion. The failure of the Shinano voyage meant that the first Ohka Model 11 operations were carried out from the Japanese islands instead of in the Philippines. While repelling the Allied invasion of Okinawa, on 21 March 1945 eighteen 'Betty' bombers took off, including sixteen with Ohka Model 11 aircraft attached. The formation was escorted by 30 fighters. The task of the suicide pilots was to eliminate three American aircraft carriers detected south of Kyushu. However, fifty miles from the American ships, the Japanese formation was intercepted by around fifty American fighters which had been alerted to their approach and guided by radar. In a short combat the F6F Hellcats shot down all the heavily-laden Japanese bombers, giving them no chance to get close to the aircraft carriers or to release their suicide aircraft.

Another attack with Ohka Model 11 aircraft was prepared for 1 April. This time the operation was more modest, comprising three G4M2e 'Betty' bombers carrying Ohka Model 11s. They took off from Kanoya, and carried out individual rather than group attacks, leading to the first, albeit uncertain, successes. The battleship USS *West Virginia* and the transport ship Alpin were damaged, but only one carrier aeroplane returned to base. Ohka Model 11s were used again on 12 April, during the operation *Kikusui* 2. This was a major mission that involved about ninety suicide aircraft, including nine Ohka Model 11s. That day, the Japanese claimed to have sunk seven enemy units, including three battleships, one of which was apparently sunk by the Ohka Model 11 flown by Lieutenant Saburo Doi. The crew of the carrier aeroplane reported upon return that Lieutenant Doi had released the suicide aircraft at an altitude of 6,000m, 18km from the target. He performed a textbook attack on the target that ended in a large explosion and a 500m high column of water. Documents proved after the war that Lieutenant Doi had actually sunk the destroyer USS *Mannert L. Abele*, rather than a battleship as claimed by the Japanese. Seven more Ohka Model 11s were used on 14 April, but this time without effect. Attacks using Ohka Model 11 aircraft continued until June 1945, with only modest results.

The Allies thus first encountered Ohka aircraft during the fighting around Okinawa. Intelligence had reported a new aircraft of unknown role, but they had been considered to be training aircraft, and therefore avoided scrutiny. Once the true role of the Ohka Model 11 was realised, they were given the unofficial name of Baka (Japanese for 'fool' or 'madman'). The Japanese tactic was to release the suicide aeroplane from the carrier some 35km away from the area of attack, at a speed of around 280-325km/h and at an altitude of 6,000 - 8,250m. After release, the suicide aeroplane glided

*One of six Ohkas found on Okinawa.*

*via. A. Lochte.*

*Last preparations for the take-off of a Mitsubishi G4M2e Model 24J carrier-aircraft with an Ohka Model 11 suicide aircraft attached under the fuselage, at Konoike airfield. The crew was led by Lt. Commander Nonaka of the 721st Kokutai. The photo was probably taken on 21 March 1945.*

at a speed of some 370km/h towards the target of choice at the optimum glide angle, usually at 5 degrees for around 35 seconds. In the last phase of the glide the suicide pilot could start his rocket engines to increase the speed to 860km/h at 5km from the target. In the final stages the pilot pushed the aircraft into a steep, 50 degree dive. The diving speed rose to 995km/h and when that speed was reached the pilot aimed directly for the target he had chosen. This flight technique was determined to be the most effective method with the highest probability of hitting the target.

Despite these carefully-researched tactics, the Ohka Model 11 was a failure in practice. The fighters that defended American ships expanded their patrol zone, preventing the Japanese carrier aeroplanes from reaching the point of release. Launching too early meant that the Ohkas failed to reach the area of attack, and getting closer to the assigned target at high altitude, only achieved by breaking through the radar-guided American fighter screen, was virtually impossible. Initial successes could be attributed to the element of surprise and the relatively small size of the suicide aeroplane. In addition to these problems, more and more aircraft suffered various failures in flight, particularly during the dive. In that phase of the flight, controlling the aeroplane and hitting the rapidly manoeuvring enemy ships was very difficult, so in the hands of an inexperienced suicide pilot the aeroplane simply crashed into the sea.

Realising the shortcomings of the Ohka Model 11, on 11 March 1945 the *Kaigun Koku Hombu* terminated its production. Until that time 155 Ohka Model 11 aircraft had been built by the Kugisho plant at Yokosuka, and 600 machines by *Dai-Ichi Kaigun Kokusho* at Kasumigaura. During the fighting at Okinawa, some 300 Ohka Model 11s were delivered to the island. After American troops captured Japanese underground hangars, three fully serviceable aircraft and two slightly damaged ones were seized, which enabled American technical intelligence to become acquainted with the new, previously ultra-secret, Japanese weapon.

*One of three MXY7 K-2 Wakazakura two-seat trainer gliders built, together with a Mitsubishi Ki-67 Hiryū aircraft aboard the aircraft carrier USS* Core *en route to the USA. The glider was covered with a protective coating.*

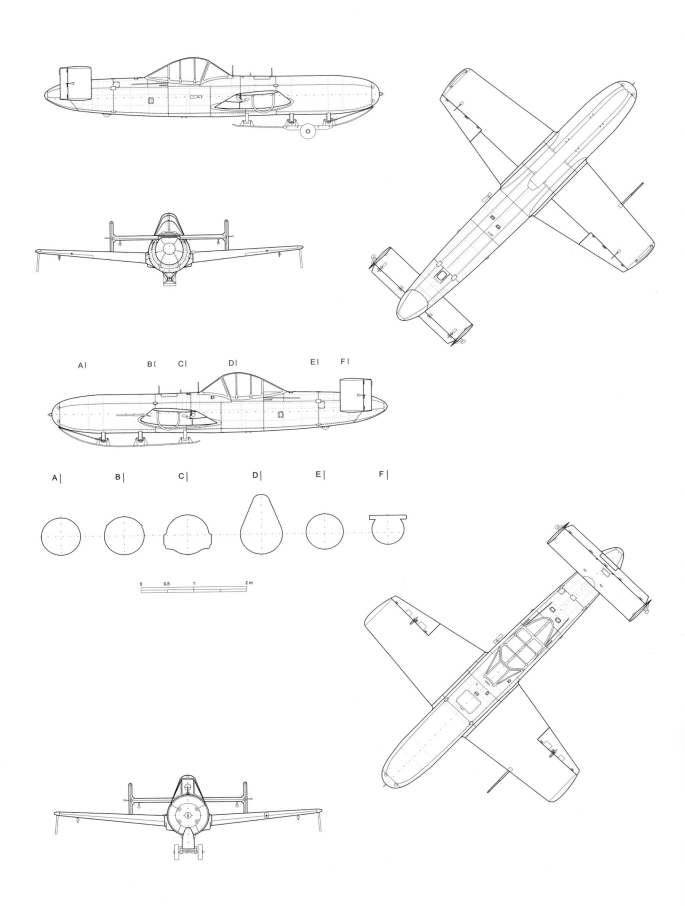

A|     B| C|     D|     E| F|

A|     B|     C|     D|     E|     F|

0    0,5    1       2 m

*Kugisho Ohka K-1*            *1/72 scale.*

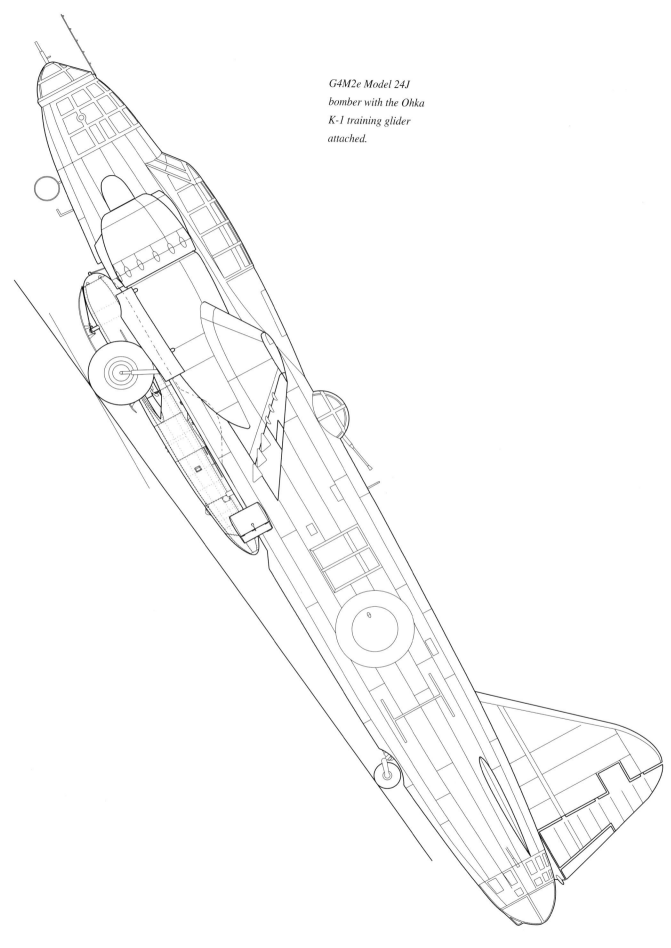

*G4M2e Model 24J
bomber with the Ohka
K-1 training glider
attached.*

*Not to scale.*

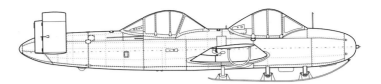

*Kugisho Ohka K-2*

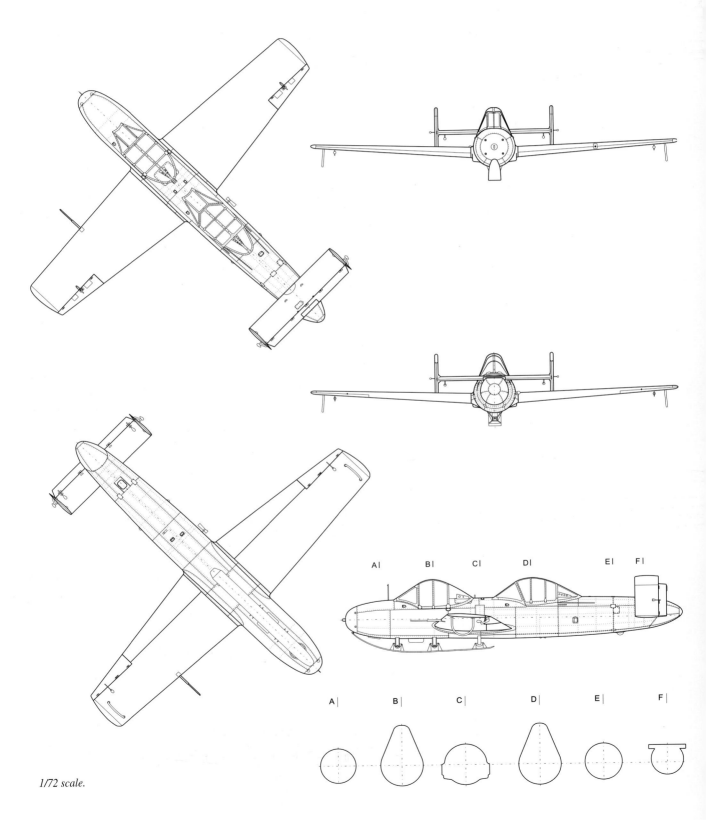

*1/72 scale.*

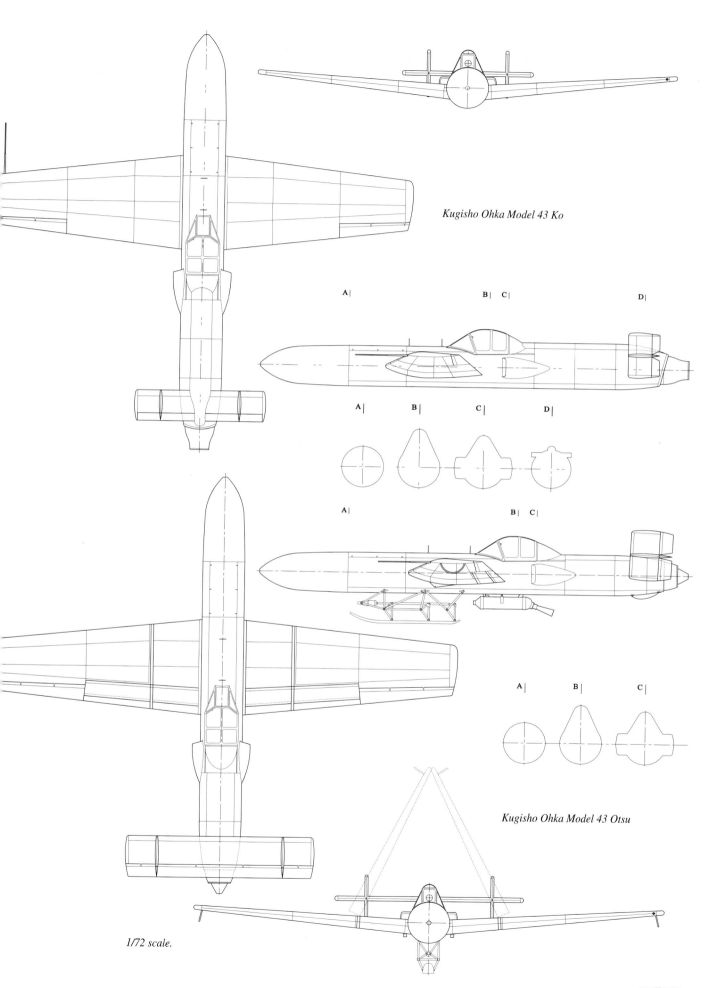

*Kugisho Ohka Model 43 Ko*

A|     B| C|     D|

A|  B|   C|   D|

A|     B| C|

A|    B|    C|

*Kugisho Ohka Model 43 Otsu*

*1/72 scale.*

163

*Kugisho Ohka Model 33*

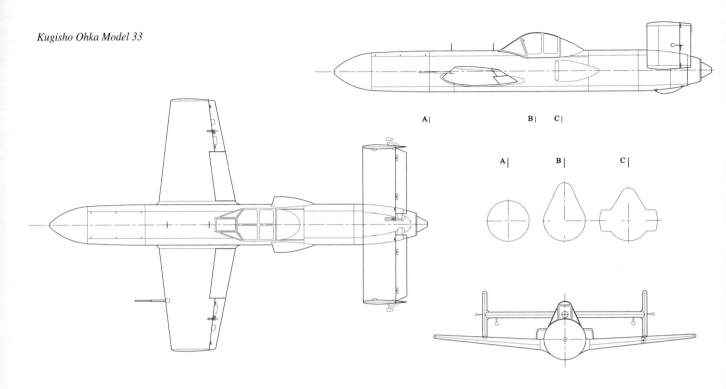

A|  B|  C|

A|  B|  C|

*1/72 scale.*

*Kugisho Ohka Model 53 wireless*
*quided missile (fantasy, a post-war*
*created)*

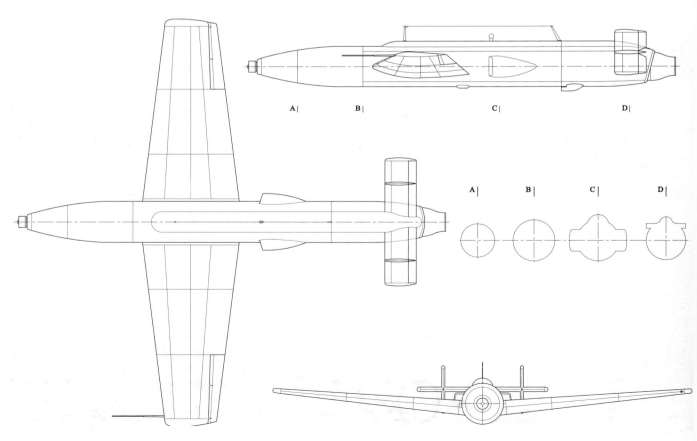

A|  B|  C|  D|

A|  B|  C|  D|

Besides the basic combat version of the Ohka Model 11, the Kugisho plant at Yokosuka manufactured training gliders, designated Ohka K-1. These carried water ballast in place of the warhead and propulsion units. Otherwise construction was almost identical to the powered version. The wings were fitted with flaps and wing-tip skids, and the outlet of the rocket engines was faired over with a metal panel. After take-off, the Ohka K-1 glider was able to land safely on a special under-fuselage shock-absorbing skid. Production of the gliders commenced in October 1944: in the first month the subcontractor built eighteen pairs of wings and the same number of tail sets, and by March 1945, 45 Ohka K-1 gliders had been built. These gliders were used for training prospective suicide pilots who had little experience in flying and navigation. After release from the carrier aeroplane, the pilot performed a flying training programme. Having completed this programme, the glider jettisoned its water ballast and landed on its skid at a speed of 152km/h. In practice, the water ballast proved difficult to jettison and some versions had water tankage removed.

Later, it was planned to fit one Type 4 1-Go Model 30 (4FH130) rocket engine, with a 9-second thrust of 400kG, designed to assist the pilot to practice his skills during rapid acceleration. The project, designated Wakazakura K-1 Kai (Young Cherry), was not put into practice.

In addition to the single-seat training version, three modified two-seater training gliders were built under the designation MXY7 K-2. The MXY7 K-2 glider featured two separate cockpits for the pupil and the instructor. The design was based on the fuselage of the Ohka Model 11 combat version, but an additional cockpit was fitted in place of the warhead. The wing span was also increased, and the wings fitted with flaps and skids. After the war, one of the captured MXY7 K-2 gliders was brought to the USA on the carrier USS *Core*.

Since the combat career of the Ohka Model 11 was so unsuccessful, designers and officers from the *Kaigun Koku Hombu* started to look for a successor. Their chief requirement was for a suicide aeroplane that could be launched further from the target to reduce the losses of carrier aeroplanes and the number of suicide aircraft destroyed before they could be launched. As solid fuel rocket engines burned too briefly, these were discarded. The jet engine concept was therefore revived. As the suicide aeroplane did not require too much power, a low-power Campini-flow Tsu-11 jet engine was selected. This, with a 110hp Hitachi GK4A Hatsukaze 11 in-line engine driving the compressor, produced a thrust of about 200kg. With this powerplant the aircraft was designated Ohka Model

*Kugisho Ohka K-2, trainer version.*

via A. Lochte

*Ohka K-1 trainer photo-graphed at Wright Field, Dayton, Ohio, shortly after the war.*

*via A. Lochte.*

22. In addition to the new propulsion unit, the new aeroplane had a shorter wing span but a longer fuselage. The warhead of the Ohka Model 22 was reduced to 600kg due to the shorter wing span. However, the longer range compensated for this. The reduction in wing span of the Ohka Model 22 was a result of a change in the carrier aeroplane, now the Kugisho P1Y Ginga ('Frances') in the specially-prepared P1Y1 Model 13 version which had an increased wing span.

The Kugisho plant at Yokosuka, together with the Aichi and Fuji companies, managed to build only 35 complete Ohka Model 22 aircraft and fifteen airframes by the end of hostilities. By the end of the war Aichi, also included in the Ohka production programme, had failed to set up an assembly line due to frequent bomber raids. Parts used to build production Ohka Model 22s were made in underground factories belonging to *Dai-Ichi Kaigun Kokusho* at Kasumigaura.

The Ohka Model 22, similar to the Ohka Model 11, was a cantilever low-wing monoplane with twin tails, of mixed construction. The wings and the tail were of wooden construction and the fuselage was monocoque, all-metal, divided into three sections, similar to the Ohka Model 11 (nose, centre, and tail). The nose section housed the 600kg explosive charge, the centre section included the cockpit, fitted with instruments similar to those in the Ohka Model 11, and the tail section housed the propulsion unit of a Hatsukaze 11 piston engine and the Tsu-11 jet, the nozzle of which extended some distance out of the fuselage. Air intakes were located on the sides of the fuselage, and the single exhaust of the piston engine protruded under the fuselage.

In February 1945, an Ohka Model 22 made a single test flight with two Type 4-1 Model 10 auxiliary rocket engines under the fuselage. The flight was not successful, as during the climb under high acceleration the pilot lost consciousness, and after the engine stopped working the aeroplane entered a dive and crashed. It took until 12 August 1945 to carry out the second test flight with another Ohka Model 22. This time, the jet engine was used as power plant. The moment the aeroplane was released, the pilot started the under-wing auxiliary rocket engines in error, and the Ohka Model 22 hit the fuselage of the P1Y1 Model 13 Ginga carrier aeroplane. In the resulting collision the Ohka Model 22 lost its tail, entered a spin and crashed, killing the pilot. Three days later, upon announcement of the armistice, trials of the Ohka Model 22 were terminated. Mass production of the aircraft at a rate of 200 machines per month had been planned.

Originally, it was planned that the Ohka Model 22 would be released as far as 130km from the target, thus significantly reducing the risk of interception and loss of the carrier aeroplane. It was also believed that the cruising speed in a glide would be 427km/h. This was not high when compared with the speeds of Allied fighters, a problem barely mitigated by the planned auxiliary rocket boosters.

American technical intelligence services reported that several two-seater training gliders based on the Ohka Model 22, but without warheads were built, similar to the earlier variant, but there is no Japanese evidence that such a version existed. No drawings or photos of this version are known.

Based on the above versions of the Ohka, Nakajima developed and built a prototype which had its wings covered with thin steel plates to reduce weight. The company also developed a new version of the aeroplane, designated Ohka Model 21, which combined the airframe of the Ohka Model 22 with the power plant of the Ohka Model 11.

Despite the operational failures, designers did not stop work on the concept. A new Ohka Model 33 was developed from the Ohka Model 22, to be powered by the Ne-20 turbojet engine with a thrust of 475kg. The warhead was to be increased to 800kg, and the carrier aeroplane would be the Nakajima G8N1 Renzan Model 11 four-engined bomber, which was intended to carry two, or even three Ohka Model 33s. However, due to delays in the production programme of the new heavy bomber, the *Kaigun Koku Hombu* gave up further development of the Ohka Model 33.

A similar fate befell the next version, designated the Ohka Model 43 Ko, which had a slightly redesigned fuselage. The aeroplane was going to be launched from *Toku-gata* (I-400) class submarines. The Ohka Model 43 Ko would take off from a catapult on the ship. The wings could be folded for storage, and the submarine would allow the suicide pilot to evade patrolling American fighters. It was planned that the Ohka Model 43 Ko would be powered by the Ne-20 turbojet engine.

In this case, too, no prototype was built, as most suitable submarines were at the time being converted to carry Kaiten manned torpedoes.

The Ohka Model 43 Otsu was another incomplete project. This time, in spite of external similarity with the preceding design, the role of the aeroplane was altered. This was going to be a special attack aeroplane catapulted from 97-metre launchers located in coastal caves. This would be a 'weapon of last resort', protecting mainland Japan. The aircraft was designed so that after the aircraft took off and reached flying speed with the aid of under-fuselage rocket engines, the pilot could jettison the wing tips in order to increase speed further.

The plan was to use the Ne-20 turbojet engine and two additional Type 4-1 Model 10 rocket engines to augment the catapult. The designers believed that, with batteries of catapults, it would be possible to launch waves of up to forty aircraft every five minutes. Work on the project commenced in April 1945, but had not progressed to the equipment stage by the end of hostilities. Only a full-scale wooden mock-up of the Ohka Model 43 Otsu was built. Trials with the launcher were carried out at Takeyama, and a catapult was also fitted on Mount Hiei near Kyoto. In July 1945, the 725th *Kokutai* was formed at Shiga, and this was going to be equipped with Ohka Model 43 Otsu aircraft.

A further variant based on the Ohka Model 43 Otsu airframe, was mooted, and designated the Ohka Model 43 Hei. This had increased wing span but jettisonable wingtips, as with the Ohka

*3/4 view showing rocket motors.*

*Rear view.*

*Side view.*

*Armor plate located behind pilot's head.*

*Tail assembly removed showing installation of rocket motors.*

*Side view of rocket units with tail removed.*

*Ground transport carriage.*

*Wing of exploded plane. All photos Stratus coll.*

Model 43 Otsu, to increase speed in the final attack. The wings could be folded for storage in underground bases and could take off from a railway trolley fitted with two auxiliary rocket boosters for acceleration to flying speed. This variant was intended to equip ground forces.

The Japanese planned to build a variant of the Ohka Model 43 Otsu, for mass training of pilots. This was a trainer with two cockpits, powered by a single Type 4-1 Model 20 rocket engine that would be able to operate for 8-10 seconds. The project received the designation Ohka Model 43 Otsu Kai.

The last version of the Ohka family was the Ohka Model 53, a development of the Ohka Model 33. This variant was to be towed to an appropriate altitude, and then released near the target. The power plant assigned was the Ne-20 jet, and the tug would be a Kugisho P1Y Ginga twin-engined bomber or Nakajima G8N Renzan. Design was entrusted to *Aichi Kokuki Kabushiki Gaisha* at Ichigisho, and development was led by the chief engineer, Norio Ozaki. Work was halted by the end of the war.

Some German sources have claimed that the Ohka Model 53 was a pilotless radio-controlled missile, and drawings supposedly back this up. However, there is no Japanese source confirming these claims, and this seems to be a post-war created fantasy. Other source mentions the Ohka Model 50 (not 53!) fitted with an undercarriage for conventional take-off but again, no Japanese source confirms this.

The originator of the Ohka suicide aeroplane idea, Sub-Lieutenant Mitsuo Ohta, unlike many of his colleagues, did not die at the controls of a Kamikaze aeroplane; he survived the war and lived as a civilian under a different name. Many years later he was located by BBC reporters, who interviewed him. Many Ohka aircraft survive to date, and are on display in various museums of the world, such as the Fleet Air Arm Museum in England and the Yasukuni Shrine Yūshūkan war museum in Japan.

**Specifications:**

Description: special attack (suicide) aeroplane Ohka Model 11, Ohka Model 21, Ohka Model 22, Ohka Model 33, or trainer glider Ohka K-1, K-1 Kai Wakazakura, MXY7 K-2, or catapulted special attack aeroplane Ohka Model 43 Ko, Ohka Model 43 Otsu, Ohka Model 43 Hei, or towed missile Ohka Model 53. All cantilever mid-wing monoplanes of mixed construction.

Crew: suicide pilot (Ohka Model 11, Ohka Model 21, Ohka Model 22, Ohka Model 33, Ohka Model 43 Ko, Ohka Model 43 Hei), or instructor and pupil (Ohka K-1, Wakazakura K-1 Kai, MXY7 K-2).

Power plant: Set of three Type 4-1-Go Model 20 (4FH120) solid fuel rocket engines with a total thrust of 800kG, and two optional auxiliary Type 4-1 Model 10 (4FH110) solid fuel rocket engines under wings with a total thrust of 540 kG (Ohka Model 11, Ohka Model 21).

One Type 4-1-Go Model 30 (4FH130) solid fuel rocket engine with a thrust of 400kG (Wakazakura K-1 Kai).

One Tsu-11 jet engine with a thrust of 200kG and one 110hp Hitachi GK4A Hatsukaze 11 (Ha-11-11) 4-cylinder air cooled in-line engine driving the compressor. Fuel tank capacity 290l (Ohka Model 22).

One Ne-20 turbojet engine with a thrust of 475kG. Fuel tank capacity 250l (Ohka Model 33, Ohka Model 43 Ko, Ohka Model 53).

One Ne-20 turbojet engine with a thrust of 475kG and two additional Type 4-1 Model 20 rocket engines under the fuselage with a total thrust of 540kG. Fuel tank capacity 400l (Ohka Model 43 Otsu, Ohka Model 43 Hei).

Defensive armament: none.

Warhead: 1,200kg (Ohka Model 11);

800kg (Ohka Model 33, Ohka Model 43 Ko);

600kg (Ohka Model 21, Ohka Model 22, Ohka Model 53).

*Ground transport carriage.*

*Fuselage and warhead of damaged Ohka.*

*One of the solid fuel rockets.*

*Rear view of Ohka.*

*Fuselage/warhead joint.*

*General view of warhead and fuselage.*

*Front view of warhead*

*Side view of warhead. All photos Stratus coll.*

| Type: | Ohka Model 11 | Ohka Model 21 | Ohka Model 22 | Ohka Model 33 | Ohka Model 43 Ko | Ohka Model 43 Otsu | Ohka K-1 | Wakazakura K-1 Kai | MXY7 K-2 | Ohka Model 53 |
|---|---|---|---|---|---|---|---|---|---|---|
| Wing span m | 5.12 | 4.12 | 4.12 | 5.0 | 8.0 | 8.972 | 5.12 | 5.12 | 7.0 | 8.0 |
| Length m | 6.066 | 6.88 | 6.88 | 7.2 | 8.15 | 8.164 | 6.434 | 6.066 | 6.434 | 8.16 |
| Height m | 1.15 | 1.16 | 1.16 | 1.16 | 1.15 | 1.15 | 1.15 | 1.15 | 1.15 | 1.13 |
| Wing area m² | 6.0 | 4.0 | 4.0 | 6.0 | | 13.0 | 6.0 | 6.0 | | |
| Empty weight kg | 1,440 | 1,535 | 1,545 | | | 1,150 | 730 | | 644 | |
| Take-off weight kg | 2,140 | 2,450 | 2,510 | 2,300 | 2,520 | 2,270 | 880 | | 810 | |
| Useful load kg | 700 | 915 | 965 | | | 1,120 | 150 | | 166 | |
| Wing loading kg/m² | 356.6 | 612.5 | 627.5 | 383.3 | | 174.6 | 146.6 | | | |
| Power loading kg/KG | 2.67 | 3.06 | 12.55 | 4.84 | 5.30 | 4.78 | - | | - | |
| Maximum speed km/h | 648 | 643 | 514 | 642 | 643 | 569 | | | | |
| at an altitude of m | 4,000 | 4,000 | 4,000 | 4,000 | 4,000 | 4,000 | | | | |
| Cruising speed km/h | 462 | 443 | 427 | | | | 200 | | | |
| at an altitude of m | 3,500 | 4,000 | 4,000 | | | | | | | |
| Diving speed km/h | 1,020 | | | | | | | | | |
| Landing speed km/h | - | - | - | - | - | - | 152 | | 130 | - |
| Ceiling m | 8,250 | 8,500 | 8,500 | | | | | | | |
| Normal range km | 37 | 112 | 130 | 278 | 200 | 278 | | | | |

Production:
A total of 855 Ohka aircraft and gliders were built:
*Dai-Ichi Kaigun Koku Gijyutsusho* at Yokosuka:
- 155 - Ohka Model 11
- 50 - Ohka Model 22
- 45 - Ohka K-1
- 3 - MXY7 K-2

*Dai-Ichi Kaigun Kokusho* at Kasumigaura:
- 600 - Ohka Model 11
- Nakajima Hikoki Kabushiki Gaisha:
- Ohka Model 11 (with steel wing skin)
- 1 – Ohka Model 21

*Ohka Model 11 s/n 1026 on Okinawa after the war. US National Archives via A. Lochte.*

*side view of rudder*

*head-on view of tail assembly*

*bottom view of horizontal stabilizer*

*bottom plan view of wing*

*top view of horizontal stabilizer with vertical stabilizer showing on each end*

*rear view of warhead showing attaching lugs two "all-ways" fuses and two impact fuses*

*All photos Stratus coll.*

**173**

# Kokukyoku Jinryu

The Jinryu ('Divine Dragon') suicide glider was one of the most mysterious Japanese aircraft of the Pacific war. It was shrouded in deep secrecy, and the little information that leaked out was sometimes very far from accurate. Several significant facts about the design were only revealed by Juichi Narabayashi, a military test pilot, in his memoirs published some twenty years after the war. Supplementary information was provided sixty years later by Koutaro Ohmura, a former member of 15-ki *Kaigun Hiko Senshu Yobi Gakusei* (the 15th Midshipman Team of Naval Aviation Reserve) from Tsuchiura *Kaigun Kokutai*. Close to the war's end he was among thousands of students undergoing flying training on Wakakusa and Hikari gliders.

In March 1944 the *Kokukyoku Koku Shikenjyo* (Aviation Testing Centre of Aeronautical Bureau) designed a private-venture experimental glider fitted with rocket-assisted take-off gear. It was a low-endurance secondary glider, equipped with three 176lb st (0.78kN) solid propellant rockets, which enabled it to take-off and climb to around 2,620ft (800m), then glide and land. The design team consisted of several engineers, in particular Shigeki Sakakibara, Yoshio Akita, Yoshikatsu Tondokoro, Tadashi Koichihara and Kazuo Kamiryo. The only prototype, called K1-Go by the factory, underwent extensive testing until March 1945. With this experience, the *Koku Shikenjyo* was to develop another rocket-powered glider – this time destined for special attack role.

In November 1944, when the Ohka operational trials programme was nearing its end, the *Kaigun Kansei Hombu* (Navy HQ) asked the *Koku Shikenjyo* to develop a wooden glider carrying a bomb to destroy enemy landing craft and M4 tanks. Soon after the first mass bombings of Japan, an urgent meeting was held with the manager of the *Koku Shikenjyo*, Mr. Komabayashi, who said: *"The present war situation is dangerous and Allied troops might land here soon. We must think of how we can prevent the Allies in their landing on our shores. One has to remember that American M4 tanks are very well armoured and cannot be destroyed with our short-range artillery. Besides, Japan is continuously bombed and there is not enough material to manufacture sufficient numbers of fighters. In this connection the Navy HQ and the Koku Shikenjyo received the task to develop tactical-technical specifications for a glider of all-wooden construction, fitted with an explosive charge, to be used against Allied landing ships and M4 tanks. Because there is no factory where such gliders could be manufactured, production should be placed where fighters for our armed*

*Jinryu glider just before the evaluation flight, seen head-on with test pilot Juichi Narabayashi at the controls. The bulges on cockpit sides contain steel blocks used to imitate some 220 lb (100 kg) of high explosives. Paint scheme was light grey overall with matt black anti-glare panel in front of the windshield.*

*(Photo by Koutaro Ohmura)*

*forces are manufactured, and wood should be considered the only material for aircraft production still available. I am under the impression that concept work should commence immediately."*

Soon afterwards, in December 1944, the special suicide glider project was prepared. This was a glider with 100kg explosive charge located in the fuselage, which would take off using rocket boosters, for example from a tunnel in a mountainside, and which would be employed to ram enemy tanks and ships attempting to land on the beaches of the Japanese islands. This was supposed to be a simple and effective weapon in case of an invasion. Prototype construction and testing were entrusted to the *Dai-Ichi Kaigun Koku Gijyutsusho* at Yokosuka. Soon afterwards, at *Koku Shikenjyo*, a technical team was established under Mr. Shigeki Sakakibara. The team was divided into individual sections responsible for the design of the fuselage, wings and tail, aerodynamics and flight trials. From the outset it was decided that the future glider would be built of wood, which would allow for series production at minimum cost. The design of the glider was such that production could be undertaken by virtually any woodworking workshop, and the number of metal parts was reduced to the absolute minimum. The gliders were intended to be stored in coastal caves, from where they would take off using rocket boosters. For that reason, the wing span had to be significantly less than that of normal gliders.

The development team originally assumed that the explosive charge of 100kg would be located in the forward fuselage, and that propulsion would be provided by a cluster of three rocket engines with a total thrust of 400kG and 10 seconds of firing time, fitted under the fuselage immediately aft of the cockpit. One of the engines would be fitted in a tubular housing in the fuselage under the tail boom, and the other two would be fitted on the sides of the fuselage. It was considered that the glider could reach a range of 4km at a free flight speed of 110km/h. The maximum speed was 275km/h. Calculations suggested that to achieve this performance, the glider would need a take-off run of at least 20m, and by the time the rockets stopped working it would achieve an altitude of no more than 400m. The glider was a cantilever high-wing monoplane of all-wooden construction. Curves were avoided so as not to complicate production. The forward fuselage was of rectangular cross-section and very simple construction. Three landing skids were located beneath the forward fuselage. The tail was conventional. Once completed, the calculations were verified by Kugisho and development work was carried out at Oppama, as Yokohama was bombed on a daily basis.

Work on the design details and construction of the prototype was contracted to Mizuno, a small company in Fukaya, in Saitama prefecture, which had almost completed construction of the first prototype by the end of May 1945. The project was developed for the most part by Yoshio Akita. Mr Tondokoro undertook structural strength calculations, while Saito used a model of the glider for wind-tunnel testing at Kizuki. Before the first prototype was flight tested, the project was criticised because its design was deemed too simple, and it was suggested that the glider may not fly at all. After many hours of discussions, the preliminary project was completely altered. In the middle of June 1945, a design team under Mr. Tondokoro began work on a completely new design. The modified project was also a very simple glider, a high-wing monoplane with broad chord (1.8m) wings and a short wing span. The glider was designed to be simple and forgiving to fly, allowing young inexperienced pilots to quickly learn to operate it. The short wing span made camouflaging the gliders and their take-off from tunnels in mountain caves significantly easier.

The wings had a symmetric aerofoil. The box-type fuselage had an all-wooden framework, stiffened with steel cables, and covered in fabric, and it had three takeoff skids fitted underneath the fuselage. The cockpit was open, with a small windscreen. Power for takeoff was to be provided by three auxiliary solid fuel rocket engines with a total thrust of 400kg and 10 seconds of firing time for take-off.

The preparation of the production documentation commenced, and almost at the same time, parts were being manufactured. In a month, Mizuno built two prototypes of the glider, and factory trials could therefore begin immediately. Before the results of the wind-tunnel trials were complete, the prototype had already commenced the next stage - test flights. This rapid rate of development was possible thanks to the efforts of the design team and the technicians who assembled the prototypes, working day and night. Nevertheless, some of the technical problems that emerged could not be solved. Above all, there were doubts about the aircraft's stability, stiffness and ease of flying. Such reservations were expressed before the first flight by the test pilot Narabayashi. He suggested, among other things, that the tail structure should be strengthened and twin fins should be introduced. However, this was not pursued, mainly due to the lack of time.

In the middle of July 1945, the glider, without the engines, was sent to the flying school at Ishioka to be tested in towed flight. At the time, the aerodrome was very often attacked by Allied aircraft, so the glider and the towing aeroplane were hidden in a nearby wood. The first test flight of the Jinryu took place at Ishioka in Ibaragi prefecture. The glider was first flown by test pilot Juichi Narabayashi, who checked the flight stability of the glider and its handling characteristics during the flight. The pilot's opinion was favourable, but the test flight was at low speed. On the following day an attempt was made to reach maximum speed in a dive. The weather on that day was favourable. The Jinryu was towed by a Tachikawa Ki-9 training aeroplane, flown by a well-known pre-war Japanese glider pilot, Saburo Fujikura.

According to the memoirs of the pilot, after a few bounces, the glider took to the air, and after a long flight on tow it reached an altitude of 2,300m, where it was to be released. For unknown reasons the cable did not release, and the pilot of the glider was forced to cut it away. Subsequently, he undertook the flying programme. He started the trial by entering a dive, gaining speed slowly. When it exceeded 300km/h, the entire glider started to shudder, to such an extent that it was not possible to gauge airspeed accurately. Upon pulling the control stick, the glider lost speed, and the shuddering stopped. As the pilot wondered what had caused this vibration, the speed rose again and the shuddering reappeared. There was still enough altitude for the pilot to attempt a controlled speed increase, to focus on the cause of the shuddering. After this trial the pilot levelled out and landed safely

It transpired that the vibrations were due to insufficient stiffness of the rear fuselage and the small fin area. It was decided to introduce the suggested design changes as soon as possible. The validity of the change was proved a few days later during another test flight, and confirmed by wind-tunnel tests, which were repeated by Saito at Kizuki. As a result of the tests, the tail was significantly redesigned and the forward fuselage was reshaped to be more streamlined. The single tail of the wind tunnel model was replaced with twin vertical tails, which led to satisfactory results

*The first prototype Jinryu glider during assembly by the Mizuno company. The centre and tail sections of the fuselage can be seen. Rocket booster attachment points are shown to advantage. Note the large wing incidence and the location of landing skids.*
*(Photo by Koutaro Ohmura)*

- but because of lack of time, this modification was not carried out on the production model. In a compromise measure, the height of the single vertical fin was increased to provide greater area.

For the next stage of trials, the Jinryu was brought to Kasumigaura Aerodrome where the trials were carried out in a corner of the aerodrome, in a box faced with sand-bags. Three rocket boosters with a total thrust of 400kG were used. The power of the rockets was more than expected, and the testing team were concerned that the glider could not endure their vibration. In the main rocket test, after some reinforcement of its fuselage, an unmanned glider was launched, with water ballast in place of a pilot. The launch was partially successful, but the glider crashed to the ground after its engines stopped. Once they had received the results of this test, the Navy ordered the start of production.

The quality and short operation time of the engines were the cause of serious concerns by the test pilot, who reported these characteristics to Major Suganuma, who was responsible for the testing of the Jinryu on behalf of the *Kaigun Kan-Sei Honbu*. Narabayashi, the pilot, reported that the Jinryu was rather difficult to fly and the glider was not suitable for ramming suicide attacks. He therefore suggested that the Jinryu should be fitted with six rocket engines, with a burning time of 30 seconds, which would allow it to achieve a maximum speed of some 750km/h. He also suggested that the glider should be armed with rocket projectiles, each more effective than 100mm field gun shells. A glider that had been modified in this fashion could make repeated attacks on enemy tanks, landing craft and B-29 Superfortress bombers. Narabayashi received no reply to his suggestions, but preparations for a powered flight continued. Major Suganami received information that the Navy was already in possession of a rocket engine able to operate for 32 seconds. He therefore started to organise a team that would develop a new rocket-powered aeroplane, Jinryu 2, and all engaged were sworn to secrecy. On 15 August 1945, the surrender of Japan was announced, but production work at the Fukaya plant of the Mizuno company, where assembly of the fifth prototype Jinryu was completed, continued until 20 August.

The development of the Jinryu with rocket engines ended at the unmanned flight stage. No manned flight with rocket engines was made because Japan ended hostilities, and in any case, many doubted that the concept of a suicide glider was viable. In accordance with the concept it was to be deployed in tunnels made in mountainsides and used in combat in beach areas during the landing of American troops and tanks.

Based on the battle experience of Iwo Jima and Okinawa, the Japanese changed their deployment plan: Jinryu was to be dismantled, with wings removed, and carried on a truck. It would initially remain at a safe distance from potential landing grounds. When the enemy landing started, the carrying trucks would move into forward areas where the Jinryu would be assembled and launched. Although it was believed that the gliders would have a gliding range of up to 4km at a speed of 110km/h, they would be useless without previous reconnaissance detailing the time and exact

*Jinryu glider immediately before landing. The overall shape of the glider.*
*(Photo by Koutaro Ohmura)*

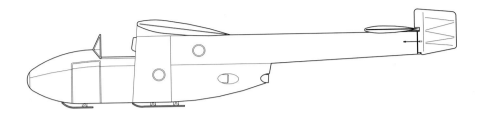

*Jinryu 1st prototype (based on the original drawing)*

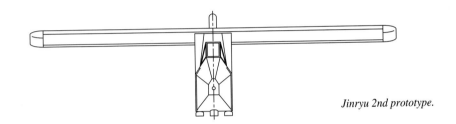

*Jinryu 2nd prototype.*

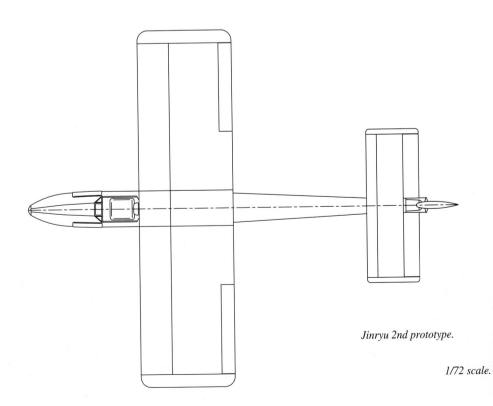

*Jinryu 2nd prototype.*

*1/72 scale.*

*Jinryu 2nd prototype.*

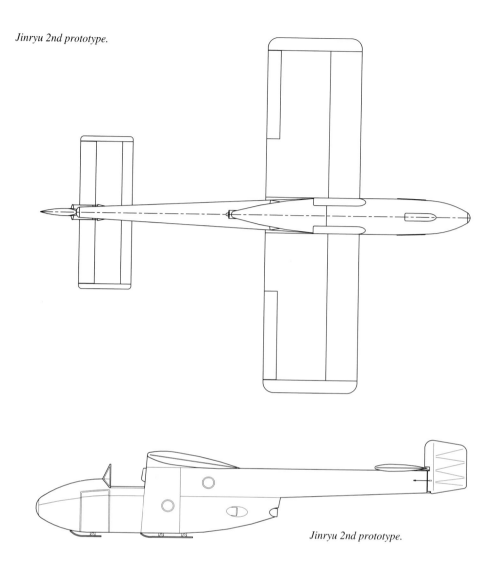

*Jinryu 2nd prototype.*

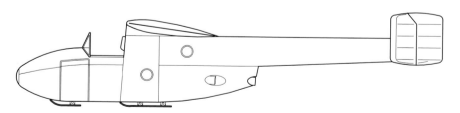

*Jinryu development project.*

*1/72 scale.*

location of the intended enemy landing. It was therefore considered that these tactics would have a very low rate of success.

Major Suganami and his team started work on a new aeroplane, which was more of an interceptor attack fighter than a suicide aeroplane. There is information of another anti-tank rocket glider project, designated "MX75". It was developed from 1941 to 1942, but no detailed information is available.

**Specifications:**

Description: single-seat cantilever high-wing monoplane suicide glider. Wooden construction.

Crew: pilot in an open cockpit.

Power plant: three auxiliary take-off rocket boosters with a total thrust of 400 kG and 10 seconds firing time.

Armament: 100kg explosive

| Type | K1-Go | Jinryu | Jinryu (with engines) |
|---|---|---|---|
| Wing span m | | 7.0 | 7.0 |
| Length m | | 8.22 | 7.6 |
| Height m | | 1.8 | 1.8 |
| Wing area m$^2$ | | 11.0 | 11.0 |
| Aspect ratio | | 3.9 | 3.9 |
| Empty weight kg | 200 | 220 | |
| Normal take-off weight kg | | 380 | |
| Maximum take-off weight kg | | 600 | |
| Useful load kg | | 54,55 | |
| Wing loading kg/m$^2$ | | 1,00 | |
| Maximum speed km/h | | 275 | 300 |
| Cruising speed km/h | | 110 | 110 |
| Ceiling m | 800 | 400 | 400 |
| Normal range km | 6 | 4 | 4 |
| Take-off run m | 20 | 20 | 20 |

Production:

• *Kokukyoku Koku Shikenjyo* developed the Jinryu glider project, while the Mizuno Glider Seisakusho company from Osaka built five prototypes that were ordered.

# Nakajima Kikka

The Nakajima Kikka, a twin jet fighter which was turned to potential suicide use quite early in its development, was a promising airframe let down by under-developed powerplants.

The story goes back to the development of the first Japanese jets. In 1920 Kohichi Hanajima, then Lieutenant and subsequently Captain, commenced research work on jet propulsion. He brought from France ten Rateau compressors, which he wanted to use as the basis for a new propulsion unit. For this purpose, the *Dai-Ichi Kaigun Koku Gijyutsusho* at Yokosuka established a special department, headed by Lieutenant Hanajima. However, there was little interest in the work.

An impulse for further research on jet propulsion was provided in the second half of the 1930s when patents by Campini in Italy and Whittle in Britain were announced in 1937, followed by press articles by Goddard in the USA. With help from the Imperial University in Tokyo and from Mitsubishi, Hanajima was able to start at last serious studies on new means of aircraft propulsion, including ramjet and rocket engines. However, once again, neither the industry nor the military expressed any significant interest in his work. Jet engine research was resumed in 1938 under Lieutenant Commander Tokiyasu Tanegashima, the head of the Aircraft Engine Research Department at the *Dai-Ichi Kaigun Koku Gijyutsusho* at Yokosuka. Although the Navy was not very interested in jet power, Lieutenant Commander Tanegashima managed to obtain orders and some funds for these experiments. Turbines were the main subject. Theoretical assistance was provided by Professor Fukusaburo Numachi, at the time the top Japanese expert in axial compressors. While developing the idea they started to use their experience in design of a jet engine. Support was provided by such companies as *Ishikawajima-Shibaura* (Turbine Factory), *Ebara Fabryca S.A.*, and Professor Stodola from the University in Zurich. Trials were carried out by a small company, *Mitsu Seiki Kogyo Kabushiki Gaisha*. Experimental work consisted of design and construction of various compressors, combustion chambers and turbines. However, unlike work in Great Britain and Germany at the time, all the work was based around the impractical Campini model of an internal combustion engine driving a compressor.

It took until 1940 before Tokiyasu Tanegashima came to the conclusion that the optimum solution would be an axial compressor linked by a free shaft to a turbine. In around 1942 Japanese scientists heard about the first flight of the jet-powered Heinkel He-178 in Germany, but did not learn any details of the power plant. For that reason they continued to work on development of their own engine-compressor concept, producing the Tsu-11 engine used to power the Kugisho MXY7 Ohka Model 22 suicide aircraft. Vice-Admiral Mitsuo Wada, the manager of the *Dai-Ichi Kaigun Koku Gijyutsusho*, issued an order about further development of jet engines according to the concept of Tokiyasu Tanegashima. The first engine was built by Ebara. Its development involved, apart from the author of the idea, Commander Osamu Nagano from the Aircraft Engine Research Department at Yokosuka and Masanori Miyata from the Electric Part Depot. The engine received the designation TR-10. Japanese language had no word for 'turbine' or 'rocket', so English terms were 'Japanised'. TR stood for Turbine Rocket. The engine was fitted with a single-stage compressor and single-stage axial turbine. In the summer of 1943 the TR-10 was started for the first time, but its performance was far from satisfactory.

To improve efficiency, the TR-10 was fitted with a four-stage axial compressor at the front. This new engine received the designation TR-12, and a lighter version, the TR-12 Otsu, was put into production. 40 engines of the type were built, and these were used to complete the trial programme. The TR-12 was going to be used to power a new special (suicide) jet aeroplane, its development contracted to Nakajima. However, further developments ruined these plans. In the autumn of 1943 the Germans presented data on their secret rocket- and jet-powered aircraft to representatives of the Japanese embassy. This show impressed the Japanese, who started protracted negotiations to purchase a licence. Eventually, in March 1944, a Japanese delegation headed by Captain Kinashi visited Adolf Hitler and gained approval to purchase a licence. Hitler awarded Captain Kinashi the Iron Cross 2nd class, ostensibly for the Japanese sinking the American aircraft-carrier USS *Wasp*.

Soon afterwards Hermann Göring gave his approval to provide the Japanese with the documentation of the Messerschmitt Me 262A-1a jet fighter and Messerschmitt Me 163B-1a rocket interceptor. In accordance with the agreement, the Germans declared they would supply blueprints and production technology for the airframes and engines. It was also arranged to deliver one airframe and engine of each type, and two similar sets in the form of spare parts and subassemblies. A party of German specialists were to be sent to Japan to help acquaint the Japanese with the new technology and assist in start-up of series production. In late March or early April a team of technicians and engineers was formed, and a complete set of documentation was prepared.

Meanwhile four Japanese 25mm Type 96 AA cannon on the submarine I-29 were replaced by German 37mm Krupp AA cannon and one 20mm *Mauser Flakvierling*. Eighteen passengers (including four Germans) embarked on the I-29. Cargo included the HWK 509A-1 rocket engine as used in the Messerschmitt Me-163 Komet interceptor, and the Jumo 004B engine used in the Messerschmitt Me-262 Schwalbe jet fighter. Captain Eiichi Iwaya also took copies of the engineering documentation of the Me-163 and the Me-262, and Lieutenant Commander Matsui obtained plans of rocket engine test beds. Other officers took care of documentation for flying bombs and radar equipment. Twenty Enigma cipher machines were also collected. Engineering documentation included also drawings of the Italian Isotta-Fraschini torpedo boat engine. A V-1 flying bomb fuselage, acoustic mines, bauxite, and mercury were also carried.

The team was split into two groups, one of which, under Captain Kikkawa, embarked on the submarine Satsuki. The second group, headed by Captain Eiichi Iwaya, was placed on the submarine I-29. Me-163 and Me-262 pattern aircraft were not taken due to lack of space. The I-29 left the port of Lorient on 16 April 1944 for Japan, escorted by seven M class minesweepers. However, the first submarine, Satsuki, was quickly detected and sunk by Allied ships.

The I-29 was luckier. After a difficult voyage, it reached Singapore on 14 June 1944. Captain Iwaya flew to Tokyo with part of the documentation. However, most of the detailed documentation remained on the ship, as it was of too great a volume to take with him. This was planned to be brought to Japan in the submarine. However, on 26 July 1944, soon after leaving the port at about 5.00 pm local time, the I-29 sailing on the surface was spotted by the American submarine USS *Sawfish*. Captain Alan B. Banister fired four torpedoes towards it. Observers on the I-29 spotted the incoming torpedoes, and Captain Kinashi attempted an evasive manoeuvre, but three torpedoes hit their target, sinking the Japanese submarine almost immediately. Three members of the I-29 crew were thrown overboard. Only one of them managed to swim to a small Philippine island and report the loss. Captain Kinashi, regarded as one of the best Japanese submarine commanders, was killed together with the crew of 105 and passengers. He was posthumously promoted Rear-Admiral.

Loss of most of the German aircraft documentation on the I-29 significantly slowed down the Japanese jet propulsion programme, but the surviving documents arrived safely in Tokyo. They were used immediately for development of the Kikka (Orange Blossom) aeroplane by Nakajima based on the Me 262, and of the J8M1 Shusui (Sword Strike) by Mitsubishi based on the Me 163.

The return of Captain Eiichi Iwaya to Japan coincided with the last preparations to start series production of the TR-12 Otsu engine, its designation changed to the Ne-12 (short for Nensho-Rocketto – combustion rocket). Having analysed surviving German documentation it was found that the BMW 003A engine was a more complex and more developed design. This fragmentary documentation was used to develop engine projects by several companies, including *Ishikawajima-Shibaura*, Nakajima and Mitsubishi. The engine project of *Ishikawajima-Shibaura* received the designation Ne-130, that of Nakajima Ne-230, and that of Mitsubishi, Ne-330. The *Dai-Ichi Kaigun Koku Gijyutsusho* at Yokosuka developed its own version, designated the Ne-20. Although the designers from Yokosuka followed the BMW 003A, their engine was 25% smaller. Therefore, many substitute parts and materials were used. The axial compressor and turbine were similar. The combustion chamber was ring-shaped, but it had 12 igniters instead of 16. Development of the Ne-20 was completed at the end of January 1945 and production of experimental examples was undertaken immediately. The first Ne-20 was run in a cave near Yokosuka on 26 March 1945.

Development of the engine was led by Captain Osamu Nakano in cooperation with Lieutenant Commander Tokiyasu Tanegashima. For security reasons their office was moved to Hanada on the southern slope of Mount Oyama. Development work concentrated on the axial compressor, which failed to produce the required pressure. Captain Nagano thought that the problem could be due to inadequate angle of attack of the blower blades, their profile following the 'Clark Y' aerofoil. To verify his guess, the blades were smoothed and fitted in the second prototype Ne-20 engine. Another problem, the tendency of the support ball bearing on the compressor shaft to overheat, was solved relatively quickly. Cracks at the base of the blades at the joint with the ring were yet another concern. This was solved by thickening the joint and reducing the number of blades. However, the change affected engine performance.

By mid-June the Ne-20 was improved so that it could run safely for five hours. At the same time preparations for series production were under way. By February 1945 nine Ne-20 engines were built at Kugisho, while the shipyard at Yokosuka assembled 12 more - though these were very poor quality. It was planned that both these manufacturers were going to build 45 Ne-20 engines monthly. Additionally, the companies *Kure-Hiro* and *Maizuru* were to supply another 20 engines monthly. There were also plans to undertake production of Ne-20 engines at Sasebo, with the capacity of that plant estimated as some 15 monthly. The situation would improve dramatically once production of the Ne-20 engines was joined by the major engine manufacturers such as Mitsubishi and Hitachi.

In parallel with the development of the engine, work progressed on the airframe. In August 1944 the *Kaigun Koku Hombu* prepared a strategic plan that called for three categories of special aircraft, known under the code name of *Kokoku Heiki* – The Emperor's Weapon. This term referred to a tactics that consisted in mass suicide attacks against enemy objects. To discuss the plan, the *Kaigun Koku Hombu* invited representatives of such companies as Kawanishi, Mitsubishi and Nakajima. After the meeting the *Kaigun Koku Hombu* placed an unofficial order with Nakajima for a jet-powered special attack aeroplane within the *Kokoku Heiki* 2-Go programme. The aeroplane received the designation 'Experimental Navy Attack Aeroplane' and the codename *Maru-Ten* (Maru - 'disc', Ten - 'sky').

Nakajima treated this order as a matter of priority. Kenichi Matsumura, the company's chief designer, was put in charge of the design, assisted by Kazuo Ohno. Work on the new aeroplane went smoothly. A meeting of Nakajima designers with representatives of the *Kaigun Koku Hombu* took place on 14 March 1945, to discuss the preliminary project. The project was developed with assistance from Eiichi Iwaya, who had been able to acquaint himself with German designs. Japanese designers followed the general layout of the German Messerschmitt Me 262, but the aircraft was an entirely new design.

Upon approval of the preliminary project the *Kaigun Koku Hombu* presented specifications of the *Maru-Ten* in accordance with the *Kokoku Heiki* 2-Go plan:

*The first prototype Kikka at Kisarazu airfield, where flying trials were conducted.*

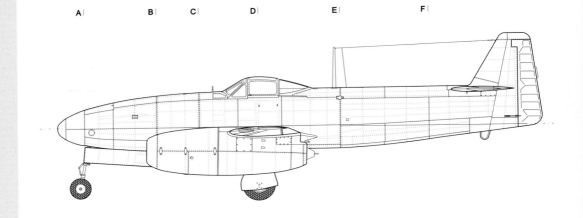

A    B   C    D     E      F

A|      B|      C|      D|      E|      F|

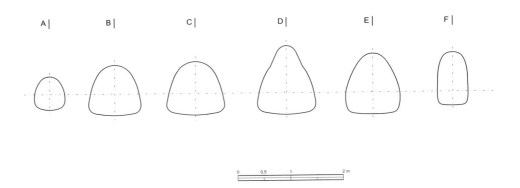

0    0,5    1      2 m

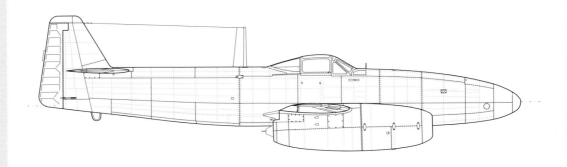

*Nakajima Kikka*

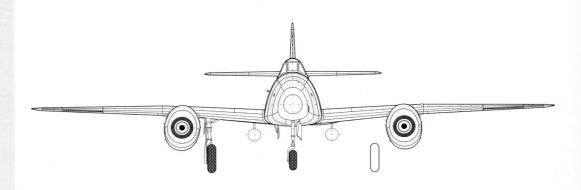

*1/72 scale.*

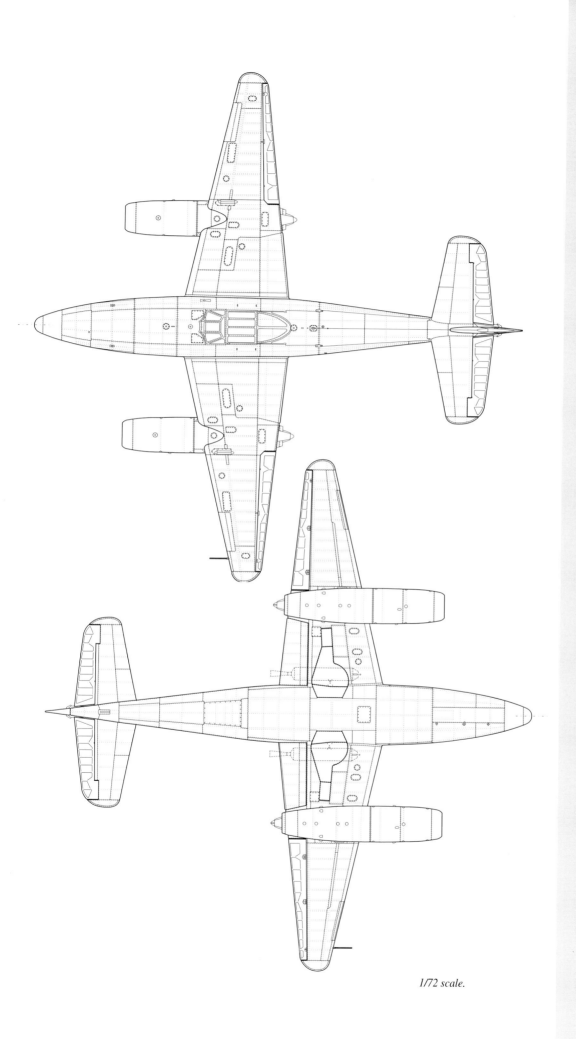

*1/72 scale.*

- Role: land-based attack aeroplane for suicide attacks against the invasion fleet, suited for mass production;
- Layout: low-wing monoplane powered by two TR-12 jet engines;
- Dimensions: as small as possible. Wing span when folded up to 5.3 m; length of the fuselage up to 9.5 m, height no more than 3.1 m;
- Crew: one;
- Performance: maximum speed with a 500kg bomb at sea level no less than 510 km/h; range with a 500kg bomb – 204 km; range with a 250kg bomb – 278 km; take-off run with additional take-off boosters – no more than 350 m; minimum speed – 148 km/h;
- Stability and control: high manoeuvrability during tight turns. At maximum speed the aeroplane must follow a constant heading towards the selected target;
- Armament: one 250 – 500kg bomb;
- Armour: 70mm thick armoured glass windscreen, 12mm thick armour plate under the seat and behind the pilot, self-sealing fuel tanks.

In accordance with the above requirements the new *Maru-Ten* was going to be a machine for suicide attacks - no undercarriage was planned, as the aircraft was intended to take off from a launcher, using rocket boosters for additional acceleration. Development work on the new aeroplane received top priority. Complete production documentation was ordered to be prepared by the end of October 1944, and by the end of November 1944 the *Kaigun Koku Hombu* planned to complete flight trials with TR-12 Otsu (Ne-12 Otsu) engines, in a Mitsubishi G4M 'Betty' bomber used as a flying testbed. Nakajima was expected to build 40 aircraft by the end of 1944, and the company did all it could to meet the deadline. On 8 December 1944 the technical head of Nakajima, Kazuo Yoshida, presented a full scale wooden mock-up of the new aeroplane to representatives of the *Kaigun Koku Hombu*. A day after the presentation during another meeting, representatives of the *Kaigun Koku Hombu* changed the original specifications regarding the role of the aeroplane. The Navy cancelled the suicide character of the aeroplane in favour of a fast fighter-bomber. In accordance with the new requirements the aeroplane would have undercarriage, increased armour around the cockpit, and other added complexities. The TR-12 engines would be replaced with Ne-20 jet engines, and the maximum speed would rise to 620 km/h. The range requirement was increased to 350 km, and the maximum bomb load to 800kg. Landing speed was reduced to 50 knots (93 km/h). The aeroplane received its unofficial codename Kikka.

Another meeting regarding the Kikka took place on 28 January 1945 at Koizumi. This was led by Admiral Misao Wada, and the subject was to prepare the Japanese aircraft industry for mass production of the Kikka. The principal problem was the raw material crisis and the lack of skilled

workers. The question of propulsion was also considered. The Ne-20 was selected as the ultimate engine, but it was suggested that the Ne-12 Otsu engines should be used for the first flight so as not to delay the development programme.

Design changes resulting from the new role were not many. The design was to be adapted to fit undercarriage from the Mitsubishi A6M 'Zero' fighter, the forward fuselage had to be modified to carry armament, and the cockpit canopy had to be redesigned. On 10 February 1945 the official acceptance of the improved wooden mock-up took place, with the future test pilot Susumu Takaoka participating in the assessment. Following approval of the mock-up, preparations for series production commenced. The first two production aircraft would also act as prototypes. No armament would be fitted to these test aircraft. Cockpit armour and self-sealing fuel tanks would be fitted from the fifth production machine onwards. As American raids mounted, on 17 February designers were forced to move from Koizumi near Tokyo to Sano. Production of the aeroplane was also dispersed. Central and rear fuselage, wings and tail, previously made by Kugisho at Yokosuka and the Nakajima plant at Koizumi, were moved to various factories in Gumma prefecture that had earlier manufactured silk fabric.

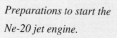

*Kikka power-plant: the*
*Ne-20 turbojet engine.*

*Test pilot Susumu Taka-oka preparing for the first flight in the Kikka.*

*Last moments before the take-off of the Kikka. Auxiliary rocket boosters can be seen under wings near the fuselage.*

*A few more remarks exchanged between the pilot and his mechanic...*

In March 1945 the final decision was taken not to use the Ne-12 Otsu engines, and consequently even the first aircraft would receive Ne-20 engines. The deadline for the assembly of the first aircraft was constantly postponed. On 20 March the Ne-20 engine was started for the first time, but it took until 20 May to deliver the first airframe for trials. At the same time that production of 25 airframes commenced, only six Ne-20 engines were ready for them at the end of May. During another meeting Admiral Misao Wada communicated that all work on the Nakajima G8N Renzan heavy bomber was to be halted and all efforts were to be shifted to the Kikka mass production programme. At the same time he announced that it was estimated that stocks of aluminium would run out in October 1945, and then only wood and steel would be available.

On 25 June 1945 assembly of the first Kikka airframe was completed, and was then partly disassembled and shipped to the plant at Koizumi, for the engines to be fitted. The following day it was announced that the Kikka was ready for take-off, and on 27 June the engines were started. The runway at the factory aerodrome at Koizumi was too short, so the airfield at Kisarazu, in Misawa air base on the coast of the Tokyo Bay, was selected for flight trials. Before the first taxiing trials took place one of the engines had to be replaced. A nut left in the engine through carelessness damaged the turbine blades. The first 'ceremonial' taxiing test was performed personally by Admiral Wada, who was later replaced by the test pilot, Takaoka. On 29 June 1945 during one of the taxiing trials speed was increased to test the effectiveness of the brakes. Ground trials were completed by 6 August, when the news of the nuclear attack on Hiroshima came in. The news of the atom bomb prompted the designers to fly the machine as soon as possible. The following day the Kikka was ready for flight. Fuel tanks were only partly filled, so that the take-off weight did not exceed 3,150kg, and there was therefore no need to use the auxiliary take-off boosters. The first flight took only 11 minutes, during which the undercarriage was not retracted.

The test pilot, Takaoka, considered the stability in flight and general behaviour of the aeroplane in the air to be good, and the engines worked properly throughout the flight.

The second flight was planned to take place on 10 August. By that time production of 25 production airframes was well advanced. Another flight was going to be the official presentation of the new type, and high-ranking representatives of the Army and Navy were invited. This time the aeroplane was going to take a full fuel load, and the take-off would be assisted by auxiliary rocket boosters. On the day of the official presentation the area around Tokyo was attacked by American carrier-borne aircraft, so the flight was postponed until the next. On 11 August, despite a strong side wind, the first flight was approved. During the take-off, the test pilot Takaoka lost control of the machine as soon as he switched on the additional take-off boosters. Thinking that the Ne-20 jet engines had stopped, he aborted the take-off. However, he failed to stop the aeroplane on the

*...and the first Kikka jet aircraft took off for its first flight.*

runway, overshot and crashed the machine in an irrigation ditch. This marked the end of the Kikka development programme.

In parallel with the design work and preparations for series production, training of personnel continued. The 724th *Kokutai*, ultimately going to be equipped with Kikka aircraft, was established on 1 July 1945. The 724th *Kokutai* was in fact a suicide unit, where Kikka tactics were to be developed. The air base in the Tateyama area on Miura peninsula, where Kikka aircraft of the 724th *Kokutai* were to be based, was located on the coast of Tokyo Bay. Aircraft were going to be housed in underground shelters protected from bomb raids. The runway was also partly located inside an underground tunnel. There the Kikkas, their wings folded, would await the signal to take-off. Reconnaissance duties would be performed by a Kawanishi E15K1 Shiun reconnaissance floatplane taking off from a nearby harbour. Its role was to locate enemy invasion ships and guide the Kikkas to them. To achieve that, the E15K1 Shiun was supposed to mark the surface of the sea with special markers upon detection of the target, and circle nearby, transmitting radio signals. Upon receiving the report that the enemy had been located, the Kikkas would scramble from their underground shelter using additional rocket boosters and, guided by radio signals received by the Kurutsu system, they would attack the enemy ships from low altitude with 500kg bombs. However, the armistice signed on 15 August 1945 halted the planned attacks.

The 25 Kikkas already in production included five two-seater trainers (Kikka 1). It was planned that by September 1945 Nakajima would build 45 Kikka aircraft, in October another 50, and in November 40 more. It was anticipated that by the end of year Nakajima would deliver 155 Kikkas. Kugisho Arsenal was going to deliver 20 machines in September, and then 30 aircraft monthly. Kyushu was going to build 25 aircraft in September, and from October on they would make 35 Kikkas monthly.

Apart from the above mentioned Kikka 1 trainer version, more development variants for various roles were in preparation. The Kikka Kai variant had already been developed. Kikka 2 fast reconnaissance aeroplane was also under development, this being essentially a conversion of the two-seater training machine.

The Kikka 2 was to be fitted with a Type 96 Model 3 radio set in the rear cockpit.

This version would locate targets and guide standard Kikkas towards them, supplanting the E15K1. It was not produced.

The Kikka 3 was planned to be a conventional interceptor, but like the Kikka 2 was destined never to leave the drawing board. Work on this variant commenced in May 1945. It was planned to be powered by modified Ne-20 engines with thrust increased by 20-30%. Armament would include two Type 5 cannon with 50 rounds each. As the interceptor version was equipped with heavier armament, the airframe structure needed to be strengthened, the fuselage had to be stretched to maintain balance, and the control system required improvements. The weight of the modified aeroplane increased with the various additions, so wing loading increased. This necessitated the use of split flaps and double slats, and an increase in wing area to improve take-off and landing characteristics. A further interceptor variant that was never build was the Kikka 5.

Kikka 4 was a version intended to be launched by catapult, and was also under development at the war's end. It would take off from a giant 200 m catapult, and at the end of it, with the main engines and auxiliary boosters on, the aeroplane would reach a speed of 222 km/h and acceleration of some 3-4g. Prototype catapults were planned to be built in Kugisho in September 1945. After take-off from a catapult and having flown about 2,000 m the aeroplane was expected to attain an altitude of 100 m.

American engineering services, having captured the Nakajima aircraft factory at Koizumi, showed much interest in the Kikka aircraft captured there. At least three machines were shipped to the USA for testing, probably including the 3rd and the 5th production aeroplane. One of the Kikkas survives, and is now on display at the National Air and Space Museum. This appears to be complete, but in fact the 'engine pods' were improvised from external fuel tanks as no Ne-20 pods were available.

*Kikka special attack aircraft on Nakajima assembly line at the Koizumi plant, Gunma prefecture.*

The Kikka did not receive an Allied reporting name, and the Japanese themselves never gave it an official alphanumeric code. According to the standard system it should have received the designation J9N1, but was never known by this.

**Specifications:**

Description: twin-engined low-wing monoplane interceptor fighter, special attack, reconnaissance or trainer aeroplane. All metal construction with fabric covered control surfaces and ailerons.

Crew: Single pilot in an enclosed cockpit (Kikka, Kikka Kai, Kikka 3, Kikka 4, Kikka 5); Crew of two (Kikka 1, Kikka 2),

Power plant: Two Ne-12 Otsu jet engines with a thrust of 475 kG (*Maru-Ten*); Two Ne-20 jet engines with a thrust of 475 kG; fuel tank capacity 725 l or 1,450 l (Kikka, Kikka Kai); Two Ne-20 Kai jet engines (Kikka 3, Kikka 4, Kikka 5),

Armament: Two 30mm Type 5 cannon in the fuselage (Kikka, Kikka Kai, Kikka 2, Kikka 3, Kikka 4, Kikka 5) ; Bomb load: 1x250kg (*Maru-Ten*); 1x500kg (*Maru-Ten*, Kikka Kai), 1x800 (Kikka)

| Type | *Maru-Ten* | Kikka | Kikka Kai | Kikka 1 | Kikka 2 | Kikka 3 | Kikka 4 | Kikka 5 |
|---|---|---|---|---|---|---|---|---|
| Wing span m | 10.0 | 10.0 | 10.0 | 10.0 | 10.0 | | 10.0 | 10.0 |
| Length m | 8.125 | 9.25 | 9.25 | 9.25 | 9.25 | | 9.25 | 9.25 |
| Height m | 2.95 | 3.05 | 3.05 | 3.05 | 3.05 | | 3.05 | 3.05 |
| Wing area m$^2$ | 13.00 | 13.21 | 13.21 | 13.21 | 13.21 | 14.52 | 13.21 | 13.21 |
| Empty weight kg | | 2,300 | | | | 2,980 | | 3,060 |
| Normal take-off weight kg | 3,014 | 3,550 | | | | 3,925 | | 4,000 |
| Maximum take-off weight kg | 3,120 | 4,312 | | 4,009 | 4,241 | 4,152 | 4,080 | 4,232 |
| Useful load kg | | 1,250 | | | | 945 | | 940 |
| Wing loading kg/m$^2$ | 231.85 | 268.74 | | | | 270.32 | | 302.80 |
| Power loading kg/kG | 3.38 | 3.74 | | | | 4.13 | | 4.21 |
| Maximum speed km/h | 565 | 670 | 687 | 722 | 722 | 889 | 713 | |
| at an altitude of m | 0 | 10,000 | 6,000 | 6,000 | 6,000 | 10,000 | 8,000 | |
| Landing speed km/h | 151 | 159 | 167 | 167 | 167 | 170 | 171 | 156 |
| Climb to 6,000m | | 12``6` | | | | 10``2` | 11``50` | 11``18` |
| Ceiling m | 10,100 | 10,700 | | | | | 12,100 | 12,300 |
| Normal range km | 428 | 582 | | | | | | 594 |
| Maximum range km | 539 | 888 | | | | | 815 | 793 |
| Take-off run m | 283 | 504 | 552 | 667 | 676 | | 470 | 470 |
| Landing run m | | 1363 | | | | | 1,250 | 1,240 |

Note: the designations of Kikka 1, Kikka 2 etc are for information only - these were not official or contemporary.

Production: from June until August 1945 Nakajima *Hikoki Kabushiki Gaisha* plant at Koizumi built two complete Kikka prototypes out of a total of 25 airframes in various stages of assembly.

*Ne-20 turbojet engine with the cowlings removed, as fitted in the second Kikka prototype.*

*Kikka airframes at advanced stages of assembly at the Koizumi plant, as found by American occupation forces.*

*Incomplete second Kikka prototype.*

# Nakajima Toka

The Nakajima Ki-115a Tsurugi, as a straightforward, dedicated suicide aircraft for the Army, also aroused interest in the Navy. The aircraft featured an extremely simplified design, allowing the use of most radial engine types. That was why the Navy decided to use the aeroplane itself. The first prototypes of the Army version were built for the March 1945 in Nakajima's Mitaka plant. However, it took until the very end of the war before the *Kaigun Koku Hombu*, urged by the Naval Aviation HQ and after inspection of the Ki-115 Ko Tsurugi design, placed orders for a similar aeroplane with Nakajima. They also bestowed their own designation 'Experimental Navy Special Aeroplane Toka' ('Wisteria Blossom').

A programme for production was prepared, calling for some 830 Toka aircraft to be built by February 1946 in the Navy shipyards at Yokosuka and Kure, and other civilian shipyards, while 250 aircraft were planned to be built by Showa.

The Toka was a single-engined, single-seat cantilever low-wing monoplane with the main undercarriage jettisoned after take-off. Its general layout was similar to a single-seat fighter. As a special attack aeroplane it could take one 500 or 800kg bomb in a recess under the fuselage, and pilot had a choice of conventional bomber attack or suicide attack.

**Specifications:** for the Toka were:

- Construction should require only around 10% of the man hours needed for the Mitsubishi A6M 'Zero' fighter, which meant roughly 1,500 man hours. The wings were to be single-spar, made up of separate assemblies – leading edges, wing centre section, and trailing edges – all connected by bolts. The fuselage cross-section was oval. The tail was of wooden construction. The main wheel legs were to be fitted with shock-absorbers.
- Any radial engine could be used as power plant. It was planned that the aircraft for the Army would be fitted with Ha-115 engines, while those for the Navy would have Zuisei 12, Sakae 12, Kinsei 41 (or 51) or Kotobuki 2 engines.
- Apart from the bomb, a radio set would be the only other equipment.

Following ground trials of the Ki-115 Ko Army version at the Nakajima aerodrome in Ota, the *Kaigun Koku Hombu* requested the following revisions:

- Engines and equipment should be approved by the Navy.
- Wing area increased by 1 m².
- Add landing flaps.
- Fit the aeroplane with auxiliary take-off rocket boosters.
- Improve visibility by repositioning of the cockpit and its hood.
- Other armament should be approved by the Navy.

A design to this improved specification was handed over to Ichigisho and the *Kansei Hombu* 4. Bu, (4th Section of the Fleet Policy Department) which was responsible for ship construction. Two Ki-115 Ko aircraft were transferred by the Army for conversion by Showa, and to prepare series production, but the war ended before any work commenced. An all-wooden Toka variant was also under consideration. There is information that Ki-230 designation was given to the Toka, which implies that the Toka was also planned to be used by the army, but no Japanese source confirms this.

**Specifications:**

Description: single-seat low-wing monoplane suicide aeroplane. Mixed construction with fabric covered control surfaces and ailerons.

Crew: pilot in a partly enclosed cockpit.

Power plant: one air cooled radial engine of any type, rated at ca. 1,130 hp (830 kW) for take-off, three-blade fixed pitch metal propeller depending on the engine type; fuel tank capacity 450 l.

Armament: one 800kg or 500kg bomb.

| Type | Toka |
|---|---|
| Wing span m | 9.72 |
| Length m | 8.5 |
| Height m | 3.3 |
| Wing area m$^2$ | 13.1 |
| Empty weight kg | 1,700 |
| Normal take-off weight kg | 2,560 |
| Maximum take-off weight kg | |
| Useful load kg | 860 |
| Wing loading kg/m$^2$ | 195.42 |
| Power loading kg/hp | 2.26 |
| Maximum speed km/h | 558 |
| at an altitude of m | 2,800 |
| Ceiling m | 6,500 |
| Normal range km | 1,200 |

Production: Showa Hikoki Kabushiki Gaisha had not started production of Toka aircraft by the end of the war, nor had it converted the two Ki-115 Ko aircraft delivered by Nakajima.

# Remote controlled flying bombs of the Imperial Japanese Army and Navy

German development and use of guided and unguided missiles in the Second World War is relatively well known, particularly the V-1 flying bomb and V-2 ballistic missile. By the last years of the war, German industry concerning these weapons had achieved a relatively advanced state. Less known, but in some ways equally advanced, was Japanese technology in this area which progressed according to a programme largely separate from that of the Germans.

In July 1944 concept work commenced on radio-controlled flying bombs. This was not for the human reason of saving pilots' lives but because it was calculated that such weapons would stand a better chance of reaching their target - as the war in the Far East progressed, Allied defences had increased to the level where most piloted Kamikaze aircraft would be shot down before they could press home their attack. The radio-controlled bombs would be much harder to intercept because of their smaller size and, in some cases, high speed.

## Army

The Army generally focused on air-to-surface flying bombs designated I-Go-1. One of these was the Mitsubishi I-Go-1 Ko flying bomb, essentially a small pilotless aeroplane with an 800kg warhead, powered by a 240 kg thrust pulse-jet. Another flying bomb, the Kawasaki I-Go-1 Otsu, was similar to the Mitsubishi project, but was much smaller and had a shorter range of action. Both these flying bombs underwent flight testing at the end of 1944 but were not used in combat.

The Rikugun I-Go-1 Hei flying bomb project, developed by the Aeronautical Faculty of the Imperial University in Tokyo, was a completely different technological solution. The control system of the I-Go-1 Hei bomb was designed to home in on shock waves from naval gunfire.

At the end of 1943 work commenced on the Ke-Go flying bomb that used heat radiation for homing. During trials some 60 bombs were dropped, but only a few of these reacted to temperature changes during the fall sufficiently to home in on their target.

A special Rikugun Ta-Go flying torpedo for coastal defence was developed to an order from the Imperial Japanese Army. The concept was that when launched by an aeroplane, it should fly just above the water. Design work also commenced on the AZ torpedo, another remote controlled weapon ordered by the Imperial Japanese Army.

# Fu-Go bomber balloon

During the Pacific war Japan carried out several attacks against the American continent. These were of rather different character to the Pearl Harbor raid of 1941.

In February 1942 the Japanese submarine I-17 shelled the fuel terminal near Santa Barbara beach and destroyed a pump house. Subsequently in June 1942 the submarine I-25 shelled a coastal fort in Oregon, damaging the net on a volleyball court, and in September the crew of the submarine assembled and catapulted a small floatplane, a Kugisho E14Y1 'Glen', which dropped a few incendiary bombs on coastal forests, starting small fires.

The fourth and last attack, during the last winter of the war, was carried out using balloons with incendiary bombs. The tactic of using balloons for military purposes was developed at the 9th Army Technical Laboratory, headed by General Sueyoshi Kusaba. It was hoped that these would start fires in the West Coast forests, some of which were close to inhabited areas. Detailed specifications were prepared by a research team headed by Major Teiji Takada. It was hoped that strong west-to-east prevailing winds at high altitudes during winter and spring could carry the bomb-laden balloons towards America. The new weapon received the codename 'Fusen bakudan', which translates as 'fire bombs' or 'fire balloons'.

The Japanese military had a history of using balloons for military purposes since 1900. In the Russo-Japanese war in 1905 balloons were employed for observation during the siege of Port Arthur. In 1944, the army balloon regiment was ordered to start the special attack by balloon against the US mainland by the Daihonei directive. The attacks were planned for November 1944-March 1945.

The aim of the operation was to drop around 7,500 15kg bombs, around 30,000 5kg incendiary bombs and around 7,500 12kg incendiary bombs on the US mainland. In the region of 15,000 balloons were to be launched, 500 in November, 3,500 in December, 4,500 in January, 4,500 in February and 2,000 in March. Daihonei designated this special attack operation 'Fu-Go Shiken' (Fu-Go Experiment). Balloons with bombs attached in this way were generally referred to as Fu-Go.

Initially the Fu-Go balloons were made of gummed silk, but it was found that better results could be gained with an envelope of mulberry paper, which was more resistant and waterproof. The envelope had a diameter of 10 m and it was filled with 540 m3 of hydrogen. Its useful load at sea level was about 400kg, and at an altitude of 10,000 m this fell to 200kg. Five 12kg incendiary bombs and one 15kg bomb with a very sensitive fuse were hung on the basket of the balloon.

Balloons carrying bombs were launched from Japan in winter, when the jet stream was strongest. The balloons climbed to an altitude of 3,000 to 6,000 m, where they were caught by the jet stream and were carried across the Pacific at a speed of some 320 km/h towards the US West Coast. The strongest jet stream developed above 9,000 m, and could carry a large balloon across the Pacific, a distance of over 8,000 km, within three days.

Balloons were usually launched in the morning, so that they could gain height - at night they became covered with dew which significantly reduced the altitude the balloon could reach. The correct flight altitude was controlled by an altimeter, actuating a mechanism which could release ballast in the form of bags of sand. When the altitude fell below 9,000 m an electric device was triggered which burnt through the ballast attachments. The sand bags were attached in groups of four under an aluminium ring below the balloon. Bags could be jettisoned in pairs on each side of the ring. Alternatively, if the balloon rose above 11,600 m, the altimeter triggered a valve to release hydrogen. Hydrogen could also be released if the pressure in the envelope grew too high.

The balloon flight altitude control system was designed to operate for three days, after which it was calculated the balloon should be over US territory. A small explosive charge automatically released the attached bombs, and the free balloon flew on, with a fuse attached on a 19.5 m cable. After 84 minutes the fuse exploded and destroyed the balloon.

Overall weight of the balloon was approx. 900kg. The envelope of the balloon consisted of triple or quadruple bonded so-called 'devil's tongues'. To make these balloons the workforce included many 10-year old girls, due to their nimble fingers. They had to wear gloves, their fingernails had

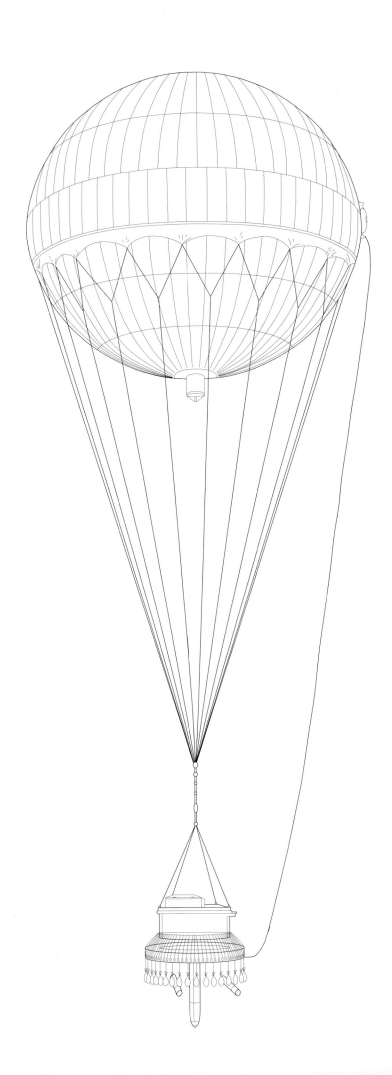

to be cut short, and they were not allowed to use pins. Sections of the paper envelopes were made in many regions of Japan. Because they were long, a large surface was required for their production, so theatres, sumo halls and large recording studios were used for the purpose.

The first trials took place in September 1944 and were successful. Before preparations to release them were completed, American B-29 bombers started their intensive bombardment of Japan.

The first balloon was released in early November 1944. Major Takada watched it for a long time as it climbed and finally disappeared beyond the horizon. The balloon was visible only for a few minutes, then it merged with the sky.

In early 1945 the Americans realised that something strange was happening in their territory. Balloons were seen, and explosions were heard in California and Alaska. Witnesses said they had seen a parachute falling at Thermopolis, Wyoming. Fragments of a bomb were found near a crater. A Lockheed P-38 Lightning shot down a balloon at Santa Rosa, California, another balloon was seen over Santa Monica, and pieces of washi mulberry paper were found in the streets of Los Angeles.

Two paper balloons were found the same day, in Modoc National Park and east of Mount Shasta. Near Medford, Oregon one of the bombs dropped from a balloon exploded near an oil drill. US Navy ships also found some floating balloons. Fragments of balloons with their equipment were found in Montana and Arizona, and in Sasketchewan, North-West Territories and in Yukon in Canada. A US Army fighter managed to hit a balloon in the air that subsequently landed intact. Its construction was analysed and photographed.

On 2 January 1945 Newsweek published an article titled 'Mysterious balloon'. That same day the Office of Censorship sent out instructions to press editors that no information about the balloons and related events should be published. Thus it was intended to cut the enemy off from any up-to-date information about the effectiveness of the balloon offensive.

In fact the balloons falling in America posed a real threat. Incendiary bombs could start widespread forest fires, but at this time of the year forests were damp and this prevented fire spreading. Nevertheless local authorities were notified about the balloons, which caused a certain nervousness, as the Americans had information about Japanese development of biological weapons. It was also feared that the incoming balloons might carry chemical weapons, which also posed a serious threat.

Nobody wanted to believe that the balloons were coming directly from Japan. It was supposed that the balloons were launched off the North American coast from Japanese submarines. There were also rumours that the balloons were launched by German prisoners of war held in camps in the USA, or by the Japanese interned in America.

*Fu*-Go *bomber balloon*

Several sand bags from 'fusen bakudan' were taken for geological analysis by the US Geological Survey military unit. This had been established in June 1942, six months after the attack on Pearl Harbor. The geological unit started co-operation with the US Army intelligence service, headed by Colonel Sidman Poole. First, microscopical and chemical analysis of the sand found in the bags was carried out, which allowed identification of the diatoms and other sea elements and the mineral content. As a result of the analysis it was ascertained that the sand could not have come from American beaches or the central Pacific, and proved that indeed the balloons must have come from Japan.

Meanwhile, the balloons continued to arrive over Oregon, Kansas, Iowa, Manitoba, Alberta, North-West Territories, Washington, Idaho, South Dakota, Nevada, Colorado, Texas, northern Mexico, Michigan and even over the Detroit suburbs. Fighters tried to intercept the balloons, but achieved no significant successes. The balloons flew at high altitudes and in the jetsream were surprisingly fast. Fighters managed to destroy fewer than twenty balloons.

Geologists continued their research and eventually identified the beaches in Japan from which the sand was taken. By that time, however, there was little point to the work - early in the spring the balloon offensive stopped.

Japanese propaganda claimed that huge fires had been started in America, society was in panic, and that there were thousands of victims. In fact, as a result of Japanese actions

*Fu-Go bomber balloon
photographed over the
ocean.*

during the Pacific war, only six people were killed in mainland America. A minister and his wife
and children, fishing in southern Oregon, found a balloon which exploded when they came close.
The minister's wife and five children were killed.

General Kusaba's unit launched over nine thousand balloons, of which about 300 have been
confirmed to have reached the USA. The Japanese estimated that some 10% of the balloons reached
their target, and perhaps a thousand may have crossed the Pacific. Two balloons landed back in
Japan, but caused no damage.

The Japanese balloon programme was large and expensive, and might have been more effective
if not for the raids of American B-29 bombers, which destroyed two out of the three hydrogen
factories built especially for the programme. One of the last paper balloons came down on 10
March 1945 near Hanford, Washington, where Manhattan project work was carried out. The balloon
became entangled in power lines leading to the reactor which made plutonium for the atom bomb
later dropped on Nagasaki. As a result of the collision the reactor was switched off temporarily.

The balloons did, however, cause US forces to divert resources to protect the mainland from
the balloons. A special top secret mission was set up on the US West Coast codenamed 'Fire Fly',
which was aimed at intercepting and shooting down the balloons by a specially formed fighter unit.
Special ground units for fighting forest fires were organised under the codename 'Smoke Jumpers'.
One of these was the 555th Parachute Battalion, known as the 'Triple Nickel'.

The navy version of Fu-Go was designated 8-Go Heiki (Number 8 Weapon), and the concept was
to launch them from submarines near the US coast. The submarine I-55 had been under construction
for the purpose until June 1944, but the plan was not carried out.

# Rikugun Maru-Ke (Ke-Go) homing bomb

In March 1944 Colonel Kyoyuu Nomura was appointed the head of the *Heiki Gyo-Sei Hombu* (Armament Supply HQ) of the *Rikugun Koku Hombu*. Soon afterwards (as recorded in his memoirs) he received a directive to "design a weapon that has not existed before, and which would decisively alter the existing war situation".

At the same time the laboratories of Tokyo *Shibaura Electronics* (Toshiba) were carrying out experiments, under Army orders, to determine the possibility of developing a detector which could recognise a man's hand using infra-red (IR) from a distance of 70m. The aim of the research was to develop a method of aiming precision fire at enemy soldiers hiding in the jungle. The task would be performed by a prototype IR sensor tested in a machine gun night sighting device. Using the results of the experiment, Colonel Nomura started to develop an 'IR weapon'. The *Rikugun Koku Hombu* immediately expressed interested in this device, and placed a ten million yen contract to develop and supply IR directed homing bombs, codenamed Maru-Ke - Ke being short for kenchiki (detector). The *Rikugun Koku Hombu* ordered preparations for mass production of at least 700 of the Maru-Ke bombs, later designated the Ke-Go, by October 1945.

In May 1944 Colonel Kyoyuu Nomura was appointed the head of the design team, and Mr. Sudo was ordered to develop an air-to-surface bomb that would home onto an IR radiation source, for use against Allied shipping in the vicinity of Japan. Colonel Nomura designed the wings and control system. The *Rikugun Koku Hombu* approved the project and, for further development, handed it over to a newly formed design team, made up of ballistics and aircraft weapon specialists, based near Tokyo. At the same time design work on the Shinyo suicide boat (codenamed Maru-Re) was started there. Both these projects involved around 400 specialists.

In March 1944 concept work had commenced in parallel on three types of homing bombs using IR detection. The bombs were designated the Ke-Go Ko, Ke-Go Otsu and Ke-Go Hei. Only work on the Ke-Go Ko was continued, as this was found to be the most promising, while work on the Ke-Go Otsu and Ke-Go Hei was soon abandoned. The Ke-Go Ko was intended to be dropped from a carrier aeroplane at moderately high altitude and then home by itself onto a surface object emitting IR radiation, such as an enemy ship. Nine versions of this weapon were produced within the Ke-Go programme, designated Model 101 to Model 109, but only the Model 101, Model 102, Model 106 and Model 107 bombs were subjected to intensive drop trials. These trials halted in July 1945, with trials of Model 108 and Model 109 bombs planned to be resumed in September 1945 - the end of the war put an end to that intention.

The Ke-Go homing bomb was a free-falling bomb, which steered itself onto a target using an IR controlled gyroscope acting on external control surfaces via electromagnetic powered hydraulics. It would be dropped from aircraft near enemy warships. The first models of the Ke-Go consisted of a warhead fitted with thermal sensor to detect IR radiation, a fuselage, four wings of cruciform design mounted on the central section, and an air brake at the tail section. The cruciform wings were fitted with ailerons to control the flight's trajectory, and to prevent spin. The main wings were attached in line with the centre of gravity.

Throughout the Ke-Go's flight, the fuselage would point vertically downwards. In later models the fuselage of the bomb was fitted with an additional cruciform-shaped tail to improve control. Some 60 bombs were dropped during trials, but only a few reacted to the temperature source. Nevertheless, the trial results were found to be sufficiently promising, and the designers were positive that their idea would lead to successful homing bombs.

The Ke-Go IR homing bomb warhead consisted of 200-300kg of high explosive. Some Japanese sources say the explosive was 600kg, but this was the total weight of the Ke-Go Model 101. Or they may have mistaken 600 pounds as 600 kg. The main structure was of wooden construction, with the exception of the nose cone, the tail (including the air brake), and metal wing attachment joints. Model 101 and Model 102 bombs were fitted with four cruciform-shaped wings, while the

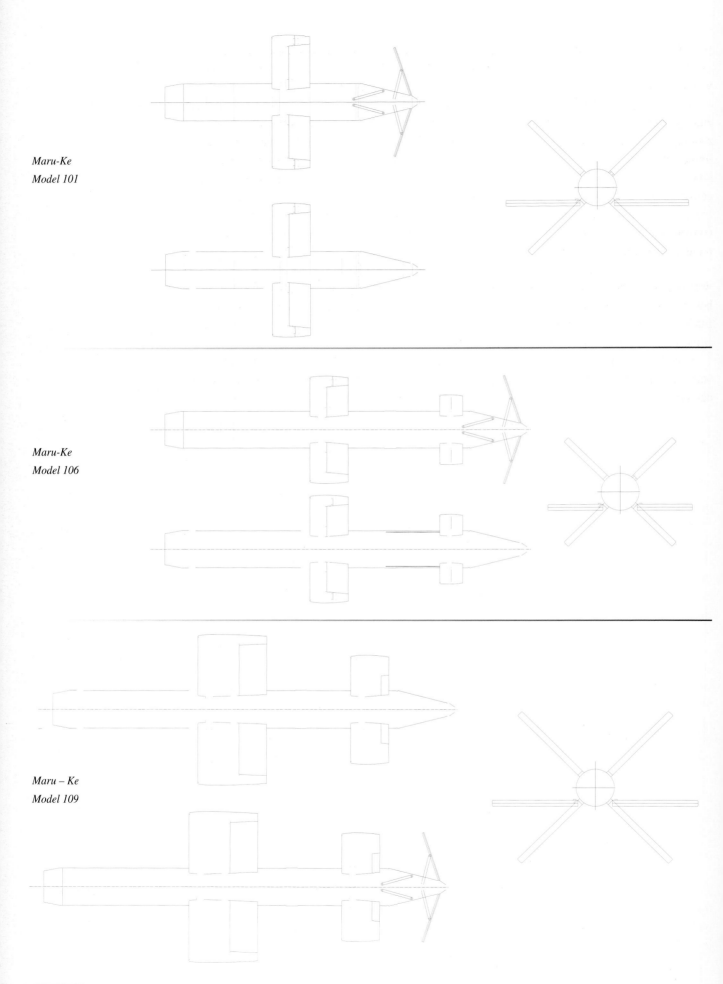

*Maru-Ke*
*Model 101*

*Maru-Ke*
*Model 106*

*Maru – Ke*
*Model 109*

remaining bombs were fitted with four main and four tail cruciform-shaped wings. The largest of these was the Model 109 bomb, with a fuselage of 0.50 m diameter 5.30 m long, and an overall weight of 800kg.

The fuselage of the Ke-Go bomb was divided into three sections: thermal head, warhead, and cylindrical aft section with air brake. Thermal head included the detection equipment - a rotating mirror, the IR detector (bolometer) and amplifier with batteries. The warhead was located immediately aft of thermal head. The main wings with four flaps and two or four ailerons, depending on the version of the bomb, were fitted further aft. The directional gyro - and control for the ailerons consisting of a spherical oil tank, electromagnetic oil valves and batteries to power them - were located between the main wings and the smaller tail wings. (Early versions of the bomb used a more conventional hydraulic system operating on only two ailerons). The rear-most section of the bomb mounted the umbrella-shaped retractable air brake.

One notable feature of the Ke-Go was the folding lower wings, which allowed Ki-67 bombers with bomb attached to take-off from unprepared airfields. On the ground the lower wings of the bomb were raised manually to a horizontal position, and maintained in that attitude by inner spring catches until immediately prior to release, when hydraulic jacks released the catches to bring the wings back into their deployed position.

Each bomb featured two instantaneous fuses in the forward fuselage, and a delayed action fuse was fitted in the tail section, which activated upon hitting the water. In all Ke-Go bombs the Ta-dan type explosive was fitted between thermal head and the main wings. The forward section was

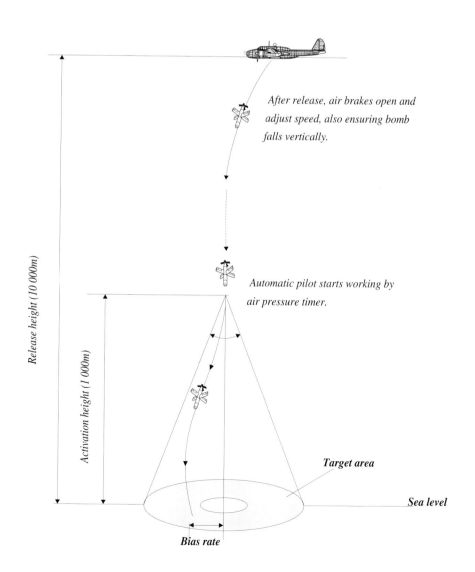

*After release, air brakes open and adjust speed, also ensuring bomb falls vertically.*

*Automatic pilot starts working by air pressure timer.*

*Release height (10 000m)*

*Activation height (1 000m)*

*Target area*

*Sea level*

*Bias rate*

*Illustration of bomb release.*

shaped in such way that the explosive had the highest force of impact, as required to penetrate the deck of any Allied ship.

Two detonation systems for the explosive were used. The purpose of the first was to cause an immediate detonation the moment the bomb struck a solid object. The system consisted of a detonator located in the rear section of the explosive charge, connected with two strike fuses fitted on long probes in the forward section of the bomb. They were armed by small propellers, which were activated by a cable attached to the mother aircraft when the bomb was released. The second system was to detonate the explosive warhead with a slight delay under water, if the bomb missed the ship, as this way it could inflict serious damage below the waterline of the target vessel. The delayed action fuses, armed by an atmospheric pressure sensor, were standard equipment. Such a detonation system was regarded as sufficient to be used in case of either a direct hit or a near miss and explosion immediately under the water, so the bomb would explode in any eventuality.

The problem of stabilising the flight was solved by a gyro system, which deflected the control surfaces as required. In the first versions, the control system of two ailerons used a hydraulic system connected with a link control system, as opposed to the later versions with electromagnetic system to control four ailerons. The Model 101 and Model 102 used electric gyros, but the high temperature they produced interfered with the amplifier of the IR detection system, so subsequent versions used pneumatic gyros which had a rotation speed of 5,000-8,000 rpm. The IR measurement device (bolometer) consisted of nickel-plated strips of various lengths, from which signals were received and transmitted to the control system. Above the bolometer was a rotating concave mirror attached eccentrically. The signal from the bolometer went via the amplifier and two relays to the hydraulic actuating mechanism, which deflected the ailerons on the wings to direct the bomb during its fall towards the detected source of IR radiation.

The IR source detection system posed the greatest technical difficulty. This was because the technology of galvanic application of a very thin layer of nickel on steel sheet in production had not been mastered. Eventually this problem was solved, too, and series production of Ke-Go homing bombs could start.

Immediately before the parent aircraft took off, all electric circuits related to bomb release had to be checked. Bombs were brought to the carrier aeroplanes using standard bomb trucks. Due to long span of the unfolded wings, when the bomb was attached in an open bomb bay, the wing tips

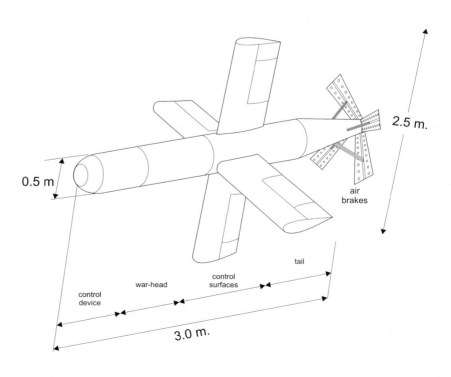

*Rikugun Maru-Ke*
*(Ke-Go) overall view.*

extended several inches beyond the aeroplane's fuselage outline. At the front and rear the bomb was supported by shock-absorbing attachments, two on each side. The bomb was attached in such way that it could not rock or swing. The lower wings were raised manually to the horizontal position, and maintained in that attitude by inner spring catches. Shortly before flight, all electric sockets were connected, the timer switched on and fuses rendered safe.

The bomb was targeted from the mother aircraft by using a standard bomb sight. Immediately before release of the Ke-Go bomb, the wings were extended and the gyro power supply switched on. Before release the timer was also switched on, and for the last 10-15 seconds of free fall flight the latter took control of the bomb. During the drop a cable attached between the bomb and the bomber was broken, and this triggered the process of opening the tail air brake and activating the fuses.

Ten minutes before bomb release the following actions had to be taken in the carrier aeroplane:
- Mechanically open the first valve to lower the wings of the bomb.
- Open the second valve to activate the hydraulic control system.
- Switch on the pneumatic gyro.
- Switch on the IR sensor amplifier (coils made of nickel-plated wire fitted inside the amplifier housing).

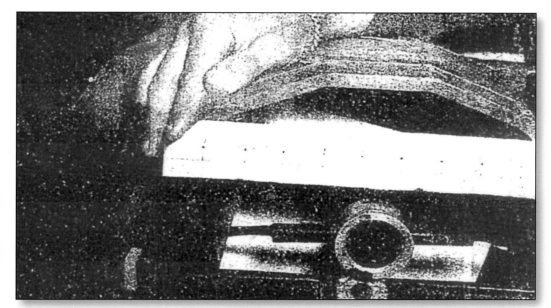

*Bolometer – IR sensor.*

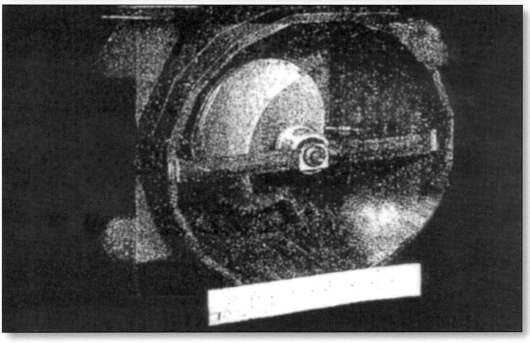

*Thermal sensor head.*

205

- Switch on the mechanically set timer, which defined the time during the fall of the bomb before control circuits were switched on. This usually took place at an altitude of 3,000 m.

The timer did not operate before the drop, but was activated upon release by an atmospheric pressure sensor - under any circumstances, the timer did not run for more than 50 seconds. The bomb aimer calculated the time required to start it at an altitude of no more than 900 m. This way he could use the full 50 seconds of timer operation. At the moment of release an electric circuit was closed, and this automatically switched on the IR sensor, including the mirror, electric motor and amplifier. Just before bomb release the speed of the carrier aeroplane was reduced to some 380-450 km/h.

Ke-Go bomb drop trials were carried out in Hamamatsu Bay from December 1944 until July 1945. The carrier aeroplane, usually a Mitsubishi Ki-67 Hiryū bomber, took off from Kujihama aerodrome near Mito in Ibaragi prefecture. The target used was a 10 x 30 m raft, on which a fire was set to provide a heat signature. About 60 bombs were dropped at night, mainly Model 106 and Model 107 versions. The bomb was taken by a carrier aeroplane to an altitude of approx. 10,000 m and released near the raft. Having detached from the carrier aeroplane the umbrella-shaped air brakes deployed almost immediately, significantly reducing the rate of fall, and above all giving it a vertical trajectory. At an altitude of between 3,000 and 2,000 m above sea level the atmospheric pressure sensor automatically activated the tracking device. The effectiveness of the drops was recorded by a cine camera on the shore - a position light on the tail of the bomb allowed the flight trajectory to be tracked for later analysis.

Only in five or six cases out of around 60 was the bomb observed to detect the IR radiation source, and manoeuvre towards it during testing. The remaining bombs failed to detect the IR source and went far from their intended path. These results were very poor, suspected to be the result of high temperature variations of the heat source, failures in the guidance system and the surrounding environment of the bomb affecting the sensitivity of IR detection. Nevertheless, the designers hoped that their subsequent design, the Model 109 (which had increased wing area) would be a success.

Although the results achieved during bomb drop trials were far from satisfactory, the *Rikugun Koku Hombu* placed an order for 700 Ke-Go bombs by October 1945. The contract was not fulfilled, however, due to the cessation of hostilities. Japanese sources quote the carrier aeroplane as the P1Y Ginga, or 'Frances' to the Allies, but as the Ke-Go project was substantially run by the Army, it is unlikely that the Navy 'Frances' would have been used as a carrier.

After the war, in 1946, American aircraft engineering intelligence found secret Japanese military documents which included drawings, photos and reports from the trials of the Ke-Go IR homing bombs. Several sub-assemblies of these bombs were found at the *Rikugun Gijyutsu Honbu Dai 7 Kenkyujyo* (Army Technical Headquarter 7th Laboratory) at Matsumoto, including two incomplete IR detection heads. All the materials were shipped to the USA.

**Specifications:**

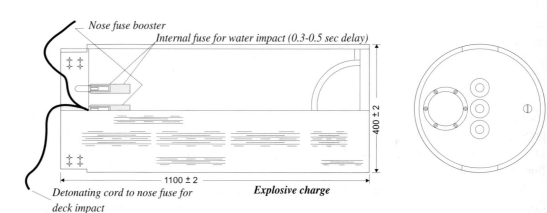

*Explosive section of Maru-Ke. It was Ta-dan (shaped-charge) type.*

Description: air-to-surface infra-red homing bomb. Mixed construction.

| Model | Ke-Go Model 101 | Ke-Go Model 106 | Ke-Go Model 107 | Ke-Go Model 108 | Ke-Go Model 109 |
|---|---|---|---|---|---|
| Wing span m | 2.65 | 2.0 | 2.0 | 2.865 | 2.865 |
| Length m | 3.0 | 4.725 | 4.745 | 5.490 | 5.3 |
| Fuselage diameter m | 0.5 | 0.5 | 0.5 | 0.5 | 0.5 |
| Wing area m² | 1.00 | | | | |
| Overall weight kg | 600 | | 726 | 800 | |
| Explosive weight kg | 200 | 200-300 | 200-300 | 200-300 | 200-300 |
| Release altitude m | 10,000 | 10,000 | 10,000 | 10,000 | 10,000 |
| Search altitude m | 3,000-2,500 | 3,000-2,500 | 3,000-2,500 | 3,000-2,500 | 3,000-2,500 |
| Hit accuracy m | ± 50 | ± 50 | ± 50 | | |
| Final descend speed km/h | | | | 620 | 676 |

Production: Several companies participated in production of Ke-Go bombs, among which the Mitsubishi *Jukogyo Nagasaki Heiki Seizojyo* (Nagasaki Arsenal at the Mitsubishi concern) made fuselages and carried out final assembly. Such sub-assemblies as gyros, bolometers, electric and mechanical components, were supplied by small specialist companies, such as Hitachi, Sumitomo, Hattori, and others. One of the bombs was tested for vibrations and another in a wind-tunnel at Tachikawa. Numbers produced of individual versions are given in the table below:

Ke-Go Production
Model 101 -     10
Model 102       5
Model 103       project
Model 104       project
Model 105       project
Model 106       50
Model 107       30
Model 108       project
Model 109       project

# Kawasaki I-Go-1 Otsu (Ki-148)

When the *Kaigun Koku Hombu* started to design the Funryu series of guided missiles for the Naval Aviation, this inspired the *Rikugun Koku Hombu* to explore options for a similar air-to-surface missile for the Army. The *Rikugun Koku Hombu* therefore asked the 1st Army Air Arsenal at Tachikawa (Tachikawa *Dai-Ichi Rikugun Kokusho*, usually abbreviated to *Kosho*) to prepare preliminary specifications for such a weapon.

In late June/early July 1944 concept work on three projects was completed, and these were handed over for production. The concept work was headed by General Enosawa, while the design was directly supervised by Lieutenant Colonel Takeo Omori from the *Koku Gijyutsu Kenkyujyo* (Army Air Technical Research Institute). On 24 July 1944 the *Rikugun Koku Hombu* passed the preliminary specifications to the Kawasaki and Mitsubishi companies, and the Imperial University in Tokyo. All the projects were built and almost until the end of the war were subject to intensive flight testing, but none were used in combat.

**Specifications:** of the missile, which received the designation 'Experimental Army Remote Controlled Flying Missile' (Ki-148) were handed over to the *Kagamigahara* plant of Kawasaki near Gifu. Jun Kitano was responsible for implementation of the programme. The missile was also known as the I-Go-1 Otsu (Model 1B – weapon). This was a small and relatively lightweight rocket-powered missile with a warhead consisting of 300kg of Ta-dan explosive (Ta-dan – short for Taisensha Dan). The Ki-48-lIb 'Lily' light bomber planned to act as the carrier aeroplane. The I-Go-1 Ko guided missile was developed by Mitsubishi in parallel.

The I-Go-1 Otsu was intended for attacks against targets that were relatively close to main air bases, mainly enemy ships concentrated around the Japanese islands. The missile was designed to be carried to an altitude of 700-900 m by a 'mother' aircraft and released some 12 km from the visible target. Following release, the guidance gyro system and the rocket engine would be started. An operator on the carrier aeroplane would guide the missile up to 4 km from the target, after which the missile would fly straight at sea level, no longer controlled by the operator.

Design work on the I-Go-1 Otsu missile commenced in July 1944 in the design bureau guided by Takeo Doi - two or three weeks later than design work on the similar project by Mitsubishi. Construction of the prototype missile was entrusted to the Akashi plant near Kobe, also belonged to Kawasaki. Nagaharu Kuroda with his team of 15 men was responsible for constructing the prototype. By the end of September 1944 a full scale model of the missile and a half-scale model were built. These were intended for wind-tunnel trials. Wind-tunnel tests of the Ki-48-IIb with a missile attached were also carried out.

The first powered I-Go-1 Otsu missile prototype was completed in October 1944. Initially it was fitted with a 100kg explosive warhead, but after some design changes the warhead was increased to 150kg, and then 300kg. By the end of October, 30 experimental guided missiles had been built for flight trials. The first flight test was carried out in October at Ajigaura beach near Mito. The I-Go-1 Otsu missile was slung under a Ki-48-II light bomber, which took off from Kamata aerodrome. After reaching an altitude of about 1,500 m the missile was released towards the Hitachi coast. Soon after release of the missile, its rocket engine was automatically started, and the missile accelerated to 600 km/h. However, the flight was not considered a success as the bomb failed to hit the target, instead crashing into Mount Mayumi. Subsequent flight trials were carried out from November 1944 until May 1945.

Most flight trials of the I-Go-1 Otsu missiles were carried out at Fusa air base (now US Air Force Base Yokota), east of Tokyo, where the *Koku Gijyutsu Kenkyujyo Kokushinsabu* (Aircraft Test Department of the Army Air Technical Research Institute) experimental unit was based. The programme of experimental trials was headed by Colonel Mitsuo Arimori, Lieutenant Colonel Takeo Omori from the *Koku Gijyutsu Kenkyujyo* (Army Air Technical Research Institute) and Major Kiyoshi Masumoto. Colonel Mitsuo Arimori was later promoted to General.

Trials of the new weapon were carried over Ajigaura beach near Mito, north-east of Tokyo, and then in Sagami Bay near Atami, south of Tokyo. The missiles were taken to an altitude of 500-1,000 m and released in level flight some 12 km from the visible target. Initial launch speed was 360 km/h. Subsequently the remote control system was switched on. At the same time the carrier aeroplane

*The radio aerial was fitted in the leading edge of the wing, which was of all wooden construction. The Kawasaki company built 150 I-Go-1 Otsu missiles.*

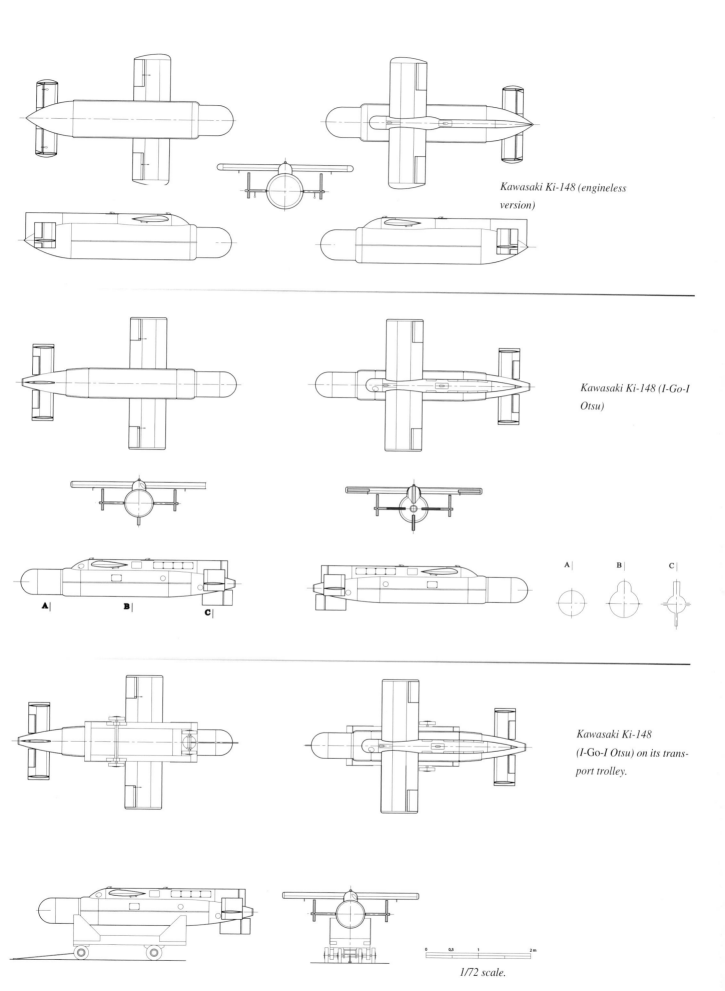

*Kawasaki Ki-148 (engineless version)*

*Kawasaki Ki-148 (I-Go-I Otsu)*

A|     B|     C|

**A**|     **B**|     **C**|

*Kawasaki Ki-148 (I-Go-I Otsu) on its transport trolley.*

0   0,5   1    2 m

*1/72 scale.*

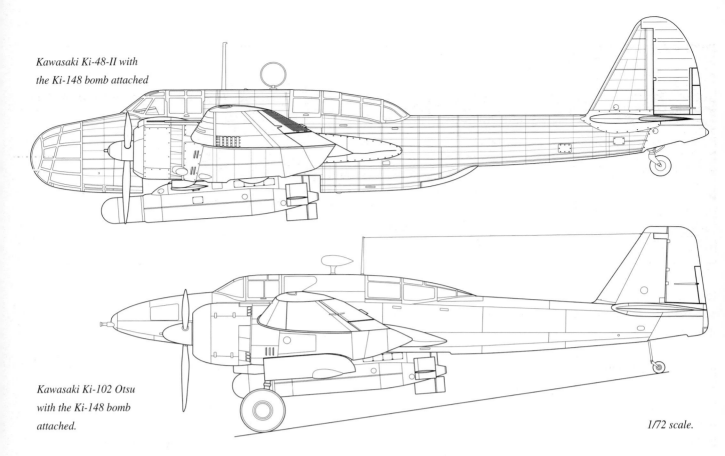

*Kawasaki Ki-48-II with the Ki-148 bomb attached*

*Kawasaki Ki-102 Otsu with the Ki-148 bomb attached.*

1/72 scale.

flew straight and level until the missile was directed onto a selected target. Following launch, the guidance system started to operate after one minute.

The guidance gyro was expected to operate for one to two minutes. Between half a second and two seconds after the missile was detached from the carrier aeroplane the flight was stabilised, and after two seconds the rocket engine started automatically. The missile accelerated to 550-600 km/h, heading towards the target. Maximum speed of the I-Go-1 Otsu missile was expected to be up to 650 km/h.

The missile flight control system was straightforward. Level flight was achieved by stabilising the missile using the gyro. The missile was controlled by operating the ailerons, which could deflect 5° up and 25° down. Upon an up or down command, the missile could change direction. If the command was stopped the missile returned to its pre-programmed flight direction. Therefore, to introduce a vertical change in flight trajectory the correction was entered gradually. To achieve a horizontal change of flight direction it was possible to deflect the rudder up to 25° to starboard or

*The negative angle of attack at which the I-Go-1Otsu missile was attached under the fuselage of the Ki-48-II Otsu carrier-aircraft was defined during wind-tunnel trials.*

to port. When the missile attempted to turn to port, the port wing aileron was deflected up, and the starboard surface down. The flight direction change mechanism was located in rear fuselage. After the control system was tuned the missile flew on the course set originally.

When in automatic flight guidance mode control was maintained not by the revolutions of the gyro, but the revolution limiter which used voltage change in accordance with the principle of the Wheatstone bridge. This was a new idea used to solve the problems with missile guidance from the carrier aeroplane. At the end of 1944 the electric altimeter was developed. This allowed the missile to fly at an altitude of 7 m over sea level. The altitude of 7 m was ideal for attacks against battleships, cruisers or aircraft carriers. However, due to many engineering problems still unsolved at the time, it was decided to continue with traditional manual guidance system by operators in carrier aeroplanes. Guidance of the missile in flight was achieved using the gyro and the radio

*The weight of the explosive in the warhead was 300 kg, while the entire I-Go-1Otsu missile weighed 680 kg. The radio remote control system was housed under the fairing at the top of the fuselage.*

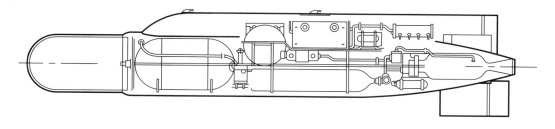

*Cut-away of the Ki-148 bomb.*

system made by Sumitomo from Tokyo. The latter system was later converted for Kawasaki. The carrier aeroplane used an improved Army type Tobi-1 radio set as a transmitter. The transmitter operated in two frequency ranges (35-46 MHz and 45-58 MHz). Both these ranges had three bands each. The transmitter could send signals to six I-Go-1 Otsu missiles simultaneously, but only one missile could be guided at any one time.

Many problems with guidance of the I-Go-1 Otsu missiles were encountered during flight trials. The speed of the missile was quite high, which made it difficult to see. In practice this made it difficult to maintain the missile missile's trajectory towards the target. Therefore some missiles were painted in bright colours during flight trials, for better visibility. This was the necessary to help the operator guide the missile to the target. By May 1945 the success rate for hitting the target rose to 75%. This result was satisfactory for the specified goal of the programme, but practical assessment was in fact less optimistic. The size of the target was 150 m long, 30 m wide. These dimensions were supposed to represent the deck of an aircraft carrier or other ship. Later the dimensions of the target were increased by 20 m in both length and width, to give better effectiveness. Before satisfactory results were achieved in the spring of 1945, a total of some 50 I-Go-1 Otsu missiles were fired in trials.

During testing at the end of 1944, I-Go-1 Otsu missiles were released during flight trials from carrier aeroplanes over Ganseki Jima (Rock Island), where the aiming point was located. During one of the trials the released missile could no longer be guided. The operator failed to notice that the

*Flying trials of the I-Go-1 Otsu missiles made use of the Kawasaki Ki-102 Otsu aircraft. Here ground crew members prepare the guided missile for a test flight.*

missile turned to the port and was headed towards Atami, a health resort town. Soon afterwards the missile hit the Tamanoi Hotel and exploded, upon which the hotel started to burn. Two hotel guests and two maids were killed in the explosion. Although the incident was covered in the media, no details were given. Development work on the missiles was secret and the press was not allowed to publicise information about the incident. After this incident the trials were temporarily halted. It was later found out that the missile turned to port due to control system damage. After detailed analysis of the flight it was found that the problem was also caused by the angle of incidence of the main wings and the tail. It was decided to build 30 engineless missiles to conduct a series of gliding trials. Later a trials station was built on Lake Biwa, the largest lake in Japan, and Ganseki Jima island was chosen as the proper point for aiming trials.

There were also many problems with engineering and guidance. One of the engineering problems was that the method of detaching the missile from the carrier aeroplane was imperfect. Very often the hydraulic catch disengaged spontaneously, due to vibrations from the carrier aeroplane. Another problem was unstable voltage in the electrical system. This affected the remote control of the missile. The flight trajectory of I-Go-1 Otsu missiles was also often curved, in the shape of a long sinusoid. This was due to high wing loading with a low aspect-ratio wing meaning that a stable flight pattern could not be achieved without constant correction.

The unpowered missile was a cantilever high-wing monoplane. Water ballast was fitted in place of the explosive charge and the rocket engine in the forward and rear sections of the round fuselage. Untapered wings with round tips were fitted with slotted ailerons.

Kamihira village in Toyama prefecture was chosen as the trial site, and the unpowered experimental missiles were delivered there. Their design allowed adjustment of the wing and tail incidence, to test it during controlled take-offs from a catapult. Each missile take-off was filmed by a number of cine cameras, each recording a flight between poles spaced at 10 m intervals. The records after each trial were immediately sent by coded signal to Tachikawa, where the flight was analysed. The trials were completed on 8 November 1944 after the optimum angle of incidence was defined. This allowed resumption of flight trials of the powered missiles.

The missile in this version was a cantilever high-wing monoplane. The forward fuselage housed a warhead with 300kg of Ta-dan explosive, while the rear section housed a rocket motor. The

*The top fairing of the fuselage, which housed the remote control system, could be removed for maintenance. The two-piece cylindrical fuselage was made of thin two-layer metal sheets, and was bolted together by 25 screws along each side.*

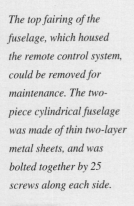

*I-Go-1Otsu missile attached under the Kawasaki Ki-48 carrier-aircraft. Note the automatic stabiliser of the height of attachment, which was later removed.*

*Wooden structure of the I-Go-1Otsu missile wings was simple and strong. It proved its worth during flying trials, when it carried very high wing loads.*

*To attach the I-Go-1Otsu missile under the fuselage of the Ki-102 Otsu aircraft, rigid attachment points were fitted and the bomb bay doors removed.*

*The Kawasaki Ki-102 Otsu aircraft was being introduced into service with combat units at the time of flight testing of the I-Go-1Otsu missiles.*

fuselage was a two-layer cylinder of 0.3 and 0.5mm steel sheets, with the outer cylinder separated from the interior of the fuselage. It consisted of two halves split along a horizontal plane connected with 25 bolts on each side. The outer cylinder was integral with the upper fuselage, which housed the automatic guidance system, the radio system, batteries, etc. Also the wings of the missile were attached to this section. The wings were of all-wood construction. The radio receiver aerial was fitted in the wing leading edge. The wing had a standard NACA 0012 symmetrical airfoil, and had 3° of incidence. The twin tails were made of wood, but were covered entirely with thin metal sheet.

The rocket engine was fitted in the rear fuselage, and the central section housed the tanks for the two-component liquid fuel. The rocket fuel mixture included two components: Ko (the German *T-Stoff* produced under licence), consisting of 80% hydrogen peroxide ($H_2O_2$) plus oxyquinoline and pyrophosphate as stabilisers, and Otsu (licence-produced *C-Stoff*) consisting of 30% hydrazine hydrate ($N_2H_4$), methanol ($CH_3HO$) and water with small amount of potassium-copper cyanides. The central fuselage also housed the compressor, fuel injectors to the combustion chamber, and the gyro control system. The Toku-Ro.1 Type 1 rocket engine, with a thrust of 130 kG, operating for 77 seconds, was located in the tail. It was based on the German Walter HWK 109-509A. Wings were fitted above the fuselage on a solid support, as were the attachments to fit the bomb under the carrier aeroplane. Control surfaces comprised ailerons, rudders and elevators, actuated by radio

*The radio control system equipment of the I-Go-1Otsu missile was fitted in the forward compartment of the Kawasaki Ki-48-II Otsu carrier-aircraft.*

signals from the carrier aeroplane. I-Go-1 Otsu missiles were brought under the carrier aeroplane on a special transport trolley, and subsequently attached to racks located in the bomb bay.

Flight trials continued until July 1945, mostly conducted over Lake Biwa. The I-Go-1 Otsu (Ki-148) guided missile was approved for series production, which was started at the Akashi plant. By the end of June 1945, 150 missiles had been built. However, the plant was completely destroyed during bomber raids on 22 and 26 June and 7 July, so series production of the missiles became virtually impossible.

All previous flight trials were carried out using the Kawasaki Ki-48-II Otsu bomber. Ultimately, the Ki-148 missiles were going to be carried by Kawasaki Ki-102 Otsu and Mitsubishi Ki-67 Hiryū bombers.

Paint scheme

Ki-148 remote controlled missiles were finished light grey overall, with a red band around the forward fuselage, and a red stripe along the fuselage.

**Specifications:**

Description: remote controlled high-wing monoplane air-to-surface missile of mixed construction. Wings and tail were made of wood, and the fuselage of metal.

Power plant: one Toku-Ro.1 Type 1 liquid fuel rocket engine with a thrust of 130 kG, gyro start-up time 0.5 s after launch, engine start-up 1.5 seconds after launch, engine operation time 77 seconds.

Explosive charge: 300kg

| Type | I-Go-1 Otsu (Ki-148) (engineless version) | I-Go-1 Otsu (Ki-148) (powered version) |
|---|---|---|
| Wing span m | 2.6 | 2.6 |
| Length m | 3.96 | 4.09 |
| Fuselage diameter m | 0.7 | 0.55 |
| Height m | 0.9 | 0.9 |
| Wing area m² | 1.95 | 1.95 |
| Empty weight kg | | 550 |
| Normal take-off weight kg | | 680 |
| Useful load kg | | 130 |
| Wing loading kg/m² | | 349 |
| Power loading kg/kG | - | 5.23 |
| Maximum speed km/h | | 550 |
| at an altitude of m | | 500-1,000 |
| Launch speed km/h | | 360 |
| at an altitude of m | | 500-1,500 |
| Ceiling m | | 500-1,000 |
| Normal range m | | 12 |

Production: a total of 180 Ki-148 (I-Go-1 Otsu) missiles, including 150 production examples, were built between October 1944 and late June 1945 at the Akashi plant of Kawasaki Kokuki Kogyo Kabushiki Gaisha.

*The remote control system was fitted in the nose of the Ki-48-II Otsu fuselage. It was activated upon release of the I-Go-1Otsu missile. Dual controls and careful visual observation were used to guide the missile during flying trials.*

# Mitsubishi I-Go-1 Ko (Ki-147)

In late June/early July 1944 preliminary specifications, codenamed I-Go, for remote controlled air-to-surface rocket-powered missiles were developed under General Enosawa. On 24 July 1944 *Rikugun Koku Hombu* passed the specifications to the Kawasaki and Mitsubishi companies, and the Imperial University in Tokyo.

This idea was derived from German experiments with remote controlled missiles during the Second World War, including the Henschel Hs-117 Schmetterling, Henschel Hs-293, Messerschmitt Enzian and others.

The remote control missile developed by Mitsubishi received the designation 'Experimental Army Remote Controlled Flying Missile' (Ki-147). The missile was also known as the I-Go-1 Ko (Model 1A weapon). Design work was headed by Kyunojo Ozawa, who had earlier designed the Mitsubishi Ki-67 Hiryū bomber. Design work on the I-Go-1 Ko commenced in August 1944, and the first prototype was ready by October. In November nine more missiles were built, but when the factory at Nagoya (*Nagoya Kenkyujyo*) was destroyed on 7 December during an earthquake, further assembly was stopped. Several missiles were assembled by Nihon Sharyo (Japanese Rail Cars). The first ground trials were carried out there, and these covered testing of stabilisation devices and gyros. A contract was placed there for a batch of 50 I-Go-1 Ko missiles and for series production, but eventually not a single missile was built as the *Rikugun Koku Hombu* terminated any further work on it.

The Ki-147 had an 800kg explosive warhead and fuse in the forward section. The central fuselage housed the radio receiver with the gyro-controlled actuating mechanism, which received signals from the carrier aeroplane. The tail section was originally planned to house the Toku-Ro 1-Go Model 1 two-component liquid fuel rocket engine, developed on the basis of the German Walter HWK 109-509A, with a thrust of 130 kG, for 77 seconds. But its thrust proved insufficient, so the modified Toku-Ro 1-Go Model 2 rocket engine with a thrust of 300 kG for 60 seconds was fitted.

The rocket fuel mixture included was the same Ko (*T-Stoff*) and Otsu (*C-Stoff*) described previously. The liquid fuel was fed to the rocket engine using compressed air from a cylinder at 150 kG/cm$^2$. When the engine was started, an electromagnetic jack released the fuel valve. Fuel tanks were made of tinned steel, and moving parts were chromium plated. Fuel system piping was made of aluminium.

The central fuselage also housed a compressed air cylinder which powered the gyro stabilisation system and servo-mechanisms as well as the fuel system. The system was problematic because whenever the rocket engine stopped working, the stabilisation system also turned off, rendering the missile uncontrollable. Before the problem could be cured the entire programme was cancelled.

Conformal tanks for the two-component rocket fuel were located above the fuselage, along with the fuel filler and the attachment for fitting the missile under the carrier aircraft. The support also held the untapered wing, which had 3° dihedral. The tail was fitted with twin fins. Both the wings and tail were fitted with control surfaces, ailerons, rudders and elevators. These surfaces were radio controlled via the gyro from the carrier aeroplane. Wings and tail had wooden framework and were plywood covered.

The I-Go-1 Ko missile was attached on two hydraulic links in the bomb bay of a specially converted Mitsubishi Ki-67 Hiryū bomber. Immediately prior to launch the missile was lowered on special extended attachments so that it did not hit the propellers on launching. The carrier aeroplane climbed to an altitude of 700-900 m with the missile attached and launched it 11 km from the visible target of the attack. Half a second after the missile was detached from the aeroplane, the stabilisers were switched on automatically, and after 1.5 seconds the rocket engine was started and fired for approximately 60 seconds. From that moment the missile was powered by the rocket engine and flew at an altitude of about 7 m above the sea at a speed of 550-600 km/h, while the carrier aeroplane followed it to within 4 km of the target. All this time the missile had to be maintained within visual range to allow it to be radio-controlled from the carrier aeroplane, until it reached its target. Guidance onto the target was achieved using the radio transmitter fitted in the forward fuselage of the carrier. This was manually controlled by the operator using twin two-position switches, which defined the commands up, down, port, and starboard. Only one command at a time could be transmitted - delays between subsequent commands constituted the main problem of the guidance system.

Before flight trials were undertaken in early September 1944 the *Rikugun Koku Hombu* ordered 25 scaled-down wooden models of the I-Go-1 Ko missiles, which were subjected to flight stability tests. A special launcher was built by Nihon Hatsuden company on an embankment near Kohara power station at Kamidaira village near Toyama. Between 5 October and 8 November 1944 experimental take-offs in the direction of Shogawa Valley were carried out. These flights allowed the design team to define the optimum wing incidence and test flight stability. Each flight was filmed, and subsequently the film was sent to Tachikawa, where flight analysis was carried out and conclusions drawn. This allowed the designers to amend their design as necessary.

At the end of October full size I-Go-1 Ko missiles were assembled, and in November they were fitted with rocket engines. Work on converting the Mitsubishi Ki-67 Hiryū to the role of a carrier was done at Fusa air base. Flight trials were carried out by the experimental unit commanded by Lieutenant Colonel Takeo Omori, based at Ajigaura on the Manazuru Coast near Mito. A series of experimental launches were carried out over Lake Biwa, with the rocky island of Ganseki Jima as the target. Just before the end of 1944 the trial programme and all development work was abandoned, as it was decided that guiding a bomb to within 4 km of the target before leaving it to continue unguided (for example a group of aircraft carriers) was impractical and unlikely to result in much success. Besides, the speed of the missile was not very high, and radio guidance onto the target by the operator required a lot of precision, all within the modest range of the radio transmitter. Mainly for these reasons the I-Go-1 Ko missile was not used in combat.

Paint scheme.

The I-Go-1 Ko remote controlled missile was painted light grey overall. Large identification letters in yellow were applied on both sides of the rear fuselage. A yellow band was also applied on the fuselage forward of the wings.

**Specifications:**

Description: high-wing monoplane air-to-surface remote controlled missile. Mixed construction: wings and tail wooden, fuselage metal.

Power plant: one Toku-Ro 1-Go Model 1 liquid fuel rocket engine with a thrust of 150 kG, gyro start-up time 0.5s after launch, engine start-up 1.5 s after launch, engine operation time 77s (project).

One Toku-Ro 1-Go Model 2 liquid fuel rocket engine with a thrust of 300 kg, gyro start-up time 0.5s after launch, engine start-up 1.5 seconds after launch, engine operation time 60 seconds (prototypes).

Warhead: 800kg

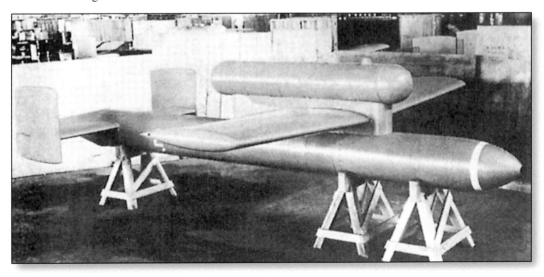

*The second prototype of the I-Go-1 Ko missile.*

*The last minutes of work for the ground crews preparing the I-Go-1Ko missile for a test flight, carried by the Mitsubishi Ki-67 Hiryū.*

*The last preparations for take-off of the Mitsubishi Ki-67 Hiryū bomber with the I-Go-1Ko missile attached under the fuselage.*

*Side view of the Mitsubishi Ki-67 Hiryū bomber, fin code no. 220, with the I-Go-1Ko missile, code no. 11, attached, during preparations for flight trials.*

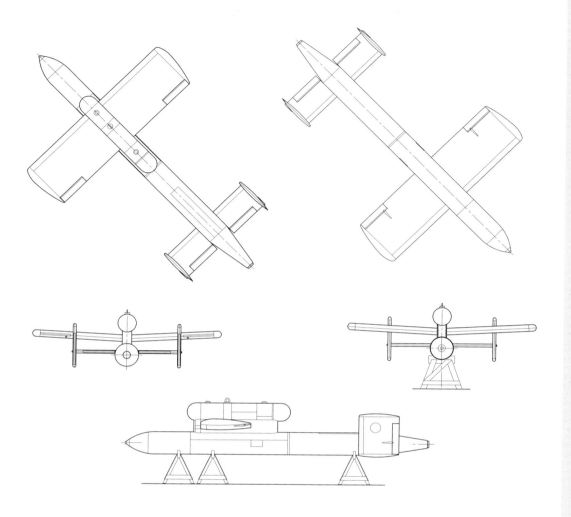

*Mitsubishi Ki-147*
*(I-Go-1 Ko)*

*1/72 scale.*

*I-Go-1 Ko missile, code
no. 11, attached in the
bomb bay of the Mitsubi-
shi Ki-67 Hiryū bomber.*

*Army aviation ground crew perform the last checks of the I-Go-1Ko missile immediately before attaching it under the carrier aircraft.*

| Type | Ki-147 (I-Go-1 Ko) |
| --- | --- |
| Wing span m | 3.8 |
| Length m | 5.77 |
| Height m | 1.055 |
| Fuselage diameter m | 0.45 |
| Wing area m² | 3.6 |
| Normal take-off weight kg | 1,400 |
| Wing loading kg/m² | 389.0 |
| Power loading kg/kG | 5.8 |
| Maximum speed km/h | 550-600 |
| Launch speed km/h | 360 |
| from an altitude of m | 700-900 |
| Ceiling m | 5,000-1,000 |
| Normal range km | 11 |
| Maximum range km | 15 |

Production: Mitsubishi Jukogyo Kabushiki Gaisha at Nagoya and Nihon Sharyo built a total of 10 Ki-147 (I-Go-1 Ko) experimental guided missiles between October and November 1944.

*During tests with the I-Go-1Ko missile the Mitsubishi Ki-67 Hiryū flew over Biwa lake near Kyoto. One of the targets "attacked" during these trials was a small rocky island near the shore of the lake.*

*Preparations for flying trials of the I-Go-1Ko guided missile attached under the Mitsubishi Ki-67 Hiryū. The trials were probably carried out at Fussa air base, now Yokota.*

The second prototype of the I-Go-1 Ko missile on trestles in the assembly hall.

For security reasons the rocket fuel components were stored in underground magazines. Here, workers dig out a shelter for the rocket fuel in the northern slope of Murayama mountain near Yokota air base.

The engineer in charge of flying trials checks his watch before take-off of the Mitsubishi Ki-67 Hiryū, under which the I-Go-1Ko guided missile prototype is attached.

# Rikugun I-Go-1 Hei

In the spring of 1944 Lieutenant General Enosawa, the head of the *Rikugun Koku Hombu*, ordered the establishment of a team to prepare specifications for unmanned remote controlled anti-ship missiles, codenamed I-Go. The team included, among others, Colonel Mitsuo Arimori, Lieutenant Colonel Takeo Omori and Major Kiyoshi Masumoto.

On 24 July the *Rikugun Koku Hombu* issued specifications for two guided missiles that received the designations Ki-147 and Ki-148, (previously described). Later these were changed to I-Go-1 Ko, I-Go-1 Otsu, respectively. Development and construction of the I-Go-1 Ko missile prototypes was contracted to Mitsubishi's Nagoya plant, while the contract for work on the I-Go-1 Otsu missile went to Kawasaki. Both these radio-controlled missile projects would be powered by Ro-Go liquid fuel rockets.

The third missile project, designated I-Go-1 Hei (Model 1C weapon), was quite different. This was an unpowered missile with a torpedo-shaped fuselage 3.50 m long and 0.50 m in diameter, with cruciform main wings and tail. The forward fuselage housed a 300kg warhead fitted with a fuse. It would be guided onto the target by one of two systems. The first was by homing on sound waves emitted by gunfire from enemy ships, by receiving aerials at the wing tips which would decide the heading, the time delay taken into account. The second system consisted of a sensor and a microphone which could detect 3-5 Hz band sound waves from naval guns. After a number of experiments with both systems the latter showed greater promise and was selected for implementation. Development was started by the *Rikugun Koku Hombu* in the spring of 1944.

Starting in March 1945 range trials commenced at Kujihama, near the airfield at Mito. The I-Go-1 Hei missile was carried on a Mitsubishi Ki-67 Hiryū heavy bomber. In March three trials of the missile prototypes were carried out, to test the effectiveness of the homing device. By July 1945 an additional 20 missiles of a modified design had been built. Prototypes were fitted with a gyro system actuating three control surfaces out of six, but modified variants had another gyro to recover the missile from inverted flight. In July 1945 launch trials of six modified prototypes, without the guidance system, were carried out over Lake Biwa, only the gyro stabilising system being tested. Trial results were satisfactory. Air-launched trials of the homing devices were intended to be carried out with the remaining 14 prototypes, but these were never performed due to end of hostilities. It was planned also that I-Go-1 Hei missiles would be launched from coastal launchers on special rocket powered trolleys, directly towards enemy landing ships.

The *Rikugun Koku Hombu* expected a lot of the I-Go-1 Hei sound-wave homing missiles, and even considered them more effective than the I-Go-1 Ko and I-Go-1 Otsu radio-guided missiles. No photos or drawings of the I-Go-1 Hei missile are known, so its exact appearance is unclear.

**Specifications:**

Description: winged air/surface-to-surface homing missile. Mixed construction.
Power plant: no propulsion.
Weight of the warhead: 300kg

| Type | I-Go-1 Hei |
| --- | --- |
| Wing span m | 3.5 |
| Length m | |
| Fuselage diameter m | 0.5 |
| Maximum speed km/h | 650 |
| at an altitude of m | |
| Launch speed km/h | 360 |
| at an altitude of m | 700-1,000 |

| Type | I-Go-1 Hei |
|---|---|
| Normal range km | 9 |
| Maximum range km | 18 |

Production: 24 I-Go-1 Hei experimental missiles were built.

# Tokyo University I-Go infra-red guided missile

Hideo Itokawa, Assistant Professor of the Second Engineering Faculty, Aircraft Structure Department of Tokyo University, was asked to make an aircraft for Tokko-tai by *Rikugun Sanbo Hombu* and *Kaigun Gunreibu*. He declined this offer, but suggested instead an infra-red guided missile, to home in on enemy warship's infra-red emissions. They accepted his offer, and it was designated as the 'I-Go Bomb', taking the I from Itokawa. Development of I-Go bomb proceeded as far as the final test stage. Tests were planned against *Gunkan Jima* (Battleship *Island*) in Lake Biwa, as this island's shape was similar to a warship. In early August 1945, an air strike killed two of the trials team. The project was stopped by the end of the war. All the material of the project was disposed of on August 16, 1945. Though the guidance systems are different, there is still a possibility that this was I-Go-1 Hei itself, or this was Maru-Ke itself.

Production: in 1945 at least one prototype was built.

# Rikugun AZ and Maru-Ko flying torpedoes

The jet-powered AZ flying torpedo was developed in 1941 to the order of the Imperial Japanese Army. Upon launch from the carrying aeroplane it would fly for a time just above the water, and upon approaching an enemy ship would submerge and hit it. The engine was removed from a Type 91 Model 3 torpedo, and a jet engine with combustion chamber and injectors was fitted in its place in the rear section. Kerosene was used as fuel, as in normal torpedoes. The torpedo received the designation AZ. Only four prototypes were built. A range of 290 m at a speed of 54 km/h was achieved during trials. Frequent problems with combustion and poor underwater stability were encountered during testing. All trials were terminated after three months.

In 1944, also to an order from the Imperial Japanese Army, another special flying torpedo was developed, designated Maru-Ko, for coastal defence. The concept was that it should be launched by a conventional torpedo-bomber and fly just above the water. The preliminary project was developed by the *Rikugun Gijyutsu Honbu Dai 7 Kenkyujyo* (Army Technical Headquarters 7th Laboratory) in cooperation with Mr. Hirasawa from the *Kaigun Kansei Honbu* (Navy Fleet Administrative Headquarters). Mitsubishi *Jukogyo Nagasaki Heiki Seizojyo* (Nagasaki arsenal at the Mitsubishi concern) was responsible for selection of the fuel. The rocket engine of the torpedo would be fed with a mixture of nitric acid and methanol. A mixture of hydrogen sulfide and ammonia would be the catalyst. Laboratory trials confirmed the suitability of the fuel, but no suitable ignition device could be found, and consequently the required ignition temperature could not be reached. Trials with ignition of kerosene in the pre-combustion chamber, and subsequent injection of the actual fuel were carried out. The prototype Maru-Ko torpedo was ready in July 1945 and awaited trials, but all development was abandoned after attempts to start the engine proved unsuccessful. The *Heiki Gyo-sei Hombu* (Weapon Administrative Headquarters) of the *Rikugun Koku Hombu* wanted to fit a control system, but frequent air attacks and the subsequent end of hostilities called a halt to development.

# Tokushu Kogata Bakugekki and Sa-Go

Two anti-aircraft missiles named '*Tokushu Kogata Bakugekki Kogata*' (Special Small Bomber Small-size) and '*Tokushu Kogata Bakugekki Ohgata*' (Special Small Bomber Large-size) were developed by the Army. Both types had a warhead of 530kg, and were propelled by rockets with between 8.3 and 9.2 seconds firing time. They were intended to attack enemy bombers by means of radio control.

A missile project designated 'Sa-Go' is said to have been a surface-to-air guided rocket under development by the army until work stopped in July 1944. Tokushu Kogata Bakugekki and Sa-Go may have been the same weapon.

The Navy went further than the Army in development of guided weapons in some respects, with work including surface-to-surface missiles and more advanced work on surface-to-air missiles, in addition to the air-to-surface devices favoured by the Army.

The Funryu ('angry dragon') series of rocket powered missiles were among the first such devices to be developed by the Navy. These were anti-ship or -aircraft missiles of increasing sophistication.

Most of the guided missiles were developed by the Kugisho design bureau in the summer of 1943, and testing continued until the end of the war. The first models were focused as an anti-ship weapon and developed as surface-to-surface, and later as air-to-surface missiles.

In addition, the Navy conducted development work on flying anti-submarine torpedoes. These would be dropped from an aeroplane and after a short diving flight they would enter the water and spiral down to 60 m below the surface. Two versions of unpowered flying torpedoes were developed, called the Kurai 6-Go and Kurai 7-Go. Due to unsatisfactory trial results they were not put into production.

A system of dropping mines from aircraft was also under development. This was carried out by the Fujikura company, which developed a special parachute to slow down the free fall of the mine. Trials terminated due to the cessation of hostilities.

## Kugisho Funryu remote controlled missile

At the end of 1943 the *Kaigun Gijyutsu Kenkyujyo* (Navy Technical Laboratory) at Meguro near Tokyo studied the possibility of replacing coastal guns with rocket missiles. A parallel analysis was done by *Kure Kosho* (Kure Arsenal), *Dai-Ichi Gijyutsu-Sho* (Navy 1st Technical Bureau) and *Dai-Ni Kayaku-Sho* (2nd Gunpowder Bureau). Within the *Kaigun Gijyutsu Kenkyujyo* the work was carried out by scientists from various branches of technology, and by the beginning of 1944 the task of developing the rocket missile was taken over by the *Dai-Ichi Kaigun Koku Gijyutsusho* at Yokosuka, *Kugisho* in short. Within its organisation the *Funshin Kenkyu-Bu* (Rocket Research

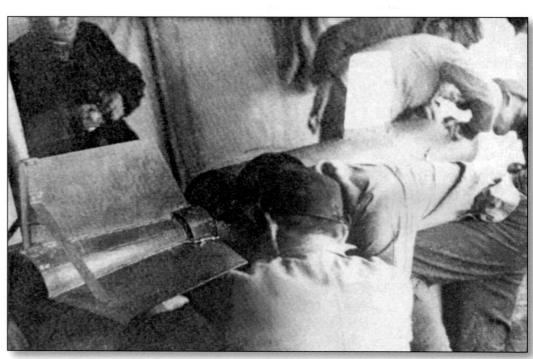

*Funryu 2-Go rocket missiles readied for take-off. Note the center wings are painted white for test purposes*

Bureau) was formed with the aim of developing new rocket-powered artillery weapons. The bureau employed some 200 technicians, and the main research was done by 40 engineering officers of the Navy and civilian engineers.

The main task of the new team was to develop remote control missiles able to destroy both enemy ships and bombers. The entire programme received the codename Funryu (Angry Dragon). The first to be developed was a surface-to-surface missile, which received the designation Funryu 1.

The Funryu 1 was a remote control missile launched from land to be used against surface vessels. It was developed in 1944 by Masao Sugimoto from the Science Research Department of the Navy Institute of Technology. The missile received the designation Toku-Gata Funshindan (rocket missile). It was powered by a solid fuel rocket engine. It later provided the basis for the Funryu 2, Funryu 3 and Funryu 4 AA missile projects.

The Funryu 1 missile was designed by Yoshinori Otsu from the Shipbuilding Research Department. It was a torpedo-shaped missile, with a fuselage 3 m long, and cruciform main wings and tail. The sole prototype was built by the *Dai-Ichi Kaigun Koku Gijyutsusho*, and the remote control system was developed by the Electric Wave Research Department.

The Electric Wave Research Department used radio control systems for remote guidance. They were used, among others, for remote control of floating targets during artillery training. Research into this type of guidance was well advanced, but designers could not master the sending of commands on various bands. The system was not fully developed, and needed two additional transmitter and radio receiver devices. One of these would be used to detect and track the target, a kind of radar, while the other would check the speed and flight direction of the missile. Eventually further development of the Funryu 1 missile was cancelled due to engineering problems.

From the very beginning it was realised that development of such a missile would be complex. Hitting a manoeuvring target such as an enemy ship, would be a particularly big problem. Furthermore, raids by Boeing B-29 bombers were becoming more and more damaging. Despite these troubles several experimental Funryu 1 missiles were ordered, and for flight trials they were going to be carried in the bomb bay of a Mitsubishi G4M 'Betty'. Soon all development work was abandoned and it was decided to design another missile, in the surface-to-air category, remotely controlled by radio, that would explode automatically on reaching the target. The designers hoped that such missile would scatter tight formations of B-29 Superfortress bombers.

When the designers of the Funryu 2, as the new AA missile was designated, commenced work they had no information for comparison. Brief reports of the German V-1 flying bombs and V-2 rockets reached Japan, but gave only a vague idea of their design. In Japan, work on solid fuel rockets only commenced in the summer of 1944. Hence, design work on the new missiles was limited to the shape of the missile itself and the remote guidance system.

Takashi Yoshika, the Engineering Manager of the 4th Department of the Navy Supply HQ, was responsible for the main warship development programmes in the Navy Science Research Institute. After the briefing on 2 July 1944, he was also appointed to the development programme of rocket missile automatic guidance systems (Funshindan).

As a result of an agreement with Iwakichi Ezaki, the development programme was immediately given priority and design work gained pace. Participating in design work were Mr. Sugimoto from the Science Research Bureau, who already had some experience working on the Funryu 1 anti-ship missile, and Mr. Otsu from the Shipbuilding Research Bureau, who prepared production documentation together with Major Urata.

At the end of 1944 the technicians, with their families (altogether some 400 people), moved to a site near the foot of Mount Asama, at Sengadaki near Karuizawa. Here they set up a trial range, to carry out firing trials with the Toku-Gata Funshindan. Additionally, in April 1945 the Rocket Studies Department, headed by General Shizuo Oyagi, was reformed into the Navy Technical Research Institute.

The Funryu 2 missile was fitted with the 3-shiki Funshin 2-gata (Type 3 rocket engine Model 2) solid fuel rocket engine, developed by the *Kaigun* Dai-Ni Kayakusho (Navy 2nd Gunpowder Arsenal).

Testing of the Funryu 2 missile was to commence with trials of the rocket engine, still without the remote guidance system. General specifications of the Funryu 2 missile with the 3-shiki Funshin 2-gata rocket engine were as follows:

- Overall missile weight: ca. 370kg (including 192kg warhead)
- Rocket fuel weight 50kg (Model FD6T two-component fuel)
- Maximum thrust 5,570 kG
- Average thrust 2,430 kG during approximately 5 seconds of operation
- Maximum range 5 km.

The shape of the Funryu 2 missile was similar to a torpedo, with cruciform wings positioned at the centre of gravity. Ailerons on the wings were deflected by a pneumatic system of servo-mechanisms, to point the flight trajectory towards a certain aiming point. The shape of the missile was selected following detailed testing in a wind-tunnel with varying conditions to simulate various phases of flight.

A simple system of commands was adopted for the guidance system, as this was considered sufficient for control in the cruciform wing layout. The radio guidance system consisted of a receiver and transmitter. Additionally, the guidance system included two pneumatic gyros responsible for stabilising the missile. A modified radio control system was used for remote guidance, similar to that planned for guidance of the Funryu 1 missile.

The missile was designed to be launched from a launcher angled at some 45 degrees. After take-off the missile would be radio controlled. Flight control was through two ailerons on the main wings and two rudders, and two gyros. The main wings were of wooden construction, with receiver aerials inside. Atmospheric pressure was used to drive the gyros, while dry batteries supplied the radios.

The first trial of the Funryu 2 missile with the radio guidance system was carried out on 25 April 1945, in the presence of His Royal Highness Prince Takamatsu and high ranking officers of the Naval General Staff from Tokyo. That day a trial was scheduled which would involve radio communication with the missile, correct radio control, flight stability, as well as measurement of range, ceiling and accuracy. Take-off of the missile took place in accordance with the plan, radio commands set the Funryu 2 in straight and level flight, and a hit near the selected target was achieved. The flight was considered an overall success, but accuracy was not as hoped as the missile struck 20 m from the target.

After analysis of the automatic flight record, in cooperation with Professor Ichiro Tani, an aerodynamicist from the Aerodynamics Faculty of the Imperial University in Tokyo, the radio guidance system was modified, the weight of the missile fuselage was reduced, the gyro operation was improved, and the radio command system was improved.

At the time funds for development of new military technology were reduced, so the Funshin Kenkyu-bu was unable to obtain the two tonnes of duralumin needed to make fuselages for the prototype batch of missiles. For this reason one of the workers stole the necessary amount of duralumin from a store at Kugisho, and in this way several Funryu 2 missiles were built, one of which was earmarked for wind-tunnel testing, and nine were handed over for further flight trials, carried out near Mount Asama. It was assumed that the trials would give proper results for an effective future weapon.

Meanwhile, work continued on another type of propulsion for the missile, a liquid fuel rocket engine. The engine would be used to power the Funryu 3 missile, a development of the Funryu 2. Only one prototype of the experimental Funryu 3 guided AA missile was built. However, due to lack of experience and funds, all development work on the Funryu 3 missile was abandoned, and soon afterwards work started on an entirely new missile, the Funryu 4.

Immediately after the first launch of the Funryu 2 missile, the *Kaigun Rocket Hishotai Kenkyu* (Rocket-Powered Aircraft Research Department) was formed. Its role was to develop a remote control missile, designated Funryu 4. Its main aim was to combat B-29 bombers. The programme team included professors and experts from Mitsubishi *Jukogyo Nagasaki Heiki Seizojyo* (Nagasaki arsenal at the Mitsubishi concern), from the Akashi aircraft plant of Kawasaki at Gifu, and from *Tokyo Keiki* (Tokyo Factory of Aircraft Instruments). The experts were based at the foot of Mount Izu where they commenced design work. The KR-20 liquid fuel rocket engine with a thrust of 1,500 kG, the same as in the Ohka special attack aeroplane, would be used in the Funryu 4 AA missile. The KR-20 rocket engine was built by the Nagasaki Arsenal and by the plant at Gifu. Inside the fuselage of the missile were two tanks with the liquid rocket fuel, an explosive charge, high-pressure container with liquid nitrogen, radio transmitter, batteries, two gyros and fuses.

In accordance with the trial programme, at the first stage of operation the KR-20 rocket engine produced 3 levels of thrust, 1,500 kg initially, 750 kg at 6,000 m, and 600 kg at 11,500 m. The fuel gave a total firing time of 1 min 55 sec, enough for the missile to reach 23,500 m under power and 25,700 m at apogee. It was assumed that the weight of the body would be 76kg, the rocket engine 140-150kg, remote control system 25kg, fuel tank 132kg, fuel 600kg, and explosive charge 50kg.

In fact, due to lack of duralumin it was not possible to make missile bodies of light alloy, so steel was used, and as a result the overall weight of the first prototype Funryu 4 rose to 1,500kg. For this reason the method of launching the missile was altered. Originally it was going to be launched vertically, but it was now to be angled at 45°. Additionally, the missile was fitted with an auxiliary solid fuel rocket engine. The combustion chamber of the liquid fuel rocket was made of soft steel, and internally it was lined with a thin layer of fireproof ceramic supplied by Toyo Toki (Oriental Ceramics Factory) at Moji.

The tank for the Ko liquid fuel was made of thin tinned steel sheets (production versions were to have tanks made of duralumin). The valves were made of stainless steel, while the valve body, valve lifter and piston were plated with a layer of chromium. The body of the valve lifter was made of acid-resistant steel, while the entire fuel system was made of internally tinned steel tubes or duralumin tubes. All connections were made of PVC, tin, aluminium, synthetic rubber, or soft

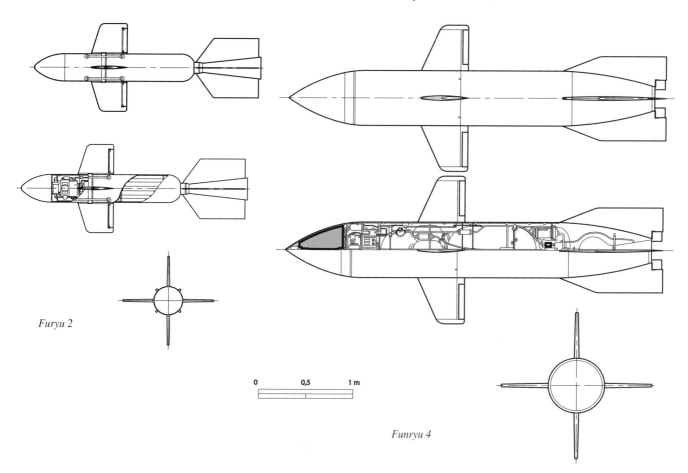

*Furyu 2*

0    0,5    1 m

*Funryu 4*

stainless steel. The fuselage of the Funryu 4 missile prototype was made by Kugisho, but series production would be undertaken by Kawanishi.

Cruciform wings of all-wooden construction were made by the Akita Mokuzai company. Hydrogen peroxide, a component of the rocket fuel, would be supplied by the Yamakita company of Edogawa, while hydrazine would come from Mitsubishi Kasei. The remote control system was going to be delivered by Dai-Ni Gijyutsu-Sho (2nd Radio Wave Armament Department).

The development department was headed by Tatsuichi Shiromi, from the staff of the Japanese Broadcast Corporation, and design work was carried out, among others, by Doctor Kenjiro Katayanagi and Hiroshi Shinkawa from the *Kaigun Gijyutsu Kenkyujyo* (Navy Technical Laboratory). The control system was designated A-2 Model 1 for AA guns and A-2 Model 2 for AA rocket missiles (Funshindan).

Guidance onto the target was by a radar control system. Two ground radars (Ko and Otsu) were used to input corrections of the rocket missile flight trajectory. The guidance signal changed depending on the frequency transmitted by the Otsu radar. There were five frequency bands changing commands every 200 Hz, broadcast by a 1,000 Hz transmitter. The signals would be intercepted by the M device, which would distinguish them and transfer to individual execution mechanisms commands of 'up', 'down', 'starboard', 'port', and 'detonate'. The control system featured a single system of direction commands, consisting of transmitting a continuous radio signal band. Each 200 Hz were followed by a short break. When the signal returned by the target was identical with the signal returned from the missile, detonation took place automatically. Effective range of guidance was 22 to 32 km, with an impact error of up to 50 m.

Two pneumatic gyros were included in the stabilising system, similar to those in the Funryu 2 missile. The servomechanisms were typical pneumatic units, which controlled wing ailerons via an electric relay supplied from dry batteries upon receiving the signal.

A firing trial of the Funryu 4 missile was planned on 16 August 1945, but the war ended before Mitsubishi *Jukogyo Nagasaki Heiki Seizojyo* (Mitsubishi Heavy Industries Nagasaki Arsenal) could supply liquid rocket fuel. It was too late for further work, so the programme was terminated, and preparations for series production were stopped. The designers were sworn to secrecy, and soldiers blew up all the stations and launchers connected with the Funryu 2 and Funryu 4 programme. The prototype liquid fuel rocket engine, auxiliary solid fuel rocket engine and Funryu 4 missile fuselage were buried in the ground at the foot of Mount Asama and Mount Tenmaru. Some were dug out by the local population in 1954.

**Specifications:**

Description: remote controlled surface-to-surface missile (Funryu 1); remote controlled surface-to-air missile (Funryu 2, 3 and 4).

Power plant: one 3-shiki Funshin 2-gata (Type 3 Model 2) rocket engine with a thrust of 2,430 kG and 5 s (Funryu 1 and 2), solid fuel.

One KR-20 liquid fuel rocket engine with a thrust of 1,500 kG and 5 minutes time of operation (Funryu 3 and 4).

Warhead: 50kg (Funryu 1, 2 and 3) or 200kg (Funryu 4) charge.

| Type | Funryu 1 | Funryu 2 | Funryu 3 | Funryu 4 |
|------|----------|----------|----------|----------|
| Wing span m | | 0.96 | 0.96 | 1.6 |
| Length m | 3.0 | 2.4 | 2.4 | 4.0 |
| Fuselage diameter m | | 0.3 | 0.3 | 0.6 |
| Empty weight kg | | 370 | | 1,900 |
| Power loading kg/kG | | 0.15 | | 1.27 |
| Maximum speed km/h | | 792 | | 1,100 |
| Climb to 10,000m | | | | 1 min. 00 sec. |
| Ceiling m | | | | 15,000 |
| Normal range km | | 5.5 | | 35 |

Production: Heiki Seizojyo built for trials at Nagasaki:
* prototype Funryu 1 experimental missile,
* Funryu 2 missiles,
* prototype Funryu 4 experimental missile.

# Kugisho Kudan flying bomb

At the end of 1944 the *Kaigun Koku Hombu* prepared specifications for an air launched rocket-powered homing flying bomb, which could be used against enemy aircraft formations. Development of the project, designated Kudan 1-Go (Flying Bomb No. 1), was entrusted to Captain Tsuruno from Kugisho in Yokosuka. Soon afterwards a model of the flying bomb was built in cooperation with Dai-Ichi Koku K.K. (The First Aviation Company). Ultimately the Kudan 1-Go bomb was going to be fitted with a rocket engine and a target homing system. The streamlined fuselage was made up of three main sections. The forward section housed the explosive, the central section supported the cruciform wings and housed the homing system, and the rear section housed the solid fuel rocket engine. The war ended while a test station was being prepared near Yokosuka.

The second guided flying bomb project, this time air-to-surface, was designated Kudan 2-Go (Flying Bomb No. 2). The project was developed by Major Tabuchi from the *Kugisho Hiko Jikken Bu* (Flight Test Department), who fitted a standard 10kg aircraft bomb with small wings. It would be dropped from an aeroplane and guided by radio control onto enemy ships. The wings, with Clark Y airfoil, had a span of 0.4 m, 0.125 m chord, and area of 0.05 m². The bomb was to be carried by an aeroplane to an altitude of 1,000 m and dropped. Subsequently, radio-controlled from the aeroplane, it glided to the target 12 km away.

Results of the first trials were unexpectedly good. Therefore, Mr. Wada, the manager of Kugisho, ordered further development work. The wing loading was about 2,000kg/m² (for fighters of the time it was 250-300kg/m²), and Major Tabuchi was worried by the lack of sufficient flight stability of the bomb. For this reason the wings were fitted with remote radio controlled ailerons, developed by Major Konishi.

At the time Major Tabuchi and Major Konishi were also engaged in trials of a new twin-engined bomber project. Both of them went missing during a test flight of the plane. Therefore, the experiments with remote guidance systems for glide bombs were not completed by the end of the war.

**Specifications:**
Description: radio-controlled flying bomb air-to air (Kudan 1-Go) and air-to-surface (Kudan 2-Go).
Mixed construction.
Power plant: rocket engine,
Warhead: (Kudan 1-Go),
10kg (Kudan 2-Go),

| Type | Kudan 1-Go | Kudan 2-Go |
|------|------------|------------|
| Wing span m | | 0,400 |
| Wing area m, | | 0,05 |
| Overall weight kg | | 40 |
| Wing loading kg/m, | | 2000 |
| Normal range km | | 12 |

Production: flying bombs Kudan 1-Go and Kudan 2-Go were built by *Dai-Ichi Kaigun Koku Gijyutsusho* in Yokosuka.

# Kugisho Kurai flying anti-submarine torpedo

The worsening military situation of Japan constantly forced the high command to look for more effective means of defence. One of these was the concept of aircraft-launched anti-submarine torpedoes, and intensive development work on these was carried out from April 1944. In accordance with the specifications prepared by the *Kaigun Koku Hombu*, issued for implementation to Kugisho in Yokosuka, the torpedo was going to be used against submarines, mainly in Tokyo Bay.

Initial plans were for a winged unpowered torpedo, launched from an aeroplane flying at 450 km/h at an altitude of 100 m, and gliding into the water, where it would make up to three 80 m spirals to reach a depth of 60 m where it would explode. The explosive charge would weigh 100kg, and it would be triggered by magnetic proximity fuses, design work on these having commenced at the time. To avoid premature detection of the magnetic field of the torpedo by enemy submarines, it was required that the design should be entirely wooden.

For this reason the designers, headed by Mr. Sano from *Hikoki Bu* (Aircraft Department), faced a serious problem of making the wooden structure watertight enough, to prevent the explosive from getting wet. Beside that they had to solve the problem of proper submersion of the torpedo. During submersion trials it was planned to fill the warhead of the torpedo with enough sand to equal the ultimate explosive charge. Apart from that, the bomb had to have a structure strong enough to endure the impact of hitting the water. The flight trials programme was going to provide solutions for all problems connected with flight stability, and define the optimum angle of entry. Possible problems were going to be solved by shifting the centre of gravity and by changing wing dihedral, which affected glide path stability and achieving sufficient speed in the air, and subsequently in the water.

The above specifications defined the external shape of the torpedo, which was named Kurai 6-Go in accordance with the rules of experimental aircraft torpedo designations. Sano built a model of the torpedo, and subjected it to tests in a water tank, to define the optimum flight path angle for the entry into the water. Mr. Nagashima from *Raigeki Bu* (Attack Torpedo Department) also participated in these trials. After the model trials, construction of the prototype Kurai 6-Go torpedo was started, and it was planned to test it in the open sea. Prototypes were built by Maruni Mokko (Maruni Wood Industry Inc.), a small woodworking shop at Hatsukaichi-shi in Hiroshima prefecture, headed by Mr. Yamanaka, with Mr. Numata as the engineering manager.

In accordance with the requirements, the design of the torpedo was wooden, with the exception of the nose fairing that took on the impact on entry into the water, and of two small attachments. The torpedo had three sections: the warhead, the body with wings, and the tail. The torpedo did not have its own propulsion, either in flight, or in the water.

The warhead, with a total weight of 100kg, was made up of a metal housing and 98kg of explosive charge with magnetic proximity fuses. The fuses would immediately arm upon release of the torpedo, the moment the cable connecting the aeroplane with the torpedo was broken.

The body of the torpedo was made of multi-layer thin strips of plywood, 30 to 50mm wide, up to 13mm total thickness of the shell. The strips were arranged cross-wise. This method produced a stiff and tight structure. Short-span wide-chord wings with a dihedral of 15°, initially, were cemented onto the body. The main role of the wing was to maintain stability of the torpedo during the glide.

The tail was also cemented onto the body, the fin attached at an angle of 8°, which caused the torpedo to make three 80 m spiral rounds in the water as it descended to 80 m below the surface. The structure of the torpedo gave it a maximum depth of submersion of 100 m. To prevent the angled rudder from affecting the flight direction during the glide, a wooden box was fitted ahead of the tail, riveted to the body with thin aluminium rivets, which were torn away the moment the torpedo entered the water.

First prototype Kurai 6-Go torpedoes were ready by September 1944, and were subjected to drop trials from Nakajima B6N1 Tenzan Model 11 or Model 12 torpedo-bomber aircraft. To test stability in flight 40 torpedoes were dropped, 15 of which rolled or rocked during the glide. The torpedoes were dropped at a speed of 440 km/h, and gliding at 15 to 20° entered the water, and there spiralled down at a speed of 9 to 11 km/h.

The first gliding and submersion trials of the Kurai 6-Go torpedoes confused the designers, because many of them lost their wings and the tail upon entering the water. Beside, it was not possible to watch the torpedo under the surface, and thus to assess its path, speed and the depth it reached. To check all these unknown items the explosive in the warhead was replaced by a colour agent, visible in the water. Colour bubbles floating to the surface marked the path of the torpedo in the water.

At the end of 1944 trials of the Kurai 6-Go torpedo were ended, their results regarded as unsatisfactory, despite the dihedral of the wings being increased to 20° in an attempt to improve stability. About 100 experimental Kurai 6-Go torpedoes were built. Metal parts were made at Kugisho, while wooden components and final assembly were made by Maruni Mokko.

Despite the failure of the Kurai 6-Ku the *Kaigun Koku Hombu* ordered development of another version, designated the Kurai 7-Go. Its design was similar, but the body and a part of the tail were made of metal. To improve stability in flight the wing span was increased, and dihedral set at 15°. Fins were fitted at 6°, and were 20mm taller than the span of the tailplanes. To give the warhead better penetration power, the thickness of the nose fairing was increased, and the weight of the explosive charge rose to 220kg, thus increasing the overall weight of the torpedo to 500kg.

In January 1945 11 trial drops were made. The Kurai 7-Go torpedo was launched from an altitude of 300 m at a speed of 400 km/h, and following a shallow diving glide at 15° it entered the water. Each time the flight stability was unsatisfactory, and the torpedoes rolled, so conclusions from the trials stipulated that the torpedo should be fitted with stabilising devices. This did not take place and no more trials were carried out by the end of hostilities.

After the war, in 1946, American engineering intelligence found secret Japanese military materials and located two mock-ups of the Kurai 6-Go aircraft torpedo. All the materials were later shipped to the USA aboard USS Barnes, and were placed in deposit at Anacostia base for final evaluation of the weapon's usefulness.

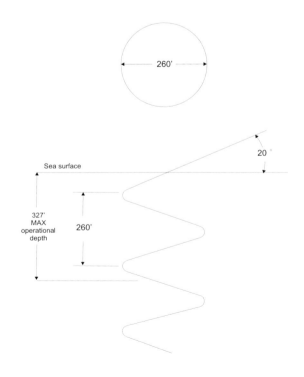

*The trajectory of gliding flight and in submersion of the Kurai gliding depth torpedo.*

### Specifications

Description: aircraft depth torpedo. Wooden construction (Kurai 6-Go) or mixed construction (Kurai 7-Go).
Power plant: none
Warhead: 100kg (Kurai 6-Go), 220kg (Kurai 7-Go).

| Type | Kurai 6-Go | Kurai 7-Go |
|---|---|---|
| Length of the body m | 3.085 | 3.085 |
| Body diameter m | 0.3 | 0.3 |
| Wing span m | 0.8 | 1.22 |
| Wing area m$^2$ | 0.93 | 1.58 |
| Overall weight kg | 270 | 500 |
| Wing loading kg/m$^2$ | 270 | 316 |

Production: between September 1944 and January 1945 about 100 Kurai 6-Go torpedoes and 11 Kurai 7-Go torpedoes were built by *Dai-Ichi Kaigun Koku Gijyutsusho* in Yokosuka and Maruni Mokko at Hatsukaichi-shi.

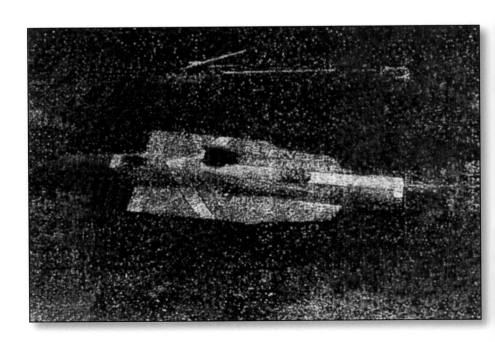

*Kurai 7-Go torpedo. The wing shape is little different from the drawings in US Navy Report. Note the white stripe marking for test purposes.*

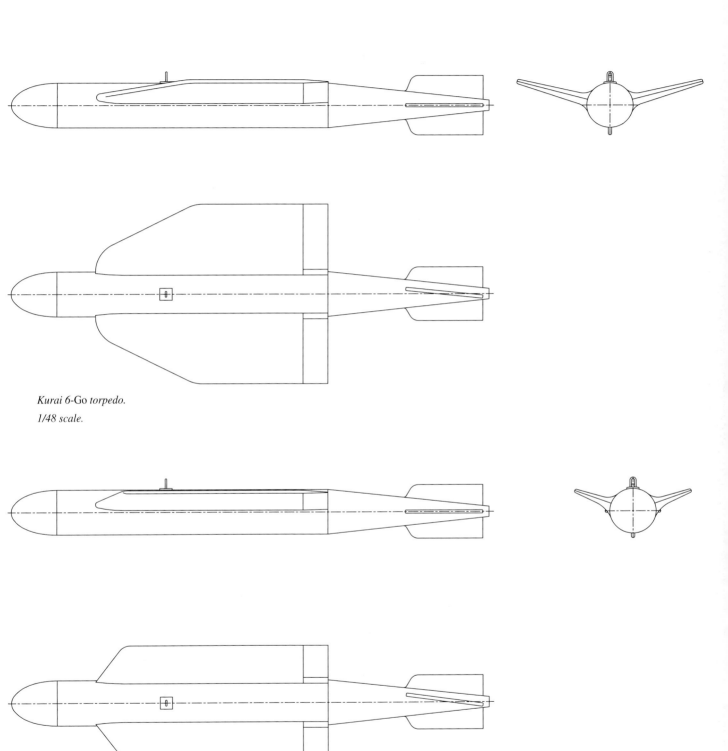

*Kurai 6-Go* torpedo.
*1/48 scale.*

*Kurai 7-Go* torpedo.
*1/48 scale.*

# Kokukyoku Shusui-shiki Kayaku Rocket

The Navy placed an order with *Kokukyoku* (Aeronautical Bureau) to develop a special interceptor. The decision resulted from more and more intensive bombardment of the Japanese home islands by American Boeing B-29 Superfortress bombers.

Design work on the new anti-aircraft missile commenced in March 1945 at *Kokukyoku*, headed by Yujiro Murakami. The Navy requirement was for a special pilotless ramming missile, controlled by means of an auto-pilot, able to intercept a large enemy bomber and ram it inflicting terminal damage, then glide safely back to base.

The Japanese designers used the Mitsubishi J8M1 Shusui design as the basis. The missile was designated the Shusui-shiki Kayaku Rocket (Shusui-type ram attack rocket).

The Shusui-shiki missile was a mid-wing design with stubby fuselage, similar in shape to an artillery shell, fitted with swept (30°) wing and vertical tail. The head of the fuselage had a pointed shape with reinforced structure, and wing leading edges were also reinforced, so as to inflict the greatest possible damage when ramming the bomber.

Since it was hoped that after the ramming the missile would be radio-guided back to the ground, it is likely that a landing skid was fitted under the fuselage, and small supporting skids were designed under the wings. The missile was designed to take-off from a rail launcher, and following launch would be powered by four 120kg solid fuel rockets. The rocket engines are thought to have been located inside the fuselage, to avoid damaging them during an attack. The missile would reach a ceiling of 9,000 metres within about 100 seconds, carry out the attack and then safely glide back to base, to take off again with new rockets. The missile carried no explosive warhead.

After stability calculations and construction of a small experimental model test were completed, production documentation started to be prepared, to be handed over to Kawasaki company. However, this work was not completed before the war ended.

Technologically this was a very challenging undertaking, with little experience of remote control equipment. As with so many projects, lack of time was the main problem.

Recently details of a similar interceptor were found along with a rough drawing in the archives of the Defence Institute. The dimensions on the drawing are almost the same except for the wing shape, which has a mean sweep-back of 45°, not the 30° of the final version. It also has a canopy and a cockpit - curious, given that a pilot could not be contained along with rockets in such a fuselage of this size. Therefore it is possible this drawing shows the small-sized experimental plane, or scale test-bed for a larger suicide aircraft. Yujiro Murakami stated that the design team tried many kinds of experiments and calculations before they reached the final version, this rough sketch may show one of many ideas in the pre-design phase. There is also a possibility that this was the rough sketch of the alternative manned type in case the unmanned type proved to be a failure.

Description: ground-to-air anti-aircraft ramming missile, mid-wing monoplane of mixed design.
Power plant: four 120kg solid fuel rocket engines

| Type | Shusui-shiki |
|---|---|
| Dimensions | |
| Wing span m | 4.000 |
| Fuselage length m | 2.800 |
| Fuselage diameter m | 0.800 |
| Wing area m$_c$ | 5.00 |
| | |
| Weights | |
| Maximum weight kg | 800 |
| Empty weight kg | 200 |
| Performance | |
| Climb to 9,000m | 100 seconds |

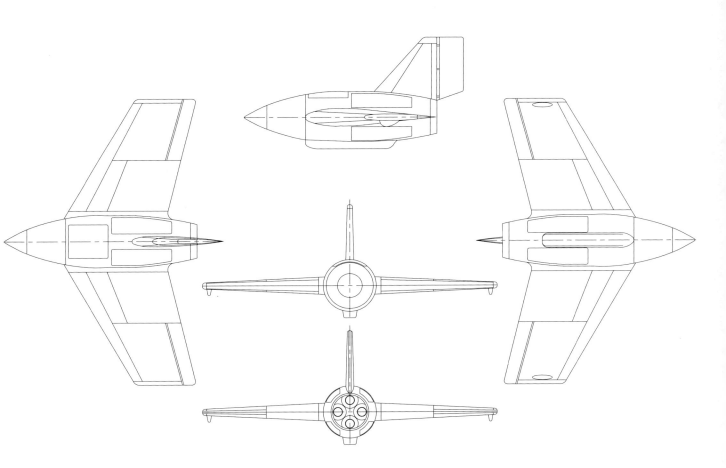

*Shusui-shiki ram attack rocket. (Hypothetical).*

*No scale.*

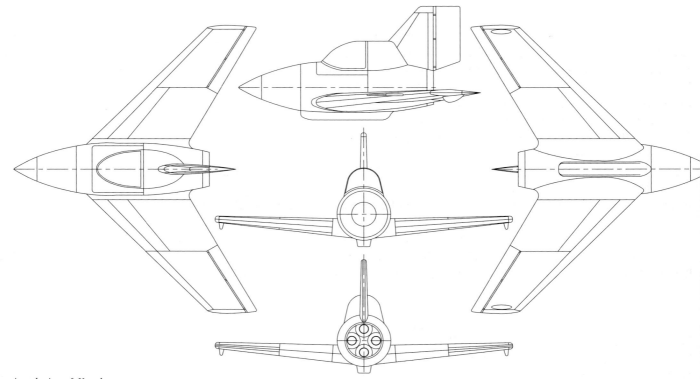

*Attack aircraft Yuyoku
Funshindan. (Hypotheti-
cal). No scale.*

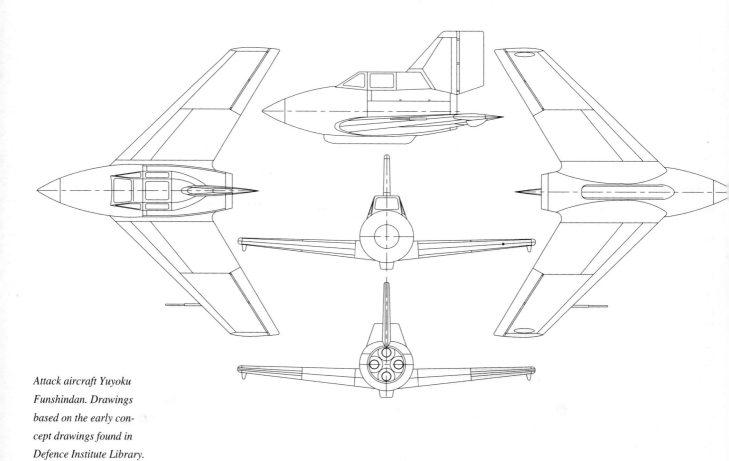

*Attack aircraft Yuyoku
Funshindan. Drawings
based on the early con-
cept drawings found in
Defence Institute Library.
(Hypothetical). No scale.*

# Bibliography

Harold Andreas – The Curtiss SB2C-1 Helldiver – Profile Aircraft No.124 – Windsor 1982

S. Arutjumow, G. Swietłow – Starzy i nowi bogowie Japan – PIW – Warsaw 1973

Ian K. Baker – Japanese Navy Aircraft Colours & Markings in the Pacific War and Before.

Charles Bateson – The War with Japan – Barrie & Rockliff – London 1968

David Brown – Kamikaze – Gallery Books – New York 1990

Richard M. Bueschel – Kawasaki Ki-61/Ki-100 Hien in Japanese Army Air Force Service – Aircam Aviation Series No.21 – Berkshire 1971

Richard M. Bueschel – Nakajima Ki-84a/b Hayate in Japanese Army Air Force Service – Aircam Aviation Series No.16 – Berkshire 1971

Richard M. Bueschel – Nakajima Ki-44-Ia,b,c/IIa, b, c in Japanese Army Air Force Service – Aircam Aviation Series No.25 – Berkshire 1971

Richard M. Bueschel – Nakajima Ki-43 Hayabusa I-III in Japanese Army Air Force – RTAF, CAF, IPSF – Service – Aircam Aviation Series No.13, Berkshire 1970

Richard M. Bueschel – Kawasaki Ki-48-I/II Sokei in Japanese Army Air Force – CNAF & IPSF Service – Aircam Aviation No.32 – Berkshire 1972

Christy Campbell – Air War Pacific – Crescent Books – New York 1990

Andrzej Celarek – Bitwa o Zatokę Leyte – Wydawnictwo Morskie – Gdynia 1960

Robert Chesneau – Aircraft Carriers – London 1984

Basil Collier – Japanese Aircraft of World War II – London 1979

Michał Derenicz – Japonia – Nippon – Nasza Księgarnia – Warsaw 1977

Robert F. Door – US Bombers of World War Two – London 1989

Robert F. Door – US Fighters of World War Two – London 1984

Zbigniew Flisowski – Burza nad Pacyfikiem (tom 1 i 2) – Wydawnictwo Poznańskie – Poznań 1986 i 1989

Rene J. Francillon – Japanese aircraft of the Pacific War – Funk & Wagnalls – New York 1970

Rene J. Francillon – Imperial Japanese Navy Bombers – Windsor, Hylton – 1969

Rene J. Francillon – The Kawasaki Ki-45 Toryu – Profile Publications No.105 – London

Rene J. Francillon – The Kawasaki Ki-61 Hien – Profile Publications No.118 – London

M.F. Hawkins – The Nakajima B5N Kate – Profile Publications No.141 – London

Imperial Japanese Army Air Force Suicide Attack Unit – Model Art. No. 451, Tokyo 1995

Imperial Japanese Navy Air Force Suicide Attack Unit 'Kamikaze' – Model Art. No. 458, Tokyo 1995

Zdzisław Kwiatkowski – Krach Cesarskiej Floty – MON – Warsaw 1975

Yasuo Kuwabara, Gordon T. Allred – Kamikaze – Ballantine Books – New York 1982

Raymond Lamont-Brown – Kamikadze powietrzni samuraje-samobójcy – Wydawnictwo Amber 2003

Michel Ledet – Les Kamikaze: Arme ultime du Japon – Batailles Aeriennes No. 19, Outreau 2002

O. Leyko – Kamikadze – Moscow 1989

Edward T. Maloney – Kamikaze – The Ohka Suicide Flying Bomb –Aero Publishers No. 7 – Fallbrook 1960

Bernard Millot – Les Chasseurs Japonais de la Deuxieme Guerre Mondiale – Docavia – Paris 1977

Bernard Millot – Divine Thunder – MacDonald – London 1971

Robert C. Mikesh – Kikka – Monogram Close Up No. 19 – Balyston 1979

David Mondey – American Aircraft of World War II – Aerospace Publishing – London 1982

Andrzej Mozołowski – Tak upadło Imperium – KAW – Warsaw 1984

Josef Novotny – Causa Kamikaze – Nase Vojsko – Prague 1991

Masatake Okumiya, Jiro Horikoshi and Martin Caidin – Zero! – Ballantine Books – New York 1979

Andrzej Perepeczko – Okinawa – Wydawnictwo Morskie – Gdynia 1965

Saburo Sakai – Samurai! – Ballantine Books – New York 1972

Donald W. Thorpe – Japanese Army Air Force Camuflage and Markings World War II – Aero Publishers – Fallbrook 1968

Jolanta Tubielewicz – Historia Japonii – Ossolineum – Wrocław 1984

Antoni Wolny – Okinawa 1945 – MON – Warsaw 1983

Takeo Yasunobu – Ah, Kamikaze Tokko Tai – Kojin-sha – Tokyo 1995

Kazuhiko Osuo – Tokubetsu Kogekitai no kiroku (Kaigun hen)(rikugun hen) – Kojin-sha – Tokyo 2005

The Great Book of World War II Airplanes – Bonanza Books – New York 1984

# U.S. NAVY SHIPS

| Code | Name | Code | Name |
|------|------|------|------|
| AG | auxiliary ship | ACM | fast minesweeper |
| AH | hospital ship | AM | minesweeper |
| AO | Oiler, or Fuel Oil Tanker | APA | Attack Transport |
| APD | High Speed Transport (ex-DD) | AT | Ocean Tug |
| AV | Seaplane Tender | BB | Battleship |
| CA | Heavy Cruiser (Gun Cruiser) | CL | light cruiser |
| CM | Minelayer | CV | Aircraft Carrier |
| CVL | Light Carrier | CVE | Escort Aircraft Carrier |
| DD | Destroyer | DE | Escort Destroyer |
| DM | Light Minelayer | DMS | High-Speed Minesweepers |
| DL | Figate | LCI(FF) | Landing Craft, Infantry (Flotilla Flagship) |
| LCI(G) | Landing Craft, Infantry (Gunboat) | LCI(L) | Landing Craft, Infantry (Large) |
| LCI(M) | Landing Craft, Infantry (Mortar ship) | LCI(R) | Landing Craft, Infantry (Rocket ship) |
| LCP(L) | Landing Craft, Personnel (Large) | LCP(R) | Landing Craft, Personnel (Ramped) |
| LCV | Landing Craft, Vehicle | LCVP | Landing Craft, Vehicle and Personnel |
| LCM | Landing Craft, Mechanized | LCS(L) | Landing Craft, Support (Large) |
| LCS(S) | Landing Craft, Support (Small) | LCT | Landing Craft, Tank |
| LSM | Landing Ship, Medium | LSM(R) | Landing Ship, Medium (Rocket ship) |
| LST | Landing Ship, Tank | LVT | Landing Vehicle, Tracked |
| LVT(A) | Landing Vehicle, Tracked (Armored) | MCB | Motor Cargo (US Coast Guard) |
| PC | Submarine Chasers | PG | Patrol Gunboat |
| PT | Motor Torpedo Boat | PTC | Lnding Sip for Lnding tTops of PC, PG and PT |
| SS | Submarine | SC | Submarine Chasers |
| IX | Unclassified Miscellaneous Unit | YMS | Motor Minesweeper |

*A6M2 of the first Kamikaze Special Attack unit - 201 Kokutai, Mabaracat Air Base in the Philippines on 25 October 1944. Aircraft flown by the unit commander, Yukio Seki.*

*Kugisho D4Y4 of 601 Kokutai, 1945. Aircraft usually carried 500 kg bomb in the bomb bay for special attack missions.*

*Kugisho D4Y4 of 701 Kokutai flown by Adm. Ugaki on 15 August 1945 in the last special attack mission.*

*Nakajima Ki-43-I Hayabusa of 47 Independent Chutai.*

*Nakajima Ki-43-III Ko Hayabusa 1 Chutai, 33 Hiko Sentai with 200 litre tank and 250 kg bomb. Aircraft so equipped were used for special attack missions in the Philippines, 1944.*

*Nakajima Ki-43-III Ko Hayabusa 250 kg bomb under fuselage.*

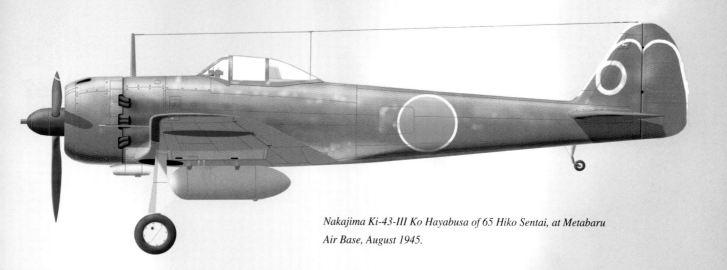

*Nakajima Ki-43-III Ko Hayabusa of 65 Hiko Sentai, at Metabaru Air Base, August 1945.*

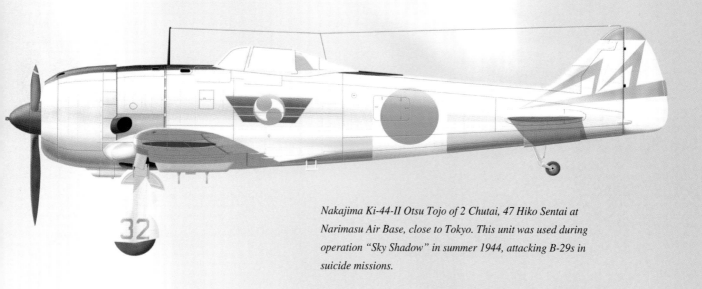

*Nakajima Ki-44-II Otsu Tojo of 2 Chutai, 47 Hiko Sentai at Narimasu Air Base, close to Tokyo. This unit was used during operation "Sky Shadow" in summer 1944, attacking B-29s in suicide missions.*

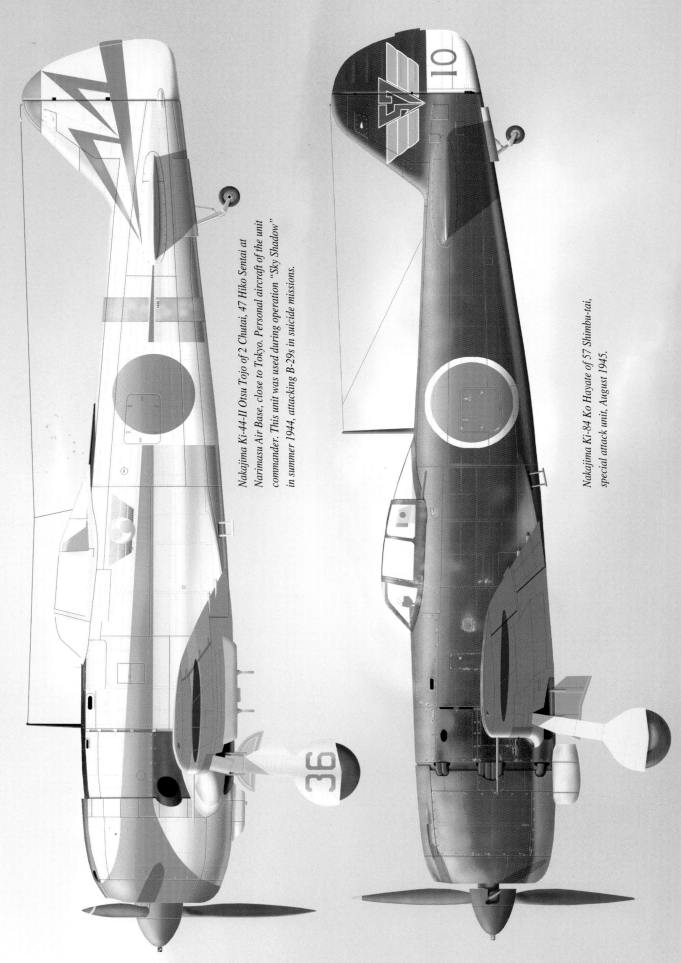

*Nakajima Ki-44-II Otsu Tojo of 2 Chutai, 47 Hiko Sentai at Narimasu Air Base, close to Tokyo. Personal aircraft of the unit commander. This unit was used during operation "Sky Shadow" in summer 1944, attacking B-29s in suicide missions.*

*Nakajima Ki-84 Ko Hayate of 57 Shimbu-tai, special attack unit, August 1945.*

*Nakajima Ki-84 Ko Hayate of 182 Shimbu-tai, special attack unit,*
*August 1945. Personal aircraft of Takeshi Imoto.*

*Kawasaki Ki-61-I Otsu Hien of 3 Chutai 59 Sentai, at Ashiya airfield,*
*Kyushu, August 1945.*

*Kawasaki Ki-61-I Otsu Hien of 149 Shimbu-tai, special attack unit, 59 Sentai.*

*Kawasaki Ki-61-I Otsu Hien of 244 Sentai.*

*Kawasaki Ki-61-1 Tei Hien of 244 Sentai.*

*Nakajima Ki-84 Ko Hayate, of 181 Shimbu-tai, special attack unit, August 1945.*

247

*Kawasaki Ki-48-II Otsu with triple probe fuse.*

*Kawasaki Ki-48-II Otsu Kai with Kawasaki I-Go-I Otsu rocket.*

Zygmunt Szeremeta '07

Zygmunt Szeremeta '07

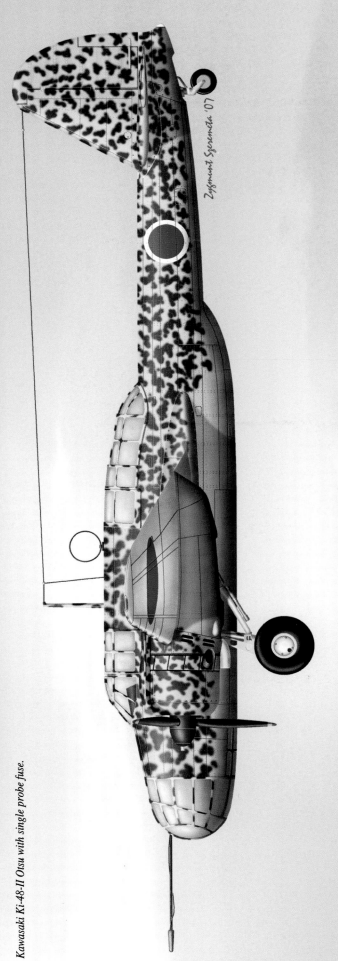

*Kawasaki Ki-48-II Otsu with single probe fuse.*

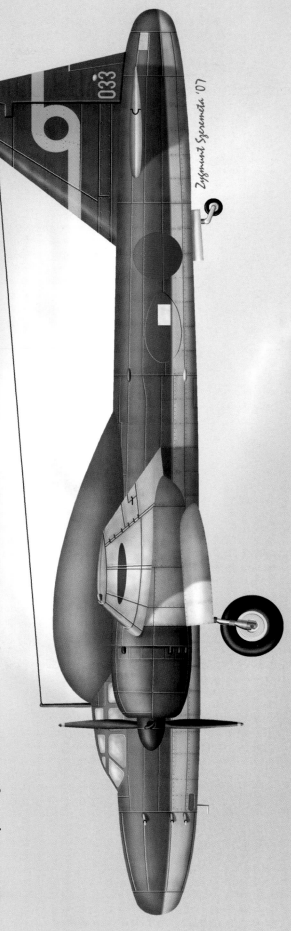

*Mitsubishi Ki-167 with shaped charge bomb Sakura-dan 2-Go. Aircraft was commanded by Yutaka Fukushima.*

249

Mitsubishi To-Go of Fugaku Sentai

Zygmunt Szeremeta '07

One of the seven D3Y1-K Model 22 delivered to Imperial Japanese Navy.

Zygmunt Szeremeta '07

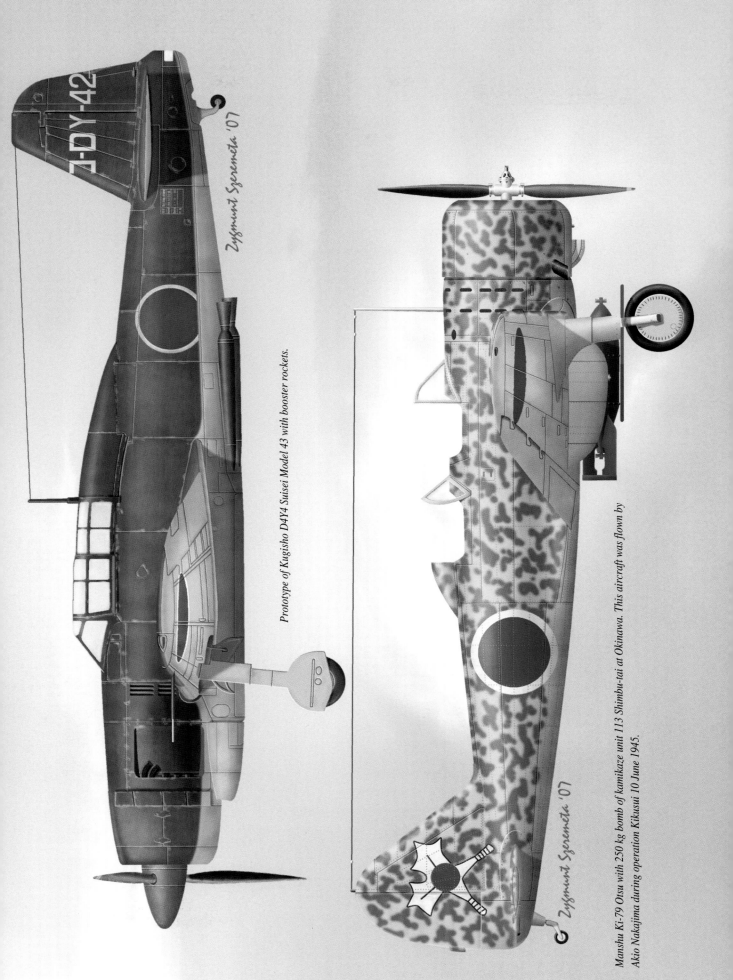

Zygmunt Szeremeta '07

Prototype of Kugisho D4Y4 Suisei Model 43 with booster rockets.

Zygmunt Szeremeta '07

Manshu Ki-79 Otsu with 250 kg bomb of kamikaze unit 113 Shimbu-tai at Okinawa. This aircraft was flown by Akio Nakajima during operation Kikusui 10 June 1945.

*Kawanishi Baika 1. Land version in different configuration..*

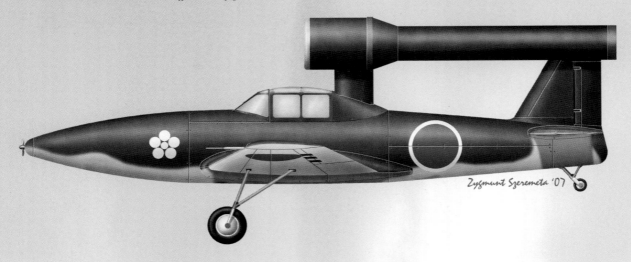

*Kawanishi Baika 2. Land version.*

*Kawanishi Baika 3 . Version planned to be used from rail catapult.*

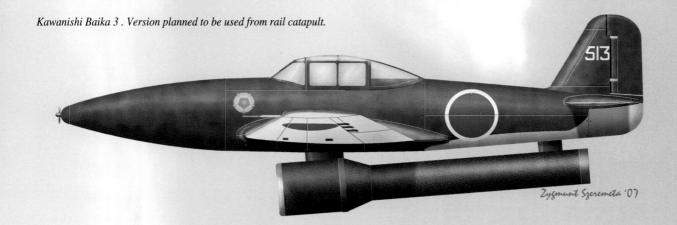

*Kawanishi Baika. Two seat training version, (hypothetical).*

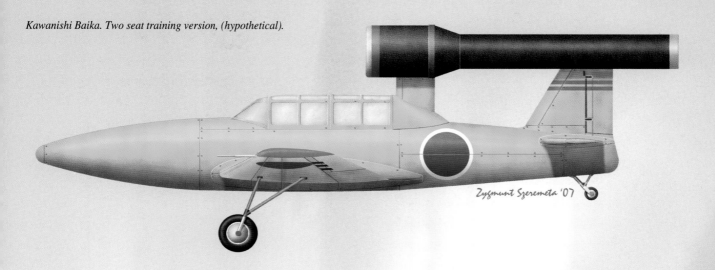

*The second prototype of Jinryu glider with three rockets.*

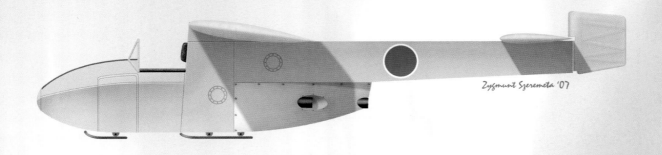

*The Experimental Single-seat Attack Aeroplane.*

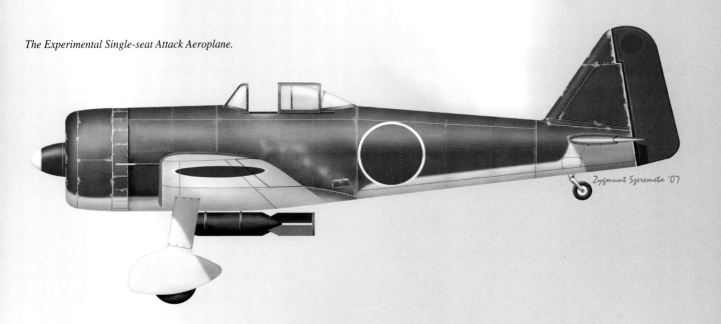

*Kawasaki Ki-102 Otsu with the Ki-148 bomb attached.*

*Zygmunt Szeremeta '07*

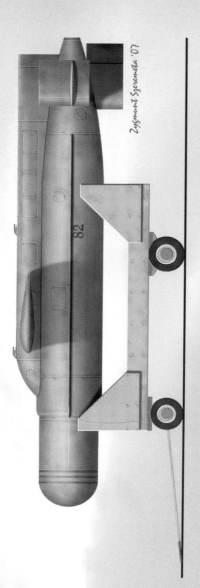

*Kawasaki I-Go-1 Otsu guided missile on handling trolley.*

*Zygmunt Szeremeta '07*

Mitsubishi Ki-67 Hiryū with Mitsubishi I-Go-1 Ko missile.

Zygmunt Szeremeta '07

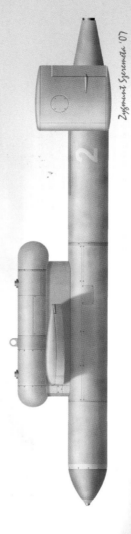

The second prototype of Mitsubishi I-Go-1 Ko missile.

Zygmunt Szeremeta '07

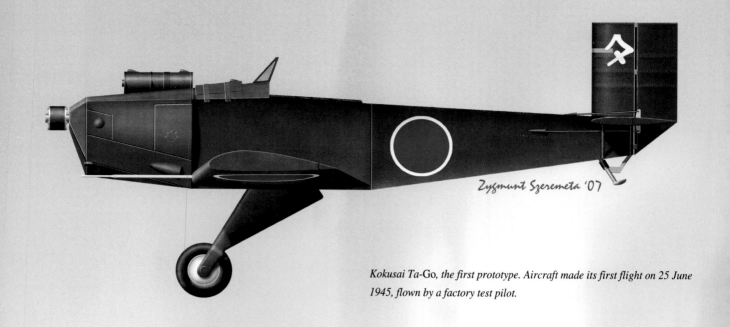

Kokusai Ta-Go, the first prototype. Aircraft made its first flight on 25 June 1945, flown by a factory test pilot.

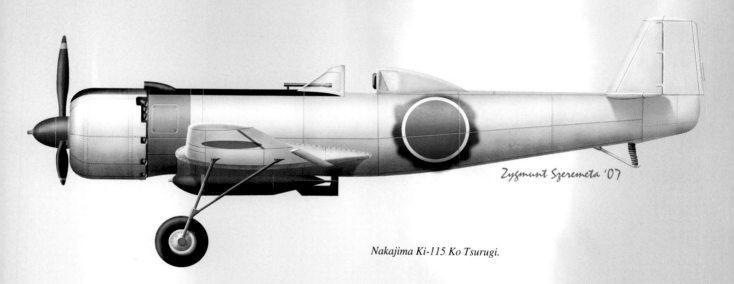

Nakajima Ki-115 Ko Tsurugi.

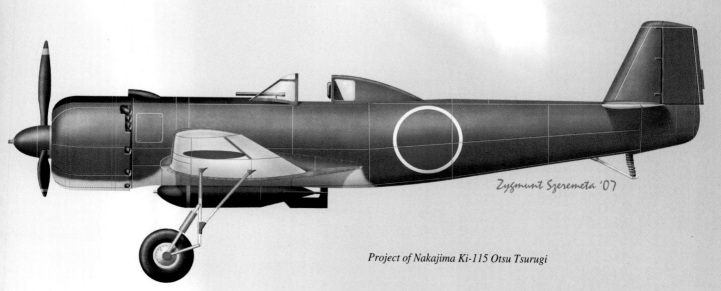

Project of Nakajima Ki-115 Otsu Tsurugi

Projects of Kokukyoku Shusui-shiki Kayaku
Rocket. (hypothetical)

Zygmunt Szeremeta

Zygmunt Szeremeta

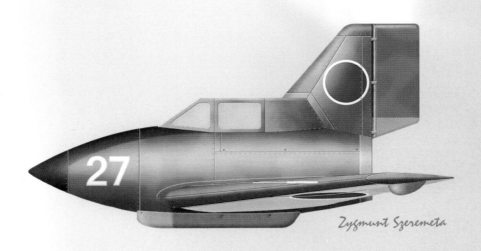

Zygmunt Szeremeta

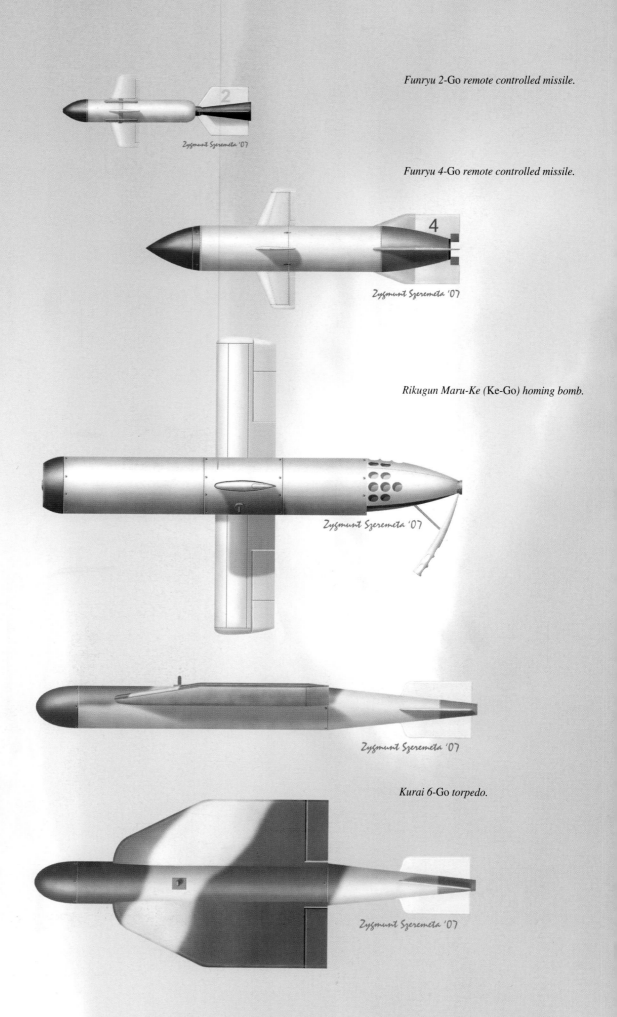

*Funryu 2-Go remote controlled missile.*

*Funryu 4-Go remote controlled missile.*

*Rikugun Maru-Ke (Ke-Go) homing bomb.*

*Kurai 6-Go torpedo.*

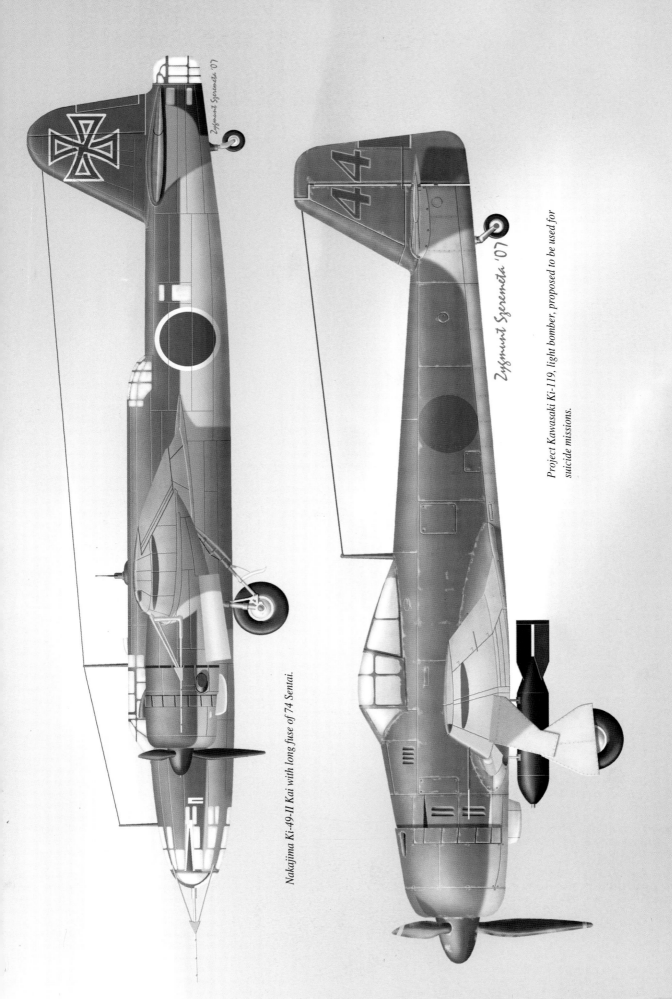

Nakajima Ki-49-II Kai with long fuse of 74 Sentai.

Project Kawasaki Ki-119, light bomber, proposed to be used for suicide missions.

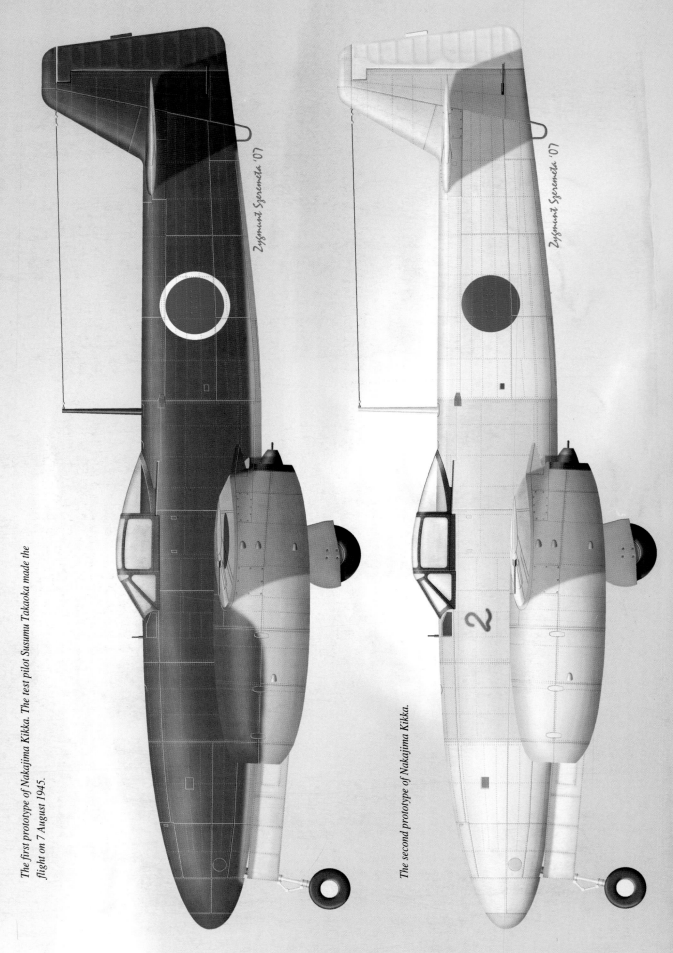

*The first prototype of Nakajima Kikka. The test pilot Susumu Takaoka made the flight on 7 August 1945.*

*The second prototype of Nakajima Kikka.*